# STUDIES IN IMPERIALISM

General editor: Andrew S. Thompson
Founding editor: John M. MacKenzie

When the 'Studies in Imperialism' series was founded by Professor John M. MacKenzie more than thirty years ago, emphasis was laid upon the conviction that 'imperialism as a cultural phenomenon had as significant an effect on the dominant as on the subordinate societies'. With well over a hundred titles now published, this remains the prime concern of the series. Cross-disciplinary work has indeed appeared covering the full spectrum of cultural phenomena, as well as examining aspects of gender and sex, frontiers and law, science and the environment, language and literature, migration and patriotic societies, and much else. Moreover, the series has always wished to present comparative work on European and American imperialism, and particularly welcomes the submission of books in these areas. The fascination with imperialism, in all its aspects, shows no sign of abating, and this series will continue to lead the way in encouraging the widest possible range of studies in the field. 'Studies in Imperialism' is fully organic in its development, always seeking to be at the cutting edge, responding to the latest interests of scholars and the needs of this ever-expanding area of scholarship.

## Knowledge, mediation and empire

Manchester University Press

# SELECTED TITLES AVAILABLE IN THE SERIES

*WRITING IMPERIAL HISTORIES*
ed. Andrew S. Thompson

*MUSEUMS AND EMPIRE*
*Natural history, human cultures and colonial identities*
John M. MacKenzie

*MISSIONARY FAMILIES*
*Race, gender and generation on the spiritual frontier*
Emily J. Manktelow

*THE COLONISATION OF TIME*
*Ritual, routine and resistance in the British Empire*
Giordano Nanni

*BRITISH CULTURE AND THE END OF EMPIRE*
ed. Stuart Ward

*SCIENCE, RACE RELATIONS AND RESISTANCE*
*Britain, 1870–1914*
Douglas A. Lorimer

*GENTEEL WOMEN*
*Empire and domestic material culture, 1840–1910*
Dianne Lawrence

*EUROPEAN EMPIRES AND THE PEOPLE*
*Popular responses to imperialism in France, Britain, the Netherlands, Belgium, Germany and Italy*
ed. John M. MacKenzie

*SCIENCE AND SOCIETY IN SOUTHERN AFRICA*
ed. Saul Dubow

# Knowledge, mediation and empire

## JAMES TOD'S JOURNEYS AMONG THE RAJPUTS

Florence D'Souza

MANCHESTER UNIVERSITY PRESS

Copyright © Florence D'Souza 2015

The right of Florence D'Souza to be identified as the author of this work has been asserted by her in accordance with the Copyright, Designs and Patents Act 1988.

Published by Manchester University Press
Altrincham Street, Manchester M1 7JA, UK
www.manchesteruniversitypress.co.uk

*British Library Cataloguing-in-Publication Data is available*

ISBN 978 0 7190 9080 6 hardback
ISBN 978 1 5261 4807 0 paperback

First published by Manchester University Press in hardback 2015

This edition published 2020

The publisher has no responsibility for the persistence or accuracy of URLs for any external or third-party internet websites referred to in this book, and does not guarantee that any content on such websites is, or will remain, accurate or appropriate.

Typeset by Servis Filmsetting Ltd, Stockport, Cheshire

*To my paternal grandmother 'Doctor Granny' (Mary Macedo-D'Souza, 1890–1959), who worked as the Zenana Lady-Doctor to two successive ruling Nawabs of Tonk in Rajasthan, from approximately 1916 to 1936.*

# CONTENTS

*List of figures* – viii
*Founding editor's introduction* – ix
*Acknowledgements* – xi

|   |   |   |
|---|---|---|
|   | Introduction: James Tod's role in knowledge exchanges with the Rajputs | 1 |
| 1 | Tod as an observer of landscape in Rajasthan and Gujarat | 20 |
| 2 | Tod as anthropologist: trying to understand | 41 |
| 3 | Tod's practice of science in India: voyages through empirical, common sense | 64 |
| 4 | Tod's use of Romanticism in his textual constructions of Rajasthan and Gujarat | 80 |
| 5 | Tod's Romantic approach as opposed to James Mill's Utilitarian approach to British government in India | 116 |
| 6 | Tod's knowledge exchanges with his contemporaries in India | 133 |
| 7 | Tod among his contemporaries in London, 1823–35 | 157 |
|   | Conclusion: Tod's sympathetic understanding of Rajput difference | 192 |

*Appendices*
  I   Thirteen letters from James Tod (and Patrick Waugh) between early 1820 and late 1822, to Maharana Bheem Singh of Mewar – 205
  II  Tod's Memorandum on the Mirs of Sind, IOR MSS EUR E 293/35 (9 folios) – 213
  III Tod's Memorandum on the Tribal Mhairs of Mhairwarra, IOR MSS EUR E 293/47 (22 folios) – 218
  IV  James Tod's Last Will and Testament, deposited by him with his solicitors on 11 August 1834, PRO/B/11/1857, folios 31–3 – 231
*Bibliography* – 238
*Index* – 250

# FIGURES

1. Temples of Gunga Bheou, Royal Asiatic Society (RAS); Raymond Head, *Catalogue of Paintings, Drawings, Engravings and Busts in the Collection of the Royal Asiatic Society*, London: Routledge, 1991, no. 037.094, p. 116.   page 2
2. Citadel of the hill fortress of Komulmer, RAS; Head, *Catalogue*, no. 037.021, p. 112.   21
3. Figures showing various occupations. Engraving by Edward Finden of a miniature after an unknown Indian artist's original, formerly owned by James Tod, RAS; Head, *Catalogue*, no. 037.064/065/066, p. 115.   42
4. Rajput princesses killing a lion, RAS; Head, *Catalogue*, no. 061.002, p. 155.   51
5. William Jones Collection: Shaikh Zayn-Al-Din, Botanical study: flower and leaves, RAS; Head, *Catalogue*, no. 025.075, p. 105.   65
6. Palace of Ranee [sic] Bheem and Pudmundi [sic], RAS; Head, *Catalogue*, no. 037.004 ii, p. 110.   81
7. Painting of the East India Company building, Leadenhall Street, London, British Library, Ref. 016802 – Source WD 2460.   117
8. Miniature attributed to Deogarh Chokha, 1817, entitled 'Captain Tod riding on an Elephant with his companions and Escort' (© Victoria & Albert Museum, London).   134
9. Five initial seals of the Royal Asiatic Society in 1823, from the uncatalogued RAS collections.   158
10. Rana Bhim Singh of Udaipur installing the image of Srinathji in a tented enclosure, RAS; Head, *Catalogue*, no. 063.029, p. 160.   193

# FOUNDING EDITOR'S INTRODUCTION

James Tod (1782–1835) was a self-educated polymath. Born in London of Scottish parents with Indian connections, he was schooled in Scotland and trained as a military engineer at Woolwich. But these bare details of his life give no hint of the fact that he was to be intellectually omnivorous in his studies of western India, of Rajasthan and Gujarat, during the peak of his career when he served as political agent in that region. He was interested in cartography and topography, in geology and botany, in both human and natural history, in philology and myth, in archaeology and architecture, and in the comparative history of societies in both Europe and India. The pursuit of his military and political duties was deeply embedded in his extensive studies. His relationships with the courts of princes gave him access to documents and libraries which he assiduously used in his search for information and ideas.

He was also very much a man of his time. Though lacking a university education, he was influenced both by the Enlightenment and by the Romanticism which was, in some senses, a reaction to it. He was well read in romantic literature and was keen, like many contemporaries, to illustrate his topographical descriptions, his visions of mythic pasts and his descriptions of heroic events with allusions to and quotations from a wide range of literary works in English. He was also fascinated by some of the dominant scientific ideas of the age as well as by the conventional artistic perceptions of the time. In all of this, he demonstrated both a sympathetic understanding of the Rajputs and a desire to fit them into a universalist concept of human society which, to a certain extent, contrasts with the harder, more hierarchical, ideas of the later nineteenth century. All of this emerged in his copious writings.

As such, he has excited the interest of a number of scholars, but none of them have cast their net as wide as Florence D'Souza. She presents an extensive picture of Tod's many interests, interpreting them in terms of the efforts at knowledge exchange that took place in the period, the genuine fascination with indigenous understanding exhibited by quite a number of East India Company employees, as well as the extraordinary networks through which such information and ideas were garnered, circulated and propagated. Tod acknowledged the help of his local helpers, notably the Jain Yati Gyanchandra. He was also in communication with the remarkable group of East India Company employees, a number of them Scots, who turned themselves into students of India in the period.

Tod's life and work also illustrate the manner in which Oriental studies were developed during his life time through the foundation of institutions and the publication of journals. He himself was employed by the Royal Asiatic Society of London, founded in 1823, and published, or was reviewed, in its *Transactions*, in the *Asiatic Journal* and the *Oriental Herald*. These developments were international, connecting for example with the Société Asiatique

**FOUNDING EDITOR'S INTRODUCTION**

de Paris and the *Journal Asiatique* or with German Orientalist scholars. Tod contributed to a remarkable flowering of studies of India, and Florence D'Souza has charted, through both her extensive research and her close studies of his works, just how significant he was. She has also provided some useful appendices of material not readily available elsewhere. Her book represents a notable addition to the literature of Orientalism while offering a significant revision to the crudely binary interpretations of some modern scholarship.

John M. MacKenzie

# ACKNOWLEDGEMENTS

This book, as it developed over many years, owes its existence to the support of a large number of persons and institutions.

The project emerged in 2004 following the encouragement given to me by Aniruddha Ray, Emeritus Professor of History at Calcutta University, to embark on a monograph on James Tod and the Rajputs, in the course of a discussion about India's pre-colonial historiography. I was further inspired by childhood memories of accounts of adventurous 'shikars' or hunting expeditions in Rajasthan, by my paternal grandfather, my father and his sister, who were all influenced by the experiences in Rajasthan of my paternal grandmother, Mary Macedo-D'Souza, to whom this work is dedicated. She unfortunately expired at the age of sixty-nine, six months after my birth in 1959. Born in 1890 in Poona, she had qualified as a medical doctor from Poona's B.J. Medical College around 1915, and obtained employment with the then Nawab of Tonk, Ibrahim Ali Khan (r.1867–1930) from around 1916, and then under his successor, Saadat Ali Khan (r.1930–47), until her retirement in Poona from 1936. Thus, Mary Macedo-D'Souza worked over some twenty years in Tonk (1916–36, approximately) as the ruling Nawab's zenana doctor, looking after the health of the wives, children and domestic staff of these early twentieth-century Nawabs. Her link with James Tod is that the ancestor of these Nawabs of Tonk, who employed her, was the Pathan military adventurer Amir Khan (1768–1834), who had been 'pacified' from his violent incursions into Rajasthan by the British Representative, Tod, in 1817, through the award of a princely state in Rajasthan, made up of Tonk, Rampura (west of Sawai Madhopur) and Neembahira, together with the title of 'Nawab'. The present Nawab of Tonk is Aftab Ali Khan, in power since 1994, whose son, Junaid Ali Khan, was born in 1986.

In preparing this book, I was able to avail myself of the invaluable assistance of staff members of the Royal Asiatic Society, especially the recently retired librarian, Kathy Lazenbatt, her assistant Helen Porter and Kathy Lazenbatt's successor, Edward Leech. At the British Library, Andrew Cook and Jennifer Howes were very helpful.

Correspondence and personal conversations with Robert Skelton, Giles Tillotson, Lloyd Rudolph and Ann Buddle of the National Galleries of Scotland helped me along my way.

Academics working on India, in particular Muzaffar Alam, Daniel Carey, Michael Fisher, Jason Freitag, P.J. Marshall, Rosane Rocher, Massimiliano Vaghi and David Washbrook, enlightened me with constructive comments.

In France, my research supervisor, Alexis Tadié, and my Orientalist colleague, Marc Rolland, provided generous support with finalising my manuscript. Encouragement from friends Beena Anand, Marie-Joëlle Ravit and Armelle Saint-Martin, as also from my brother Leslie, kept my spirits up over the slow maturing of this project.

## ACKNOWLEDGEMENTS

Without the unhesitating defence of my publication proposal by John M. MacKenzie, the founding editor of the Manchester University Press Studies in Imperialism series, following upon my chance meeting with him at a lecture he was invited to give in Paris, the book would never have got off the ground. I am also indebted to Emma Brennan and Polly Bentham of Manchester University Press, for their constant vigilance and kindness throughout the production of this work.

Finally, to my life partner, mentor and guide, Guy Deleury, my deep gratitude for his unquenchable optimism, through thick and through thin.

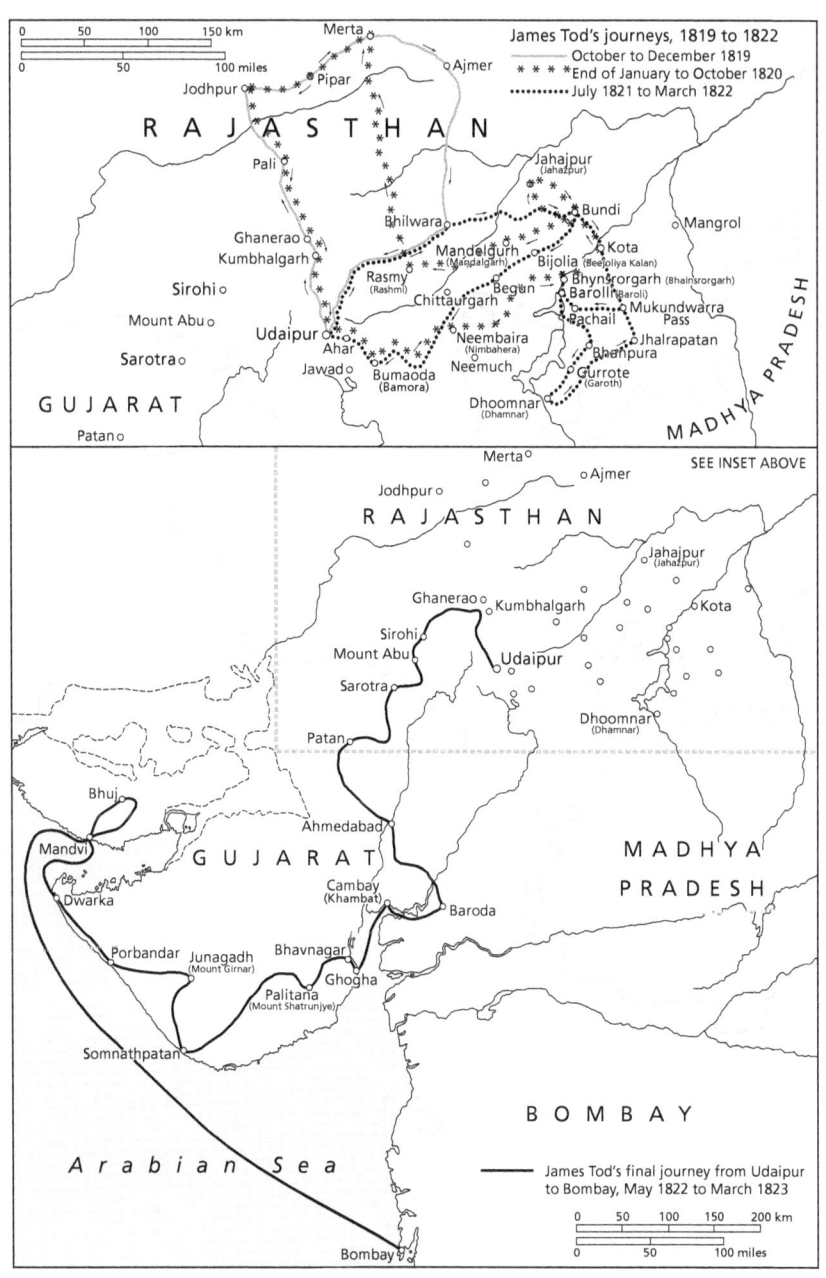

A map of James Tod's journeys through Rajasthan and Gujarat.

# INTRODUCTION

# James Tod's role in knowledge exchanges with the Rajputs

In a context of the expanding presence of the East India Company in India in the early decades of the nineteenth century, James Tod (1782–1835) had the opportunity to be in close contact with the Rajputs in central and northwestern India between 1800 and 1822. He chose to learn their language (a dialect of Urdu) and to observe their way of life, their history and their social institutions attentively throughout his stay of twenty-two years in India. After his return to England in 1823, Tod assembled the information he had gathered on the Rajputs in a series of publications that appeared in London between 1827 and 1839. It is these publications by Tod that form the basis of my study of Tod's role as a participant in knowledge exchanges with the Rajputs for the benefit of the reading public of Britain and Europe.

Tod's publications fall into two groups: first his two major works that appeared in 1829, 1832 and 1839 (posthumously), and then a set of shorter studies on specific points of Rajput history and culture that had interested him, which were published in learned journals in Britain and France. The work by which he is mainly remembered occupied him over the better part of a decade (1823–32). It is entitled *Annals and Antiquities of Rajasthan*, and is in two volumes. The first volume of Tod's *Annals* was published in 1829 by Routledge & Kegan Paul Ltd, in London, in a leather-bound quarto format, with a series of engravings of scenes from Rajasthan (mainly sketched by Tod's assistant and kinsman Captain Patrick Waugh in Rajasthan). It contains a dedication to King George IV, the author's introduction, a geography of Rajasthan, a history of the Rajput tribes in eight chapters, a sketch of a feudal system in Rajasthan in five chapters with an appendix, the 'Annals of Mewar' in eighteen chapters, a section of six chapters on the religious establishments, festivals and customs of Mewar and finally a 'Personal Narrative' or the journal of Tod's travels to Marwar between October and December 1819, in six chapters. The volume ends with appendices

1 Temples of Gunga Bheou.
(By kind permission of the Royal Asiatic Society of
Great Britain and Ireland)

including translations of seven inscriptions fixing eras in Rajput history, and the text of the treaty between the East India Company and the Rana of Udaipur, dated 13 January 1818.

The second volume of Tod's *Annals and Antiquities of Rajasthan* appeared in 1832 with the same publisher (Routledge & Kegan Paul Ltd) in London, in the same leather-bound quarto format as the first volume. It comprises a dedication to King William IV (George IV had died in 1830), a brief introduction by the author, the annals of Marwar in sixteen chapters, the annals of Bikaner in three chapters, the annals of Jaisalmer in seven chapters, a sketch of the Indian desert in two chapters, the annals of Amber or Dhoondar (Jaipur) and the Shekhawat Federation in seven chapters, and the annals of Haravati, with a first section of four chapters on Bundi, while the following seven chapters are on Kota. The final section of volume II contains again a 'Personal Narrative' in fifteen chapters. It is made up of the journal of Tod's second journey out of Mewar (to Bundi and Kota) in eight chapters, from 29 January 1820 to 27 October 1820 (over nine months), and the events of Tod's third journey out of Mewar, in seven chapters, between late July 1821 and 8 March 1822 (over some seven and a half months), when Tod visited Bundi (after the death from cholera of Bundi's Raja Bishen Singh), and Kota (as a result of the fateful battle at Mangrol in October 1821). After his return to Udaipur from Kota, at the end of this third journey, in March 1822, Tod decided to leave Rajasthan and

INTRODUCTION

India. The second volume of Tod's *Annals* contains seven appendices. They include a letter dated 1728 from Raja Jai Singh of Amber (Jaipur) to Rana Singram Singh of Mewar, concerning the pargana of Edur, disputed at the time between the parricidal Raja Abhay Singh Rathore of Marwar and his Rathore brother Anand Singh, followed by a series of six treaties between the various states of Rajasthan (except Mewar, whose treaty was included in volume I) and the East India Company, signed between January 1815 and December 1818.

The second volume closes with two genealogical tables, the first table from 2200 BCE to 1100 BCE, and the second table from 1100 BCE to 720 CE, of the Suryavanshi and Chandravanshi races, starting with the divinities Brahma, Vishnu and Narayana, proceeding via various sages, and then descending through different dynasties.

Tod's second major work, entitled *Travels in Western India, embracing a visit to the sacred mounts of the Jains, and the most celebrated shrines of Hindu faith between Rajpootana and the Indus; with an account of the ancient city of Nehrwalla*, appeared posthumously in 1839, with the London publisher W.H. Allen & Co. It is in fact the travel journal of Tod's last peregrination in India (over nine months from 1 June 1822 to the end of February 1823), through the south of Rajasthan (Mount Abu) and across Gujarat from east to west. It ends with his final boat journey from Mandvi (in the Cutch peninsula in Gujarat) to Bombay in March 1823, where Tod boarded a ship that carried him back to Britain. The text is made up of twenty-three chapters and is motivated by the same goal as Tod's *Annals and Antiquities of Rajasthan*, 'the hope of making the Rajpoots known by their works'.[1] Tod had intended the volume to close with fifteen appendices, these being translations of inscriptions he had found along his way. Of these fifteen inscriptions the publisher was unable to trace three among Tod's posthumous papers, leaving twelve that he published. These inscriptions are mainly from Somnathpatan and Mount Girnar (Junagadh), and illustrate Tod's fervent antiquarian interest, visible throughout his travels. This second full-scale, published work contains nine engravings of pencil drawings of scenes of Mount Abu and Gujarat by Mrs William Hunter Blair (the wife of a British colonel of the Bombay Army who visited these regions in the late 1820s, a few years after Tod had been there). These are acknowledged in Tod's dedication to Mrs William Hunter Blair: 'so greatly indebted to your exquisite pencil for its illustration'.[2] Tod's second work is also completed by twelve inset sketches and miniature vignettes that show the layout, ground plan or bird's-eye view of several sites described in Tod's text.

Tod's shorter compilations are made up of twelve articles. Of these, seven were published in the *Transactions of the Royal Asiatic Society*,

London (three in volume I in 1827, three in volume II in 1830 and one in volume III in 1835). Of the remaining five articles by Tod, two appeared in French in the *Journal Asiatique* of the Société Asiatique of Paris, in volume 11 of its first series, in the first half of 1827, and the three others appeared in the *Asiatic Journal or the Monthly Register*. Not only was Tod the official librarian of London's Royal Asiatic Society from 1824 to 1834, but he personally read his seven papers which were published in the *Transactions* before the members between 1824 and 1830. The *Asiatic Journal or the Monthly Register* was connected with the East India Company in London,[3] while the Société Asiatique of Paris, founded in 1825, was a regular forum for European scholars who worked on Asia and the Orient. Thus from the names of the journals where Tod's short essays were published, we can note that he had become a member of scholarly Orientalist circles in Europe after his return to Britain from India in 1823. These essays covered varied topics: a Sanskrit inscription relative to the last Hindu monarch of Delhi;[4] comments on an inscription on marble and three grants inscribed on copper plates found at Ujjain;[5] Greek, Parthian and Hindu medals found in India;[6] the Asiatic origin of some of the former tribes of Europe settled on the banks of the Baltic Sea;[7] the religious establishments of Mewar;[8] certain sculptures in the cave temples of Ellora;[9] observations on a gold ring of Hindu fabrication found at Montrose in Scotland;[10] and a comparison of the Hindu and Theban Hercules, illustrated by an ancient Hindu intaglio.[11] 'The Feudal System in Rajasthan' appeared in the *Asiatic Journal and Monthly Register for British and Foreign India, China and Australasia*.[12] 'Géographie du Rajasthan' was published in *Journal Asiatique*.[13] 'Indo-Grecian Antiquities' came out in the *Asiatic Journal and Monthly Register for British and Foreign India, China and Australasia*.[14] Finally, a translation by Tod of a section of the twelfth-century bard Chand's *Prithviraj Raso*, on 'The Vow of Sunjogta', was published posthumously in the *Asiatic Journal or the Monthly Register*.[15]

## Aim of the book

My aim through the following chapters of this book is to analyse Tod's role in knowledge exchanges with the Rajputs, through his published writings, unpublished correspondence and personal documents, in order to elucidate what stand he took in relation to the Rajputs: whether his designation as the Political Resident for the Western Rajput states of the British Government in India led him to function from a position of superiority over his Rajput interlocutors, imposing British knowledge and viewpoints on them, or whether his

## INTRODUCTION

curiosity to acquire historical, topographical and social knowledge about the Rajput states under his jurisdiction inspired him to establish human relationships of trust with ordinary Rajputs as also with learned Rajputs in positions of authority, in order to obtain from them authentic information about their history, geography and social customs. Tod's position, such as it can be discerned from his writings, is one of a self-elected spokesman trying to defend and illustrate the cause of the Rajputs through his publications on information he had gathered about them, before the literate tribune of the world at large (mainly in Europe and Britain). This study will try to analyse some of the complexities and contradictions that such a position presented. My goal is to demonstrate that there were no clear-cut camps opposing authoritarian colonisers against dominated and humiliated colonised people, since human relationships and affectionate bonds of loyalty could and did develop across any such eventual divides. Here, certain ideas expressed by Salman Rushdie in his lecture-essay 'Step across this line' are helpful in understanding Tod's daring, pioneering move to step across the line of his supposed white man's camp into the camp of the Rajputs.[16] Rushdie states that stepping across a frontier involves 'an opening of the self' and 'an increase in what it is possible for the voyager to be'.[17] In this expansion of the self in the encounter with difference, there is 'shape-shifting' and 'self-translation' involved,[18] an adventure that makes change and new opportunities viable.[19] Even if this transformation includes 'a darker meaning'[20] provoking violent conflicts, alternations between expansion and retreat[21] and 'a recurring uncertainty',[22] Rushdie seems to affirm that the risk is definitely worth taking, since 'the dance of history' inevitably implies stepping across 'fixed and shifting lines'.[23] This book through the following chapters tries to illustrate that Tod was undeniably a stepper across lines and frontiers.

Jason Freitag has shown that Tod's use of the travel diary genre in his 'Personal Narrative' sections, at the periphery of his historical annals of past generations of Rajputs, not only permits an emotional identification of the reader with the author,[24] but in Tod's case also demonstrates a rhetorical manoeuvre whereby Tod asserts himself in an authoritative, insider position (in close contact with the Rajputs), in order to use this traveller's position as a reliable observer in order to further the political argument present throughout the body of his works. In fact, according to Freitag, Tod's political agenda was to show that the Rajputs had a historical sensibility and awareness, which made them capable of acceding to modernity and nationhood.[25] Tod was thus politically attempting to place the Rajputs on an equal footing with the peoples of Europe, while fighting against any efforts to relegate them to the inferior position of rude, uncivilised and backward peoples without any sense of history, which would justify their total subjugation by a conquering, colonising power. I perceive this position adopted by Tod as a deliberate choice on his part. I will use it in this study as an example of his constant efforts to incite among the British authorities concerned with India a recognition of the need to enlist an active support for British rule from the Rajputs and from other Indian powers, through a respect by the British for the Indians' sense of pride and honour, so as to preclude any Indian rejection of what they might perceive as a humiliating imposition of external British domination. This political message of tolerance and mutual respect, in fact, went against the dominant British way of thinking at the time (as can be seen in Tod's frictions with his British hierarchical superiors), and also situates him as a man who refused to conform to simplistic, binary oppositions of power, or race or nation.

The present analysis of Tod's writings on the Rajputs is limited exclusively to the background and reception of Tod's texts during Tod's time. Jason Freitag in *Serving Empire, Serving Nation: James Tod and the Rajputs of Rajasthan* chose a wider angle of approach, covering not only the period of the initial publication of Tod's text on Rajasthan, but extending across the nineteenth century and the early twentieth century, with a study of varying interpretations and reutilisations of Tod's account by authorities of the later British Raj in India and by nationalist leaders of the Indian Independence movement:[26]

> What makes Tod and his *Annals* unique, however, is the lasting effect the work has come to have. The *Annals* has taken on a life of its own far outside the context of empire, and in an ironic twist, served the ends of anti-imperialist, nationalist discourse in late nineteenth- and early twentieth-century India. ... Finally, this book spans more than one hundred years, and almost the entire width of the subcontinent, reaching late nineteenth and early twentieth century nationalist writers and activists, particularly in Bengal. The image and stories of the heroic Rajputs in Tod's *Annals* had become transformed into inspirational historic images in the rhetoric and literature of the nationalist movement.

In contrast with Freitag's book on Tod's two volumes on Rajasthan, my study attempts to look closely at the knowledge explorations that went into the construction and contemporary reception of Tod's two volumes on the Rajputs, while including also (as opposed to Freitag) Tod's account of his travels through Gujarat and his shorter compilations that appeared in learned journals of his time.

Two other scholars who have published studies on Tod are Lloyd Rudolph and Norbert Peabody. Lloyd Rudolph, a specialist in political

## INTRODUCTION

science, has used Tod's work on Rajasthan directly and indirectly in wider studies of politics and governance in Rajasthan.[27] He has also reflected on Tod's contribution to the historiography of the Rajputs,[28] while elsewhere contrasting Tod's pro-Rajput views on British governance in India with what Rudolph reads as James Mill's systematically anti-Indian views in his *History of British India*.[29] My approach to Tod's writings, although also incorporating a chapter on Tod and James Mill (Chapter 5), attempts to be less diametrically clear-cut than Lloyd Rudolph's study of Tod and James Mill, since I acknowledge that while Tod expressed clear differences with James Mill's views, he was nevertheless an imperialist who did not wish for the withdrawal of the British Empire from India but hoped instead for material improvement through the means available via Britain's administrative and logistical presence in her Indian territories. Not being a political analyst myself, my study is also less political than Lloyd Rudolph's publications on Tod, as I focus more on literary and aesthetical aspects (landscapes, the use of poetical quotations, Tod's attention to rhetoric). From another angle, Norbert Peabody's publications on Tod's writings manifest a leaning towards the links between Rajput polity on the one hand and religious practices[30] and social anthropology concerning questions like feudalism on the other.[31] I have found Peabody's insights into Tod's perceptions of Rajput feudalism very helpful in writing about Tod as anthropologist (Chapter 2).

Thomas R. Metcalf, in his study *Ideologies of the Raj*,[32] explains the complexities of the varying political positions of specific British authorities at any given time, as also the shifts in differing formulations of the official British stand over different moments in time, as stemming from an absence of any coherent, overall British Raj ideology.[33] He identifies two overlapping poles around which the different British imperial policies can be understood: sameness and difference.[34] Although he finds a major shift in British attitudes to India after the 1857 Indian uprising, when views prioritising difference can be seen to have taken precedence, he also points to contradictions in the application of views of a universal similarity of all of humanity in the period between 1757 and 1858, since already during this first century of British rule in India, certain inferiorising stereotypes of Indian behaviour went hand in hand with a belief in the superior improving potential of impersonal British laws and British notions of private property, when combined with a limited, rational British form of government.[35] Although Metcalf's understanding of British attitudes to India between 1757 and 1835 tends to fall in a little too neatly with Edward Said's polarising interpretation of the role played by the early British Orientalists in solely and wholly consolidating British imperial rule,[36] Metcalf expresses a useful insight in his portrayal of 'the

Romantics in India' (identified by him as including Thomas Munro, John Malcolm, Mountstuart Elphinstone and Charles Metcalfe) as opposed to a Whiggish, Cornwallis-type distant and reformist regime:[37]

> With its concern for individual introspection, its focus on the emotions and the glories of the past, its distrust of artifice, uniformity and abstract learning, Romanticism necessarily challenged much in the Cornwallis system, with its faith in impersonal laws and limited government. ... Sensitive to history as an organic expression of a society's character, anxious to conserve the enduring institutions, as they saw them, of India's past, these men endeavoured to rehabilitate and reclaim for the Raj, what they conceived of as the Indian tradition of personal government.

In particular, on the subject of Tod's perception of the British intervention in Rajputana, Thomas Metcalf outlines the ambivalence on the part of the British in their official policy, as well as the ambivalence of Tod's particular reactions at the grassroots level, in contact with the local Rajput chiefs:[38]

> According to James Tod, British generosity had rescued the Rajputs from destruction by the Afghans and the Marathas. But British alliance with them contained the danger of laying prostrate these ancient relics of civilisation. So Tod saw a need for British non-interference in her alliances with the Rajputs, as a means to perpetuate this oasis of ancient rule.

Even if Metcalf telescopes this Romantic approach further into the nineteenth century, where he perceives its manifestation in the British collector as the compassionate father and mother of the peasantry (which goes beyond the scope of the present study), his classification has the merit of underlining the multiple inspirations that came into play in the formulation of British policies in India. In such a light, Tod can be situated roughly among the Romantics in India, although as I will show later (in Chapter 5), Tod's position also included certain utilitarian ideas of capitalist improvement for his beloved Rajasthan.

In an illuminating article entitled 'Imperial history and post-colonial theory', Dane Kennedy attempts to bridge the gulf between the two very different methods adopted by imperial historians and by post-colonial theorists:[39]

> What, then, does post-colonial theory offer to imperial history? With its mind-numbing jargon, its often crude essentialisations of the West and the Other as binary opposites, and, above all, its deeply ingrained suspicion of historical thinking, one might well wonder if it has anything to offer. ...
> It [post-colonial theory] has raised provocative, often fundamental questions about the epistemological structures of power and the cultural

foundations of resistance, about the porous relationship between metropolitan and colonial societies, and the construction of group identities in the context of state formation, even about the nature and uses of historical evidence itself. ...

Post-colonial theory, then, has contributed to the task of restoring the relationship between centre and periphery, of recovering the connection between the history of Britain and the history of its imperial dependencies – in effect, of putting Humpty-Dumpty back together again. It has done so by demonstrating that imperialism was a process of mutual interaction, of point and counterpoint that inscribed itself on the dominant partner as well as the dominated one. And it has made it clear that any assessment of this interaction which ignores the cultural dimension – that is, the realm of mutual representations of the self and the other – is one that misses what may well be the most persistent and profound legacy of the imperial experience.

This study of Tod's writings attempts to execute some of Dane Kennedy's hints about the useful application of certain insights from post-colonial theory to studies of documents compiled during British rule in India. In particular, I have tried to move beyond essentialised, binary oppositions between British colonial officials and Indians in exploring the porous relations and mutual interactions between these two groups in the process of knowledge constructions about the Rajput states, while also paying attention to the cultural dimension of these exchanges which resulted in mutual representations of the self and the other, on both sides of the colonial gulf.

In a similar vein to Dane Kennedy, David Washbrook[40] takes a firm stand against the exclusionist and exclusivist views of Colonial Discourse Theory and Critique as advocated by Edward Said, Gayatri Spivak, Dipesh Chakrabarty, Gyan Prakash, Ranjit Guha and Gauri Viswanathan. Applied to the historiography of the British Empire, Washbrook sees such an approach as functioning within 'a closed system of reasoning', and by 'a circular process of logic',[41] highlighting only the inverted self-images and consolidations of European domination supposedly produced by all colonial knowledge undertakings. According to Washbrook, Colonial Discourse Critique ignores internal differences within European thoughts on the Colonial Other, such as European praise of non-Europeans, or European hostility to European colonialisms,[42] and it anachronistically uniformises all of European colonial cultural experience into a monolith.[43] It also occludes the positive contributions to colonial power structures and knowledge systems by certain groups among the colonised, and above all, appropriates European concepts such as modernity, freedom, progress or the Romantic rebellion against rigid rationality, paradoxically to reject

Europe while consolidating ascriptive hierarchies and traditional forms of authority within non-European societies.[44] As a way of countering these regrettable consequences of Colonial Discourse Theory and Critique, Washbrook proposes a 'dialogic' approach inspired by Mikhail Bakhtin,[45] in order to take on board dissonance and many-voiced, finely graded differentials of power[46] in our attempts to understand the functionings of the British Empire and in order to give due recognition to the contribution of non-European bodies of knowledge in the forging of world science, world capitalism and world politics, before, during and after periods of colonialism:[47]

> In this [dialogic] focus, emphasis has shifted away from the epistemic closures of 'discourse' to the more open-ended interplay of meanings implied by the concept of 'dialogue'.
> The application of 'dialogics' is in its early stages, and some tension exists between two different understandings of the concept. On the one hand, some scholars evoke it in a post-modernist, Bakhtinian sense, to suggest dissonance in the way that the many 'pieces' of which colonial cultures were comprised, fitted together. But on the other hand, other scholars use the term in a more Enlightenment sense to suggest effective syncretisms and cross-cultural rationalisations. The tension between the two usages is, itself, insightful and may reflect the difficulty of handling complex colonial situations in which not just two but many voices, coming from positions marked by finely graded differentials of power, were speaking. ...
> In shattering Europe's monolithic conceits, 'dialogics' may come to offer a more far-reaching critique of European world centrality and dominance than Discourse Theory ever managed. This critique may also, perhaps, more clearly re-authorise the universalist principles of Reason and Freedom, though not necessarily in their specific European forms.

In this study of Tod's texts on the Rajputs, Washbrook's formulation of a 'dialogic' approach helps me to focus attention on the many-voiced and multi-faceted currents that constitute them, in order to better be aware of the complexities and contradictions at work in Tod's context, rather than simplistically collapsing all his textual constructions into binary oppositions where a monolithic colonisers' discourse is pitted against an erased and inferiorised colonised people. C.A. Bayly has also advocated the use of the notions of 'dialogism' as conceptualised by Mikhail Bakhtin and of 'hybridity' according to Homi Bhabha in his article on Indian informants in Benares under British rule.[48]

Another recent study on knowledge constructions under British rule in north India by Michael S. Dodson has inspired me with pertinent strategies to consider the processes involved in these knowledge exchanges between colonisers and colonised:[49]

## INTRODUCTION

Many writers have attempted to destabilise perceptions of the representational authority of 'science' or colonial discourse, often through an acknowledgement of the importance of accounting for interpersonal 'contact' between formerly disparate socio-cultural groups, together with the need to define colonial encounters within the bounds of a specific historical geographic locality. Homi Bhabha's work, in particular, has foregrounded the inherent instability of colonial discourse when enunciated within the geographical space of colonialism. His essay 'Signs taken for wonders', for example, argues that colonial discourse is inherently ambivalent, and as such, can never be as authoritative as it purports to be, for there is always a 'slip' in meaning, or a hybridisation, during its articulation and reception across socio-cultural boundaries, allowing for both a misunderstanding as well as a subversive redeployment. [Author's note: Homi Bhabha, 'Signs taken for wonders', in: *The Location of Culture*, London: Routledge, 1994.] 'Resistance' is produced, in essence, through recognising a refusal to accept the subject positions inscribed for the colonised in colonial discourse, destroying the Self–Other dialectic which is fundamental to European domination. Despite the many critiques of Bhabha's work [by Robert Young, Bart Moore-Gilbert, Benita Parry], the notion of 'hybridity' he deploys allows for a dynamicism in knowledge and culture, and, importantly, recognises meaning as negotiated and contested, rather than as a unilateral and authoritative imposition.

In the light of Dodson's reading of Homi Bhabha's concept of 'hybridity', Tod can be understood to have gone to the extent of subversively deploying the historical accounts and other details he had gleaned from the Rajputs in their defence. Besides, by developing ties of friendship with his Rajput interlocutors he also refused to accept the subject position (of inferiority) inscribed for the colonised in the official colonial discourse of his day (as visible in the instructions he received from the British Resident in Delhi, David Ochterlony, and from the Governor-General's office in Calcutta, for example). Thus by deliberately subverting in several ways the Self–Other dialectic upon which British colonial domination was founded, Tod was apparently perceived as a threat to the correct functioning of the British administration in India by his British hierarchical superiors, which would explain his feeling of marginalisation and exclusion from official favour, and in all probability this led him to decide to retire prematurely from his post in Rajasthan.

In a pioneering collection of articles, Daniel Carey and Lynn Festa have assembled pertinent suggestions on ways to draw together the concepts and approaches embodied by the terms 'Enlightenment' on the one hand and 'Postcolonialism' on the other.[50] So far, little attention has been given to the two-way interactions that are in fact common to these two fields of study, since the specialist scholars of each of these domains have tended to regard the other domain as hostile, impermeable and irrelevant to their own research. The general aim of the volume seems to be to circumvent the lack of attention to colonialism by Enlightenment scholars, while also attempting to overcome reservations about the universality of Enlightenment categories like 'reason' and 'science' among scholars of Postcolonial Critique. Carey and Festa believe that considering these two fields together can open up alternative historicisations of categories, events and ideas, and in this way lead both fields towards new understandings of the phenomena they study. Since Tod lived astride the end of the Enlightenment period and the emergence of the Romantic period, and since his writings are testimonies of events under the British colonial regime in India, Carey's and Festa's suggestions are helpful for their study. To begin, Carey and Festa advocate a study of diverse practices and specific texts rather than a focus on umbrella concepts like 'race' or 'rationalism'. Indeed, Tod's specific writings are more informative about an individual British colonial officer's attitudes and difficulties, in his specific circumstances, than about general ideas in circulation at the time. Also, Carey and Festa suggest a making plural of 'Enlightenment' as well as of 'Colonialism'. By comparing Tod's travel texts to the travel writings of other British travellers of his time, and by parallel readings of Tod's official dispatches with the dispatches by other contemporary British officials, the positions Tod adopted can be understood as individual and not particularly paradigmatic of any monolithic coloniser's mindset (see Chapters 1 and 6). This corroborates Carey's and Festa's view that there were many possible understandings of facts and experiences through the Enlightenment and Romantic periods. Another suggestion by Carey and Festa is to make contrapuntal readings of individual texts. By searching for textual omissions or varying formulations of the same events within Tod's accounts, I have attempted to bring to light some of the difficulties Tod was up against, for example in his handling of the Kota crisis in October 1821 (see Chapter 6). Carey and Festa advise a use of the dialogic form of analysis (as does Washbrook, above) in order to take into account the voices of the natives, or voices with alternative views, for example. Here, Tod's letters in the Urdu dialect of Mewar to Rana Bheem Singh illustrate two-way personal bonds, outside the official register. An example of shifting alignments within colonies (which according to Carey and Festa can serve to render appropriately complex any monolithic perception of the reactions of the colonised peoples), can be observed in the rivalries between the kingdoms of Marwar and of Jaipur for greater influence at the court of Mewar, as visible in the tragic death of Princess Kishna Kumari of

INTRODUCTION

Mewar (studied here in Chapters 2 and 4). Unplanned uncertainties and reversals that appear in the documents studied also help to avoid teleological, unilinear readings of colonial and postcolonial history according to Carey and Festa. Such a reversal appears in Tod's abrupt departure from Rajasthan after only four and a half years as British political agent to the Western Rajput states, although he gives evidence everywhere of having enjoyed and grown attached to this position (see end of Chapter 6). Finally, Carey and Festa suggest that attention to the many facets and changes in colonisers' representations of the natives can help avoid a unitary understanding of the colonial situation. This can be seen in Tod's sometimes contradictory portrayals of the Rajputs he describes: while he mentions their bonds of loyalty to their local lands, thanks to notions like 'swamdherma' or loyalty to the local chief,[51] and unswerving attachment to the 'bapota' or patrimonial land,[52] he also does not hesitate to allude to counterproductive subdivisions of the frérage or *bhyad*.[53] Here is a summing-up of Carey's and Festa's recommendations on ways of blending together postcolonial theorists' approaches and the methods of scholars of Enlightenment colonialisms:[54]

> The need for sustained engagement between histories of 18th century colonial activity, Enlightenment and postcolonial theory arises from an imperative to think through how the relative value of these forms of Difference [in scientific, theological and anthropological discourses] is produced, not just what these forms of difference might be. The [object is] not to create a history of diversity – comparing pre-given objects of ethical, aesthetic or ethnological interest in order to display, appreciatively, the relativism of all knowledge – but instead address HOW historical and cultural differences are structured. The point is not to reify what constitutes identities in order to compare them, but to address HOW they are made, examining processes of differentiation rather than celebrating differences.

Thus, by interrogating some of the processes and the HOWs of colonial encounter and its results, as suggested by Carey and Festa, in the case of Tod and his Rajputs, this study aims to arrive at a balanced postcolonial understanding of the paradoxical interactions and complex stakes that were present in Tod's experience of Rajasthan.

## *Outline of the book*

This book is made up of an introduction, seven chapters and a conclusion. The five initial chapters cover specific aspects that constitute Tod's two major published texts. Then the two final chapters make a study of Tod's personal exchanges with his contemporaries in India and of his shorter compilations after his return to London.

Chapter 1, 'Tod as an observer of landscape in Rajasthan and Gujarat', based mainly on the 'Personal Narrative' or travel journal sections of *Annals and Antiquities of Rajasthan* and on Tod's *Travels in Western India*, compares Tod's depictions of landscape scenes with the ways in which Tod's contemporaries Francis Buchanan Hamilton and Bishop Reginald Heber deal with landscape in their respective travel accounts. This enables an understanding of the specificity of Tod's overlapping use of existing aesthetic and ideological frameworks in his textual portrayals, to make accessible to his European readers those aspects of the Rajput and Gujarati landscapes that struck him the most.

Chapter 2, 'Tod as anthropologist: trying to understand', studies Tod observing the Rajputs and the Gujaratis in a context of attention by thinkers of the Scottish Enlightenment and French Enlightenment philosophers to kinship systems, social customs, gradations and hierarchisations among different human groups. Tod seems to have tried to adapt his reports to his field observations of the manners and customs, and the relation to history of the Rajputs and the Gujaratis, rather than to project a preconceived grid of interpretation on their social practices with the sole object of consolidating the superiority of Western societies and justifying British colonial intervention in India. Whether it was concerning different tribes, ethnic groups and dynasties, varying interpretations of rights to the land, the social status of women or local histories, Tod seems to have spent his energy mainly in trying to understand, and then in presenting to his European readers, the complexities of his observations on the social practices of the Rajputs and Gujaratis, rather than in situating them in any abstract, hierarchical scale of civilisations.

Chapter 3, 'Tod's practice of science in India: voyages through empirical, common sense', situates Tod in the scientific context of the first two decades of the nineteenth century in Britain, which were the occasion of the institutionalisation of major earth sciences like topographical surveying, geology and botany. In India, colonial British scientists practised empirical field observations in these physical sciences in an overall theoretical framework of classifications and causatory explanations, inspired by the common-sense philosophy of the Scottish Enlightenment. With the help of his British companions, his Indian assistants and Western scientific instruments, Tod recorded notations of relative topographical situations of places, geological formations and botanical specialities of the regions he traversed. Since he was not a trained scientist himself, Tod's scientific remarks include utilitarian reflections on the economic potential of the natural resources of

## INTRODUCTION

Rajasthan and Gujarat, but also show that in his own way, he participated in the introduction of ideas of Western science into Indian contexts.

Chapter 4, 'Tod's use of Romanticism in his textual constructions of Rajasthan and Gujarat', shows that Tod's use of a heroic Romantic register and of quotations from Romantic writers like Byron and Scott in his published works can be compared with the recourse to literary quotations by some of his British contemporaries in India like James Forbes and Bishop Heber. Tod's renderings of heroic legends from Rajput bardic chronicles can be understood to have been inspired by Romanticism's idealisation of the heroic spirit and its nostalgia for a chivalrous past. Tod's use of quotations from Romantic poets and novelists, while not extraneous and moralising like the quotations used by James Forbes, resembles Heber's deliberate incorporation of literary references into the body of his travel narrative in order to heighten its emotional impact and to render more comprehensible to his British readers his experiences in India. However, Tod differs from Heber in his greater sympathy and serious attention to the proud past and ideals of the Rajputs in their own right. Tod's use of literary Romanticism can be classified under three types, according to David Arnold:[55] first, a sentimental, nostalgic Romanticism, which would include Tod's allusions to bleak ruins; second, a dark and brooding Orientalist Romanticism which would incorporate Tod's literary mentions of cosmic elements and an epic register; and finally, a heroic, Byronic Romanticism which would encompass Tod's poetic meditations on death and the futility of life, and paradoxically also on human love. Finally, Tod's use of quotations from Romantic literary texts seems to play a double role: an aesthetic role of making strange settings and events familiar by establishing cultural bridges through well-known literary favourites; and then an ideological role of advocating a flexible colonial regime that would respect age-old Rajput customs and the Rajput sense of honour, while awakening in Britain 'a sympathy for ... the interesting people of Rajasthan'.[56]

Chapter 5, 'Tod's Romantic approach as opposed to James Mill's Utilitarian approach to British government in India', puts side by side the ideological contexts and publications of James Mill (1773–1836) and James Tod (1782–1835), which appear on the surface to be diametrically opposed. Mill never visited India, adhered to Jeremy Bentham's rational Utilitarian philosophy and published in 1817 his *History of British India*, which, while tracing the arrival and expansion of the British in India (1600–1805), attributed what James Mill considered as India's low and rude state of civilisation in the 1800s to an absence of reliable historical records and to a too great submission to superstition and despotism. James Tod, on the other hand, spent twenty-two years in India, respected the non-European uniqueness of Rajput historical chronicles and spent much of his energy in establishing a coherent narrative of the past exploits of the various Rajput clans, with a view to securing policies that would ensure Rajput support for the British Government in India. In 1831–2, in their recommendations to the British Parliament in the context of the renewal of the East India Company's Charter, the respective views of Mill and Tod again seem poles apart: concerning the mixed system of British subsidiary alliances, on the levying of land taxes and the collection of duties on agricultural products, and about the relations of the East India Company with native Indian employees. However, the advocates of both the Romantic and the Utilitarian approaches were inspired by similar high ideals of achieving the most advantageous way of governing India, and had to face the same multiple political, bureaucratic and human pressures in Britain and in India. In fact, James Mill can be understood to have supported innovative reforms and genuinely liberating change for India, while Tod can be seen to have combined an ethos of Romanticism with a Utilitarian agenda of down-to-earth improvements.

Chapter 6, 'Tod's knowledge exchanges with his contemporaries in India', aims to arrive at as complete a picture of Tod as possible through his written mentions of and exchanges with his contemporaries. Tod's family had Scottish connections, and his two maternal uncles, named Heatly, were members of the Bengal Civil Service in India. Mentions of encounters with wild animals, hunting and fishing in India provide light entertainment for Tod's readers, in the midst of his dense historical and political accounts. Allusions to tensions about British appointments and responsibilities, and a textual ellipsis in the travel narrative of Tod's third journey from Mewar (June 1821 to March 1822) reveal official distrust between Tod and his hierarchical superior David Ochterlony. Similarly, the very few mentions of illness during the early years of Tod's stay in Rajasthan (1819–20) contrasted with more frequent experiences of ill health from 1820 onwards, indicating official pressures and professional worries that intervened later. Tod's field account book covering thirty months, from November 1819 to April 1822, provides concrete details on the precise amounts Tod had to spend in his official capacity, in his dealings with British and Indian subordinates, in his contacts with local Indian chiefs and as part of a punctilious British bureaucracy. A series of eleven letters in the local Urdu dialect, written from various field positions in Rajasthan and Gujarat, by Tod to Rana Bheem Singh of Mewar, between March 1820 and November 1822, cover Mewar political matters and the personal friendship between Tod and Rana Bheem Singh. Through his Scottish

INTRODUCTION

links, his firm defence of his personal views on Rajput affairs and the numerous transactions and human relationships he entered into during his years in Western India, we catch glimpses of a tormented but committed Tod.

Chapter 7, 'Tod among his contemporaries in London, 1823–35', closes the volume with a look at Tod's twelve shorter essays, presented by him before learned societies in London and Paris, between 1824 and 1835. In two steps concerning these shorter essays, an analysis is made of (a) Tod's deployment of an apparatus of erudition and (b) Tod's attention to language. By unfolding parallels and comparisons between the Rajput coins, artefacts, sculptures, inscriptions and religious land grants, which he was presenting on the one hand, and similar inscriptions, coins, ancient texts, mythologies, religious practices and sculptures from a whole host of other ancient and medieval cultures on the other hand, Tod was deliberately setting Rajput history and culture alongside those other ancient and medieval cultures evoked, as equally worthy of scholarly attention. Tod's inclusion of personal connections to other scholars, texts and places of learning in his shorter compilations gives these writings the emotional stamp of an authentic eyewitness, putting forward reliable information for a scholarly readership in Britain and Europe. His careful treatment of the rhetorical structures and poetical expressions in the original Rajput texts he translated into English shows his keen respect of all things Rajput. To conclude this seventh chapter, a brief overview of the reviews that Tod's various publications received in the learned journals of his time is presented in order to illustrate the contemporary reception of the published results of his knowledge gathering on the Rajputs and Western India.

In the conclusion to the volume, 'Tod's sympathetic understanding of Rajput difference', an overall assessment is made of Tod's place in his own time among the learned circles of Britain and Europe, as a participant in knowledge exchanges with the Rajputs, with the aim of defending them as a historically grounded people fully capable of moving into the modern world, without however questioning the beneficial effects of prolonged British rule in India. This deliberate choice on Tod's part explains his political efforts to incite among the British authorities concerned with India a recognition of the need to enlist an active support for British rule from the Rajputs and from other Indian powers, through a respect by the British for the Indians' sense of pride and honour, so as to preclude any Indian rejection of what they might perceive as a humiliating imposition of external British rule. Thus, Tod can be seen to have been simultaneously a defender of the Rajputs and a defender of the British Empire in India. This political message of tolerance and mutual respect, which went against the dominant

British way of thinking at the time, also situates Tod as an individual who refused to conform to simplistic, binary oppositions of power, or race or nation. A few, rapid comparisons of Tod's trajectory with other scholarly British traveller-philanthropists, in the Middle East for example, are undertaken in order to permit a clearer understanding of the particularities of Tod's role concerning knowledge constructions about the Rajputs and the Gujaratis.

## Notes

1 James Tod, *Travels in Western India*, London: W.H. Allen & Co., 1839, 'Advertisement', p.vii.
2 Tod, *Travels*, p. v.
3 See Jason Freitag, *Serving Nation, Serving Empire: James Tod and the Rajputs of Rajasthan*, Leiden: Brill, 2009, pp. 132–3.
4 *Transactions of the Royal Asiatic Society*, 1 (1827), 133–54.
5 *Transactions of the Royal Asiatic Society*, 1 (1827), 207–29.
6 *Transactions of the Royal Asiatic Society*, 1 (1827), 313–42.
7 *Journal Asiatique*, 1.11 (January–June 1827), 277–309.
8 *Transactions of the Royal Asiatic Society*, 2 (1830), 270–325.
9 *Transactions of the Royal Asiatic Society*, 2 (1830), 328–40.
10 *Transactions of the Royal Asiatic Society*, 2 (1830), 559–72.
11 *Transactions of the Royal Asiatic Society*, 2 (1835), 139–59.
12 *Asiatic Journal and Monthly Register for British and Foreign India, China and Australasia*, new series, 5.17 (May–August 1831), 40–8.
13 *Journal Asiatique*, new series, 8 (July–December 1831), 46–66.
14 *Asiatic Journal and Monthly Register for British and Foreign India, China and Australasia*, 17.65 (May–August 1835), 9–15.
15 *Asiatic Journal or the Monthly Register*, 25.1 (January–April 1838), 101–12; 197–211; 273–86.
16 Salman Rushdie, 'Step across this line', in: *Step Across this Line: Collected Non-fiction 1992-2002*, London: Jonathan Cape, 2002, pp. 407–42.
17 Rushdie, 'Step across this line', p. 409
18 Rushdie, 'Step across this line', p. 434.
19 Rushdie, 'Step across this line', pp. 415, 419.
20 Rushdie, 'Step across this line', p. 421.
21 Rushdie, 'Step across this line', p. 424.
22 Rushdie, 'Step across this line', p. 425.
23 Rushdie, 'Step across this line', p. 425.
24 See Jean Viviès, *Le récit de voyage en Angleterre au XVIIIe siècle*, Collection Interlangues Littérature, Toulouse: Presses Universitaires du Mirail, 1999, p. 167: 'De même que ce que découvre le voyageur au terme de son voyage n'est pas vraiment un autre monde mais un moment du sien, de même "l'autre" du texte, narrateur, personnage, voyageur, nous renvoie, par réfraction, une image de ce que nous sommes sans le savoir. La lecture réunit ce qui était disjoint et permet au lecteur, non plus de se reconnaître, mais véritablement d'apprendre sur lui-même.'
25 Jason Freitag, 'Travel, history, politics and heritage: James Tod's "Personal Narrative"', in: Carol E. Henderson and Maxine Weisgrau (eds), *Raj Rhapsodies: Tourism, Heritage and the Seduction of History*, Aldershot: Ashgate, 2007, pp. 47–59.
26 Freitag, *Serving Empire, Serving Nation*, pp. 10, 18.
27 Lloyd Rudolph and Susanne Hoeber Rudolph, 'Rajputana under British Paramountcy: the failure of Indirect Rule'. *Journal of Modern History*, 38 (1966), 138–60. Also Lloyd Rudolph and Susanne Hoeber Rudolph, 'Occidentalism and

## INTRODUCTION

Orientalism: perspectives in legal pluralism', in: S.C. Humphreys (ed.), *Cultures of Scholarship*, Ann Arbor: University of Michigan Press, 1997, pp. 219–51.
28 Lloyd Rudolph, 'Writing and reading Tod's Rajasthan: interpreting the text and its historiography', in: Jos Gommans and Om Prakash (eds), *Circumambulations in South Asian History: Essays in Honour of Dirk H.A. Kolff*, Leiden: Brill, 2003, pp. 251–82.
29 Lloyd Rudolph, 'Tod vs. Mill, clashing perspectives on British Rule in India and Indian civilization', in: Giles Tillotson (ed.), *James Tod's Rajasthan: The Historian and His Collections*, Mumbai: Radhika Sabavala for Marg Publications on behalf of the National Centre for the Performing Arts, 2007, pp. 122–33; simultaneously published as *Mārg*, 59.1 (2007).
30 Norbert Peabody, *Hindu Kingship and Polity in Precolonial India*, Cambridge: Cambridge University Press, 2003.
31 Norbert Peabody, 'Tod's *Rajast'han* and the boundaries of imperial rule in 19th century India'. *Modern Asian Studies*, 30.1 (1996), 185–220.
32 Thomas R. Metcalf, *Ideologies of the Raj*, Cambridge: Cambridge University Press, 2001 (1995).
33 Metcalf, *Ideologies of the Raj*, 'Preface', p. xi.
34 Metcalf, *Ideologies of the Raj*, 'Preface', p. x.
35 Metcalf, *Ideologies of the Raj*, Chapter 1, pp. 23–4.
36 Edward Said, *Orientalism*, New York: Vintage Books, 1979 (1978).
37 Metcalf, *Ideologies of the Raj*, pp. 24–5.
38 Metcalf, *Ideologies of the Raj*, pp. 73, 79–80.
39 Dane Kennedy, 'Imperial history and Post-Colonial Theory'. *Journal of Imperial and Commonwealth History*, 24.3 (1996), 345–63.
40 David Washbrook, 'Orients and occidents: colonial discourse theory and the historiography of the British Empire', in: Robin W. Winks and Alaine Low (eds), *The Oxford History of the British Empire*, vol. V, *Historiography*, Oxford: Oxford University Press, 1999, pp. 596–611.
41 Washbrook, 'Orients and occidents', p. 597.
42 Washbrook, 'Orients and occidents', p. 603.
43 Washbrook, 'Orients and occidents', pp. 603–4.
44 Washbrook, 'Orients and occidents', pp. 605, 608.
45 Mikhail Bakhtin, *The Dialogic Imagination: Four Essays*, Austin & London: University of Texas Press, 1981.
46 Washbrook, 'Orients and occidents', p. 609.
47 Washbrook, 'Orients and occidents', pp. 609–10.
48 C.A. Bayly, 'Orientalists, informants and critics in Banaras, 1790–1860', in: Jamal Malik (ed.), *Perspectives of Mutual Encounters in South Asian History, 1760–1860*, Leiden: Brill, 2000, pp. 97–127.
49 Michael S. Dodson, *Orientalism, Empire and National Culture: India 1770–1880*, Basingstoke: Palgrave Macmillan, 2007, pp. 8–9.
50 Daniel Carey and Lynn Festa (eds), *The Postcolonial Enlightenment: Eighteenth-Century Colonialism and Postcolonial Theory*, Cambridge: Cambridge University Press, 2009, pp. 1–33.
51 James Tod, *Annals and Antiquities of Rajasthan*, vol. I, London: Routledge & Kegan Paul Ltd, 1829; repr. Delhi: Rupa & Co., 1997, p. 139.
52 Tod, *Annals*, vol. I, p. 382.
53 Tod, *Annals*, vol. I, p. 141.
54 Carey and Festa (eds), *The Postcolonial Enlightenment*, pp. 24–5.
55 David Arnold, *The Tropics and the Travelling Gaze: India, Landscape and Science, 1800–1856*, Seattle: University of Washington Press, 2006, pp. 94–8.
56 James Tod, *Annals and Antiquities of Rajasthan*, vol. II, London: Routledge & Kegan Paul Ltd, 1832; repr. Delhi: Rupa & Co., 1997, p. vii.

# CHAPTER ONE

# Tod as an observer of landscape in Rajasthan and Gujarat

The years during which James Tod was in central and western India (1800–22), as also the years when he wrote the accounts of his experiences in India after his return to London (1823–35), were years of economic, political, aesthetic and scientific transformation in Great Britain and Europe. The Industrial Revolution in Britain was changing the traditional rural, agricultural economy into an urbanised economy centred on factory production; there were moves for electoral reform, in order to extend the right to vote to a larger part of the population; the Napoleonic wars changed the European political scene; and there were new empirical approaches in fields of scientific investigation such as geology, geography, botany, zoology, chemistry, physics and anatomy.

In the aesthetic field of artistic production also, there was a shift towards more direct observation of the objects and scenes depicted, a greater emphasis on atmospheric effects through contrasts of light and shade, with a preference for rough and ragged colouring in what came to be labelled as the 'Picturesque'. This picturesque mode of pictorial representation stood halfway between the earlier classical aesthetic categories of the Sublime (which inspired terror through imposing size or darkness) and the Beautiful (which incited pleasure through reassuring harmonies).[1] Picturesque depictions of landscapes, in trying to provoke astonishment and delight, also took inspiration from seventeenth-century classical landscape artists like Claude Lorrain and Salvator Rosa, who had experimented with light and shade effects, from a narrow, low viewpoint in a restricted range of tones, to create a brooding, moody atmosphere. These picturesque landscape characteristics had been taken up in the late eighteenth century by neo-classical explorers like Winckelmann and d'Hancarville in connection with Greece and Egypt.[2] Transposed into the colonial setting of the East India Company's activities in India, British landscape depictions showed emphasis chiefly on topographical accuracy linked to military

2 Citadel of the hill fortress of Komulmer.
(By kind permission of the Royal Asiatic Society of Great Britain and Ireland)

surveying and a utilitarian approach to exotic species of vegetation and geological strata. Nevertheless atmospheric effects and melancholy meditations on ruins also had their place among British visual portrayals of India around Tod's time, as for example in scenes drawn by William Hodges and Thomas and William Daniell.[3]

Tod resorted to comparisons with familiar landscape elements from the Scotland of his family ancestors, in order to textually render novel landscape details he observed in Rajasthan and Gujarat. That Tod was completely a man of his time can be seen in the occurrences of the terms 'picturesque' and 'sublime' in the accounts of his travels in Rajasthan and Gujarat, which appear in the parts labelled 'Personal Narrative' in each of the two volumes of his *Annals and Antiquities of Rajasthan* and throughout his posthumous *Travels in Western India*.[4] Tod makes several textual depictions of picturesque and sublime landscapes associated with their visual representations by his able assistant and kinsman Captain Patrick Waugh (1788–1829), who accompanied Tod throughout his peregrinations in Rajasthan from 1819 to 1823, being also a gifted watercolourist. Tod's text on Gujarat was illustrated with engravings of sketches made by Mrs Eliza Blair, wife of Colonel William Hunter Blair of the Bombay Army, in the 1820s.[5] In studying Tod's observations of Rajasthani and Gujarati landscapes, we will proceed chronologically through the two sections of his 'Personal Narrative' in his two volumes on Rajasthan, and then through his account of his travels across Gujarat. We will focus first on three sites from Tod's first volume on Rajasthan: Kumbhalgarh, north of Udaipur, followed by the sacred lake of Pushkar, near Ajmer, and then Udaipur itself, a presentation of which closes Tod's first volume. In our second section, we will look at three sites from Tod's second volume on Rajasthan: the Mukundwara Pass, south of Kota, followed by the temples of Ganga Bheva in the forest of Puchail in eastern Mewar and finally the temples of Menal (Mahanal), between Bijolia and Begun, west of Kota. We will end this chapter with an analysis of Tod's presentation of a few sites he observed in Gujarat. Our aim here is to analyse the textual strategies Tod uses to convey impressions of picturesque or sublime scenes. In order to establish points of comparison with Tod's landscape depictions, we will mention the travel narratives of two of Tod's contemporaries: Francis Buchanan Hamilton and Bishop Heber.[6]

## Scottish landscape terms

To begin with Tod's use of Scottish terms to refer to landscape details that he observed in Rajasthan, we can note 'crag' (from the Gaelic 'craig', 'creog' or 'carraig', meaning a rough, steep rock or point) and its adjective 'craggy' (meaning rugged, made up of broken rocks); 'glen' (from the Celtic term 'gleann', meaning a narrow valley worn by a river or alternatively a depression between hills); and 'cairn' (from the Celtic 'carn', meaning a heap of stones raised specifically over a grave or more generally a stone landmark on a mountain top; in addition, the Cairngorms mountain range in the Scottish eastern highlands produces a type of quartz, crystal rock called 'cairn').

The first observable use of 'crag' by Tod is in a comparative context to point out the universality of human inventiveness in circumventing practical problems between Nathdwara and Sumaicha on his way to Kumbhalmer in October 1819:[7]

> Here we have proof that ingenuity is the same, when promoted by necessity, in the Jura or the Aravulli. Wherever soil could be found, or time decomposed these primitive rocks, a barrier was raised. When discovered, should it be in a hollow below, or on the summit of a CRAG, it is alike greedily seized on; even there water is found, and if you leave the path below and ascend a hundred feet above the terraces, you will discover pools or reservoirs dammed in with massive trees,

which serve to irrigate such insulated spots, or serve as nurseries to the young rice-plants.

In his second volume on Rajasthan, we find 'craggy summits' where the Boondi range of mountains is viewed from Talera in the Kotah region in September 1820:[8]

> The country and roads, as usual, flat, with an apparent descent from Talera to the base of the Boondi range, whose CRAGGY and unequal summits showed it could be no buttress to the table-land with which it unites. The general direction of the range is east-north-east, though there are diverging ridges, the course of which it is impossible to delineate.

In both these examples, the Scottish terms 'crag' and 'craggy' underline the roughness of the rocky peaks in question.

Tod uses the term 'glen' in connection with the narrow valleys at Kumbhalgarh (or Komulmer), an ancient capital of the Chohan Rajputs and with the lake at Pushcoonda encountered when descending from Mundore, the former, ancient capital of the Marwar Rathores of Jodhpur. The contrast in altitude between the steep hill faces and the bottom of the glen at Kumbhalgarh is clearly expressed: 'Noble forest trees covered every face of the hills and the bottom of the glen, through which, along the margin of the serpentine torrent, which we repeatedly crossed, lay our path.'[9] The sound of rushing water 'towards the banks of the stream, the roar of whose waters was our guide,' 'the tumultuous rush', 'the voice of the waters of a deeper and hoarser tone', further underline the impression of steep, mountainous terrain. At the glen of Pushcoonda also, the term 'glen' highlights Tod's depiction of declivity: 'Let us now descend by the same causeway to the glen of Pushcoonda, where there is much to gratify both the lover of the picturesque and the architectural antiquary.'[10]

In his *Travels in Western India*, Tod uses the term 'glen', along with 'dale' and 'dell' to portray narrow river valleys between hills. At Gurriah, between Palitana and Junagadh, in the Kathiawar peninsula of Gujarat, Tod appears sensitive to the picturesque landscape of glens:[11]

> [We] marched nearly seven miles over this wild upland scenery, picturesque and interesting, in the highest degree. Small rivulets pour their pellucid waters from the dark clefts through well-wooded glens, at every mile of our route.

A little further into Gujarat, Tod qualifies the 'wild dell' in Babriawar [Babra], a sterile and mountainous area between Palitana and Junagadh, where the giant named Tulsishyam is reputed to have conducted his legendary combat, with at its base a hot-well called 'Seeta-Coond', as 'presenting some pretensions to the picturesque'.[12] As he approached the peaks of Mount Girnar, in the pastoral plains of Kowrewar and Goreedur [Gariadhar], Tod is sensitive to the beauty of the landscape, with its alternation of hill and dale:[13]

> Soon after we passed over the Sangavari, and another Machandri, near Goreedur. Here is fine exercise for the pencil; the village is surmounted by its castle and quadrangular towers, black with age upon a rock, and overlooking a noble expanse of hill and dale. On one side the five peaks of Girnar; on the other, the towns upon the sea-coast, whose rocky bound is elevated so as to exclude a view of the ocean.

Similarly, Tod comments on the topographical situation of Goomli, the ruined capital of the Jaitwas, northeast of Porbunder, between Junagadh and Dwarka, especially on its appearing ensconced in 'a dell or valley': '[Goomli] may be said to be buried in a dell or valley, bounded to the south and east by the Burrira hills, rising about six hundred feet from their base, and the rest is concealed by a low ridge.'[14] Tod's mentions of 'glens' and 'dells' in the course of his journeys can be understood to express his awareness of natural beauty, particularly in scenes where the sloped landscape offered contrasting heights.

'Cairn' features several times in Tod's text, always to refer to tombstones of Rajput warriors. At Mundore, the former Rathore capital in Marwar, in November 1819, Tod uses several synonymous terms for 'cairn' without mentioning the word 'cairn' itself:[15] 'cenotaphs of the Rathores', 'these necrological monuments', 'monumental relics', 'dewuls' or 'domestic temples', all indicating the stone memorials in the cemetery of the Rathores. While describing the ramparts of Mundore proper, Tod draws a comparison with the ancient Etruscan cities of Cortona, Volterra and Todi, situated in today's Tuscany, near Florence. Tod sees in the walls of the ancient Tuscan cities and in Mundore 'the same ponderous character' termed 'Cyclopean' in ancient Etruria. Here, it is through a detour via ancient Italy that Tod expresses the giganticness of the walled fortifications of Mundore.

During his second journey to Kotah and Bundi in 1820, Tod noted the 'cairn' of a Rajput on the banks of the Bunas River and made the gesture of participating in the customary homage to the dead warrior by adding a stone to the heap.[16] Between Bhynsror and Kotah, at Dabi, during the same journey in 1820, Tod uses both the Scottish term 'cairns' and the Rajasthani term 'pallia', as well as the Latin term 'tumuli', to indicate the tombstone of a Charun bard who was slain with other Rajputs as they defended their cattle, by bandit-like tribal Meenas who 'dwell amidst the ravines of the Bunas'.[17]

Tod notes 'the cenotaphs of the Haras' at Kotah in September 1820, at the end of his six-month stay in Kotah, as 'trophies of their sires' and 'a tribute to virtue'.[18] Here again, the word 'cenotaphs' takes the place of the term 'cairns', with the same commemorative meaning.

Finally, Tod lets the reader in on one of his erroneous traveller hypotheses about the possible meaning of a strange feature encountered along the way. It is about stone pillars between Bhynsror and Barolli in August 1821, during this third journey from Udaipur:[19]

> We descended along a natural causeway, the rock being perfectly bare, without a particle of mould or vegetation. Small pillars, or uninscribed tablets, placed erect in the centre of little heaps of stone, seemed to indicate the scene of murders, when the Bhil lord of the pass exacted his toll from all who traversed his dominion. They proved, however, to be marks placed by the *Bunjarris* to guide their *tandas*, or caravans, through the devious tracks of the forest.

Here, though the Scottish term 'cairn' does not appear, Tod's conjectures about the possible meaning of these 'uninscribed tablets' show his efforts to make sense of unfamiliar landscape features.

In his *Travels in Western India*, Tod resorts to a variety of terms (both in English and in local Indian languages) to refer to funeral monuments: 'cairn', 'pallia', 'than', 'joojurh' and 'tomb' for funeral monuments of Muslims, as well as more general terms like 'cenotaphs', 'necropolis' and 'tumulus'. Tod reports the sacred mount of Shatrunjaya near Palitana, southwest of Bhavnagar, as bearing the Muslim tomb of Henga Peer, the 'pallia' or sepulchral stone of a Jain sweetmaker and devotee of Adnath, a Hindu 'than' or commemoration monument in honour of Lord Krishna's six brothers who had been massacred by the evil King Kansa, and the 'joojurhs' of a large number of Hindu Rajput warriors, with their allegorical *relievi* showing the social class of the fallen braves.[20] This endows the sacred mount with a multi-religious atmosphere, in a spirit of typically Indian syncretism.

In *Travels in Western India*, Tod also mentions the 'pallias' of three Gujarati dynasties. First, the 'pallias' of the Jaitwas in their ruined capital of Goomli, northeast of Porbunder, from which he deduces that the date of the destruction of Goomli can be situated in the middle of the eleventh century (between 1056 and 1063 CE), corresponding to a few decades after the invasion of Gujarat by Mahomed of Ghazni (around 1026 CE).[21] Then, two tombs of pirates of the Badhail clan, at Aramra, near Dwarka, indicate through their sculptured inscriptions and high reliefs that these Gujarati pirates engaged in combat in their ships and lost their lives on the high seas.[22] And finally, from the humble 'pallias' at the necropolis of the Jhareja Raos of Cutch, in their capital of Bhuj, in the farthest western corner of Gujarat,[23] Tod concludes that the Jharejas had developed their own monumental particularity in their 'pallias': enclosure of the necrological monument within 'a stone screen or lattice, as if to keep out the profane', which did not exist in the Rajput 'pallias' which Tod had had occasion to observe.

By situating these new phenomena through connections with familiar Scottish terms, or well-known European architectural monuments or through imagined meanings, later rectified by information gleaned from local people, Tod manifests a typical Enlightenment-influenced approach of proceeding rationally through ground observation, and verifying hypotheses against evidence obtained along the way.

This brings us to the second part of this chapter, where we will study Tod's textual descriptions of certain 'picturesque' and 'sublime' sites he visited in Rajasthan and in Gujarat.

## *Kumbhalgarh, Pushkar and Udaipur*

Arriving at Kumbhalgarh (or Komulmer), a fortified complex on a rocky summit in the Aravalli mountains between Udaipur and Jodhpur, in October 1820,[24] Tod spends seven pages of his text describing the natural setting, the different ruins and fortifications, and the historical legends around the famed Prithviraj, who was allegedly poisoned by a jealous kinsman, shortly before the Mughal invasion of India, and his beloved Solanki wife, Tara Bai of Bednore (Bidnaur), who committed sati on the pyre of her deceased young husband at the place of the shrine subsequently built in their honour, 'on the opposite side of the valley, and almost in the gorge of the pass'.[25] Tod compares this 'simple monumental shrine' to the 'Sybilline temple of Tivoli' (near Rome), and comments on its unpretentiousness. In contrast to this vignette of refined plainness, he sketches verbally the imposing height of the Kumbhalgarh peak:

> The spot where I encamped was at least five hundred feet lower than Arait Pol, the first of the fortified barriers leading to Komulmer, whose citadel rose more than seven hundred feet above the *terre-pleine* [sic] of its outworks beneath.[26]

Further on, Tod specifies that 'the peak of Komulmer will be 3,353 feet above the level of the ocean'.[27] He then describes his descent from this exalted, natural grandeur:

> For nearly a mile there was but just breadth sufficient to admit the passage of a loaded elephant, the descent being at an angle of 55° with the horizon and streams on either side rushing with a deafening roar over their rugged beds. ... For another mile it became more gentle, when we passed under a tower of Komulmer, erected on a scarped projection of the rock, full five hundred feet above us. The scenery was magnificent; the

mountains rising on each side in every variety of form, and their summits, as they caught a ray of the departing sun, reflecting on our sombre path a momentary gleam, from the masses of rose-coloured quartz which crested them. ... Notwithstanding all our mishaps, partly from the novelty and grandeur of the scene, and partly from the invigorating coolness of the air, our mirth became wild and clamorous: a week before, I was oppressed with a thousand ills; and now I trudged the rugged path, leaping the masses of granite which had rolled into the torrent.[28]

Here, Tod underlines the 'variety of form' and the contrast between 'a momentary gleam' from the setting sun and the shade of 'our sombre path'. These typical characteristics of the picturesque – variety and contrasts between light and shadow – are further heightened by the sudden exuberance of Tod and his group.

On his return journey from Jodhpur to his headquarters in Udaipur, Tod halted at the Pushkar Lake near the city of Ajmer in December 1820.[29] Tod alternates observations on the striking colours of the geological strata of the surrounding mountains – a 'rose tint' on one side and a 'greyish granite' on the other, with 'white quartz about their summits' – with a description of the visible structures around the lake:

> Pushkar is the most sacred lake in India: that of Mansurwar [Mansarovar] in Thibet may alone compete with it in this respect. It is placed in the centre of the valley, which here becomes wider, and affords abundant space for the numerous shrines and cenotaphs with which the hopes and fears of the virtuous and the wicked amongst the magnates of India have studded its margin. It is surrounded by sand-hills of considerable magnitude, excepting on the east. ... Every Hindu family of rank has its niche here, for the purposes of devotional pursuits when they could abstract themselves from mundane affairs.[30]

Here Tod has perspicaciously remarked on the Indian version of the frequent blend of involvement in 'mundane affairs' like politics, trade, amassing wealth or resolving family disputes on the one hand, alongside absorption in 'devotional pursuits' on the other. To these empirical observations, Tod adds accounts of the mythological legends of the origin of the sanctity of Pushkar. Being the site of the Creator Brahma's primordial sacrifice, 'before Creation began', it contained the 'sole tabernacle dedicated to the One God' throughout India, built only four years prior to Tod's visit there, that is around 1816, by a devout minister of the Maratha chieftain Sindhia. Tod explains through popular folklore the *teeba*s or sand-hills in the valley around the lake:

> During these rites [i.e. Brahma's primordial sacrifice], Mahadeva, or, as he is called, Bhola Nath, represented always in a state of stupefaction from the use of intoxicating herbs, omitted to put out the sacred fire,

[ 27 ]

which spread, and was likely to involve the world in combustion; when Brimha extinguished it with the sand, and hence the *teeba*s of the valley. Such is the origin of the sanctity of Poshkur.[31]

Tod's last comment shows his deliberate refrainment from any value judgements on the belief systems he was inventorying. A little later in the same paragraph though, he confesses his 'heretical' disbelief of the local brahmins' claim to possess 'a copper plate grant from the Purihara prince of the lands about Poshkur'.

Apart from his three journeys across different parts of the region in 1819, in 1820 and in 1821–2, Tod spent most of the time he was posted in Rajasthan at Udaipur, the Mewar capital.[32] Tod's description of Udaipur features at the end of his 'Personal Narrative' in volume I, marking his return there after his two-month journey to and from Jodhpur, via Kumbhalgarh and Ajmer, at the end of 1819. This description divides into three parts: first, a panoramic description of the Mewar capital with its chain of fortresses as viewed from the east; then, an evocation of the ancient, adjoining site of Ahar containing the cenotaphs of all the Mewar rulers down the ages; and finally, Tod's reflections on the surprising juxtaposition of Jain and Shaivite images in the monuments at Ahar.

In the first part, Tod chooses to underline the contrast between the 'airy elegance' of the Udaipur palace complex, with the heavy solidness of 'the pierced battlements of the city beneath'. Tod notes 'the same aspect of decay' that enveloped 'these castellated heights'.[33] Here, we have a blend of picturesque contrast and a Romantic preoccupation with ruins. In the second part of Tod's description of Udaipur, devoted to the necropolis of Ahar, as a faithful Orientalist, gathering as much information as possible, Tod gives a brief history of the site: from the Tamba-Nagri of the Tuar ancestors of Vikramaditya, to the Anundpoor or 'happy city' founded by Asa-ditya, the direct ancestor of the Mewar ranas, and finally to 'Ahar', whence the patronymic Aharya of the Guhilot clan of Mewar.[34] Finally, Tod concludes his description of Ahar with reflections on its undoubted antiquity:

> But the most superficial observer will pronounce Ar to have been an ancient and extensive city, the walls which enclose this sepulchral abode being evidently built with the sculptured fragments of temples. Some shrines, chiefly Jain, are still standing, though in the last stage of dilapidation, and they have been erected from the ruins of shrines still older, as appears from the motley decorations where statues and images are inserted with their heads reversed, and Mahavira and Mahadeva come into actual contact: all are in white marble. Two inscriptions were obtained; one very long and complete, in the nail-headed character of the Jains; but their interpretation is yet a desideratum. A topographical map

of this curious valley would prove interesting, and for this I have sufficient materials.[35]

As always, Tod appears here as the indefatigable topographer and devoted collector of ancient inscriptions, sensitive to the successive sedimentation of historical evidence in ancient human sites, somewhat similar to the sedimentation of the earth's strata. This unifying approach to research and human knowledge was typical of the Enlightenment period, which preceded the later nineteenth-century specialisation and separations between exact sciences, life sciences and social sciences.

## *Mukundwara, Ganga Bheva and Menal*

In the second volume of *Annals and Antiquities of Rajasthan*, Tod recounts his second trip out of Udaipur from January to October 1820, when he visited Kota, Bundi and Mandalgarh, as well as his third journey from July 1821 to February 1822, when he visited Bundi, Kota, Mukundwara, Baroli, Dhamnar and Jhalrapatan. It is during this third trip, in November 1821, that Tod describes the Mukundwara Pass through the Puchail mountains and forest that separate Harawati (including Kota and Bundi) from 'the fine plains of Malwa' to the south.[36] It is the area through which the upper Chambal River flows north-eastwards to join the Jumna (Yamuna). Here is how Tod describes it:

> The sun rose just as we cleared the summit of the pass, and we halted for a few minutes at the tower that guards the ascent, to look upon the valley behind. The landscape was bounded on either side by the ramparts of nature, enclosing numerous villages, until the eye was stopped by the eastern horizon. We proceeded on the terrace of this table-land, of gradual ascent, through a thick forest, when, as we reached the point of descent, the sun cleared the barrier which we had just left, and darting his beams through the foliage, illuminated the castle of Bhynsror, while the new fort of Dangermow appeared as a white speck in the gloom that still enveloped the Pathar [or tableland].
> [...]
> As we continued to descend, enveloped on all sides by woods and rocks, we lost sight of the towers of Bhynsror, and on reaching the foot of the pass, the first object we saw was a little monastery of Atteets, founded by the chiefs of Bhynsror: it is called Jhalaca. We passed close to their isolated dwelling on the terraced roof of which a part of the fraternity were squatted round a fire, enjoying the warmth of the morning sun. Their wild appearance corresponded with the scene around; their matted hair and beard had never known a comb: their bodies were smeared with ashes (*bhaboot*), and a shred of cloth round the loins seemed the sole implication that they belonged to a class possessing human feelings.[37]

What is striking in Tod's textual evocation of the Mukundwara Pass is the contrast between the occasional beams of sunlight through the foliage and the gloom in which the tableland was plunged, creating an effect of chiaroscuro. There is also variety in the man-made lookout tower guarding the ascent alongside of 'the ramparts of nature'. Finally, his allusion to the 'wild appearance' of the Atteet ascetics, in seeming correspondence with the natural setting of 'woods and rocks', completes the typical ruggedness of picturesque tableaux. In addition, Captain Waugh's watercolour of the Mukundwara Pass shows ruined columns amid exotic vegetation, conveying with more formally Romantic visual means the isolated unkemptness of the scene.[38]

Between Bhynsror (Bhynsrorgarh) and Bhanpura, alongside what is now the Rana Pratap Sagar, Tod halted at a ruined temple complex called Ganga Bheva, or 'the circle of Ganga', from the spring that feeds the temple pond, considered to be 'an emanation of Ganga'.[39] Tod describes the approach to Ganga Bheva as a surprise: 'through rocks and thickets, until a deep grove of lofty trees enclosed by a dilapidated wall, showed that we had reached the object of our search'. Transported by these 'mouldering fragments of ancient grandeur' of this 'retreat for the votaries of Mahadeva', he situates the site for the reader as a main temple in the centre of a quadrangle of smaller shrines, in differing architectural styles ranging from very ancient to more recent. According to Tod, the most primitive structure of the Ganga Bheva complex is its portico, partly collapsed, with an upper frieze (or 'entablature') exhibiting 'a profusion of rich sculpture'. He finds the structures and embellishments 'similar' to those at Baroli (to the west, near Chittor), 'though not in so finished a style'. In his usual empirical way, Tod goes on to make surmises as to the likely date of the construction of the Ganga Bheva complex, based on an inscription he found there, with the name of a votary on it, and to attempt a chronological classification of Hindu sculpture and architecture:

> Whatever the age of this temple (and we found on the pavement the name of a votary with the dates 1011 or 955 CE), it is many centuries more recent than those which surround it, in whose massive simplicity we have a fine specimen of the primitive architecture of the Hindus. ... [Even so] the sculpture of all these is of a much later date than the specimens at Barolli, and of inferior execution, though far superior to anything that the Hindu sculptor of modern days can fabricate.[40]

Here Tod expresses the conservative view that older constructions are aesthetically superior to more modern ones. He comments on the utter desertion of the spot, even describing the existence of a gigantic 'koroo' tree in the main hall of the principal temple, its 'immense roots' having 'rent it to its foundations'. He concludes with down-to-earth pragmatism:

> It would require a month's halt and a company of pioneers to turn over these ruins, and then we might not be rewarded for our pains. We have therefore set to work to clear a path, that we may emerge from these wilds.[41]

Towards the end of his third journey, in February 1822, Tod passed through Menal (or Mahanal, meaning 'great chasm') on the western face of the Kota-Bundi *pathar* or tableland.[42] Tod appears impressed by the gloomy grandeur (which he compares to Erebus or the dark caverns of the lower world, between earth and the Hades of the ancient Greeks) of this 'abyss of about four hundred feet in depth, over which, at a sharp re-entering angle, falls a cascade, and though now but a rill, it must be a magnificent object in the rainy season'. He comments on the choice of the spot:

> It is difficult to conceive what could have induced the princely races of Cheetore or Ajmer to select such a spot ... which in summer must be a furnace owing to the reflection of the sun's rays from the rock; tradition, indeed, asserts that it is to the love of the sublime alone we are indebted for these singular structures. ... On the very brink of the precipice, overhanging the abyss, is the group of mixed temples and dwellings, which bear the name of Pirthiraj; while those on the opposite side are distinguished by that of Samarsi of Cheetore, the brother-in-law of the Chohan emperor of Delhi and Ajmer, whose wife Pirtha-Baé, has been immortalised by Chund, with her husband and brother.[43]

Tod seizes upon the relentless bareness of the rocks to make a connection with the tragic fall of two of Rajasthan's most illustrious heroes during the Muslim invasion by Muhammad Ghori in 1192 CE. It is thus the 'melancholy charm' linked to the romanticised history of the Rajputs that Tod emphasises in his meditations on the sublime aspects of Mahanal.

## *On leaving Rajasthan: Guru Sikhra on Mount Abu and Nukhi Talao*

Tod maintains a sublime vein in his descriptions of Mount Abu and Nukhi Talao. He appears struck by the grandeur of the natural scene at Guru Sikra on Mount Abu:[44]

> The picture was equally grand and novel: masses of cloud floated under our feet, through which the sun occasionally darted a ray, as if to prevent our being dazzled with too much glory. ... At length however, Surya

burst forth in all his majesty, and chasing away the sable masses, the eye swept over the desert, until vision was lost in the blending of the dark blue vault with the dusky arid soil. All that was required to form the Sublime was at hand; and silence confirmed the charm. ... [T]he remains of the castle of the Pramars ... the clustering domes of Dailwarra ... All was contrast – the blue sky and sandy plain, the marble fanes and humble wigwam, the stately woods and rugged rocks.

It is the same awe-inspiring aspect that is foregrounded in Tod's description of Nukhi Talao, the lake situated on the slope descending from the summit of Mount Abu:[45]

At a little distance, we saw the Nukhi-Talao, a beautiful lake, about four hundred yards in length. ... Those who have seen the lake three miles above Andernach on the Rhine [between Koblenz and Bonn] have beheld its counterpart. It is surrounded by rocks, wooded to the margin, while the water-fowls skim its surface unheeding and unheeded by man. ...

A tremendous abyss was before us, and the only mode of descent was over dislocated fragments of rock, while but a narrow ledge was between us and perdition. This is the wildest scene on the surface of Aboo. ... [T]he effect was sublime. ... Salvator Rosa would have selected the scene for a chef d'oeuvre of his pencil.

## *Gujarat proper: Ghoga, Mount Shatrunjay, Mount Girnar, the Hills of Bhuj in Cutch*

Inside Gujarat, Tod alternates between his admiration for picturesque landscapes and his sensitivity to the sublime in mountainous vistas. For example, the fortifications of the port of Ghogha (south of Bhavnagar) on the western side of the gulf of Cambay, although in a state of decay, strike Tod as venerably picturesque:[46]

Still Gogo has a venerable air, and its dusky walls, which must have defended it against the pirates always abounding in these seas, give it an imposing grand picturesque aspect. The southern face, with its numerous round towers of unequal height, cannot be less than 1200 yards in length; yet this is much less than the western [sic] side, where the fortifications have been destroyed, apparently undermined by the sea.

The shrine of Adnath, at Mount Shatrunjay, near Palitana, venerated by the Jains, appears to Tod to be situated on a particularly sublime site, subject to impressive effects of light and shade:[47]

[The first of their prophets] could not have selected a spot more calculated to assist the mind's devotion, and to elevate it, 'through Nature, up to Nature's God'. The prospect was sublime, and though clouds obscured the view on the land-side, a beam of the sun burst over the ocean, irradiating the ancient Gopinath and Madumvati (now Mhowa), on the south-eastern shore of the peninsula. .... And lastly, Palithana itself, with its minarets towering through the dense foliage, and its lake east of the town, were lighted by gleams of occasional splendour.

The majestic Mount Girnar, near Junagadh, towards the south-centre of the peninsula of Kathiawar inspires Tod to some forty pages of presentation.[48] A selection of his impressions will enable us to perceive his sensitivity to the sublime aspect of this sacred mountain:[49]

> From the northern face the view is imposing. Girnar is seen towering in isolated grandeur through the opening of the range, one of whose natural portals bears the appropriate name of Doorga, the turreted Cybele, while the 'gold-flowing' Sonarica is seen gliding through its gorge toward the castle-walls, which when she quits, her face is darkened by the shadow of the deep woods covering both sides of her ample margin. ... The views from the bridge [across the River Sonarica] are sublime: in front, seen through the range called the portal of Doorga, is the mighty cone of Girnar, towering in majesty, while behind, the 'ancient castle' lowers 'in proud decay', seeming as if erected as an outwork to defend the pass leading to the holy hill.

In his brief comparison between the sites of Mount Abu and Mount Girnar (above) with its ancient palace of Junagadh and its ruined palace of Khengar 3,000 feet above Junagadh, Tod shows his preference for the rugged ponderousness and relative proximity to the ocean of Mount Girnar.

Tod's last halt in Gujarat before he travelled by sea to Bombay in order to board his ship for his final return journey to England, was at Bhuj in Kutch, the seat of the Jhareja clan:[50]

> As the day broke, the hills of Bhooj appeared in sight, their wavy, barren summits covered with walls and towers, evincing little skill in the Jhareja engineer, though they give a picturesque character to this otherwise, desolate-looking valley. The last earthquake [in 1818] had been almost their only assailant, and had effected sundry breaches, which the present administration has had the sense not to repair.

Till the very end of his journeys through western India, Tod seems to have followed the same goals: making recordings of his personal visual perceptions, contextualised with historical and mythological details, with the express aim of making available to readers in Britain and Europe what he found to be the unique characteristics of the land and the society of the Rajputs and Gujaratis he had encountered.

Tod's later publication on Gujarat (published posthumously in 1839) succeeded his first work on Rajasthan (1829, 1832) by several years, which were shadowed by illness and advancing age. A greater maturity, emphasised by his personal distancing from the Indian arena, as well as from his official duties as the librarian of the Royal Asiatic Society in London, perhaps encouraged a deeper synthesis of the myriad impressions he had gathered along his final journeys through Rajasthan and Gujarat ten years earlier. This can be observed in his comparisons and his ways of distilling his personal reactions to landscapes with his probably recently acquired knowledge of contemporary aesthetic concerns (like the picturesque, the sublime and attention to light effects, for example) with apparently better mastery in his later volume.

A brief comparison of Tod's representations of Indian landscapes with the approaches to landscape in the published accounts of some of his British contemporaries who lived and travelled in India, such as Francis Buchanan Hamilton (1762–1829) and Bishop Reginald Heber (1783–1826), will help us to appreciate the specificity of Tod's writings on landscape.

Francis Buchanan Hamilton, a qualified medical doctor who studied at Edinburgh University, had arrived in India in 1795 and served in the British administration in Calcutta till 1815. He is known for having made surveys, under instructions from the Bengal Board of Trade and the British Governor-General, Lord Wellesley (1798–1805), of the botanical and agricultural resources of Chittagong and southeast Bengal (in an unpublished report of 1798), south India (in 1800–1, published in 1807) and Nepal (1802–3, published in 1819), and later under Lord Minto (1807–13) of various districts of north Bengal and Bihar (published posthumously in the 1830s). Buchanan Hamilton lived in retirement in Scotland from 1815 till his death in 1829.[51] Given his Scottish origins, and his publications on India in the early decades of the nineteenth century,[52] it is probable that Tod knew of him. However, the type of publication that Tod and Buchanan Hamilton selected respectively differed greatly. Buchanan Hamilton was among the first British officials to publish detailed information on rural areas, in what came to be known as the genre of 'statistical surveys'. He had in mind as a model *The Statistical Account of Scotland* in twenty-one volumes (1791–9) by Sir John Sinclair, in which local parish information (including on Buchanan Hamilton's own native parish of Callander) was compiled with a view to land improvement, poverty eradication and better welfare.[53] As a result of his official instructions,[54] with their demands for accuracy and public utility, combined with his imitation of Sinclair's *Statistical Account*, Buchanan Hamilton's portrayals of landscapes in south India appear strictly utilitarian, with emphasis on the types of soils and the agricultural yield per acre. He gives very limited topographical descriptions and does not appear at all sensitive to landscape beauty.[55]

## TOD AS AN OBSERVER OF LANDSCAPE

In closer affinity to Tod's depictions of landscapes, Bishop Reginald Heber devotes attention to the picturesque and sublime aspects of the river and mountain scenes he traversed during his journey through the upper provinces of India in 1824–5. A few examples will suffice to illustrate Heber's manner of introducing landscape elements into his travel account. Among the river scenes Heber crossed is the Coomercully River in Bengal, on 30 July 1824:[56]

> About halfpast five we arrived at the mouth of the Comercolly; the wind had now in a considerable degree died away; it was still however, enough to carry our boats a full west course by my compass, across the opening of the Comercolly (which is about as wide at this season as the Thames at Vauxhall) and some small distance along the right bank of the main river, where we brought to on the margin of a fine dry pasture of fiorin grass, one of the airiest and best stations which we have had during the voyage. At a short distance was a collection of very poor huts, with a herd of cattle round them.

Heber's comparison of the mouth of the Comercolly with the Thames at Vauxhall resembles gestures by Tod to compare scenes in western India with scenes in his native Scotland. Heber also shows concern for the living conditions of the local villagers.

At another crossing across the Mahi River towards the village of Vasad, between Anand and Vadodara in Gujarat today, Heber touches on the dangers of tigers and robbers in the region, showing admiration for the river's steep banks:[57]

> As day closed we left the open country, and entered some extremely deep and narrow ravines, with sides of crumbling earth, the convexity of which was evidently the work of the waters of the monsoon in their annual course to the Mhye. ... [N]or could a more favourable place be desired to favour the spring of a tyger, or the arrows of an ambushed band of robbers. ... Nothing could be more picturesque than this 'passage of the Granicus'. ... [T]he other torches which our guides carried, and which shone on groups of men, horses and camels, as wild and singular as were ever assembled in the fancy of a Salvator Rosa.

Heber deliberately underlines the picturesque aspect of the riverside scene with its contrasts of light and shadow, through a mention of Salvator Rosa.

Between Bhagalpur and Monghyr in Bihar, Heber perceives the Kharagpur Hills in the distance, and compares them to mountains in Wales and western England:[58]

> As we advanced, we passed at Janghera two very pretty rocks projecting into the river, with a mosque on the one, and a pagoda on the other;

while, in the distance, were the Curruckpoor hills, not so tall or striking as the Rajmahal, but not inferior to the Halkin mountains, and the range above Flint and Holywell. Such as they are, they are very refreshing to the eye in these vast regions of level ground.

It is amusing to note Heber's acknowledgement of the similarly less imposing nature of low hills in Bihar and in Wales (Mount Halkin is in Flintshire, near the southwestern bank of the mouth of the River Dee, some 16 miles from Liverpool).

Heber tries to express his wonder at his view of the Himalayan peaks from a distance, when he was between Moradabad and the Kumaon foothills (while travelling through Rampur, Shishgarh, Rudarpur), comparing the pinnacles of Bhadrinath and Gangotri to the summits of Cotopasi and Chimborazo (in South America), admitting that the Clwydian chain of north Wales with its Carneth Llewellyn and Snowdon, though beautiful, did not inspire the same kind of awe:[59]

> The Clwydian chain, indeed is not crowned by such noble pinnacles as Bhadrinath and Gangotree, but I could not help feeling now, and I felt it still more when I began to attempt to commit the prospect to paper, that the awe and wonder which I experienced were of a very complex character, and greatly detached from the simple act of vision. The eye is, by itself, and without some objects to form a comparison, unable to judge of such heights at such a distance. Carneth Llewellyn and Snowdon, at certain times in the year, make, really, as good a picture as the mountains now before me; and the reason that I am so much more impressed with the present view, is partly the mysterious idea of aweful and inaccessible remoteness attached to the Indian Caucasus.

Here Heber perspicaciously points out the importance of comparisons in perceiving the specific character of natural landscapes, as well as the role of certain notions such as remoteness and already acquired book knowledge about similar natural phenomena.

In the Kumaon foothills, between Bhimtal and Dhikala, Heber, travelling in the company of Sir Robert and Lady Colquhoun, on 6 December 1824, refers to Salvator Rosa to communicate the charm of the scene (now near the Corbett natural park):[60]

> Salvator Rosa never painted glens more wild and romantic than we threaded today in our path to Dikkalee, nor did mules or poneys often pass a worse road. We emerged at length again on the valley of the Koosilla. ... The banks are exceedingly beautiful, high rocks crowned with woods, and broken into all the capricious forms which lime-stone in a rainy climate assume. The valley is broader and more stony, and the features in general are in a grander and more savage style. ... [T]his is by far the most beautiful passage into or out of the Kemaoon ... except the

gorge of mount Gaughur, which is without a rival, nothing is seen on the Beemthal road which equals the valley of the Koosilla.

Again, Heber resorts to comparisons, this time with other natural sites in the same region within India (Mount Ghaghar, other places along the Bhimtal road) to underline the exceptional beauty of the Koosilla valley he is describing. Perhaps Tod's allusions to Salvator Rosa can be explained as an attempt to emulate Heber's mentions of this seventeenth-century painter of picturesque landscape scenes.

A final example of Heber's care in conveying the particular atmosphere of the natural scenery he met in his travels in India is his description of the Bhor Ghat between Khopoli and Khandala, near Bombay:[61]

> [27 June 1825] The views offered from different parts of this ascent [from Khopoli to Khandala, up the Bhor Ghat] are very beautiful, and much reminded me of some parts of the Vale of Corwen. The mountains are nearly the same height (from 2000 to 3000 feet above the level of the sea,) with the average of Welsh mountains; and the freshness and verdure which clothes them during the rains, as well as the fleecy clouds continually sweeping over them, increased their likeness to the green dells and moist climate of Gwyneth.

Heber's parallel between the average height, verdure and fleecy clouds of Bhor Ghat and those of the hills of Gwynedd (a northwestern district of Wales), with his passing salute to the 'aweful depth and gloom' of the waterfall near Khandala, lend a simultaneously picturesque and sublime atmosphere to his evocation of the Western Ghats near Bombay.

These examples of Heber's incorporation of landscape features into his travel account almost seem to pave the way for Tod's textual digressions into landscape descriptions in his two published works, in particular through two characteristics: the tendency to compare new landscapes discovered by the traveller with known landscapes from his home environment, and the attention to picturesque (ruggedness, contrasts of light and shadow) and sublime (huge dimensions, frightening) aspects. Despite the great distance that separated Tod from Heber (Tod was a military man while Heber was an ecclesiastic with markedly sectarian religious preoccupations; Tod had no university education while Heber was the product of a thoroughly classical background; Tod was sensitive to the particular human qualities of his Indian interlocutors while Heber was obsessed with improving the lot of the Indians he met through conversion to Christianity), distinct similarities are apparent in their treatment of landscapes in their respective travel accounts.

## Conclusion

To conclude, in comparison with the travel writings of some of his British contemporaries, Tod's various descriptions of landscapes in his *Annals and Antiquities of Rajasthan* and *Travels in Western India* seem to give priority to the contemporary picturesque aesthetic designed to provoke astonishment and delight in the viewer, rather than to any overt colonialist agenda of proving the inferiority of the colonised or the superiority of the coloniser, though Tod also never for a moment forgot his role as the British Governor-General's political agent to the western Rajput states. A colonialist approach is much more evident in Francis Buchanan Hamilton's focusing on the soil qualities, with the agricultural and commercial potential of the regions he surveyed. As for Bishop Heber, despite his undisguised ecclesiastical mindset, he seems to have played the role of a model for Tod in his depictions of landscapes, through his comparisons with mountains and rivers in Britain and his admiration for picturesque and sublime natural settings in his travels across India. In Tod's tendency to compare features of Rajasthani and Gujarati landscapes with features of Scottish topography (crags, glens, cairns), with certain well-known European archaeological sites (like the cities of ancient Tuscany) or with European mythology (such as the lower world of Erebus), we can observe an eighteenth-century civic humanism which sought to include the entire planet under a common humanity with local variations, rather than the stricter hierarchisation of cultures of the later nineteenth century. Also, instead of feminising the oriental landscapes of Rajasthan and Gujarat, Tod seems to be drawn by virile scenes of mountain peaks and sublime waterfalls,[62] and to identify with its princely heroes of the past. So, in this transitional period between the end of the eighteenth century and the Victorian heyday of the British Empire, Tod's portrayals of landscapes seem to manifest an overlapping of the prevailing discursive frameworks:[63] Renaissance empiricism, an interest in rational objectivity, as well as an aesthetic concern with moving scenes of ancient monuments and imposing natural phenomena.

## Notes

1 See Edmund Burke, *A Philosophical Enquiry into the Origin of our Ideas of the Sublime and the Beautiful*, Oxford: Oxford University Press 1998 (1757); and Charlotte Klonk, *Science and the Perception of Nature: British Landscape Art in the Late Eighteenth and Early Nineteenth Centuries*, New Haven, CT: Yale University Press, 1996, pp. 28–9 and 67–100.

2 See Nigel Leask, *Curiosity and the Aesthetics of Travel Writing, 1770–1840*, Oxford: Oxford University Press, 2002, pp. 51, 107–8, 121–2, 274.

## TOD AS AN OBSERVER OF LANDSCAPE

3 Mildred Archer and Ronald Lightbown, *India Observed: India as Viewed by British Artists, 1760–1860*, London: Victoria and Albert Museum in association with Trefoil Books, 1982, pp. 8–10, 12–13.
4 The edition referred to in this chapter (abbreviated as *Annals*) is an Indian reprint of Douglas Sladen's 1859 edition, issued by Rupa & Co., Delhi, 1997. The 'Personal Narratives' appear in vol. I, pp. 519–621 and vol. II, pp. 477–613. For uses of 'picturesque' see vol. I, pp. 529–31, 543, 573, 579, 614; vol. II, pp. 504, 535, 539; for uses of 'sublime' see vol. I, p. 532; vol. II, p. 573. Also James Tod, *Travels in Western India*, London: W.H. Allen & Co., 1839 (posth.); repr. Delhi: Munshiram Manoharlal Publishers, 1997.
5 Raymond Head, *Catalogue of Paintings, Drawings, Engravings and Busts in the Collection of the Royal Asiatic Society*, London: Routledge, 1991, p. 109. See also Tod's dedication to Mrs Colonel William Hunter Blair at the beginning of *Travels*, p. v.
6 Francis Buchanan Hamilton, *A Journey from Madras through the countries of Mysore, Canara and Malabar*, London: T. Cadell & W. Davies, 1807, 3 vols, repr. New Delhi: Asian Educational Services, 1999, 3 vols. Also Reginald Heber, *Narrative of a Journey through the Upper Provinces of India, from Calcutta to Bombay, 1824–1825, with notes upon Ceylon*, London: John Murray, 1828, 3 vols, repr. New Delhi: Asian Educational Services, 1995, 3 vols.
7 Tod, *Annals*, vol. I, p. 528.
8 Tod, *Annals*, vol. II, p. 536.
9 Tod, *Annals*, vol. I, pp. 536, 538, 543, 545.
10 Tod, *Annals*, vol. I, p. 573.
11 Tod, *Travels*, p. 315.
12 Tod, *Travels*, p. 320.
13 Tod, *Travels*, p. 322.
14 Tod, *Travels*, p. 405.
15 Tod, *Annals*, vol. I, pp. 568–71.
16 Tod, *Annals*, vol. II, p. 521.
17 Tod, *Annals*, vol. II, p. 529.
18 Tod, *Annals*, vol. II, pp. 533–4.
19 Tod, *Annals*, vol. II, p. 563.
20 Tod, *Travels*, pp. 292, 293, 301.
21 Tod, *Travels*, p. 408.
22 Tod, *Travels*, p. 431.
23 Tod, *Travels*, p. 458.
24 An engraving after Waugh's drawing appeared in the original (1829/32) edition of *Annals*, vol. I, facing p. 669.
25 Tod, *Annals*, vol. I, p. 533.
26 Tod, *Annals*, vol. I, p. 530.
27 Tod, *Annals*, vol. I, p. 531.
28 Tod, *Annals*, vol. I, p. 536.
29 Engraving Tod, *Annals* (original quarto edition), vol. I, facing p. 774.
30 Tod, *Annals*, vol. I, p. 606.
31 Tod, *Annals*, vol. I, p. 607.
32 Engraving Tod, *Annals* (original quarto edition) vol. I, facing p. 211. Engraving Tod, *Annals* (original quarto edition) vol. I, facing p. 653.
33 Tod, *Annals*, vol. I, p. 620.
34 Tod, *Annals*, vol. I, p. 620.
35 Tod, *Annals*, vol. I, pp. 620–1.
36 Tod, *Annals*, vol. II, pp. 563.
37 Tod, *Annals*, vol. II, pp. 563–4.
38 Engraving Tod, *Annals* (original quarto edition), vol. II, facing p. 740.
39 Tod, *Annals*, vol. II, p. 574. Engraving, Tod, *Annals* (original quarto edition), vol. II, facing p. 716.
40 Tod, *Annals*, vol. II, p. 574.
41 Tod, *Annals*, vol. II, p. 575.

42 Engraving, Tod, *Annals* (original quarto edition), vol. II, facing p. 746.
43 Tod, *Annals*, vol. II, pp. 596–7.
44 Tod, *Travels*, pp. 80–1.
45 Tod, *Travels*, pp. 115–16.
46 Tod, *Travels*, p. 250.
47 Tod, *Travels*, p. 287.
48 Tod, *Travels*, pp. 359–401.
49 Tod, *Travels*, pp. 363, 370, 400.
50 Tod, *Travels*, pp. 457–8.
51 See Willem van Schendel (ed.), *Francis Buchanan in Southeast Bengal: His Journey to Chittagong, the Chittagong Hill Tracts, Noakhali and Comilla*, Dhaka: Dhaka University Press, 1992, 'Introduction', pp. ix–xxiv.
52 Francis Buchanan Hamilton (as mentioned in Marika Vicziany, 'Imperialism, botany and statistics in early nineteenth-century India: the Survey of Francis Buchanan (1762–1829)'. *Modern Asian Studies*, 20.4 (1986), 625–60) published four papers in the *Transactions of the Royal Asiatic Society*: (a) vol. 1 (1827), article no. XI, pp. 201–6, ' "Inscriptions upon rocks in South Bihar", described by Dr. Buchanan Hamilton, Member of the RAS, and explained by Henry Thomas Colebrooke, Esq., Director of the Royal Asiatic Society'; (b) vol. 1 (1827), article no. XXVIII, pp. 523–6, ' "Description of temples of the Jainas in South Bihar and Bhagalpur", by Dr Francis Buchanan Hamilton, Member of the RAS' (read by Henry Thomas Colebrooke); (c) vol. 1 (1827), article no. XXIX, pp. 531–6, ' "On the Srawacs or Jains", by Dr Francis Buchanan Hamilton, Member of the RAS'; (d) vol. 2 (1830), article no. II, pp. 40–51, ' "Description of the ruins of Buddha Gaya", by Dr Francis Buchanan Hamilton, Member of the RAS'.
53 Vicziany, 'Imperialism, botany and statistics', pp. 635, 648–9.
54 Buchanan Hamilton, *A Journey from Madras*, vol. I, introduction by the author, pp. vii–xiii.
55 Buchanan Hamilton, *A Journey from Madras*, vol. I, p. 357; vol. II, p. 150; vol. III, p. 478.
56 Heber, *Narrative of a Journey*, vol. I, pp. 228–9.
57 Heber, *Narrative of a Journey*, vol. III, pp. 21–2.
58 Heber, *Narrative of a Journey*, vol. I, p. 289.
59 Heber, *Narrative of a Journey*, vol. II, p. 153.
60 Heber, *Narrative of a Journey*, vol. II, p. 240.
61 Heber, *Narrative of a Journey*, vol. III, pp. 107–9.
62 See Harriet Guest, 'Curiously marked: tattooing, masculinity and nationality in 18th-century perceptions of the South Pacific', in John Barrell (ed.), *Painting and the Politics of Culture: New Essays on British Art, 1700–1850*, Oxford: Oxford University Press, 1992, pp. 101–34.
63 See Klonk, *Science and the Perception of Nature*, pp. 35 and 99–100.

CHAPTER TWO

# Tod as anthropologist: trying to understand

Apart from his military role as an officer of the army of the East India Company in India, Tod also carried out land surveys with the help of Indian teams and gathered historiographical artefacts and bardic accounts about local ruling families. Since Tod did not know Sanskrit and only learned the locally spoken Urdu language in the field, through his contact with Indians, his published text on Rajputana[1] shows his regular recourse to Indian interpreters. It also shows Tod's tendency to piece together fragments of historical evidence, and his careful attention to human relationships (of family ties, of neighbourly proximity or of official protocol) between Indians of the same ethnic origin, as well as of different ethnic origins. His efforts to rewrite the information he gathered could have been with the aim of better comprehending the objects of his observations.

I would like to approach Tod's handling of the 'self and other' question from the point of view of anthropology, defined as a study of 'the principal characters of our species, its perfection, its accidental degradations, its unity, its race and the manner in which it has been classified' (*Oxford English Dictionary*, definition dated 1861). Although anthropology became a formal social science only in the late nineteenth century, thanks to the inspiration of researchers like Radcliffe-Brown and Durkheim, as Michèle Duchet, who studied the meaning of anthropology in the Enlightenment period, pointed out, the Swiss philosopher Albert de Chavannes was the first person to formally use the term 'anthropology' in his study *Anthropologie ou Science Générale de l'Homme*, published in 1788.[2] Then, whether through the thinkers of the Scottish Enlightenment or French Enlightenment philosophers, the term gradually came to include a comparative analysis of genealogies, systems of kinship and social customs among different human groups, placing specific societies in a hierarchised, universal scale, going from savage to civilised through a series of progressive stages. According to

**3** Figures showing various occupations. Engraving by Edward Finden of a miniature after an unknown Indian artist's original, formerly owned by James Tod.
(By kind permission of the Royal Asiatic Society of Great Britain and Ireland)

Michèle Duchet, this concealed the racialist paternalism of a colonialist ideology that was present right from the eighteenth century, and subsequently crystallised into a rigid division between 'warm societies' with an awareness of their own historical past, and 'cold societies' that did not keep any track of their past, as a result of greater primitivism and lack of access to writing. This separation is visible in the writings of Hegel and of Claude Lévi-Strauss for example.[3] It would appear that this hierarchisation only consolidated the 'comfortable assumptions of superiority' with which European overseas travellers had begun their filling in of 'the great map of mankind' from the sixteenth century onwards.[4] In relation to India, several scholars have followed the trend set by Edward Said's claim:[5] that Western scholars intentionally constructed an imaginary Orient in order to prove the superiority of the West. One such case is Ronald Inden, whose treatment of 'Tod's Rajputs' as an instance of Oriental feudalism and Hindu kingship[6] is rather one-sided, since it pays no attention to the process of two-way negotiation involved in the discursive construction of difference.

I would like to argue here that perhaps Tod did not have a preconceived grid of interpretation when he set out to describe the genealogies and social practices of the Rajputs and the Gujaratis. To do so, concerning the Rajputs, I will proceed in two steps: first, Tod's pragmatic adaptations to the conditions of his field observations of Rajput manners and customs; then, Tod's portrayal of the Rajputs' relation to history and his own textual constructions of the information he gathered on them in the field. Following this, concerning the Gujaratis, I will first look at Tod's gathering of historical details on the various dynasties who ruled in the various regional capitals of Gujarat, which details Tod then organised and classified into a coherent narrative; then, Tod's field observations of the social practices of the Gujaratis of his time (often improvised and the result of a blending of practices from various sources). It must be kept in mind that Tod seems to have been favourably disposed towards non-Brahmanical Hindus, while manifesting a certain mistrust of the Muslim and Maratha authorities he encountered. This would explain why Tod allotted relatively limited space in his texts to the Muslim governors of Gujarat, as well as to the Maratha Gaikwads of Baroda, with whom the British authorities nevertheless had to negotiate in order to introduce their British residents and political agents in those areas of Gujarat under the control of these latter potentates.

## *Tod as anthropologist in Rajasthan*

To begin with Tod's pragmatic adaptations for his observations of Rajput manners and customs, he resorted regularly to the services of

Rajput scholars. At the beginning of the first instalment of his personal travel narrative through Rajputana, Tod mentions a highly cultured nephew of his host the Rana of Mewar, the crown prince of Marwar Zalim Singh, who resided in Deopoor in Mewar under the protection of his maternal uncle, the Rana of Mewar, as a result of 'domestic quarrels' in Marwar:[7]

> We passed Deopoor, once a township of some consequence, and forming part of the domain of the *Bhanaij*, Zalim Singh, the heir of Marwar, whose history, if it could be given here would redeem the nobles of Rajpootana from the charge of being of uncultivated intellect. In listening to his biography, both time and place were unheeded; the narrator, my own venerable *guru*,\* had imbibed much of his varied knowledge from this accomplished chieftain, to whom arms and letters were alike familiar. [Tod's note: \* My guide or instructor, Yati Gyan Chandra, a priest of the Jain sect, who had been with me ten years [1809–19]. To him I owe much, for he entered into all my antiquarian pursuits with zeal.]

On his return journey from Kotah and Bundi to Udaipur in February 1822, Tod halted at Beejoliya Kalan, where there were ruins of a castle and five Jain temples. Tod reports the sketching and copying of inscriptions carried out by his Indian assistants:[8]

> One of my scribes, who has a talent for design, is delineating with his reed (*culm*) these stupendous piles, while my old Jain Guru is hard at work copying what is not the least curious part of the antiquities of *Bijolli*, two inscriptions cut in the rock; one of the Chohan race, the other of the *Sankh Puran*, appertaining to his own creed, the Jain.

Among Tod's observations on Rajput manners and customs he notes the political intervention of women in matters of state, through the traditional Hindu offering of a sisterly bracelet to a potential male ally of their husband's or brother's court. This bracelet of affection is presented by sisters to brothers at the Hindu coconut festival in August each year. Tod relates the offering of the sisterly bracelet by the widowed queen Kurnavati of Rana Sanga (who reigned in Mewar, 1509–28, and who had died defending Chittore against the attacks of the Mughal invader Babar at the Battle of Kanua in 1528) to Babar's son, Emperor Humayun. This 'invested him with the title of brother, and uncle and protector to Kurnavati's infant son Oody Sing'.[9] Although Kurnavati and 32,000 Rajputs of Chittore were slain during the attack on Chittore in 1535 by Bahadur Shah, the Sultan of Gujarat, the infant prince Uday Singh was protected by the Raja of Bundi, while Humayun honoured his pledge of protection to Queen Kurnavati after her death, by expelling Bahadur Shah from Chittore and restoring Rana Bikramjeet (one of the sons of Rana Sanga) on the

Mewar throne. Tod adds in a note at this point, his own experience of the Rakhi or sisterly bracelet:[10]

> [The author] was the *Rakhi-bund bhaé* of, and received 'the bracelet' from three queens of Oodipoor, Boondi and Kotah, besides Chund-Bae, the maiden sister, of the Rana; as well as many ladies of the chieftains of rank, with whom he interchanged letters. The sole articles of barbaric pearl and gold which he conveyed from a country where he was six years supreme, are these testimonies of friendly regard.

After the sudden death from cholera in July 1821 of the Bundi Raja, Rao Raja Bishen Singh, Tod was summoned to the Bundi court to sort out the succession proceedings of the eldest, eleven-year-old Prince Lalji Ram Singh. Here is how the eldest Bundi queen mother enlisted Tod's care over her princely son:[11]

> Although the festival of the *rakhi* was not until the end of the month, the mother of the young prince sent me by the hands of the *Bhut*, or family priest, the bracelet of adoption as her brother, which made my young ward henceforth my *Bhanaij* or nephew. With this mark of regard, she also expressed, through the ministers, a wish that I would pay her a visit at the palace as she had many points to discuss regarding Lalji's welfare, which could only be satisfactorily argued *viva voce*. Of course, I assented; and, accompanied by the *Bohora* [chief minister of Bundi] and the confidential eunuchs of the *Rawula* [palace], I had a conversation of about three hours with my adopted sister, a curtain being between us. Her language was sensible and forcible, and she evinced a thorough knowledge of all the routine of government and the views of parties, which she described with great clearness and precision. ... During a great part of this conversation, the *Bohora* had retired, so that her tongue was unrestrained. With *Utr-Pan* and her blessing (*asees*) sent by one of her damsels, she dismissed me with the oft-repeated remark, 'Forget not that Lalji is now in your lap'.

From this, we can sense that far from being perceived as an untrustworthy coloniser, Tod was accepted as a part of the family at several Rajput courts. Tod also notes a quaint measure of adaptation by some of his British troops after the British takeover of the Rajputana states in January 1818, when he halted at the former commercial entrepôt of Bhilwara:[12]

> The author had passed through Bhilwara in May 1806, when it was comparatively flourishing. On this occasion (Feb. 1818), it was entirely deserted. It excited a smile in the midst of regrets, to observe the practical wit of some of the soldiers, who had supplied the naked representative of *Ad-Nath* [the Jain deity] with an apron – not of leaves, but scarlet cloth.

Tod applauds the 'progress' in terms of a passage from savage marauding and plundering in the hills between Mewar and Marwar, of a tribe known as Mairs, to a more civilised subordination to the Rajput suzerain and regular tax payment between 1818 and 1821. Tod attributes this social evolution, of course, to the presence of British troops. However, in this, Tod also makes clear his awareness of internal differences in degrees of settled law-abiding existence between specific groups of Rajpoots:[13]

> A corps of these mountaineers [Mairs], commanded by English officers, has since been formed, and I have no doubt may become useful. Notwithstanding their lawless habits, they did not neglect agriculture and embanking, as described in the valley of Shero Nullah,[14] and a district has been formed in Mairwarra, which in time may yield a lakh of rupees annually to the State ... the chiefs of the districts being brought to the Rana's presence, presented *nuzzerana* [tribute], swore fidelity, and received according to their rank, gold bracelets or turbans. It was an era in the annals of Mewar to see the accumulated arms of Mairwarra piled upon the terrace of the palace at the capital [Udaipur].

In October 1820, while returning from Kota to Udaipur, Tod observes settled groups in the urban centres of Jehazpoor and Kachola (Kujoori) of formerly semi-barbarous tribals known as Meenas. Traditionally, Meenas were nomadic *kumptas* or 'bowmen'[15]. In 1820, their chief or *tynati* at Jehazpoor maintained 'a very respectable troop of cavalry', superior in Tod's opinion even to the Rana of Mewar's own cavalry, at the time of the British takeover in 1818. Tod here notes with approval a common response to human kindness among 'semi-barbarians' as also among 'more civilised habitants':[16]

> At present [in October 1820], I could by signal have collected 4000 bowmen around me, to protect or to plunder; though the Meenas, finding that their rights are respected, are subsiding into regular tax-paying subjects, and call out with their betters *'Utul Raj'*! ('May your sway be everlasting!') We had a grand convocation of the Meena *Naiques* and, in the Rana's name, I distributed crimson turbans and scarfs; for as through our mediation the Rana had just recovered the district of Jehajgurh, he charged me with its settlement. I found these Meenas *true children of Nature*, who for the first time seemed to feel they were received within the pale of society, instead of being considered as outcasts.

A final instance of Tod's attempts to observe Rajput manners and customs through comparisons with similar phenomena in Europe is observable in his notes on Rajput feudalism. Much has already been written on Tod's perception of feudalism among the Rajputs.[17] Here I would simply like to draw attention to Tod's awareness of the overlapping of several different land tenure systems in the Rajputana of his time, and his cross-referencing of various Indian and European texts in his efforts to understand the nature of the Rajputs' attachment to their land. That Tod was not solely occupied with extorting the maximum amount of revenue from Rajput lands for the British colonial government can be seen in his dedication to George IV at the beginning of his first volume on Rajasthan, where he requests the British monarch to consider 'the restoration of their former independence' to the Rajput princes.[18] Hardly an orientalising coloniser's stand! Tod gives foremost importance to the oldest form of Rajput attachment to the land: the hereditary right of the tiller-cultivator to the land tilled by his forefathers or *Bap*, known therefore as *Bapota*, or 'belonging to the father'.[19]

Tod compares Rajput *Bapota* with medieval Europe's 'allodial property' or 'land descended by inheritance subject to no burthen but public defence', as exposed by the early nineteenth-century English Whig historian Henry Hallam.[20] Tod then analyses the nature of Rajputana's feudal fiefs as top-down grants from the local monarch to loyal military chieftains implying links of loyalty between the feudal lord and the vassal as the result of 'long gradations and mutual duties'.[21] Tod concludes that the Rajput system meets four of Hallam's six criteria of feodality – relief or military assistance, escheats or forfeiture of land for want of an heir or by confiscation, aids or taxes levied, and wardships of infant successors, while excluding marriage and alienation as they were practised in Europe in relation to feudal land ownership.[22] Thus, according to Tod, the blend of allodial or freehold tenantry and feudal militia in Rajputana meant paying a quit-rent to the crown, performing local but limited service and being available to the prince for defence in exchange for daily rations only in case of invasion.[23] While detailing the links and disputes over sub-infeudation between holders of great 'puttas' or patents of estates[24] and minor vassals, Tod quotes the Anglo-Saxon division of land into 'ploughs' and 'hides', referring to the Scottish historians John Millar and David Hume.[25] Tod thus seeks to distinguish between the bonds of solidarity and 'devotion ... to the *Solum Natale*' of Rajput feudalism,[26] as distinct from the more arbitrary or despotic land grants (*jagirs, wuttuns* and *meeras*) of the Muslim invaders[27] and the predatory extortions of the Maratha plunderers in Rajasthan.[28] Tod also juxtaposes quotations from the ancient Sanskrit text *ManavaDhermashastra* with popular Rajput proverbs like 'Bhog Ra Dhanni Raj Ho: Bhom ra Dhanni Ma Cho' (the government is the owner of the rent (or tax), but I (the tiller) am the master of the land), to illustrate how ancient statutes and evolving customary laws combined to consecrate the Rajput notion of *Bapota* or patrimonial land inheritance.[29] He further develops the unstable zone of multiple possible interpretations of rights to the land in his allusions to his own arbitrations of land disputes, as political agent of the British

Governor-General. For example, Tod had to weigh the impulse of self-interest against the dictates of reason and justice when settling the claims of the Rana of Mewar's vassal from Bheendir in February 1818.[30]

British strategic interests came into play when Tod alienated the Mewar fief of Neembaira in favour of a henchman of a Muslim ally of the British, the Pathan Khan of Tonk, in February 1820.[31] Tod declares he upheld the sacred right of *Bapota* of a Mewar vassal at Nuddowaé, over the usurpations of the Maratha chief Holkar of Indore in February 1820.[32] Thus, Tod seems to have devoted careful attention to the complexities of land ownership in Rajputana and to have tried to keep in mind the various contradictory claims to the land, while personally arbitrating land disputes. He certainly seems to have sought to avoid essentialising binary oppositions between cultivators and revenue collectors, or between recently acquired military claims and older ancestral land rights.

## Tod's portrayal of the Rajputs' relation to history

This brings me to the second part of this chapter, where I will try to look at Tod's portrayal of the Rajputs' relation to history and his own textual constructions of the information he gathered on Rajput history in the field.

Tod's enthusiasm for piecing together Rajput history seems to stem from an intention to prove to the world that the Rajputs were precisely *not* a people without history, a category that would relegate them to the lower, more primitive end of the scale of civilisation conceptualised by Scottish philosophers of the Enlightenment (like William Robertson, John Millar and Adam Fergusson)[33] and eighteenth-century French philosophers like Montesquieu, D'Holbach and Voltaire.[34] He states this historiographical aim in his Introduction to volume I of his work on Rajasthan: to correct the false but widely circulated axiom 'that India possesses no national history',[35] and thereby 'to enlighten my native country on the subject of India'.[36] Tod also describes his method as historian-anthropologist:[37]

> For a period of ten years I was employed, with the aid of a learned Jain, in ransacking every work which could contribute any facts or incidents to the history of the Rajpoots, to diffuse any light upon their manners and character. Extracts and versions of all such passages were made by my Jain assistant into the more familiar dialects (which are formed from the Sanscrit) of these tribes, in whose language my long residence among them enabled me to converse with facility. At much expense, and during many wearisome hours, to support which required no ordinary degree of enthusiasm, I endeavoured to possess myself not merely of their history,

## TOD AS ANTHROPOLOGIST

but of their religious notions, their familiar opinions and their characteristic manners, by associating with their chiefs and bardic chroniclers, and by listening to their traditionary tales and allegorical poems.

Here in a nutshell is Tod's *modus operandi* as historian-anthropologist among the Rajputs and the aims he chooses to express are those of 'throwing some light upon a people scarcely yet known in Europe and whose political connections with England seemed to me to be capable of undergoing a material change, with benefit to both parties'.[38] Thus, Tod had in mind both the filling in of gaps in the archive of humankind, without however losing sight of the political and colonial nature of the presence of his British employers in India. I would like to argue here that Tod seems to have gone to considerable lengths to frame his presentation of historical information on the Rajputs with familiar references and comparisons drawn from European culture, perhaps in order to render his text comprehensible to European readers.

For example, Tod appears to have tried to bridge the ambiguous gap between myth or legend on the one hand, and factual history with genealogies of flesh and blood dynasties on the other. For example, at the end of his volume II on Rajasthan, he includes two lengthy tables of genealogies of the divinely begotten races of the Sun (Surya Vansa) and of the Moon (Chandra Vansa, also known as Indu Vansa). The first table goes from 2200 BCE to 1100 BCE, beginning with the divinities Narayan, Vishnu and Brahma, descending via mythical sages like Kashyapa and Atri and terminating with mythical characters like Ramchandra and the five Pandava brothers from the two great Indian epics, the *Ramayana* and the *Mahabharat*, the whole with a very serious-looking date scale on the right and a numbering of the successive generations on the left. Tod's second table spans the period from 1100 BCE to 720 CE, and traces the supposed descendants of the characters of the Hindu epics through several generations to end with the solar Gehilote dynasty of Mewar which seized Chittore from the Mori race, in 720 CE, the lunar dynasty that tried in vain to attack Indraprestha or Delhi, the capital of the famed King Vikramaditya who ruled in 56 CE, while including also another branch of lunar dynasties who ruled in Magadha (Bihar). Tod's meticulousness and attempt at rationalisation amidst a welter of muddling details is striking. Now, whether Tod was trying to prove the inferiority of the Rajputs or genuinely trying to understand their world view and their explanation of their own origin is, of course, open to debate.

In an interesting chapter on the dissimilarity of manners in the various races of Rajasthan in the section on 'Religious Establishments, Festivals and Customs of Mewar' in his volume I on Rajasthan, Tod refers to a French historian of customs and laws among different peoples, named Antoine-Yves Goguet, who together with Antoine-Charles Fugère had published at La Haye in 1758 a work later translated into English and published in Edinburgh.[39] According to Goguet:[40] 'The manners of a people ... always bear a proportion to the progress they have made in the arts and sciences.' Tod thus separates 'the manners of a nation' from its 'moral causes and results':[41]

> Such a picture would represent the manners, which are continually undergoing modifications, in contradistinction to the morals of society: the latter having a fixed creed for their basis, are definite and unchangeable.

Then in a flurry of Indian and European references (for example Menu, Valmika, the comte de Ségur, Montesquieu, H.T. Colebrooke and Horace Hayman Wilson),[42] Tod reflects on the position of the female in Rajput society (known at the time in Britain and Europe from travellers' accounts for committing sati, to avoid dishonour or widowhood):[43]

> The superficial observer, who applies his own standard to the customs of all nations, laments with an affected philanthropy, the degraded condition of the Hindu female, in which sentiment he would find her little disposed to join. He particularly laments her want of liberty and calls her seclusion imprisonment. Although I cordially unite with Ségur [who opposed all restraints] who is at issue with his compatriot Montesquieu [who favoured seclusion of women] on this part of discipline, yet from the knowledge I do possess of the freedom, the respect, the happiness which Rajpoot women enjoy, I am by no means inclined to deplore their state as one of captivity.

A painting from Bundi, c. 1820, entitled 'Rajput princesses killing a lion' illustrates Tod's point about the dynamism and the autonomy possessed by Rajput women. Thus Tod advances his field experience as a sound basis for his verdict that Rajput women were not unhappy despite their segregation from male society.

Tod uses yet another device to make his accounts of Rajput history intelligible to an European audience – he liberally incorporates parallels from the well-known figures of ancient Europe. For example, Tod sketches a parallel with ancient Greece in General Monson's retreat from Gurrote, northwards to the Mokundwarra Pass, near Kotah, where the Kotah Regent Zalim Singh offered ready shelter, in 1803–4, while the adversary of Rajputana and the British, the Maratha Jeswunt Rao Holkar of Indore (r.1797–1808, d.1811),[44] advanced from the south from Pertabgurh to Mundisore. Tod does not hesitate to compare Monson's retreat to a narrow miss of a repetition of the 480 BCE battle of Thermopylae, where the Spartan leader Leonidas I dispersed

**4** Rajput princesses killing a lion.
(By kind permission of the Royal Asiatic Society of
Great Britain and Ireland)

his troops to avoid them being massacred by the invading Persian hordes led by Xerxes, the Spartan leader standing in firm resistance himself with 300 Spartan braves, all of whom were killed in the battle. Tod draws a further parallel with Xenophon's retreat at the Battle of Cunaxa, 401 BCE, where Cyrus the Great was defeated by his own brother Ataxerxes II, having allowed his Greek general Xenophon to retreat with his 10,000 Greek mercenary soldiers.[45] Such parallels are probably made with the aim of underlining the importance of certain military battles in the history of the Rajputs.

## Tod as historical anthropologist in Gujarat

In his account of his last journey from Udaipur to Bombay, via Gujarat, from June 1822 to January 1823 (published posthumously in 1839 as *Travels in Western India*), Tod first went from the north to the south of eastern Gujarat (from Mount Abu and Sirohi in south Rajasthan to Palanpur in Gujarat proper, Sidhpur, Patan or the former Anhulwarra Patan, Ahmedabad, Baroda and Cambay); then he moved westwards in Gujarat (through Bhavnagar, Palitana, Amreli, Somnathpatan, Junagadh, Porbunder, Dwarka, Okha, Mandvi in the Cutch peninsula, Bhuj, back to Mandvi and finally by boat to Bombay, for his final departure for Britain.)

The first ancient capital of Gujarat at which Tod halted was Chandravati (due south of Mount Abu, southeast of Girwur and Sarotra, to the south of the Aravulli Mountains), although it was almost buried under wild undergrowth in 1822. Tod points out that Chandravati was chosen as a capital of refuge by Raja Bhoj Pramara of Dhar (in Malwa in central India) when Dhar was attacked by Muslims in 619 CE. In its turn Chandravati was attacked by Allaudin Khilji between 1296 and 1303, and again in the fifteenth century by the second autonomous sultan of Gujarat, Ahmad Shah I (who founded the city of Ahmadabad, and reigned from 1411 to 1441). In addition, according to Tod, Chandravati had been abandoned in 1405 when Rao Subboo founded his capital of the Deoras in Sirohi (west-northwest of Udaipur). Thus by studying the chronicle *Bhoj Charitra* of the Pramara kings of Dhar and the Annals of the Deora Rajputs of Sirohi, Tod gives a quick sketch of the zenith (619–1296 CE) and fall of Chandravati (after 1405), with a rational explanation for its state of advanced decay in 1822. Indeed, Tod found only remains of pillars of ruined temples in white marble, with statues of dancing nymphs and of Shiva with many arms, in 1822.[46]

Tod also stopped at Patan in the north of Gujarat, as it was the capital of three different Gujarati dynasties between 746 and 1298 CE, before the Muslim conquests in the region. These dynasties were the Chavdas, the Solankhis and the Waghelas. Tod chooses as his guiding figure at Patan the king Komar Pal Solankhi, who was a relative of the Chohan Gehlotes of Ajmer and who reigned between 1133 and 1166 CE. He was the hero of the bardic chronicle *Komar Pal Charitra*. Tod concludes from this text that under the Balhara-Solankhi dynasty, Gujarat experienced a prosperous period of religious tolerance and flourishing trade.[47]

In November 1822, Tod reached Somnath Puttun, near Diu and Veraval (to the south of the Saurashtra peninsula). Again, based on the *Komar Pal Charitra*, since this Solankhi king was reputed to have reconstructed the Somnath temple around 1150, some 140 years after its destruction by Mahmud of Ghazni in 1008 CE.[48] Tod also refers to a Persian manuscript entitled 'The Fall of Puttun' (undated in Tod's text), as well as to Abul Fazl's late sixteenth-century *History of the Deccan*. Tod mentions two other dates when Somnath Puttun was plundered: 609 CE, probably by the Arabs from Sindh, and in 746 CE, by the Persian Caliph Harun Al-Rashid.[49] Tod confesses that he was

## TOD AS ANTHROPOLOGIST

unable to find in India any copy of the *Tarikh Mahmud-i-Ghazni*, although copies of this text were available in Europe at the time,[50] and also that he encountered no local legend about the destruction of Somnath by the invader from Ghazni, which seems surprising.[51] In addition, on two occasions in this chapter, Tod denounces the destructions in south Gujarat by the Portuguese, despite their so-called religion of love and charity:[52]

> [Billawul or Veraval] suffered, as did all the cities of this coast, from 'the idolaters of Europe', whose rapacities and cruelties were not surpassed by those of the Tartars in the tenth, or of the Afghans led by Alla in the thirteenth century.

Tod describes Junagadh (although it was under the control of a Muslim governor when Tod passed through in 1822) as the former capital of the Khengar family, of the race of the Yadu-Balharas, who were Jains, and who reigned in Ballabhi and Deoputtun (the present city of Diu) between 145 and 745 CE, before being forced to retreat to Anhulwarra Putun in north Gujarat, by invaders. Tod obtains confirmation of these details thanks to an inscription at Singirkote, situated in the sacred heights of Mount Girnar.[53]

Further on, Tod meditates on the legends of the origins of the tribe of the Jaitwas, then in power at Porbunder. Among the recognisable legends of this tribe, Tod perceives a very democratic intention to disguise the humble and possibly barbarian origins of these Pooncheria Ranas, or Ranas with a long tail:[54]

> But as distinction is transmitted *ex parte paterna*, the mother, as the witty Gibbon remarks, going for nothing, the patriarchal JAITWA bore one of the physical characteristics of his sire [i.e. the monkey god Hanuman] in an elongation of the spine, which like that of the races described by Lord Monboddo and Dr. Plot [in Africa and in the islands] has gradually worn away in the succession of many generations, and the degeneracy of his posterity; so that the family had found some difficulty in solving the question, whether the present incumbent had aught beyond the title of 'Pooncheria', though he stoutly contended for a superfluity of *down* in Prince Sontan [Jaitwa], only four generations ago.

Tod declares he drew this myth of the origins of the Jaitwas of Porbunder from the book of their genealogy (or *Buhae Vansa*) with the assistance of their family bard,[55] while adding that the Jaitwas, because of their more ancient origins, tended to look down upon their immediate feudal chief, the Gaikwad of Baroda, whose relatively recent social ascension was due only to violent military exploits.

The last Gujarati dynasty to which Tod alludes is that of the Jharejas of Bhuj (in the Cutch peninsula at the western extremity of India).

Again Tod mentions as his source the chronicles or *Bakhars* of the Jhareja family and their book of genealogy or *Vanshanali*.[56] He begins by denouncing the disorderly confusion in the *Vanshanali*, where 'three thousand years of mythical genealogies' mingled with barely 'three hundred years of truly historical facts'.[57] Tod gives details on the possible Marwar-Rathore origins of the Jharejas of Bhuj, on their migrations to the west, where they became the *Sinde-Summas* or Bhatti-Summas in the province of Sindh. The constant upsetting of the history of this dynasty by Muslim invasions (in 746, 904, 1075, 1193 CE, when Raedhun Jhareja shifted from Multan to Bhuj, and 1537, when Rao Khengar Jhareja founded his capital in Bhuj).[58] Tod underlines that the Jharejas' conversion to Islam deprived them of any right to marry or make alliances with the other Rajput clans (as religious conversion away from their tutelary Hinduism was frowned upon by the Rajputs).[59] Tod makes the following comment on the ambivalent status of the Jharejas among the Rajput tribes: 'It would have been well had the whole race remained Moslem, nor attempted to regain a place within the pale of Hinduism; now, they are neither one nor the other.'[60] Tod was therefore able to observe the Jhareja community who intermarried within a closed group, and thus saw their numbers dwindling with the passing years – literally a vanishing species.

So Tod shows himself to be an assiduous historian and an astute observer concerning the capitals and local histories of the different princely families of Gujarat. I will close this section on Gujarat with a few of Tod's observations on his own historiographical method. On the one hand, he was acutely aware of the constant overlapping of historical facts and mythological factors and magical elements in the bardic chronicles he consulted.[61] On the other hand, as a scholar influenced by the Enlightenment, he tried to look for synchronical corroborations or collateral proofs to consolidate the historical narrative he was constructing.[62] He summarises as follows his historical method:[63]

> [Referring to various bardic chronicles, extensive chains of pedigree and fables about the origin of the Jaitwa tribe, Tod declares:] Passing over the improbable period, and taking the more rational Charun [bard] as my assistant, we must endeavour to reduce these wild chronologies to something like *reason* and *common sense*.

## Tod on the social practices of the Gujaratis

This brings me to Tod's anthropological observations on the social practices of the Gujaratis of his time. One element that appears several times in Tod's text is his admiration for the collections of old Jain

## TOD AS ANTHROPOLOGIST

documents, known as 'Jain Pothi Bhandar'. Tod came across one such collection in Anhulwarra-Patan in north Gujarat. He observes that the underground location of this Jain library was a possible explanation for its having escaped destruction during the attacks of Allaudin Khilji on Anhulwarra-Patan in 1298:[64]

> The collection is the property of the *Khartra* sect ... Though everyone, lay or clerical, bearing the name of *Khartra*, has a property in the library, it is in strict charge of the *Nagar-Seth*, and the *Panch*, or chief magistrate and council of the city, while its immediate superintendence is confided to some Yutis spiritually descended from Hemacharya, the senior of whom has some pretensions to learning. ... Above all, until we have formed some acquaintance with the dignitaries of the Jain sect and their learned librarians we are not in a condition to appreciate the intellectual riches of the Jains, and can only pity the overweening vanity which has prompted the assertion, that the Hindus possess no historical records, and which seeks to quench the spirit of enquiry, by proclaiming such research a vain labour.

At Cambay, Tod dreams of discovering unrevealed secrets on the past of the Jains by penetrating into the Jain Pothi Bhandar of this port town:[65]

> Here, as wherever the Jains are numerous, is a library of considerable importance belonging to the community, and if proper measures were taken to examine its contents, without exciting alarm, something new might be elicited as to their tenets, and the past history of their patrons, for it is from individual biography that we must draw the materials for history. But this can only be affected by great caution and patient inquiry, never by a shew of authority. The best plan of investigation would be to take a Jain priest as moonshee, one whose *patravali* might trace Hemacharya or Amra, amongst his spiritual ancestry; through his means the bolts would fly open. A Brahmin must never be employed; even a Mooslem would have better chance of success.

At the sacred mount of Shatrunjye at Palitana, Tod alludes to a Jain book and knowledge festival, *gyan punchamee*, a festival where many pilgrims gathered at the temple of Adinath at Mount Shatrunjye:[66]

> [I]t is on occasion of these *sungs* or assemblies, that the literary riches are brought forth for contemplation, and to receive the homage of the learned doctors (*acharyas*), and other wise men amongst the Jains ... [on this occasion] the contents of the Jain libraries throughout India are conveyed in solemn pomp from their hidden retreats to the light of day, cleaned, worshipped and replaced. The *Bhindar* or treasury, whether literary or worldly wealth, is in the safeguard of Adinath himself, adjoining his statue.

Tod was struck by the few examples he noted of Rajputs practising sea trade, an incongruous and unusual blend, in his eyes. For example, in the Jain temple dedicated to Parswanath in Dilwarra (south of Mount Abu), when he was leaving Rajasthan to enter Gujarat, Tod observed sculptured frescoes which contained sailing trade boats:[67]

> Amidst the complicated sculptures of these vaulted roofs, (no less than ninety in number), of satyrs, gods, demi-gods and heroes, there were ships; indicating that the wealth of the founders was derived from maritime commerce, at a period when the proud city of Anhulwarra, and her prouder kings, the Balharaes, basked in the full sunshine of prosperity, their ships visiting all the adjacent kingdoms, and diffusing the products over the entire Hindu land.

Referring to the visit to Anhulwarra-Puttun by the Arab traveller of the twelfth century El-Edrisi (at the end of the reign of Sidh Raj Solankhi and at the beginning of the reign of Komar Pal Solankhi, 1133–66 CE), Tod quotes El Edrisi, who had noted the prosperity of the kingdom of the Solankhis, as a result of their maritime trade, with Hindu and Muslim sailors, at the ports of Goga and Mandavi and even with a fleet commander from Hormuz.[68]

At Bhavnagar, under the domination of the Gohils, Tod mentions that piracy was the main occupation of this princely family.[69] He notes among them the same blend of sea trade and piracy and attributes a mixture of sea brigandry and religious saintliness as the occupation of the Waghairs, a branch of Macwahana-Rathores, who had settled on the island of Beyt, near Dwarka, at the western tip of Cutch.[70]

The most exemplary case of a Rajput with maritime preoccupations is Rao Ghor of Mandavi (d.1822) in the Rann of Cutch. Not only had he encouraged the construction of ships by introducing a naval shipyard at Mandavi, but he had sent one of his own ships to England:[71]

> Even now there are between two and three hundred vessels in the *Khary* and roadstead, one of them three-masted, belonging to the prince of Cutch. In Rao Ghor [of Mandavi] and the Gohil chief of Bhaonugger, we have two conspicuous instances of the pliancy of the human mind, and its adaptation to circumstances, for nothing in nature is more anomalous than the association of ships and trade with the Rajput.

In *Annals and Antiquities of Rajasthan*, Tod had compared the right to patrimonial lands among the Rajputs or *bapota* to the 'allodial property' of medieval Europe, or 'land possessed by inheritance and subjected to no obligation or due [as opposed to the 'fief' of feudal serfs] except a duty of public defence'. The English historian of the Whig school, Henry Hallam, had studied in the early nineteenth century the system 'of slow gradations and mutual duties' that governed the links of loyalty between a feudal lord and his vassals in Europe.[72] Tod had seen a parallel between the system of feudal lands in Europe and the donations of land from the top of the Rajput hierarchy to military subordinate Rajputs, even if these Rajput military chiefs continued to hold, at the same time, their patrimonial lands or allodial *bapota*.[73] Tod had thus noticed an overlapping of an allodial system (free land ownership, without dues) and a feudal system (property with dues to the chief) in the distribution of landed property in Rajasthan. However, Dirk Kolff has since demonstrated that in eighteenth-century north India, in fact, a mercenary system of shifting, nomadic military services held sway (proving that long-term feudal land ownership could not apply in eighteenth-century Rajputana),[74] with a gradual sedentarisation of land links from the sixteenth century on, as Rajput military chieftains started institutionalising kinship bonds (*Bhaibandh*) along the lines of the Mughal aristocracy, in what was later labelled 'the Rajput Great Tradition'. In corroboration of such shifting relationships of military service, Tod notes in Palitana a local Gohil chief named Khanda Bhye, under the immediate control of the local Raja of Bhavnagar, subjected in his turn to the authority of the regional lord, the Gaikwad of Baroda. What was more, this local chief of Palitana had to put up with regular plundering raids by the Kathi tribes and had also to satisfy the demands of a troop of Arab mercenaries that he had himself employed for the defence of Palitana.[75] Tod was thus witness to a surprising arrangement under which the local chief of Palitana, having reserved for his own annual expenses an annuity of Rs. 40,000, had hypothecated all the land revenues of his domain of Palitana to a Gujarati banker, in exchange for the immediate advance of the sums required to terminate the services of the Arab mercenaries who were causing him so much trouble. Tod is not sure he has quite understood the logic of such a system:[76]

> How the system works, the facts, collected in a day's halt, afforded not the means of judging. It is manifestly the interest of the renter, who has a ten years' lease, to improve the lands and encourage the prosperity of the cultivator; but the reign of terror has been of such lengthened duration, and the internal policy so ephemeral in its nature, that they have yet to learn how much their own interests are involved in the welfare of the community. At present, cultivation is scanty in the environs, although the soil is rich, with much of that kind, which here as in central India, they denominate *mal*, a black friable loam, whence the name of Malwa is derived.

Tod observes another variation of the system of land ownership among the Jharejas of Bhuj (in Cutch). If the thirteen nobles of Bhuj indeed made up a brotherhood or *bhyad'* around the Raja of Bhuj in the same way as the nobles of Mewar, or of Marwar or Amber, around their respective sovereigns, with land donations in exchange for revenue or military dues, Tod noticed that the vassals of Cutch enjoyed to a greater extent their allodial rights (free ownership in full autonomy) and paid very limited feudal dues to their sovereign.[77] On the other hand, Tod found that in contrast with the sovereigns of Rajputana, the Jhareja sovereign of Cutch enjoyed little authority, having as his only prerogative, the right to arbitrate disputes of sub-infeudation. However, according to Tod, the nobles of Cutch intervened in the decisions of their Cutch sovereign, like a Council of State, thus avoiding any abuses of power by the Cutch sovereign. Tod concludes that the only link that in fact held the brotherhood of Bhuj-Cutch together was a collective fear of danger and an awareness of strength in solidarity.

Other differences between the Cutch regime and the regimes of Rajputana arose, according to Tod, from the relative isolation of Cutch, which might have protected Cutch from the intrigues and incursions of armed neighbours, as well as their geographical position between the coasts of India and the Muslim places of pilgrimage, ensuring Cutch of the constant support of all the Muslim princes of India in exchange for free annual transport for all the Indian Muslim pilgrims to Mecca.[78] Tod ends this comparative study of land rights in Gujarat by congratulating himself on the explicit request expressed by the Jhareja *bhyad* to the British authorities for the introduction of a subsidiary British armed force for the protection of the kingdom of Cutch.[79] This had been implemented when Tod passed through Cutch in January 1823.

Tod was also sensitive to the mixture and superposition of different architectural styles in the monuments he visited in Gujarat. In Palitana, after the incursions of Mahmud of Ghor in 1193 CE, a mosque had been constructed near the city ramparts. Tod saw in this mosque an aesthetically pleasing mixture of the Hindu style of construction and of Muslim architecture:[80]

> But this, as well as the other Mooslem remains in Palithana, gives evidence of the genius and taste of the Hindu architect, even to the *Mambar*, or pulpit of the Moollah, which has on either side the *Torun* sacred to Siva.

In Junagadh, not far from a Hindu temple to Bageshwar Mata,[81] and a Jain temple to Neminath,[82] Tod sees a mosque on Mount Girnar, attributed to Sultan Mahomed Begada (who reigned in Gujarat, 1459–1511). Tod perceived in this mosque on Mount Girnar a blend of different styles:[83]

[F]or whether mosque, musjid or eedga, the incongruous mass, though Mooslem in design, is Hindu in all its parts and materials. When I term it incongruous, I do not mean to deny it or its founders the merit justly due to it as a work of art; for, singular as its construction is, the architect has produced a fabric which, for uniformity, extent, solidity, and simplicity, deserves the epithet of magnificent.

In the same way, while descending from Mount Girnar, Tod stopped within a cave complex in the side of the hill, at a cave devoted to a Hindu Robin Hood, named Khopra Choor, where there was also a funerary monument to a Sufi Muslim saint: 'The process of transmutation is visible here, the Islamite having converted the unhallowed abode of Khopra into the Durgah of Shekh Ali Dervesh.'[84]

An extension of this hybridisation of architectural styles and ways of life appears in the princely palaces of three Gujarati chiefs whom Tod visited: at Bhavnagar, at Amreli (between Bhavnagar and Junagadh) and at Bhuj.

In Bhavnagar, at the palace of the Gohil chief Beeji Singh, Tod was taken by the incorporation of Arabic and European elements in the décor:[85]

A band of Arab tabors, instead of the Dholi minstrel of his forefathers, chaunted their renown, preceding the Thakoor in the state procession, which altogether presented a singular though not unpleasing medley. The like incongruities pervaded the *durbar*, when we paid our visit at the place in the afternoon, and whether of things animate or inanimate, the conclave was the most motley I ever beheld. Arabian and Rajpoot costumes were here commingled, and everything had a sort of amphibious aspect. The hall of reception was embellished by handsome glass lustres, but these were hoisted by double-blocks, evidently belonging to the dockyard, and which might have reeved the halyards of a first-rate top-gallant sail. The ceiling was clustered with mirrors as close as they could stow, in which were reflected from the walls portraits of princes, whose memory was associated with everything English – among them, George III and his Queen.

In the middle of the arid plains of Kathiawar, Tod halted at the rural place of Rae Govind Rao of Amreli (between Bhavnagar and Junagadh):[86]

I cannot conceive anything more calculated to surprise the European traveller, than his introduction into the habitation of the satrap of Saurashtra, more especially if fresh from his own land. We were ushered into a hall about fifty feet in length. ... Immediately in front was a *jet d'eau* in full play, through whose irradiant and mist-like medium, we looked upon a brilliant display of fireworks let off from the grand court. Verily, we were not a little surprised at this scene from the Arabian Nights, in the heart of this wild region.

Tod also describes the Palace of Mirrors (*Sheesh Mahal*) and the Durbar Palace of the Raja of Bhuj:[87]

> This gorgeous bauble ... implies neither taste nor judgment in the founder, Rao Lakhan, who thus dissipated the treasure accumulated by the frugality of his predecessor. Its interior is of white marble, literally inlaid with mirrors, each separated by gilded ornaments ... and a strange anomalous collection of portraits adorns its walls; Raja Jagat Sing of Mewar in contact with the Empress Catherine of Russia! Raja Bukt Sing of Marwar and Hogarth's election, with other Flemish, English, and Indian subjects, intermingling with the princes of Cutch, from the first rao, Khengar, to the present time.

In Gujarat, then, Tod greatly appreciated the ethnic and religious diversity of Saurashtra:[88]

> In fine, for diversity of races, exotic and indigenous, there is no region in India to be compared with Saurashtra, where they may be seen of all shades, from the fair and sometimes blue-eyed Catti, erect and independant as when his fathers opposed the Macedonian of Mooltan, to the swarthy Bhil, with keen look, the 'offspring of the forest'. Besides this field for the enquirer into the natural history of man, there is one equally wide for investigating the history of all the religions which have swayed the human mind within this sea-girt corner of Asia.

## *Conclusion*

To conclude, Tod's deliberate attempts to situate both his observations of Rajput and Gujarati manners and customs, and his perception of their version of the histories of their countries in a wider, comparative picture, bringing in inner divisions and complexities between different Rajput or Gujarati groups and European parallels, as well as the Romantic assembling by the Rajputs and Gujaratis of heroic or tragic narratives about their past, can be interpreted as Tod's open-minded approach to all things Rajput and Gujarati, rather than as his adopting a unilinear, teleological intention of showing the Rajputs and Gujaratis in a systematically inferior light, in contrast to their superior British colonisers. This is borne out by his painstaking attention to detail, by the fact that he drew criticism and opposition from his British superiors, such as the British Resident in Delhi, Sir David Ochterlony,[89] and the Bengal government, as also by the genuine ties of affection he was later remembered by among the Rajputs.[90] In fact, Tod seems to have actively undertaken to assemble and make available to a British reading public a narrative, as complete and faithful as possible, of the history and manners of the Rajputs and the Gujaratis that he encountered personally.

## TOD AS ANTHROPOLOGIST

## Notes

1. James Tod, *Annals and Antiquities of Rajasthan*, vol. I, London: Routledge & Kegan Paul Ltd, 1829; repr. Delhi: Rupa & Co., 1997; James Tod, *Annals and Antiquities of Rajasthan*, vol. II, London: Routledge & Kegan Paul Ltd, 1832; repr. Delhi: Rupa & Co., 1997.
2. Michèle Duchet, *Anthropologie et histoire au siècle des lumières*, Paris: Flammarion,1978, 'Preface'.
3. Duchet, *Anthropologie et histoire*, 'Conclusion'.
4. Peter James Marshall and Glyndwr Williams, *The Great Map of Mankind: British Perceptions of the World in the Age of Enlightenment*, London: J.M. Dent, 1982, p. 20.
5. Edward Said, *Orientalism*, New York: Vintage Books, 1979 (1978).
6. Ronald Inden, *Imagining India*, London: Hurst & Co., 2000 (1990), pp. 172–80.
7. Tod, *Annals*, vol. I, p. 521.
8. Tod, *Annals*, vol. II, p. 595.
9. Tod, *Annals*, vol. I, p. 251.
10. Tod, *Annals*, vol. I, p. 251, n.1.
11. Tod, *Annals*, vol. II, p. 559–60.
12. Tod, *Annals*, vol. I, p. 375, n.1.
13. Tod, *Annals*, vol. I, pp. 542–3. See also Appendix III, below, 'Tod's Memorandum on the Mhairs'.
14. Tod, *Annals*, vol. I, p. 528.
15. Tod, *Annals*, vol. II, p. 539.
16. Tod, *Annals*, vol. II p. 541; also Norbert Peabody, 'Tod's *Rajast'han* and the boundaries of imperial rule in 19th century India'. *Modern Asian Studies*, 30.I (1996), 185–220, esp. pp. 201–4.
17. See anonymous reviews of Tod's volumes on Rajasthan, *Edinburgh Review*, 52 (October 1830–January 1831), 86–108; 56 (July 1832–January 1833), 73–98; see also Inden, *Imagining India*, pp. 172–80; and Peabody, 'Tod's *Rajast'han*'.
18. Tod, *Annals*, vol. I, 'Dedication', p. xii,
19. Tod, *Annals*, vol. I, pp. 132, 137.
20. Henry Hallam, *A View of the State of Europe during the Middle Ages*, 2nd edn, London: John Murray, 3 vols, 1819, vol. I, p. 144.
21. Hallam, *A View*, vol. I, pp. 200, 320.
22. Tod, *Annals*, vol. I, p. 132, quoting Hallam, *A View*, vol. I, p. 190, vol. II, p. 429.
23. Tod, *Annals*, vol. I, pp. 137, 529.
24. Tod, *Annals*, vol. I, p. 381.
25. Tod, *Annals*, vol. I, p. 140; quoting John Millar, *A historical view of the English government from the settlement of the Saxons in Britain to the accession of the House of Stewart*, London: J.Mawman, 4 vols, 1787, vol. I, p. 85, and David Hume, *The History of England from the invasion of Julius Caesar to the revolution in 1688*, London: A. Millar, 8 vols, 1767, vol. II, Appendix ii, p. 291.
26. Tod, *Annals*, vol. I, p. 382.
27. Tod, *Annals*, vol. I, pp. 379, 392.
28. Peabody, 'Tod's *Rajast'han*', pp. 209–11.
29. Tod, *Annals*, vol. I, pp. 391–2.
30. Tod, *Annals*, vol. II, p. 486.
31. Tod, *Annals*, vol. II, p. 503.
32. Tod, *Annals*, vol. II, p. 515.
33. Norbert Waszek, *The Scottish Enlightenment and Hegel's Account of 'Civil Society'*, Dordrecht and London: Kluwer Academic Publishers, 1988, pp. 84–141; Anand C. Chitnis, *The Scottish Enlightenment: A Social History*, London: Croom Helm, 1976, *passim*; David Allan, *Virtue, Learning and the Scottish Enlightenment: Ideas of Scholarship in Early Modern History*, Edinburgh: Edinburgh University Press, 1993, pp. 147–213.
34. Michèle Duchet, 'Introduction', in: *Le partage des savoirs: Discours historique et discours ethnologique*, Paris: La Découverte,1985.

35 Tod, *Annals*, vol. I, p. xiii.
36 Tod, *Annals*, vol. I, p. xix.
37 Tod, *Annals*, vol. I, p. xviii.
38 Tod, *Annals*, vol. I, p. xvii.
39 A.Y. Goguet and A.C. Fugère, *The Origin of Laws, Arts and Sciences, and their progress among the ancient nations, translated from the French*, Edinburgh: G. Donaldson and A. Donaldson, 1775 (1758).
40 Tod, *Annals*, vol. I, p. 484.
41 Tod, *Annals*, vol. I, p. 483.
42 Tod, *Annals*, vol. I, pp. 484–9.
43 Tod, *Annals*, vol. I, p. 485.
44 Govind Sakharam Sardesai, *A New History of the Marathas*, vol. III, *Sunset over Maharashtra, 1772–1848*, Bombay: Phoenix Publications, 1968, pp. 408, 437.
45 Tod, *Annals*, vol. II, p. 582. Also *Annals*, Vol.I, p.xviii; and *Annals*, Vol.I, p.471.
46 James Tod, *Travels in Western India*, London: William Allen & Co., 1839 (posth.); repr. Delhi: Munshiram Manoharlal Publishers, 1997, pp. 128, 133.
47 Tod, *Travels*, pp. 210–11.
48 Tod, *Travels*, p. 345.
49 Tod, *Travels*, p. 352.
50 Tod, *Travels*, p. 350.
51 Tod, *Travels*, p. 344.
52 Tod, *Travels*, pp. 335, 353.
53 Tod, *Travels*, p. 361.
54 Tod, *Travels*, pp. 410–11.
55 Tod, *Travels*, p. 409.
56 Tod, *Travels*, pp. 451, 462.
57 Tod, *Travels*, p. 462.
58 Tod, *Travels*, pp. 451, 466, 471, 477, 479.
59 Tod, *Travels*, p. 472.
60 Tod, *Travels*, p. 476.
61 Tod, *Travels*, pp. 184, 273, 428, 453, 470, 483.
62 Tod, *Travels*, pp. 151, 186, 204, 410.
63 Tod, *Travels*, p. 411.
64 Tod, *Travels*, pp. 233, 234, 235.
65 Tod, *Travels*, p. 249.
66 Tod, *Travels*, p. 295.
67 Tod, *Travels*, p. 111.
68 Tod, *Travels*, pp. 220–1.
69 Tod, *Travels*, p. 266.
70 Tod, *Travels*, p. 426.
71 Tod, *Travels*, p. 453.
72 Hallam, *A View*, vol. I, pp. 144, 200, 320.
73 Tod, *Annals*, vol. I, pp. 132, 190; vol. II, p. 429.
74 Dirk Kolff, *Naukar, Rajput and Sepoy: The Ethnohistory of the Military Labour Market in Hindustan, 1450–1850*, Cambridge, Cambridge University Press, 1990, pp. 71–4.
75 Tod, *Travels*, p. 300.
76 Tod, *Travels*, p. 300.
77 Tod, *Travels*, p. 484.
78 Tod, *Travels*, p. 489.
79 Tod, *Travels*, p. 490.
80 Tod, *Travels*, p. 297.
81 Tod, *Travels*, p. 370.
82 Tod, *Travels*, p. 366.
83 Tod, *Travels*, p. 365.
84 Tod, *Travels*, p. 368.
85 Tod, *Travels*, p. 261.

86 Tod, *Travels*, p. 307.
87 Tod, *Travels*, p. 460.
88 Tod, *Travels*, p. 257.
89 Tod, *Travels*, p. xxxvi.
90 Tod, *Annals*, vol. I, p. 621; vol. II, p. 612; Reginald Heber, *Narrative of a Journey through the Upper Provinces of India, from Calcutta to Bombay, 1824–1825, with notes upon Ceylon*, London: John Murray, 1828, 3 vols; repr. New Delhi: Asian Educational Services, 1995, vol. II, p. 42.

CHAPTER THREE

# Tod's practice of science in India: voyages through empirical, common sense

The first two decades of the nineteenth century, when James Tod was in India,[1] was a period of great changes in the field of science in Britain, in particular with the institutionalisation of botany and geology in British universities, learned societies, botanical gardens and museums.[2] The British colonial authorities in India, who had been expanding their territorial domination through a series of wars since the Battle of Plassey in 1757, introduced British scientific methods in their Indian territories from the 1760s, in particular for geodetical purposes of military surveying and mapping,[3] for inventorying the varied geological structures and rock compositions across India[4] and also for making collections of botanical specimens of India's vast flora.[5] A large number of the British military surveyors, geologists and botanists in India, including James Tod, were of Scottish origin, for example Colin Mackenzie, who surveyed Mysore between 1799 and 1810; Francis Buchanan, who assembled herbariums and statistical surveys of Burma and South India in 1796 and 1807; several of the superintendents of the Calcutta Botanic Garden founded in 1786 under encouragement from Joseph Banks, President of London's Royal Society from 1778 to 1820; and Captain James Franklin (1783–1834), who published papers on the geology of central India in the journal entitled *Asiatick Researches*, published by the Asiatic Society of Bengal, to name only a few. This is why I will try to explore the application in India, through James Tod's travels and writings, of the paradoxical relation between empirical field observation as applied to the physical sciences in Britain in the early nineteenth century on the one hand, and the simultaneous theoretical framework of the Scottish common-sense philosophical school which searched for more abstract connections, causes and positionings of observed phenomena in an overall evolutionary scale on the other hand.[6] This explains the use side by side of the terms 'empirical' and

5 William Jones Collection: Shaikh Zayn-Al-Din, Botanical study: flower and leaves.
(By kind permission of the Royal Asiatic Society of Great Britain and Ireland)

'common sense' in the title of this chapter. While there was a conscious effort on the part of Tod and other British field scientists in India, to gather concrete information on India's topography, geology and botany, there was also perhaps an inadequate attempt to adapt and extend the theoretical models of scientific classification and explanation then in use in Britain to the diversity of the Indian context. The wide range of James Tod's field observations and comparisons of observed facts with aspects of other known societies, in his two published works,[7] could be perceived as a groping towards a more perceptive and better-informed scientific acquaintance with the Rajput and Gujarati territories, typical of the numerous 'Scottish Orientalists' scouring the Indian countryside in the early nineteenth century, as opposed to the more rigid and prejudiced views expressed by James Mill and other British experts on India in the later nineteenth century.[8] I will proceed in three steps, juxtaposing the consolidation of institutions for scientific research with Tod's scientific observations in the following fields: first, geodetical surveying, then geology and finally botany. My aim is to explore how far the existing British scientific frameworks influenced or failed to influence Tod's practice of science. The importance of Tod's contributions to British imperial science in India probably lies in his having been in the field during a period of transition, when new fields of scientific inquiry were only just emerging in Britain, making India a good arena for testing and illustrating the new methods and hypotheses elaborated in the metropolis, while the need to impose British superiority was perhaps not as yet firmly in place.

Tod's two published texts furnish us with some sparse details about his intellectual formation. Apparently he left for India in March 1799, after barely one year's training at the Royal Military Academy at Woolwich, which was where the East India Company's cadets were educated, before the establishment of the Company's Institution at Addiscombe.[9] He seems to have acquired the rest of his education in scientific subjects on the ground in India, showing from the outset 'the promise which his talents afterwards realised',[10] sparing no energy in his surveying tasks, and using every possible opportunity to 'enlarge his knowledge of the geography of the country'.[11] The anonymous author of the 'Memoir of the Author' at the beginning of Tod's *Travels in Western India*, makes the following assessment of Tod's intellectual capacities:[12]

> [H]is features were expressive, and in the discussion of literary or scientific subjects, especially relating to India and to Rajpootana, they were lighted up with extraordinary animation. His general knowledge was various; his writings indicate a very wide range of inquiry. ... With the Sanscrit and learned languages of the East he was not, perhaps, so intimately acquainted as with the Western dialects of India, which were the vehicles of oral communication and the depositaries of the history and science of Rajpootana.

Tod's British companions through his trips across Rajasthan between 1819 and 1822 were as follows:[13]

> The escort consisted of two companies of foot, each of one hundred men, with half a troop of cavalry. The gentlemen attached to the mission were Captain Waugh (who was secretary and commandant of the escort), with Lieutenant Carey as his subaltern. Dr. Duncan was the medical officer.

Captain Patrick Waugh (1788–1829) was not only Tod's kinsman, but also a gifted artist. His pencil drawings and watercolours of various landscape scenes in Rajasthan[14] (many of which illustrated the first folio edition of Tod's text on Rajasthan) make up an important part of the Tod Collection at the library of the Royal Asiatic Society of London.[15]

Tod had also obtained permission from the Governor-General, Lord Hastings, in 1821 for his cousin John Tod (1799–1821), 'an excellent classical scholar, well-versed in modern languages and every branch of natural history',[16] to join him as a research assistant in Rajasthan. Unfortunately John Tod died six months after his arrival in India, at the young age of twenty-two, before having ever exercised the research post he had been summoned for.[17]

Tod mentions his Indian research assistants, individually and collectively, at various points in his texts. His closest Indian companion was his Jain guru, named Yati Gyanchandra, who faithfully helped him in transcribing and translating Indian texts over ten years (1812–22)[18].

He mentions the services of Yati Gyanchandra in obtaining for him a copy of the *Siva Purana* at the shrine of Eklingji (a form of Shiva) near Udaipur,[19] and the local temple legend of the mother goddess at Palode near Morwan, southeast of Chittaur in February 1820.[20] Tod also refers to his Brahmin assistants: a certain Balgovind, an 'antiquarian pioneer',[21] and Baba Mohes, who kept a diary of perambulator measurements.[22] An Indian artist, named Ghassi, made sketches for Tod of architectural temple structures at Barolli, Chandravati and Chittore.[23]

Among the groups of Indian researchers trained by Tod, he mentions his 'flying detachments', obtained and instructed locally 'for deciphering, and others for collecting whatever was the object of research'.[24] He claims to have gathered eleven folio volumes of journey books of observations,[25] through his 'surveying parties' or 'parties of discovery', made up for example of 'jemadars of dâks, or superintendents of posts, which were for many years under my charge when at Sindia's court [1805–17], extending at one time from the Ganges to Bombay, through the most savage and little-known regions of India'.[26]

Tod's scientific agenda seems to have been linked to a utilitarian improvement programme, as Professor David Arnold has pointed out in his section on Tod in his book on India, landscape and science.[27] Tod dreamed of establishing detailed records of Rajasthan's natural riches and topography in the hope of using them to bring prosperity and modernity to the region (in a spirit of British, industrialising, capitalist modernisation):[28]

> In short, I know no portion of the globe which would yield to the scientific traveller more abundant materials for observation than the alpine Aravulli. ... I should know no higher gratification than to be of a scientific party to anatomise completely this important portion of India. ... The 'Aravulli delineated' by the hand of science, would form a most instructive and delightful work.

This improvement trend is visible, for example, in Tod's plans for a modern canal to link Udaisagar Lake at Udaipur to the ancient capital of Chittore, along the bed of the Berach River, thus enabling more efficient boat transport for merchandise instead of the existing transport of goods on the backs of oxen, and making possible modern irrigation to shut out famine from the area, instead of continued dependence on the 'cranking Egyptian wheel' for the distribution of water.[29]

## Geodetical surveying

To begin with geodetical surveying, it can be noted that the 'Great Trigonometrical Survey of India' only officially came into being in 1818, under William Lambton and George Everest, though surveying of territory with perambulators, barometers and thermometers, to measure distances, heights and relative temperatures, was practised right from 1765 in Bengal and north India, by the pioneer cartographer James Rennell.[30] In 1815, Colin Mackenzie was appointed for the first time Surveyor-General of all-India, uniting the surveying initiatives of all the three presidencies of Calcutta, Madras and Bombay, and from 1830 onwards, George Everest occupied simultaneously the office of Surveyor-General of all-India as well as of Superintendent of the Great Trigonometrical Survey of India (which accumulated 700 volumes of survey reports between 1790 and 1833). These institutions for land surveying in India can be seen as attempts to imitate the British Government Board of Longitude and the British Ordnance Survey, both established in London in 1791.[31] A precedent in statistical land surveying had also been set in Scotland by John Sinclair (1754–1835), on the basis of reports from Scottish parish ministers (1791–9). The same John Sinclair also founded the British Board of Agriculture (1799–1844), for the improvement of British agricultural techniques.[32] In India also, land surveying by the East India Company authorities was linked to military strategy and to agricultural revenue collection.

During James Tod's travels through Rajputana and Gujarat in western India, several geodetical observations appear in his travel narratives. Certain aspects of Tod's land surveying methods are striking. For example, he seems to set great store by the relative accuracy made possible by the use of Western scientific instruments like the barometer for air pressure readings and calculations of altitude, compass bearings at specific points to fix the observer's position in relation to other specific points, the thermometer for temperature variations[33] and the perambulator, which consisted of a pair of wheels on a frame fitted with a dial to register the distance covered.[34] Thus, thanks to his barometer, he recorded the precise height above sea level (3,353 feet or approximately

1,100 metres) of the peak of Kumbhalgarh (northwest of Udaipur) on his way from Mewar to the desert region of Marwar in October 1819.[35] A few days later, however, Tod reports that the quicksilver in his surviving barometer had 'contrived to escape', depriving him of 'the opportunity of comparing the level of the desert with the plains of Marwar'.[36] On his final journey through Gujarat prior to his departure for good from India, Tod confesses that his recording of the height of Mount Abu (west of Udaipur) in June 1822 is only 'a rough estimate', since one of his two barometers had broken on leaving the temple of Akhileshwar (one of the temples on Mount Abu), making a counter-reading impossible. Here is Tod's conclusion as an honest surveyor:[37]

> [T]he true height, therefore, of Aboo, must remain a desideratum until I reach the shore of the ocean, or be otherwise able to test its accuracy. The elevation, however, as thus indicated, accords with my own rough estimate, formed from the time occupied in ascent, the judgment of the eye, and the extent of vision over the surrounding region.

Tod also frequently resorted to the comparative method to corroborate the geodetical details he observed. For example he compares his own readings of the latitude and longitude of Ajmer on his return to Udaipur from Marwar in December 1819, to those made by James Rennell, the pioneer British cartographer in India between 1765 and 1777:[38]

> By a medium of several meridian observations, I made the latitude of Ajmer 26° 19' north; its longitude, by time, and measurement from my fixed meridian, Oodipoor, 74° 40'; nearly the position assigned to it by the father of Indian geography, the justly celebrated Rennell.

On his final journey via Mount Abu in mid-1822, Tod geologically compares the absence of visible volcanic sediments at the lake called Nakhi-talao near this mountain site to the rocks and 'volcanic scoriae' at the Laachersee in the Rhine Valley in Germany, between Koblenz and Bonn:[39]

> At a little distance, we saw the Nuki-talao, a beautiful lake, about 400 yards in length, which merited a day of itself; but time pressed and I was forced to content myself with a glance *en passant*. Those who have seen the lake three miles above Andernach, on the Rhine have beheld its counterpart. It is surrounded by rocks, wooded to the margin, while the water-fowls skim its surface, unheeding and unheeded by man. ... Its waters are said to be fathomless, but I observed no traces of volcanic scoriae.

Here we can also note Tod's easy juxtaposition of land surveying observations with geological notations. Perhaps in order to appear more serious and scientific to his reader, Tod compares the temperatures, vegetation and estimated elevation of Mount Abu to those of

Mount Sinai and thereby puts himself in the same category as the Swiss explorer Johann Ludwig Burckhardt (1784–1817), who visited Syria, Egypt, Nubia and Arabia between 1810 and 1817, and became famous posthumously as a heroic scientific explorer with Joseph Banks's African Association.[40]

Finally, among Tod's topographical remarks, there are a few mentions of his frequent reliance on Indian assistants and on certain evidence of Indian methods of recording distances. For instance, at Amba (different from Amber, the traditional name for Jaipur), between Kota and Udaipur, on 21 October 1820, Tod states that fever and ague having left his own mind 'in a sorry state', his Indian amanuensis, named Baboo Mohes, kept a diary of barometer and perambulator readings, adding 'and on his intelligence I can depend'.[41] Tod notes also with some personal surprise in Saurashtra in Gujarat in December 1822, the relative accuracy among Indians in estimating local distances, despite local variations in the 'coss' (a unit of approximately 3 kilometres) resulting from the autonomy enjoyed by individual rajas to fix their own standards in currency, weights and measures:[42]

> Amongst the many points which present themselves to the reflection of a traveller in India, one which ought to strike him with surprise is, the general knowledge possessed by all classes of the distance of places within their immediate neighbourhood; and, however the standard may vary in different countries, yet within their own, a most singular uniformity and correctness prevail. ... It is, in fact, a remnant of that ancient civilisation, which ... is not yet altogether obliterated, neither from tradition or written throughout India. This alone can account for the surprising facility which exists for laying down a champaign (or open) country from verbal estimation, with all the exactitude of the chain and theodolite.

So, although Tod preferred to use Western scientific instruments himself in his land surveying in India, he was willing to acknowledge the existence of a certain scientific acumen and certain scientific techniques practised by the Indians of his time, even if he tended to consider these indigenous capacities and techniques as less reliable and less accurate than British scientific acumen and British scientific techniques.

## Geology

This brings me to the institutional frameworks of the study of rocks and soils, emerging in the early nineteenth century in Britain as the science of geology. In London, the English surveyor William Smith triggered a dispute in 1790, when he published *A Tabular View of the British Strata*, based on a study of organic remains in the west of England. The dispute was between partisans of the Scottish geologist James Hutton (1726–97), who from 1788 had been advocating an igneous vulcanist theory to explain the earth's rock formations, and the disciples of the German geologist from Freiburg, Abraham Gottlob Werner (1749–1817), who linked the stratigraphical diversity of rocks to fossils, floods, silting, erosion and the withdrawal of oceans in his aqueous or Neptunist explanation of rock and earth configurations. Around the same time in the 1790s, London's Society of Arts (founded in 1757), began offering premiums for mineralogical maps. With encouragement from Joseph Banks, the new Royal Institution in London, founded in 1799, offered geological courses by Humphry Davy and W.T. Brande to elite amateurs, while a British Mineralogical Society came into existence in the same year (1799) to encourage fieldwork (collection of specimens, the mapping of stratigraphical structures for drainage and canal building) among members of the merchant and artisan classes.[43] The British Mineralogical Society closed down in 1807 and fused into the Geological Society of London in the same year. George Greenough was elected its first president after his geological tour of Scotland in 1805. The Geological Society attempted to find a middle path between the pure empiricism of the artisan mineral surveyors and the purely abstract speculation of the elite mineral collectors, and began publishing its learned journal, the *Transactions of the London Geological Society* from 1811. In Edinburgh, a Wernerian Natural History Society flourished for some twenty years (1808–30), under the direction of Robert Jameson, while the Royal Society of Edinburgh (founded in 1783) started its own Geological Committee in 1811. In the mean time, Charles Francis Greville (1749–1809), nephew of the British diplomat, William Hamilton, became a private mineral collector, and through the English East India Company's affairs and as a member of the London Board of Trade corresponded in 1782 with a British natural historian in Calcutta, named Dr Percy, who had studied natural history in Edinburgh under Professor Black. Later, in 1818, another British natural historian in Calcutta, Major-General Hardwicke, corresponded with the Geological Society in the hope of establishing links between the London learned society and the Asiatic Society of Bengal.[44] In Calcutta, right from 1814, the botanist Nathaniel Wallich suggested to the British authorities in Bengal a Natural History Museum of British India, with a section on minerals and fossils.[45] In fact, a Museum of Economic Geology only opened in 1840 in Calcutta, and in 1856 was transferred to the new Indian Museum, as part of the official Geological Survey of India, which was inaugurated in Calcutta by the Irishman T. Oldham in 1851. In between, in 1818, a gifted British doctor, Dr H. Voysey, was attached to the surveyor William Lambton's Great Trigonometrical Survey of India. For five years, until his death in India in 1823, Voysey conducted pioneering geological expeditions in the diamond mines and territory around Hyderabad, as well as in the Nilgiri Hills further south. Two of his geological research papers were included in the special volume on Indian geology of the Asiatic Society of Bengal's official publication *Asiatick Researches*.[46] This issue on geology was the result of the creation in 1828 of a separate Physical Committee within the Asiatic Society of Bengal, aimed at promoting 'knowledge of natural history' and 'scientific investigation' in India.[47]

Within this new, expanding institutional framework of geological science in India, James Tod included certain observations on the chemical composition of rocks and soils, on the effect of earthquakes and floods, as well as on geological resources that could be lucratively extracted, in his two published travel texts. On leaving Udaipur for Marwar in October 1819, Tod observes the geological formation of the Nathdwara ridge, due north of Udaipur:[48]

> The country is much broken, with irregular, low ridges, of micaceous schist in the shape of a chine [*OED*: spine or ridge or crest] or hog's back, the crest of which has throughout all its length a vein of quartz piercing the slate, and resembling a back-bone; the direction of these veins is uniformly NNE and the inclination about 75° to the east.

Further on, during the same journey, near Jodhpur, at Pipar, Tod takes advantage of the deep wells to note the various geological strata,[49] observing at the deepest level: 'stalactic concretions of sandstone and quartz'.

According to the note at the bottom of his page about Indawur, which he visited in late November 1819, Tod indicates that he consulted a geologist of the Royal Asiatic Society in London, named Mr Stokes, about the precise nature of 'an unctuous indurated clay', that lay between a layer of red sandy earth and a layer of sand-rock. Apparently, the London geologist pronounced the oily, hardened clay of Indawur (near Jodhpur) to be a form of steatite or soapstone, a hydrous silicate.[50]

About the effect of earthquakes and floods, Tod does not appear to adhere either to the vulcanist theory of the Huttonians, or to the Neptunist theory of the Wernerians. He contents himself with observing the ravage caused by both these natural phenomena along his way. For example, he pays tribute to human ingenuity that somehow overcomes natural adversity, be it in the Jura or the Aravalli: to irrigate agricultural terraces on steep mountain slopes, to dam up little pools of water with massive trees at high altitudes and even to start from scratch after sudden floods: 'Not unfrequently, their labour is entirely destroyed, and the dykes swept away by the periodical inundations;

for we observed the high-water mark in the trees considerably up the acclivity (or rising slope).'[51] Tod admits the limits of his own geological knowledge when noting the still visible 'ashes of a volcanic eruption' at the Rajput burial site at Ahar near Udaipur:[52]

> The vestiges of immense mounds still remain to the eastward, called the *Dhool-Kote*, or 'fort' destroyed by ashes (*dhool*) of a volcanic eruption. Whether the lakes of the valley owe their origin to the same cause which is said to have destroyed the ancient Ahar, a more skilful geologist must determine. The chief road from the city is cut through this mound.

During his journey through Gujarat, Tod noted two places where imposing monuments had been destroyed by earthquakes. In Palanpur in north Gujarat, Tod learned that two lofty columns of the Rudra Mala temple had been brought down by the 1819 earthquake,[53] and at Mandvi in the Kachchh peninsula, the palace of the Gohel chief had been shaken to pieces by an earthquake, although Tod does not specify when the earthquake occurred in Mandvi.[54] Tod does not draw any particular conclusions about the local geological structures from his observations of earthquakes in the region.

Like most practitioners of science in colonial contexts, Tod appears particularly sensitive to the economic potential of profits from the geological reserves of Rajputana and Gujarat. The abandoned copper mines at Dariba 'filled with water and the miners all dead' (approximately southwest of Bhilwara and northeast of Udaipur, between Rashmi and Jasma) make Tod dream of reviving these mines and thus restoring prosperity to the region.[55] He also alludes to reopening other tin and silver mines at Jawad unfortunately squatted by Bhils to Tod's regret (due east of Udaipur and north of Nimach) as one of his 'favourite' projects.[56] At another point on his journey back to Udaipur from the desert-like Marwar, east of Pur (to the northeast of Udaipur, southwest of Bhilwara) as well as 'on the southern frontier of Kishangarh and Ajmer' (NNE of Udaipur), Tod found 'garnets imbedded' in the blue slate rock in December 1819.[57] As always, Tod's conjectures move along lines of profits to be had from the lucrative trade of metal ore extractions and semi-precious stones.

Tod's practice of geology in western India shows some attention to rock types and rock formations, while also attaching importance to the utilitarian exploitation of the region's mineralogical deposits that could be organised.

Apart from land surveying and geology, another natural science that developed considerably in London and in India in the early decades of the nineteenth century was botany. In Britain, between 1777 and 1788, William Curtis published several volumes of his *Flora Londinensis*.

In 1781, George III purchased Kew Gardens, where a Royal Botanical Garden was launched. In 1788, a young Scottish botanist, James Edward Smith (1759–1828), was elected the first President of the new Linnean Society of London to foster botanical collections and plant taxonomy. This learned society began its own scientific journal, *Transactions of the Linnean Society of London*, to circulate the findings of botanists. Since the 1780s botany had been formally taught at British universities. It so happened that several botanists who practised botany in India trained in London, Edinburgh or Glasgow. For example, Professor John Hope of Edinburgh University trained William Hooker (head of Kew Gardens from 1841 to 1865), William Roxburgh (head of the Calcutta Botanic Garden from 1793 to 1814), Francis Buchanan (who made several botanical expeditions in northeast India and south India between 1790 and 1805) and James Edward Smith (first President of the Linnean Society from 1788 to 1828).[58] Professor John Lindley of University College London taught botany to William Griffiths (head of the Calcutta Botanic Garden from 1835 to 1838) and John Ellerton Stock, who joined the Bombay Medical Service in 1847.[59] Professor Robert Graham (brother of Maria Graham, who toured India from 1809 to 1811) taught botany at Edinburgh University in the 1820s to Hugh Falconer (head of the Calcutta Botanic Garden 1829–37 and 1849–55), while Professor William Hooker (later Head of Kew Gardens from 1841 to 1865) taught botany at Glasgow University from 1830 to 1841, and had among his students Thomas Thomason (head of the Calcutta Botanic Garden from 1856 to 1859).[60] On a suggestion from Joseph Banks (1743–1820), President of the Royal Society in London from 1778 to his death in 1820, the East India Company opened a Botanic Garden in Calcutta in 1786, with the aim of cultivating rare plant species and developing commercially profitable plant products.

In addition, the East India Company had Botanic Gardens in Sibpur (north of Dacca, in what is Bangladesh today), at Samalkot, near Kakinada in the Northern Circars on the Coromandel Coast, and at Saharanpur (south of Dehra Dun, north of Delhi) from 1823, while between 1804 and 1808, Governor-General Wellesley started an 'Institution for promoting the Natural History of India' at Barrackpur near Calcutta, with a menagerie and an aviary.[61] The two methods in use during this period for naming and classifying plants were Linnaeus's system and Jussieu's system. The method of Carl Linnaeus (1707–78) consisted of binomial nomenclature, using the flower and the number and arrangements of stamens and pistils, to group plants into twenty-four classes, further divided into orders, genera and species. Linnaeus used two-word names for species of plants within a group, with a specific name for everyday use and a descriptive name for better identification of each species.

This consistent two-word nomenclature for plants brought uniformity to the system of botanic names through the second half of the eighteenth century.[62] Antoine-Laurent de Jussieu (1748–1836), a nephew of the elder Antoine de Jussieu, introduced a new 'natural' method for naming plants which took into account the natural conditions in which the plant grew (type of soil, type of climate, altitude and especially the type of zone, either tropical, temperate or alpine) in attributing a name to it.[63]

Two characteristics are salient in Tod's occasional practice of botany during his travels. First, he observes the tripartite division of vegetation according to zone types: tropical, temperate and alpine,[64] following Jussieu's natural system of classification rather than Linnaeus's Latin binomial labels, while also treading in William Jones's footsteps,[65] by giving the local Indian plant names wherever possible.[66] As Professor David Arnold has observed, Tod's enthusiasm for Indian categories and concepts, his use of 'ethno-botany' or incorporation of vernacular terms, local names and indigenous topographical markers, in his allusions to Rajasthani plant species, shows his basic empathy for the region of his adoption. On the other hand, Tod always adopts a utilitarian approach to plants, considering them only for their potential use, without bothering to make exhaustive lists of all the plant species he encountered for the purely disinterested expansion of human scientific knowledge!

On 18 October 1819, between the Nathdwara ridge and Kailwara in the valley of Gogunda, Tod observes first the 'prickly shrubs' of this dry region by their Indian names: *khyr*, *khureel* and *babool*; and then comments on the relative lushness of 'the alpine valley called Sheroo Nullah':[67]

> The *Goolur* or wild-fig, the *Sitaphal* or custard apple, the peach or *Aroo-badam* (almond-peach) are indigenous and abundant; the banks of the stream are shaded by the withy [*OED*: a flexible, willow-kind of twig], while the large trees, the useful mango and picturesque tamarind, the sacred peepul and burr are abundantly scattered with many others, throughout.

Barely half a page later, indicating a change of vegetation in the same 'alpine valley called Sheroo Nullah', therefore, Tod observes the crops being cultivated, with an eye to agricultural revenues for the British Government, and an ear to the difficulties of the cultivators:[68]

> The rice crop was abundant, and the *joar* or maize was thriving, but scanty; the standard autumnal crop which preceded it, the *makhi* or 'Indian corn', had been entirely devoured by the locust. The sugar-cane, by far the most valuable product of this curious region, was very fine

but sparingly cultivated, from the dread of this insect, which for the last three years had ravaged this valley ... and dread of the *farkas* [a species of locust] deters speculators from renting this fertile tract, which almost entirely belongs to the fisc. Its natural fertility cannot be better demonstrated than in recording the success of an experiment, which produced five crops, from the same piece of ground, within thirteen months.

While descending from the 'alpine' Aravalli to the 'fertile plains of Godwar', Tod learns some local folklore about the natural boundary between fertile Mewar (Udaipur) and arid Marwar (Jodhpur) from the local Rana's envoy Kishendar:[69]

> [F]or nature has marked our limit by stronger features than mountains. Observe as you advance, and you will find to the further limit of the province every shrub and flower common to Mewar; pass that limit but a few yards and they are lost:
> *Aonla aonla Mewar:*
> *Bawul bawul Marwar.*
> Wherever the aonla puts forth its yellow blossoms, the land is of right ours; we want nothing more. Let them enjoy their stunted Babools, their Khureel and the Ak; but give us back our sacred peepul and the aonla of the border.' In truth the transition is beyond credence marked.

Here Tod's incorporation of the local Indian plant names underlines the exoticness of the different species while also highlighting the contrast between the blossoming plants of the better-watered region and the uninviting bareness of the thorny plants of the more arid region.

On Tod's last return to Udaipur on 8 March 1822, after his journey to Kota and Bundi, with his own final departure from Rajputana imminent (for health reasons), Tod shares with the reader his personal pleasure at seeing fruit and vegetable plants planted by him, thriving at his private secondary residence at Merta (between Ajmer and Jodhpur) and also within Udaipur at the former residence of a retired female singer and dancer named Rung-Peari, which had served Tod as his 'home' for the last four years (1818–22):[70]

> I halted a few days at Mairta, and found my house nearly finished, the garden looking beautiful, the *Aroo* or peach-tree, the *Seo* or apple, the *Suntra*, *Narinji* and *Nimboo*, or various orange and lime-trees, all in full blossom, and showing the potent influence of *Surya* in these regions; the *Sureefa* or *Seetaphal* (fruit of Seeta) or custard-apple, the *Anar*, the *kela*, pomegranate, plantain, and various indigenous fruits, were all equally forward. These plants are mostly from Agra, Lucknow or Cawnpoor; but some of the finest peaches are the produce of those I planted at Gwalior, – and I may say their grandchildren.
> When I left Gwalior in 1817, I brought with me the stones of several peach-trees, and planted them in the garden of Rung-Peari, my residence

at Oodipoor; and more delicious or more abundant fruit I never saw. The stones of these I again put in the new garden at Mairta, and these again exhibit fruit, but it will require another year to prove whether they maintain the character they held in the plains of Rarew, or in this city. The vegetables were equally thriving: I never saw finer crops of Prussian-blues, of *Kobis*, *Phool-Kobis*, or cabbages and cauliflowers, celery and all that belongs to the kitchen-garden and which my Rajpoot friends declare far superior to their indigenous race of *Sae*, or greens: the *Dewanji* (Rana) has monopolised the celery, which he pronounces the prince of vegetables.

Here, apparently Tod was practising reverse exoticism by cultivating English lettuces and celery in his Udaipur garden, to the joy of his Rajput friends!

## *Conclusion*

To conclude, James Tod's voyages cross Rajputana and Gujarat between 1819 and 1823 enabled him to apply the empirical methods in practice in Britain at the time, namely of precise measurements and detailed field observations, in the newly emerging physical or natural sciences such as land surveying, geology and botany. Tod also manifested some, if only a limited, awareness of the recent theoretical innovations like searching for causes and explanations for phenomena, situating the details noted in an overall evolutionary framework and more flexible systems of naming and classification. While Tod moved across territory in his travels, he also helped to move ideas of Western science into Indian contexts. Whether this was part of the 'epistemological violence' of colonialism and whether Tod's dreams of material 'improvement' in the territories he helped to supervise for the British Governor-General in Calcutta boiled down simply to exploitative colonial impositions are questions best left to others. What does appear from Tod's texts, however, is that though he had no formal scientific training, he valiantly made scientific readings and notes in several different fields of science, while also doing his duty as a colonial representative of the British Governor-General. Being in a position of subordination himself, both administratively and scientifically, he perhaps had no choice but to follow the dominant scientific trends set in Britain at the time, leaving his indigenous assistants and their indigenous scientific techniques in a 'doubly subaltern' position – in relation to the British colonial scientists in India and in relation to the British metropolitan scientists in Britain.[71] This can be understood as perhaps just one of the many 'paradoxes' of the scientific 'progress' that Tod seems to have believed in so firmly.

## Notes

1 Note on James Tod (1782–1835), by Stephen Wheeler and Roger T. Stearn, in: *Oxford Dictionary of National Biography*, Oxford: Oxford University Press, 2004, www.oxforddnb.com/view/article/27486.
2 G.S. Rousseau and Roy Porter (eds), *The Ferment of Knowledge: Studies in the Historiography of Eighteenth-Century Science*, Cambridge: Cambridge University Press, 1980, including Roy Porter, 'The terraqueous globe', pp. 285–324, esp. p. 301.
3 R.H. Phillimore, *Historical Records of the Survey of India*, Dehra Dun: Office of the Geodetic Branch, Survey of India, 1945, 1950, 1954, in 3 vols.
4 P.N. Bose, 'The history of the Asiatic Society of Bengal, 1784–1883', Part III, 'Natural Science, section of Geology', in: *Centenary Review of the Asiatic Society of Bengal from 1784 to 1883*, published by the Society, Calcutta: Thacker, Spink & Co., 1885, pp. xcvi–109.
5 Ray Desmond, *The European Discovery of the Indian Flora*, Oxford: Oxford University Press, 1992, pp. xii, 355.
6 Alexander Broadie, 'Conclusion', in: *The Tradition of Scottish Philosophy: A New Perspective on the Enlightenment*, Edinburgh: Polygon, 1990, pp. 127–31.
7 James Tod, *Annals and Antiquities of Rajasthan*, vol. I, London: Routledge & Kegan Paul Ltd, 1829; repr. Delhi: Rupa & Co., 1997; James Tod, *Annals and Antiquities of Rajasthan*, vol. II, London: Routledge & Kegan Paul Ltd, 1832; repr. Delhi: Rupa & Co., 1997. James Tod, *Travels in Western India*, London: William Allen & Co., 1839 (posth.); repr. Delhi: Munshiram Manoharlal Publishers, 1997.
8 Jane Rendall, 'Scottish Orientalism: from Robertson to James Mill'. *Historical Journal*, 25.1 (1982), 43–69. For example, James Mill, *The History of British India*, London: Baldwin, Cradock & Joy, 1817, 3 vols, quarto; Richard Burton, *Sind, and the races that inhabit the valley of the Indus*, London: W.H. Allen, 1851; George Campbell, *Modern India: a sketch of the system of civil government, to which is prefixed some account of the natives and native institutions*, London: John Murray, 1852; Henry Sumner Maine, *Ancient Law, its connexion with the early history of society and its relation to modern ideas*, London: J.Murray, 1861; James Talboys Wheeler, *The history of India from the earliest ages*, London: Trübner, 1867–81, 4 vols in 5; all these authors tended to justify European superiority on the basis of racial difference.
9 Tod, *Travels*, p. xviii.
10 Tod, *Travels*, p. xviii.
11 Tod, *Travels*, p. xxi.
12 Tod, *Travels*, p. lvi.
13 Tod, *Annals*, vol. I, p. 375, n.5; vol. I, p. 520.
14 Tod, *Annals*, vol. I, pp. 536–7.
15 See Raymond Head, *Catalogue of Paintings, Drawings, Engravings and Busts in the Collection of the Royal Asiatic Society*, London: Royal Asiatic Society, 1991, pp. 107–22
16 Tod, *Annals*, vol. I, p. 538, n.2.
17 See Head, *Catalogue of Paintings*, p. 109.
18 Tod, *Annals*, vol. I, p. xviii.
19 Tod, *Annals*, vol. I, p. 412.
20 Tod, *Annals*, vol. II, p. 497.
21 Tod, *Annals*, vol. II, p. 505.
22 Tod, *Annals*, vol. II, p. 547.
23 Tod, *Annals*, vol. II, pp. 566, 587, 607.
24 Tod, *Annals*, vol. I, p. 552.
25 Tod, *Annals*, vol. II, p. 233, n.1.
26 Tod, *Annals*, vol. II, p. 245, n.1.
27 See David Arnold, *The Tropics and the Travelling Gaze: India, Landscape and Science, 1800–1856*, Seattle and London: University of Washington Press, 2006, pp. 92–3.

28 Tod, *Annals*, vol. I, pp. 538–9.
29 Tod, *Annals*, vol. II, p. 504.
30 James Rennell, *Memoir of a Map of Hindoostan*, 2nd edn, London, 1792 (1783). See also Phillimore, *Historical Records*, vol. III, chapter I, 'General Narrative'.
31 Porter, 'The Terraqueous Globe'.
32 John Sinclair, *The Statistical Account of Scotland drawn from the communications of the ministers of the different parishes*, Edinburgh: William Creech, 1791–9, 21 vols.
33 Tod, *Travels*, p. 422.
34 Tod, *Annals*, vol. I, p. 579; vol. II, p. 605.
35 Tod, *Annals*, vol. I, pp. 530–1.
36 Tod, *Annals*, vol. I, p. 545.
37 Tod, *Travels*, pp. 121–2.
38 Rennell, *Memoir*; see also Tod, *Annals*, vol. I, p. 614.
39 Tod, *Travels*, p. 115.
40 See Nigel Leask, *Curiosity and the Aesthetics of Travel Writing 1770–1840*, Oxford: Oxford University Press, 2002, p. 131.
41 Tod, *Annals*, vol. II, p. 547.
42 Tod, *Travels*, p. 355.
43 See Roy Porter, *The Making of Geology: Earth Science in Britain, 1660–1815*, Cambridge: Cambridge University Press, 1977, and Paul Julian Weindling, 'Geological controversy and its historiography: the prehistory of the Geological Society of London', in: Ludmilla Jordanov and Roy Porter (eds), *Images of the Earth: Essays in the History of the Environmental Sciences*, London: British Society for the History of Science, 1997 (1979), pp. 247–68.
44 Weindling, 'Geological controversy'.
45 Bose, 'History of the Asiatic Society of Bengal', *passim*.
46 *Asiatick Researches*, 18 (1833), special volume on geology. Calcutta: Printed at the Bengal Military Orphan Press, by G.H. Whitmann.
47 See *Asiatick Researches*, 18 (1833), part I, 'Introduction', pp. i–iv.
48 Tod, *Annals*, vol. I, p. 525.
49 Tod, *Annals*, vol. I, p. 579.
50 Tod, *Annals*, vol. I, p. 581.
51 Tod, *Annals*, vol. I, p. 528.
52 Tod, *Annals*, vol. I, p. 620.
53 Tod, *Travels*, p. 140.
54 Tod, *Travels*, p. 447.
55 Tod, *Annals*, vol. I, p. 618; vol. II, p. 549.
56 Tod, *Annals*, vol. I, p. 222; vol. II, p. 505, n.1.
57 Tod, *Annals*, vol. I, p. 618.
58 See Desmond, *European Discovery*, *passim*.
59 See Arnold, *Tropics and the Travelling Gaze*, p. 158.
60 Arnold, *Tropics and the Travelling Gaze*, p. 159.
61 Mildred Archer, 'India and natural history: the role of the East India Company, 1785–1858', *History Today*, 9.11 (November 1959), 736–43.
62 See www.linnean.org/index.php?id=147.
63 Antoine-Laurent de Jussieu, *Genera Plantarum Secundum Ordines naturales disposita*, Paris: Académie des Sciences, 1795.
64 Arnold, *Tropics and the Travelling Gaze*, p. 196.
65 William Jones (1746–94) lived in Calcutta from September 1783 to 1794, was a scholar of Greek, Latin and Sanskrit and founded in 1784 the Asiatic Society of Bengal.
66 Arnold, *Tropics and the Travelling Gaze*, p. 178.
67 Tod, *Annals*, vol. I, p. 528.
68 Tod, *Annals*, vol. I, pp. 528–9.
69 Tod, *Annals*, vol. I, p. 547.
70 Tod, *Annals*, vol. II, p. 611.
71 Arnold, *Tropics and the Travelling Gaze*, pp. 180, 225, 231.

# CHAPTER FOUR

# Tod's use of Romanticism in his textual constructions of Rajasthan and Gujarat

At the time when Tod returned to England (in early 1823) and was compiling his works on Rajasthan and Gujarat, the Romantic poetry of Byron, Coleridge, Southey and Thomas Moore was in fashion. The Romantic movement was a reaction against the hyperrationalism of French classicism and the Enlightenment. It began in Germany in the 1770s as a movement of 'Storm and Stress' and was spearheaded by writers like Herder, Fichte, Schiller and Schelling. The common ground among them was an idealisation of freedom, unbridled self-invention, delight in artistic creation through self-invented ideals, a turn towards the unattainable infinite through subjective introspection, a rejection of a rigid, pre-ordained reality and a search for symbols and myths to replace established religion,[1] visible in the Romantics' attention to folk-songs and folk customs. This revolt against the straitjacket of logical causality through communion with the vastness of nature spread from Germany to Britain and other countries of Europe between 1790 and 1830. In this new pitting of the individual against all the cosmic forces, there was an oscillation between an optimistic yearning for an unobtainable harmony and a paranoiac, suicidal angst. Among the leaders of the Romantic movement in Britain were Byron and Walter Scott. For reasons known only to himself, Tod chose to highlight his texts on India with quotations from various British Romantic writers, in particular Byron and Scott.

It is true that the Romantics were famous for their neo-classical philhellenism and for their receptivity to Oriental themes,[2] both of which aspects were important to Tod. The heroes of Byron's poetical creations are known for their indomitable will, which propels them forward despite the absence of any intelligible structure in the world. Scott's novels sought to contest the contemporary values of the emerging industrial society in Britain, by placing the characters alongside idealised past values of the medieval world. The heroes of his historical

## TOD'S USE OF ROMANTICISM

6 Palace of Ranee [sic] Bheem and Pudmundi [sic].
(By kind permission of the Royal Asiatic Society of
Great Britain and Ireland)

novels illustrated constant movement and activity, with either an imaginative move towards the past or a withdrawal within the self to circumvent the absence of human order.[3]

Contemporary British officials who had published accounts of their experiences in India, like Bishop Reginald Heber (1783–1826)[4] and James Forbes (1749–1819),[5] had used quotations and references to various literary and biblical sources, including Scott and the Romantics, probably in the hope of heightening the enjoyment of their readers. My hypothesis is that Tod wished to align his texts in the tradition of these Romanticist writers on India, in order perhaps to distance himself from the other strong current of thought and writing on India, embodied by James Mill and the Utilitarian disciples of Jeremy Bentham, and exemplified among the India observers by Francis Buchanan[6] and William Tennant.[7]

My aim in this chapter is to study the role played by Tod's use of romanticised, heroic legends drawn from the local bardic chronicles, and to analyse the functions of Tod's recourse to quotations from the literary creations of British Romantic poets and novelists, in his textual constructions of his experiences and explorations into the past of Rajasthan and Gujarat.

Various possible reasons have been put forward to explain why Tod adopted a heroic register in his texts, especially since such a framework is absent from the travel texts of many of Tod's contemporaries (like Buchanan and Tennant). For example, Jason Freitag suggests that Tod was perhaps appealing to the reader's desire for a nostalgic return to the times of the European medieval and Gothic periods.[8] Lloyd Rudolph points out three models visible in Tod's evocations of Rajasthan: medieval feudalism (with its accompanying ideals of honour and loyalty), romantic nationalism (associated with young heroes sacrificing their lives tragically) and the Scottish Enlightenment (with its universal stages in the realisation of civilisational progress).[9] I would like to propose the hypothesis that Tod was probably trying to target an elite London readership, and had as a model before him while composing his text on Rajasthan Bishop Reginald Heber's travel narrative in north and south India, which went through several editions between 1826 and 1830. Heber resorted generously to quotations from Walter Scott, Robert Southey and biblical texts.[10] In this literary gesture of including British poetic quotations and of rendering his accounts heroic, Tod can be understood to have been trying to build bridges between the Rajput culture he was describing and the British culture of his readership. He seems almost to be blending the two cultures together, by stressing their similarities and by drawing parallels between these disparate cultural spheres. Tod's use of heroic legends based on the chronicles of local Rajput bards can be classified into three groups: first, allusions to usurpations and bloody succession conflicts; second, the marriages and sati sacrifices of Rajput princesses; and third, reconstitutions of famous battles.

In Tod's relations of the respective local histories of Mewar, Marwar, Bikaner, Jaisalmer, Amber, the Shekhawut Federation, Bundi-Haravati and Kotah-Haravati, as well as in his 'Personal Narrative' in each of his two volumes on Rajasthan, and also in his report on the various little kingdoms of Gujarat, he painstakingly evokes the succession of sovereigns in each of these kingdoms, with the conflicts and remarkable events of each reign. One recurrent theme that strikes the reader in the evocation of all these royal reigns, is the discontented uncle or jealous brother who usurps the throne of his young nephew on the demise of his brother, the earlier reigning sovereign, in the style of Shakespeare's Richard III. There are also instances of vengeful parricides and other types of succession conflicts. Among the annals of Mewar, a memorable parricide is that of Rana Koombho. Koombho reigned from 1419 to 1469, and van-quished Mahmud Khilji of Malwa in 1440, constructing a victory pillar at Chittor on the occasion.[11] In his *Annals* Tod narrates the killing of Rana Koombho by his own son, Ooda Hatiaro or Ooda the Assassin, himself then struck down by lightning.[12]

Another dramatic assassination of a young prince is that of Pirthi Raj in 1508, son of Rana Raemul (r.1474–9) and brother of Rana Sanga (r.1509–28). Pirthi Raj died of poisoning by the husband of his sister, Pabhoo Rao, the Raja of Sirohi, who resented Pirthi Raj reprimanding him for maltreating his wife (Pirthi Raj's sister). Tod's rendering of the sixteenth-century Pirthi Raj's untimely death rings with heroic nostalgia, since Pabhoo Rao presented Pirthi Raj with a poisoned sweetmeat while Pirthi Raj was his trusting guest at Sirohi.[13]

Closer to Tod's time is the usurpation of the throne of Mewar at Udaipur by a brother of Rana Pertap II (r.1752–5), after the death of the son of Rana Pertap II, named Rana Raj Sing II (r.1755–62). The usurper uncle named Ursi ruled from 1762 to 1772, stoking several feuds in Mewar: against the Pretender son of Rana Raj Sing II, an infant Rutna Sing, and against the Raos of Bundi. Ursi left two sons in 1772, Hamir II, who ruled as a minor in Mewar from 1772 to 1778, and his brother Bheem Sing, who ruled for fifty years from 1778 to 1828, having become Tod's good friend after 1818. Rana Ursi, however, covered his name with horror because he murdered his saintly uncle Nathji,[14] the brother of Ursi's own father, Rana Jagat Sing (r.1734–52), and was murdered himself in 1772 by Prince Ajit Sing Hara of Bundi, during the Ahairea spring festival hunt. This only confirmed the old proverb that warned against the Rana of Mewar meeting for celebrations with the Rao of Bundi on the occasion of the Ahairea festival,[15] since on several occasions in their history, tragedy had resulted from the encounter of these two princes,[16] Tod reports the unease of both the people of Mewar and the people of Bundi at this cold-blooded murder of a little-loved usurper, because of a petty boundary dispute, leaving the feud between the two houses unresolved.[17]

In the other royal houses of Rajasthan also, there are instances of usurpations and assassinations. A famous parricide took place in Marwar when Abhé Sing Rahtore took the life of his own father Raja Ajit Sing Rahtore of Marwar in 1725 (r.1710–25). Abhé Sing ruled from 1725 to 1750, and was succeeded by his son Ram Sing Rahtore (r.1750–65; Ram Sing Rahtore died in exile in Jaipur in 1773). From 1765, the other branch of Rahtores, descended from Ajit Sing's brother Bukhta Sing, seized the throne of Jodhpur, with Beejy Sing Rahtore (r.1765–96), succeeded by his son Bheem Sing Rahtore (r.1796–1802), succeeded by his son Maun Sing Rahtore (r.1802–28), thus excluding totally from the Marwar throne the descendants of Ajit Sing. Tod makes a gloomy about feudal dominion giving ambivalent results that include noble deeds and deep crimes.[18]

Tod describes at length his own intervention in sorting out the competing claims to the throne and administration of Kotah in 1821. On the one hand, there was the descendant of the Maharaos of Kotah, the legitimate Hara rulers, embodied from 1819 in Maharao Kishore Sing Hara of Kotah. On the other hand, there was the Foujdar or minister of the palace, of Jhala origin, in the person of Raj Rana Zalim Sing Jhala of Kotah (b.1739, r.1758–1824).[19] Kishore Sing had to face rival claims for his throne from his two brothers, Pirthi Sing and Bishen Sing. On Raj Rana Zalim Sing's side, his two sons, Gordhun Das (deported to Delhi by the British in May 1820) and Madhu Sing, were both competing to succeed him. In October 1821, things came to a head when Maharao Kishore Sing and his troops, the Raj Rana Zalim Sing and his troops and the British forces under Tod met at Mangrol near the Caly Sind River. The Maharao having been defeated and forced to withdraw to Baroda,[20] Tod was able to establish a truce and obtain the return of the Maharao to Kotah, with the continuation of the Raj Rana's descendant Madhu Sing in the Raj Rana's position of minister-counsellor at Kotah, with special provisions to 'prevent all collision of interests'.[21]

During his travels through Gujarat, Tod observed the various dynasties who had ruled in the region. While passing through Anhulwarra, Tod points out the overlapping of two dynasties, the Chaora dynasty (746–932 CE), and the Solankhi-Chaluc dynasty of Kalyan (on the Konkan coast) who moved to Anhulwarra in 932 CE in the person of Moolraj Solankhi (r.932–88), whose mother was a Chaora princess, the Chaoras having no male heir in 932 CE. The Solankhis ruled in Anhulwarra Puttun for 270 years, 932–1193 CE.[22] This change of dynasty was executed without any bloodshed. Here Tod takes advantage of his halts at the various dynastic capitals to fill his reader in on historical details.

Another succession in which Tod was able to intervene in 1817–18, to the satisfaction of one of the competing Rajput parties, was the principality of the Deoras of Sirohi, at the foot of Mount Abu, south of Udaipur, against an unjustified takeover by the Raja of Marwar, who was supported by David Ochterlony, Tod's hierarchical superior in Delhi, thanks to Tod's own 'historical knowledge of the complicated international politics of these regions'.[23]

If succession conflicts make up one of the fascinating threads of Tod's incorporation of heroic legends into his texts, another consists of the marriages and wifely life sacrifices of the Rajput princesses. When Prithviraj Chohan, King of Delhi, was arming to meet the vast army of Shahbudin Mahmud of Ghor in battle in 1192 CE, one of his wives, Sunjogta, Princess of Kanauj, whom he had abducted against the wishes of her father, exhorted Prithviraj to war for the honour of the Chohans, although she knew he would probably not return alive from the confrontation.[24]

Similarly, when Jeswunt Sing of Jodhpur with his Rahtore troops followed the Rana Raj Sing I of Mewar in battle against Aurungzeb, probably at Futtehbad, south of Ujjain in 1658,[25] after 10,000 Rajput soldiers were slain, Jeswunt Sing Rahtore's Mewari queen exhorted him to uphold his honour by further battle against Aurungzeb. Tod quotes the conclusion on the courage of the Rajput women and the custom of sati drawn by the seventeenth-century French traveller Bernier, who was present in north India in 1658: 'There is nothing which opinion, prepossession, custom, hope, and the point of honour, may not make men do or suffer.'[26]

As a generic example, omitting to mention the date and the name of the Muslim Khan of Bhopal in question, Tod compares the Rajput queen of Ganora to Lucretia of ancient Rome (emblematic of virtuous wifehood, who after being raped by the son of the tyrant Etruscan King of Rome in 509 BCE committed suicide because of her loss of honour), having clothed the imposing Khan with a poisoned garment.[27]

In the same emblematic vein, the queen mother of Rao Soorajmul of Bundi (r.1534–5) is cited by Tod as having expressed pride rather than sorrow at news of the heroic death of her son in warrior confrontation with Rana Ruttun of Chittor (r.1528–35), since it was an accomplishment of the Rajput ideal of chivalry and of 'aveng[ing the] father's feud'.[28]

An analysis of Tod's textual strategies in presenting these succession conflicts reveals a deliberate conciseness which underlines the tragic drama of the events. Tod also incorporates vernacular words in a literal or translated form, like *hatiaro* (meaning assassin) or 'the regions of the sun' (the English equivalent of *suryalok*), expressing some of the cultural specificities of the Rajputs. A solemn and portentous tone conveys the fateful aspect of the incidents recounted, including even Tod's own role therein, while at the same time pointing to the tone of the Rajput bardic chronicles Tod used as his sources. This conciseness and fateful tone can be observed in the examples cited above. For instance: '[A] flash of lightning struck the *hatiaro* (murderer) to the earth, whence he never arose. The bards pass over this period cursorily, as one of their race was the instrument of the crime.'[29] Or at: 'Her resolution was soon formed; the pyre was erected, and with the mortal remains of the chivalrous Pirthi-Rey in her embrace, she sought "the regions of the sun".'[30] As also: '[A]nd the contests between their issue have moistened the sands of Marwar with the richest blood of her children. Such is the bane of feudal dominion.'[31] Tod thus uses language strategies (solemn terms of vocabulary, contrasts, metaphors, a concise, paratactic sentence structure) to convey specific tragic and dramatic effects.

The marriages of Rajput princesses to Muslim sovereigns like Emperor Akbar and his son Jahangir have long occupied the attention of historians and commentators. That such marriages caused divided feelings among the Rajputs is apparent in the example of Rana Raj Sing I of Mewar (r.1654–81) who is reported to have carried off the Marwar Rahtore princess of Kishengurh and Roopnagurh around 1680, in order to avoid her forced union with the Muslim emperor Aurungzeb.[32] However, Akbar is said to have had at least two Rajputni wives: a Marwar princess named Joda Baé, daughter of Jodhpur's Rao Udai Sing Rahtore (r.1584–98), espoused by Akbar on his invasion of Marwar in 1561 during the reign of Udai Sing's father Rao Maldeo Sing Rahtore (r.1532–69),[33] often confused with Jahangir's Rajputni wife named Joda Baé, supposed to have been the mother of Shah Jahan, and recently the subject of controversy in the Indian press when the very existence of the Marwar princess Joda Baé was questioned, on the release of the film *Joda-Akbar* (directed by Ashutosh Gowariker, 2008); and a princess of Jessulmer who happened to be the sister of the Jessulmer wife of Raja Rae Sing of Bikaner (r.1573–1632).[34] Akbar's son, Emperor Jahangir (r.1605–25), is reported to have had three Rajputni wives: a Bikaner daughter of Rae Sing of Bikaner (r.1573–1632) remembered as the mother of Prince Purvez[35] and as having been responsible for the raising of the Cuchwaha prince Jai Sing I to the throne of Amber-Jaipur;[36] a Jaipur Cuchwaha princess, daughter of Raja Bhagwandas Cuchwaha, remembered as the mother of Prince Khosroo;[37] and another Jaipur Cuchwaha princess, mother of Prince Khurrum, later Shah Jehan,[38] perhaps named Joda Baé and supposedly buried at Secundra, near Agra.[39] It may, however, be noted that no Mewari princess at any time is known to have married a Muslim sovereign[40]. This confirms that if there was frequent intermarriage between the different kingdoms of Rajasthan, it was only on some rare occasions that the Rajput Rajas considered it politically astute and beneficial to give their sisters or daughters in marriage to the Muslim sovereigns under whose rule they had to live.

Among other romantic legends of Rajput princesses and their sati sacrifices, Tod mentions the love story between Prince Nala of Nishida-Jaipur and Princess Damayanti of 295 CE of Vidarbha,[41] which celebrates the constancy of Princess Damayanti, who is able to recognise her lover-husband despite several gods adopting his very form and appearance and despite his later being transformed into a dwarf. The story ends with the happy reunion of the separated lovers.

An interesting instance of a curse emitted by a dying Rajput princess in the act of wifely sacrifice or sati in the fourteenth century appears with the Hara princess of Bumaoda betrothed to the heir of

Chittore, Kaitsi (r.1361–5). Prince Kaitsi of Chittor challenged his Hara father-in-law to a duel because the latter was believed to have provoked the suicide of a holy bard from Benares, Bheemsen Bardai, by covering him with lavish gifts that left the bard immersed in remorse and self-loathing, resulting in his suicide:[42]

> Alike prepared for the fight or the feast, the Hara accepted the unequal combat and the father and lover of the bride rushed on each other spear in hand, and fell by mutual wounds. ... It was on this event that the imprecation was pronounced that 'Rana and Rao should never meet at the spring-hunt (*ahairea*) but death should ensue'.

In his travels through Gujarat, at the island of Peerum adjacent to the city of Goga (between Palitana and Broach), under the Gohils from before the Muslim invasions of the region, Tod recounts the brave resistance and death of Akhi Raj Gohil of Goga during the attacks of Allaudin Khilji on Chittore in 1303, accompanied by the sati of his Mewari wife, Soojan-Kumari.[43]

Similar to the love legend of Nala and Damayanti, though more tragic, is the tale of the star-crossed lovers Sadivaeh and heroine Sawalinga, associated with the baori-well of Palitana. Sawalinga was the daughter of a merchant from Paithan on the banks of the Godavari River, settled in Palitana in Gujarat. She was in love with Sadivaeh of Palitana through their common guru-acharya of the Kalka-Devi temple in Palitana. But Sawalinga's family had married her off to a merchant kinsman of Parkur, Marwar. Forced to depart from Palitana to join her wedded husband's home in Marwar, Sawalinga exchanged vows of constancy with her Palitana lover Sadivaeh at the shrine of Kalka Devi. The end of the story was lost by Tod, but the last he tells us of Sadivaeh is that he wandered in the Marwar desert in desperate search of his lost beloved, Sawalinga.[44] Tod's conclusion from this love romance is interesting: 'India abounds with such narratives, having generally some historical incident for their basis, and familiar alike to the peasant and the prince.'[45] One of Tod's reflections on the various shrines and monuments to mythical-historical characters is: 'There is no moving in this region without meeting at each step some objects interesting in themselves, or which have become so from association with the mingled history and mythology of past ages.'[46]

Tod seems to use the accounts of the marriages, sati sacrifices and motherly interventions of various Rajput women to underline their active role in the valorous history of their region, contrary to what might be inferred from their segregated life, isolated from the public eye. Towards this end, he deploys a paradoxical juxtaposition of terms in order to highlight the courage of the Rajput princesses in the face of an inexorable fate. For example the politically advantageous but unhappy marriages between Rajput princesses and Mughal princes are qualified with terms such as 'valorous subjects' opposed to 'unfortunate' fruit of this marriage.[47] In Tod's description of the Mughal siege of Ahmadnagar in 1596–9, the Hara's 'intrepidity' and the 'desperate assault' by Rao Bhoj of Bundi is recounted alongside the pitiless slaughter of Chand Bibi and her 700 female subordinates, who were 'slain, gallantly fighting'.[48]

Also, the heroic warrior-like intervention of the concubine queen of Rana Udai Singh of Udaipur against Akbar's attack on Chittore in 1568 ends in her being put to death by the Rana's jealous chiefs, and in a supreme paradox, encourages Akbar to repeat his attack: 'Internal discord invited Akber to re-invest Cheetore.'[49] Here again then, under the heading of marriages and wifely life sacrifices, Tod is careful to choose contrasting and paradoxical terms to express the heroic but tragic role of the brave royal Rajput women in public affairs.

In continuation of these inspiring tales of male and female heroism are the famous battles that dot the entire history of Rajasthan. Tod's accounts of these battles irrepressibly convey his partisan viewpoint on the Muslim and Maratha adversaries of the Rajput Rajas, portrayed by him as depredators and villains. He sets the tone on several occasions by comparing the battles of the Rajputs to the Battle of Thermopylae in 480 BCE, mentioned before, when the Spartan leader Leonidas I ordered his Greek mercenary troops to withdraw against the powerful and numerous army of the Persian Xerxes, while 300 Spartans valorously stood their ground unto death behind him. For example, in his 'Introduction' to volume I of his work on Rajasthan, he announces a series of heroic battles of the same epic register as those of the ancient Greeks, with an allusion to Greeks and Rajputs attaching great symbolic importance to their sword: '[T]here is not a petty state in Rajasthan that has not had its Thermopylae, and scarcely a city that has not produced its Leonidas.'[50]

After Jeswunt Sing Rahtore of Marwar (r.1638–81) was banished by Aurungzeb to the distant land of Afghanistan around 1670, his posthumous son Ajit Singh Rahtore (b.1681, r.1711–25) was protected at Ajmer by the faithful Rahtore Doorgadas, who led the Marwar forces against Aurungzeb at the Battle of Nadole in Godwar, Marwar, in 1681. Tod adds in a note to his description of this 1681 Battle of Nadole,[51] 'The heroes of Thermopylae had not a more brilliant theme for the bard.'

In a further reflection on the parallel between the Greek retreat at Thermopylae recounted later by Xenophon and the violent confrontations in India, Tod extends the analogy to a retreat by the British

General Monson, in 1804, from Gurrote on the Kotah Pathar to the Mukundwara Pass, while his adversary, the Maratha Holkar, advanced from Pertabgurh in Malwa towards Mundisore.[52] As he does throughout his texts, here Tod defends the weaker, losing side, admiring their valour in the face of their difficult circumstances, and Xenophon's account of the retreat in 480 BCE provides an appropriate paradigm.

In order to trace Tod's manner of representing the famous battles fought by the Rajputs down the ages, I will select a few memorable examples which continue to reverberate in the collective memory of today's Rajputs and indeed of all Indians. To begin, the Gehlotes of Chittor had to face the incursions of Mahmud of Ghazni between 997 and 1008 CE:[53]

> Towards the close of this [tenth] century [Subektegin, governor of Khorassan] made his last invasion, accompanied by his son, the celebrated Mahmood, destined to be the scourge of the Hindu race who early imbibed the paternal lesson inculcating the extirpation of infidels. Twelve several visitations did Mahmood [of Ghazni] make with his Tatar hordes, sweeping India of her riches, destroying her temples and architectural remains, and leaving the country plunged in poverty and ignorance.

Another momentous invasion of north India took place (in fact *two* centuries later) under Shahbudin Mahmud of Ghor in 1192 CE and was the occasion of heroic resistance from Pirthi Raj Chohan, King of Delhi and Ajmer at the time. In the course of his travels, Tod uses his halt at Mahanal, between Beejoliya Kalan and Beygun, on 21 February 1822, where there are monuments to the memory of Pirthi Raj Chohan, his brother-in-law Samarsi Chohan of Chittor and Samarsi's Chohan wife Pirtha Bae who was Pirthi Raj's sister, to expatiate on the tragedy of their deaths in 1192 CE during the battle against Shahbudin of Ghor on the banks of the Caggar (in Afghanistan):[54]

> If we may believe, and we have no reason to distrust, the testimony of Chund, had Pirthiraj listened to the counsel of the Ulysses of the Hindus (in which light Samarsi was regarded by friend and foe), the Islamite never would have been lord of Hindusthan. But the indomitable courage and enthusiastic enterprise of Pirthiraj sunk them all; and when neither wisdom nor valour could save him from destruction, the heroic prince of Cheetore was foremost to court it. Both fell on the banks of the Caggar, amidst heroes of every tribe in Rajpootana.

The twelfth-century bard Chund's 'Pirthi Raj Raso' or account of the heroic deeds of Pirthi Raj Chohan, was the focus of much of Tod's attention. He brought back at least two copies of it to London, and while in India, with the help of his Jain guru Yati Gyanchandra, tried to summarise or translate around 10,000 of its 60,000 verses, compiled in sixty-nine books in all.[55]

Another important milestone in Rajput history is 1303 CE, when Allaudin Khilji of Afghanistan attacked Chittor, then under Rana Bhimsi and his beautiful wife Padmini:[56]

> The fair Pudmani closed the throng, which was augmented by whatever of female beauty or youth could be tainted by Tatar lust. They were conveyed to the cavern, and the opening closed upon them, leaving them to find security from dishonour in the devouring element.

Then, Rana Bheemsi, satisfied that his only surviving son, Ajeysi, was safely in Kailwarra, was followed by his devoted clans to the plains, where with reckless despair they threw themselves into the crowded ranks of Allaudin Khilji's army, to their own inevitable destruction. On visiting Chittor in February 1822, Tod mentions in his 'Personal Narrative' that he visited the site of Padmini's *Johar* of 1303.[57]

The eldest son of Rana Raemul of Mewar (r.1474–1509), named Sanga (r.1509–28), was called upon to face the invasion of the Moghul Baber in 1528 CE at the Battle of Kanua:[58]

> Devotion was never more manifest on the side of the Rajpoot, attested by the long list of noble names amongst the slain as well as the bulletin of their foe, whose artillery made dreadful havoc in the close ranks of the Rajpoot cavalry, which could not force the entrenchments, nor reach the infantry which defended them. ... Sanga retreated towards the hills of Mewat [sic], having announced his fixed determination never to re-enter Cheetore but with victory. Had his life been spared to his country, he might have redeemed the pledge; but the year of his defeat was the last of his existence, and he died at Buswa, on the frontier of Mewat [sic], not without suspicion of poison.

Although the Battle of Kanua was a defeat for Rana Sanga, Tod's version insists on the 'devotion' of the Rajputs, on Sanga's determination to regain victory for Chittor, and on the tragedy of his unnatural death in the prime of his life. To reassure the reader about the completeness and objectivity of the facts related, Tod points out that he has used the Rajput annals of Mewar, as well as the autobiography of Baber, a compilation known as the *Babur Nameh*.

During the reign of Akbar, this Mughal emperor captured Chittor in 1568 and then had his son Salim (the future Emperor Jahangir) confront Rana Pertap of Mewar at the Battle of Haldighati in 1576. Both these battles occupy an important place in the narratives of Rajasthan's past. Recounting the heroic sacrifice in 1568 of Rana Udai Sing's (r.1542–71) loyal vassals, Rahtore Jeimul of Bednore and Chondawut Putta of Kailwa, aged only sixteen at the time, Tod alludes to the huge massacre involved, comparing it to the massacre by the Carthaginian Hannibal of the Romans at Cannae (southeast Italy) in 216 BCE:[59]

> Akber entered Cheetore, when thirty thousand of its inhabitants became victims to the ambitious thirst of conquest of this 'guardian of mankind'. ... When the Carthaginian gained the battle of Cannae [216 BCE], he measured his success by the bushels of rings taken from the fingers of the equestrian Romans who fell in that memorable field. Akber estimated this, by the quantity of cordons (*zinar*) of distinction taken from the necks of the Rajpoots, and seventy-four mans and a half are the recorded amount.

Tod is aware here of the unforeseeable interpretations and impressions retained of historical accounts by their receivers, underlining the symbolic effect of the figure 'seventy-four and a half' mans of Rajput sacred cordons or *zinar*, and 'three and a half' bushels of Roman rings. His use of the parallel between the Battle of Cannae and the conquest of Chittor gives his rendering a universal resonance, since he deliberately places the two events on the same level of tragedy and importance. His use of irony concerning Akbar's reputation as a compassionate 'guardian of mankind' shows clearly on whose side he is in this case.

The Battle of Haldighati in 1576 resulted in a double victory (a few months apart) for Prince Selim (Akbar's son and heir), while it reduced Rana Pertap (r.1571–97) to ten years of nomadic exile (1576–86) before he could regain his capital of Udaipur thanks to the generous financial aid of a rich Rajput merchant:[60]

> There is not a pass in the alpine Aravulli that is not sanctified by some deed of Pertap, – some brilliant victory or, oftener, more glorious defeat. Huldighat is the Thermopylae of Mewar; the field of Deweir [where Pertap confronted Shabaz Khan] her Marathon.

Tod seems clearly to be making the point that the Rajputs excelled in their dignity and valour in the very circumstances of defeat and loss. The rhetoric throughout Tod's depiction of the Battle of Huldighat presents the defeated Pertap as the ultimate hero of Rajput resistance.

Like Emperor Akbar, Aurungzeb and his immediate successors marked the memory of the Rajputs by the battles they conducted against them. The three most outstanding of Aurungzeb's battles against the Rajputs are Futtehbad, south of Ujjain, in 1658; Nadole, in Godwar, Marwar, in 1681; and Jajow-Dhaulpur, south of Agra, in 1708. Tod evokes the heroic role of Rahtore Jeswunt Sing of Marwar (r.1638–81, in Kabul from 1670), under the reign of Rana Raj Sing I of Mewar (r.1654–81) at the Battle of Futtehbad in 1658, contrasting Moghul perfidy with Rajput loyalty:[61]

> In the civil war for empire amongst the sons of Shah Jehan, when Arungzeb opened his career by the deposal of his father and the murder of his brothers, the Rajpoots, faithful to the [deceased] emperor, determined to oppose him [Aurungzeb]. ... The Rajpoots behaved with their usual bravery; but were surrounded on all sides, and by sunset left ten thousand dead on the field.

The energies of the same Rana Raj Sing I of Mewar (r.1654–81) were exhausted at the Battle of Nadole in the region of Godwar, Marwar, in 1681, although it began with victories for the Rajputs in the mountain passes of Marwar. Aurungzeb conducted the battle on several fronts at the same time (Marwar, Chittor, Gujarat, Malwa) and reduced Rana Raj Sing I of Mewar to sue for peace.[62]

In the Moghul succession conflict that followed Aurungzeb's death in 1707, the Rajputs were again involved in bloody battles, as vassals of the emperor. In 1708, a memorable conflict took place at Jajow, near Dhaulpur south of Agra.[63] The singularity of the battle of Jajow is that it opposed two Rajput clans, Rao Budh of Bundi (r.1707–19) supporting Shah Alum (later Emperor Bahadur Shah I, r.1708–13), against Rao Ram Sing of Kotah (r.1686–1708), who sided with Prince Azim Shah and lost his life at Jajow in 1708.[64]

Here, Tod's presentation of Jajow-Dhaulpur in 1708 highlights the complexity of the stakes – a longstanding rivalry between the two Hara clans of Bundi and of Kotah, combined with the rivalry between two sons of Aurungzeb for the throne of Delhi. The reader cannot but be struck by the high price of heroism in battle – bloodshed and loss of life.

Numerous battles were conducted by the Maratha forces in Rajasthan from 1747 onwards. This was the date of the Battle of Rajmahl, where Rana Jagat Singh II of Mewar (r.1734–52), supported by Malhar Rao Holkar, was defeated by one of the pretenders to the Jaipur throne on the death of Sowae Jey Sing II of Jaipur (r.1699–1743), Esuri Sing of Jaipur (r.1743–47), who despite being supported by the Maratha Peshwa's forces under Appajee Sindia committed suicide soon after, in 1747.[65] Tod does not mince his words in dating 'the decline of Mewar' to this Maratha intervention of 1747 in Rajput affairs, which he then computes to a period of seventy years, till 1817, when, according to him, the Pax Britannica permitted the Ranas of Mewar to regain their lost dignity.[66]

This serious allegation about the negative influence of the Marathas on the Rajputs is borne out in all of Tod's renderings of Maratha battles in the region. Whether this was a way for him to justify British intervention is open to debate, but that he consistently adopts this position throughout his texts is obvious. In fact, my argument throughout this chapter is that Tod's approach in championing the valour of the Rajputs despite their internal dissensions, defeats and losses can be understood to serve two purposes: on the one hand, Tod seems keen to illustrate the brave existence of the Rajputs down the ages as a full-fledged, autonomous, political entity, while on the other hand, he demonstrates exactly how the British intervention in Rajasthan could be perceived as an attempt to restore the declining honour and autonomy of the Rajputs, within a flexible and supportive British administration.

In 1788, the joint forces of Marwar and Jaipur defeated Mahadji Sindhia's troops at Lalsot (southeast of Jaipur), though this Rajput victory was soon neutralised by Ahalya Bai Holkar of Indore, who quickly brought all the Rajput towns recently reconquered by the allied Rajput forces of Lalsot under Maratha domination again. Tod attributes this setback after victory for the Rajputs to their sense of 'misplaced security': 'The newly made conquests were all rapidly lost. ... Thus terminated an enterprise which might have yielded far different results but for a misplaced security.'[67]

Tod's repetition of the term 'check' in 'Sindia received a signal check' and in Ahilya Bai's initiative 'to check this reaction of the Rajpoots' shows the struggle for ascendancy between the Rajputs and the Marathas in Rajasthan. The allusions to the former glory of the Rajputs in the expressions 'to resume their alienated territory' underline their reluctant submission to Maratha domination. The contrast between the adverbs 'newly' and 'rapidly' in 'the newly made conquests were all rapidly lost' draws the reader's attention to the precarious circumstances of the Rajputs, completely at the mercy of the Marathas at the time.

Tod makes only a brief mention of the battles of Patun (1790) and Merta (1791),[68] in his 'Annals of Mewar', using them to underline the slow infiltration of the Rajput political stage by the Maratha forces from the 1780s.

If this description of two very famous defeats at Patun (1790) and at Merta (1791) of the Rajput forces by the Marathas appears surprisingly brief, Tod makes up for this in his 'Personal Narrative' at the end of his volume I on Rajasthan. Here, referring to local folklore, in the form of a popular stanza on the humiliating role of the Jaipur Cuchwahas subordinated to the Marwar Rahtores in the Battle of Lalsont (1788),[69] Tod claims the Jaipuris were provoked into revenge against their military superiors the Rahtores, resulting in an alliance between the Jaipuris and the Marathas, against the Jodhpur Rahtores during the battle of Patun (1790).[70] Concerning the 1791 Battle of Merta, Tod attributes the defeat of the Rahtores to the household jealousies between the

Jodhpur civil minister and the Rahtore military chiefs, while he cites only in passing and in a note at the end of his account of these battles the role of Sindhia's French military Commander, de Boigne, whom Tod visited at Chambéry in 1826.[71] De Boigne's memoir points out his eighty pieces of European-style artillery (as opposed to the meagre twenty-five cannon of the Rahtores), and then underlines his European military strategy of the 'hollow square', which enabled Sindhia's infantry to present an invincible front to their Rajput adversaries, whatever side they were attacked from. In his main text, Tod prefers to lay stress on the heroism and internal divisions of the Rahtores:[72]

> Thus, owing to a scurrilous couplet of a bard, and to the jealousy of a contemptible court-faction, did the valiant Rahtores lose their independence – if it can be called lost – since each of these brave men still deems himself a host, when 'his hour should come' to play the hero. Their spirit is not one jot diminished since the days of Tonga [Lalsont] and Mairta.

While rendering sincere homage to his colleague Colonel James Skinner of Hansi, Tod reminds his reader of the long succession of battles fought in north India by the British forces, in particular against the Marathas: '[Skinner] has passed through the ordeal of thirty years of unremitted service, and from the glorious days of Delhi and Laswari under Lake [1785] to the last siege of Bhurtpore [1815], Skinner has been second to none.'[73]

Tod makes a comment about civil wars among the Rajput clans while summing up the early history of Mewar through a parallel drawn from Gibbon's history of Europe in the Middle Ages:[74]

> We may close these remarks on the fifteen princes, from Khoman to Samarsi, with the words of Gibbon on the dark period of Guelphic annals: 'It may be presumed that they were illiterate and valiant ...' and, we may add, continued bickering with their vassals within, when left unemployed by the enemy from without.

Tod's comment in his chapter on Rajput feudalism, on the possible political utility of keeping the different clans of Mewar feuding against one another (as with the example of the Chondawuts and the Suktawuts in the reconquest of Chittore when occupied by Emperor Jehangir, r. 1605–25) reveals his honest desire to acknowledge the validity of the Rajput system of government in its own right, including all its contradictions, without dubbing it 'primitive' or 'despotic', though he concedes its distortion by subsequent, more powerful regimes like the Moghul Empire and the Marathas.[75]

Some examples of such salutary internecine friction appear in Tod's travel experiences through Gujarat. An instance is the armed retaliation by the Rajput chief of Jerole (under Mewar) against an incursion by the Bhil leader of Ogunah and his bowmen, when the Rajputs with their scanty twenty-five horse charged a 'dense mass' of Bhil bowmen, defeated them 'with slaughter' and plundered their town of Ogunah before triumphantly departing.[76] Although Tod does not give the date of this event, it illustrates the frequent bloody clashes between the various populations in Mewar, viewed by Tod as a self-regulating system of maintaining the balance of power in the region.

So also, in the case of a border principality being conquered by a princely lineage of Rajasthan different from the initial Rajput sovereigns acknowledged by its inhabitants, Tod observes in Godwar (which included the famous site of the 1681 Battle of Nadole, as well as Beejipur and Balli, being situated to the west of Mewar, between Udaipur and Sarohi) the Rajput instinct for survival and diplomatic manoeuvring, despite forced submission: '[I]f asked to whom their "AN" or allegiance is due, it will be seen how easily Rajpoot casuistry can reconcile service to two masters.'[77]

An emblematic example of a Rajput leader recklessly 'aveng[ing his] father's feud', concerns the Chaluc-Balhara-Solankhi king of Anhulwarra Patan, contemporary with the great Pirthi Raj Chohan of Delhi in the twelfth century. Bhola Bhimdeo of Anhulwarra Patan (r.1169–72) began his reign by attacking and killing the Chohan chief Someshwar of Sambhur (west of Jaipur), father of the great Pirthi Raj Chohan, in revenge for Chohans having earlier killed the Jhala chief of Jhalore (northwest of Udaipur).[78] In an epic battle, at Anhulwarra Patan in 1172 CE, Pirthi Raj Chohan, in his turn, avenged his father's violent death, by vanquishing and killing the Solankhi king Bhola Bhimdeo. Tod quotes from the bard Chund's poetic text to draw a conclusion on its role of stimulating further heroic exploits.[79]

Tod draws parallels between the paradise promised to war heroes by Rajputs, Muslims and Scandinavians, apparently in order to direct the reader's attention to how poetic texts can motivate young warriors to sacrifice their lives for their nation and their people.

Interweaving heroic legends of bloody Rajput succession conflicts, inspiring accounts of marriages and wifely sati sacrifices of Rajput princesses and moving renderings of epic Rajput battles into his piecing together of his study and experiences of the Rajput past and present, Tod appears determined to convey to his reader a humane and honourable impression of the Rajputs in general. Jason Freitag sees in this attempt by Tod to restore the Rajputs' history to public consciousness (in India and in Europe), 'a distinctive type of Orientalist discourse' that constructs a shared cultural past and a common racial heritage for Europe and her Others, within a framework of an ennobling, classical approach that always holds ancient Greece and Rome as the ultimate ideal civilisation. Even if this can seem unduly one-sided in favour of Europe, Freitag does however allow that Tod's texts finally incorporate multiple discourses (colonialist, humanist, antiquarian, anthropological ...), open in their turn to various interpretations and appropriations.[80] My argument is that Tod was perhaps primarily concerned with assembling an attractive text for a British readership increasingly exposed to striking accounts of varied peoples from all over the globe in the early nineteenth century. It must not be forgotten that his two volumes on Rajasthan and his posthumous volume on his travels through Gujarat made up his life's work, his legacy to posterity, and he can be credited with having done his best to channel all his knowledge and talent to ensure that they were successes, both epistemologically and commercially. Throughout his writings on Rajasthan and Gujarat, Tod can be perceived as a cultural intermediary, transposing and making intelligible for his British readership the nuances of Rajput politics and social institutions.

## The aesthetic function of Tod's quotations of poetic and literary texts

In the second part of this chapter, I would like to dwell on the aesthetic function of Tod's numerous quotations of poetic and literary texts. Could he have been minimising the singularity of the history and monuments of the Rajputs in an effort to include them in a recognisable universality? Or was he trying to spruce up their beauty and inspirational force through his literary additions? Since for the most part these quotations are drawn from contemporary British Romantic poets and writers, they could be interpreted as contributing to the creation of a particular, visual and emotional impression for the reader, through the roving imagination and literary background of the author.[81] This was perhaps a way of connecting Rajput history and poetical legends with European history and literature. Whether it amounts to an Orientalist appropriation of Rajput imaginative territory, or a genuine attempt to render strange details familiar to European readers, likely to be discovering them for the first time, remains open to discussion. What cannot be disputed, however, is that there is a deliberate choice of European literary texts that have been inserted into Tod's writings. Indeed, some of the quotations come from poetic texts probably published after Tod's death, so we could even perceive these late quotations as additions from Tod's publisher, or from some well-meaning, external hand.[82]

## TOD'S USE OF ROMANTICISM

As points of comparison, I will briefly analyse the use of quotations from Romantic texts in their respective travel narratives by Tod's contemporaries James Forbes(1749–1819) and Bishop Reginald Heber (1783–1826).

To begin with James Forbes, he resided in Bombay, Anjengo and Gujarat from 1765 to 1784, with a furlough of one year in England for health reasons in 1776–7. So, his stay in India amounted to a total of eighteen years.[83] His *Oriental Memoirs*, published in 1813, some twenty-nine years after his return to England, in a luxuriously illustrated quarto edition in four volumes, included his own experiences in forty-two chapters, recompiled from a series of letters he had written along his journeys, and ninety-three engravings from his own drawings of monuments, various people encountered by him and specimens of the flora and fauna of western India, since James Forbes was especially interested in botany and zoology. Each of his forty-two chapters is preceded (and sometimes also closed) with a poetical quotation, drawn mainly from contemporary writers of his period. These literary quotations form an extraneous subtext, since they have only a distant, general link with the specific experiences he recounts in his chapters. In fact, Robert Southey, in his review of Forbes's *Oriental Memoirs* in the *Quarterly Review*,[84] criticised Forbes for giving too much space to these quotations.

The themes that recur among these quotations are: empires and ruins, the great chain of being, natural law, the value of travellers' observations, nature's wonders, the triumph of good over evil and the harmony and unity that prevail despite human diversity. All these literary references are morally edifying, establishing a link between James Forbes's having trained as an Anglican ecclesiastic,[85] and his commitment to furthering the British Empire in India. As an example, Forbes closes chapter 35 at the end of volume III, which marks the end of his own experiences in India, with a quotation from James Thomson's *The Seasons*:

> All now are vanish'd! VIRTUE sole survives,
> Immortal, never-failing friend of man,
> HIS GUIDE TO HAPPINESS ON HIGH!

About his inclusion of quotations from well-known authors, Forbes admits he has selected authors for their respectability and superior talents, hoping to 'add value and authenticity' to his own text through this parallel network of literary quotations.[86] It was thus an attempt at prestige-seeking and overall generic enhancement of the major work of his life, published at his own cost, upon which he was embarked. I will point out later in this chapter that in comparison with Forbes,

Tod's literary quotations were perhaps more closely knitted into the fabric of his text and served a more universalistic purpose of establishing humane, cultural and anti-tyrannical connections between the subjects of his writings and his readers.

Bishop Heber was widely read and had had a university and ecclesiastical education before his appointment as Bishop of Calcutta in June 1823. He arrived in Bengal in October 1823 (while Tod had left the shores of western India from Bombay in February 1823). Two important reviews of Heber's travels appeared in the *Quarterly Review* and in the *Edinburgh Review* in 1828.[87] Both reviews, however, accord no importance at all to Heber's use of literary references in his travel narrative. Both compare Heber to Malcolm and Elphinstone for the degree of understanding he achieved in his exchanges with native Indians. J.J. Blunt in the *Quarterly Review* highlights Heber's anthropological observations on the outward appearance of various Indians, life in Calcutta, the decadent courts of the Raja of Sibnibashi, the Nawab of Dacca in Bengal and the city of Benares. Francis Jeffrey in the *Edinburgh Review*, in similar fashion, underlines Heber's attention to his Indian subordinates, his encounter with a learned Brahmin with a large following in Gujarat, the death of his fellow traveller Stowe, Indian architecture, the character of the Indian people, the need for friendly intercourse between British officials and natives of rank along the lines adopted by Malcolm and Elphinstone, together with mentions of Heber's reports on the Indian press, the state of education and the administration of justice in India. Jeffrey concludes that Heber's account is 'an amusing book of travels', constituting 'the most instructive and important publication that has ever been given to the world on the actual state and condition of our Indian Empire'.

Despite the fact that Heber's numerous allusions to literary texts did not attract the attention of the reviewers in either of the two above-mentioned journals, these literary quotations play a significant role in the reader's perception of Heber's experiences in India.

In fact, Heber's constant excursions into the imaginary terrain of Scott's novels or Southey's Oriental romances as well as Thomas Moore's *Lalla Rookh*, Anne Radcliffe's gothic castles, Ker Porter's painting *The Storming of Seringapatam* and Ariosto's *Orlando Furioso* seem to play a deliberately constructed aesthetic role. Unlike James Forbes, Heber does not limit his use of literary texts to a morally edifying role, but incorporates his literary references into the very body of his travel narrative, and deploys them in order to heighten the emotional impact of the experiences he is conveying. Tod can be understood to have followed Heber's example in this aspect of his use of literary quotations.

Heber's allusions to literary texts can be grouped under three headings: (a) references to Robert Southey; (b) references to Walter Scott; (c) and references to other well-known Romantic literary characters and representations.

Among Heber's references to Robert Southey's Orientalist creations, there are several mentions of *The Curse of Kehama*, one mention of Southey's poem 'The Crocodile Island' and one allusion to Southey's *Thalaba the Destroyer*. It is mainly in connection with landscapes and storms that *The Curse of Kehama* comes to Heber's mind. For example, near the Sundarbans at the mouth of the Ganges, Heber witnesses a storm and is reminded of Southey's netherworld of 'Padalon' with its horrible shore which was the grave of all who remained near it.[88] Apart from landscapes and storms, when Heber was in Kashi (Benares) his encounter with a formidable wizard brought to his mind the 'Lorrinite' in *The Curse of Kehama*, this Southeyan character being a witch with magic weapons.[89] The allusion to Southey's poem 'The Crocodile Island' occurs at Jaffiergunge near the mouth of the Ganges on the Comarcolly River,[90] where a sandy island and a sandy beach, accompanied by the capture of a large Iguana by his boatmen, made Heber think of Southey's poem on the grieving mother whose son had been devoured by a crocodile and who sought justice from the king of crocodiles on the Crocodile Island, to no avail, of course. Southey's *Thalaba the Destroyer* is introduced during Heber's visit to the ruined capital of the kingdom of Sibnibashi in Bengal,[91] the desolation of the place having reminded Heber of Thalaba in the deserted ruins of the Babylonian palace during his epic journey to destroy the destructive sorcerers of Domdaniel, who had put to death his own family during a conflict with Harun-al-Rashid of Baghdad. Not only is Heber extraordinarily familiar with Southey's creations, but he uses them adroitly to create resonances with his own experiences in India in his readers' minds. This 'rendering familiar' is a strategy also adopted by Tod in his use of literary references.

Walter Scott's novels take pride of place among Heber's literary excursions in the course of his travel narrative. Apparently Heber considered Scott's fictional characters to be sufficiently familiar to his readers for them to constitute convenient cultural links between Britain and the exotic terrains he was visiting in India. The most memorable example is the elderly chamberlain or 'Muktar' of Raja Oomichund of Sibnibashi, whom Heber compares to Scott's character Caleb Balderstone in *The Bride of Lammermoor* (1819). Both the Muktar and Caleb Balderstone were loyal retainers of a formerly powerful family reduced to poverty, provoking in them an obsequious courtesy and numerous apologies for the absence of sufficient decorum in the hospitality accorded to the visitor concerned. Heber uses Scott's fictional character here to convey to his readers his own emotion at the impoverished circumstances of this formerly powerful Raja of Sibnibashi.[92] Then, Heber compares the Puharees or hill peoples of the Rajmahal hills in Bihar, in particular a local chief at Jowrah, and the Bheels of southeast Rajasthan (between Neemuch, Pertabgurh and Banswarra), to Scott's outlawed Scottish clansmen in *Rob Roy* and *The Lady of the Lake*, because of their being in conflict with the armed forces of the ruling powers.[93] Heber was obviously counting on his readers being acquainted with the adventures of the marginalised Rob Roy against the mainstream MacGregor clansmen, before the Jacobite rebellion of 1715, and with the battles of Roderick Dhu against the royal Scottish troops of James V, at a period before the Union of the Crowns in 1603. Heber also mentions Scott's novel *The Heart of Midlothian* in connection with a change from flat land to mountainous terrain in Bihar,[94] quoting Scott's character Jeanie Deans's comment on moving from the uphills of the Yorkshire Dales to the flatlands of Nottinghamshire and Lincolnshire: 'the haill country seemed to be trenched and levelled'. Although Heber was moving in the opposite direction towards hilly areas, as opposed to the southward journey towards flatlands of Jeanie Deans, he uses the parallel with Scott's character in order to underline the contrast in the terrain he was traversing. Similarly the busy streets of Lucknow bring to Heber's mind the busy streets of London in Scott's novel *The Fortunes of Nigel*,[95] in which the Scottish laird of Glenvarloch, Nigel Olifaunt, fights a duel in London in order to retrieve his Scottish estate from an evil intriguer. It is interesting to note that the provincial town of Lucknow appeared sufficiently busy to justify in Heber's eyes a comparison with the British capital London, as opposed to Britain's less busy provincial towns. In short, Scott's fictional characters can be seen to be put to a variety of textual purposes by Heber: the unifying factor in their appearance in Heber's narrative lies perhaps in their capacity to ring a familiar bell in the minds of his readers, and thus to establish parallels and bridges with the persons and situations he encountered in India, making the Indian situations understandable for Heber's British readership.

Apart from Southey and Scott, Heber also refers to other well-known contemporary authors in the course of his travel narrative. For example, at the Chunar fort near Benares, the ornamented windows and deep well remind Heber of 'Mrs. Radcliffe's castles'.[96] During his audience with the Mughal emperor at Delhi, Heber catches sight of a Persian inscription among the pillars and arches of the white marble pavilion in which he was received by the Delhi emperor, and quotes Thomas Moore's *Lalla Rookh*,[97] exclaiming 'If there be an Elysium on earth, It is this! It is this!'.⁹⁸ The Rajput palace at Amber (near Jaipur) appears to Heber as an enchanted castle, leading him to form a profound appreciation of its carvings, inlaid ornaments and romantic singularity, and to wonder about 'what magnificent use Ariosto or Walter Scott would have made of such a building'.⁹⁹ The reformed Pathan bandit, Ameer Khan, to whom the British awarded the townships of Rampura and Tonk in exchange for the surrender of his arms in 1818, is compared by Heber to the robber-turned-saint Woggarwolfe in Miss Baillie's novel *Ethwald*, since Ameer Khan was rich but deprived of his army, being thus reduced to telling beads and reading the Koran,¹⁰⁰ instead of pillaging the countryside as he had earlier been wont to do. The former Mewari Rajput capital of Chittore evokes memories in Heber of Ariosto's *Orlando Furioso*, where Agramant, the King of Africa, sought to marry Angelica, the daughter of the eastern King of Cathay, in connection with Akbar seeking to marry one of the queens of Udaipur's Rana,¹⁰¹ both incidents having tragic consequences. When he was in Lucknow in October 1824, the Lucknow king's troops brought to Heber's mind the British troops at the Battle of Seringapatam (during which Tipu Sultan was killed in 1799), as portrayed in Ker Porter's painting *The Storming of Seringapatam*, painted in 1801, which depicts a panoramic view of the battle scene at Seringapatam in 1799 and illustrates simultaneously the horror and marvel of war.¹⁰²

On the whole, Heber's use of literary and artistic associations to illustrate, enhance and make more decipherable for his readers his own text appears, at first sight, similar to Tod's use of literary quotations. In particular, both Heber and Tod show a similar humane touch in their appeal to the universality of human societies, and in their manner of aesthetically situating particular events in a wider cultural context, with specific emotional connotations, via their respective use of literary quotations. Tod thus seems to follow Heber's example in incorporating well-known literary figures and poetical passages as a means of transposing and rendering comprehensible to a British public the adventures, contexts and personages he came across in India. However, at no moment did Heber try to defend or champion the cause of the Indian peoples he visited. This marks a difference between his portrayal and Tod's depiction of the Rajputs. Tod seems to have advanced much further than Heber did in sympathising with and taking seriously the proud past and ideals of the Rajputs, going to the extent of hoping that Britain would grant the Rajputs 'the restoration of their former independence', paradoxical as this might seem from the pen of an official of the British Empire.¹⁰³

The quotations in Tod's texts include allusions to prose fictions, to learned sources (the Bible, Greek and Latin authors, Shakespeare,

Milton and Gibbon, for instance), as well as to eighteenth- and early nineteenth-century poetical creations. To follow Professor David Arnold's regrouping of these literary allusions as types of Romanticism, they would correspond to (a) sentimental Romanticism with nostalgia and allusions to human sensory perceptions; (b) Orientalist Romanticism, with dark representations of the tropical world and the fabled Orient; and (c) Byronic Romanticism, with references to intrepid heroes impelled by incessant activity.[104] Thematically they fall under the following three headings: (a) nostalgic meditation on ruins and bleak battlements, (b) dark, cosmic elements and death; and finally (c) a heroic, epic register. I will analyse examples from each of the above three subdivisions and try to make explicit their function in Tod's texts on Rajasthan and Gujarat. My claim through this presentation of Tod's use of literary quotations is that they can be interpreted as playing an aesthetic role of familiarisation of Rajput events and society for a British public, as well as an ideological role of extolling the heroic qualities of the Rajputs, despite their having suffered so many invasions and military attacks through their history, and in Tod's time despite their being subjected to a British colonial administration. This reveals Tod in an ambivalent position of official agent and upholder of the new British regime on the one hand, while on the other hand also showing his sympathy for and championing of the honour and right to independence of the Rajputs. It is difficult in this light to consider Tod's introduction of European cultural references as being intended to denigrate or degrade the Rajputs in his portrayal of them. The relatively large number of quotations from Byron's poetry and Walter Scott's novels can be understood to show Tod's partiality for these authors' respective defence of the Greek nationalist cause against Ottoman dominance, and admiration for the Scottish nation's identity grounded in an ancient history and distinct cultural customs. In addition, Tod's frequent literary ruminations can be seen to illustrate Tod's personal political stand, which would correspond to a liberalism that upheld a Herderian type of respect for national specificities and local heritage, without ignoring the welfare of the local population through material progress. Tod's brand of Romanticism would therefore be a sort of pragmatic Romanticism, while Heber's Romanticism would be an exclusively aesthetic Romanticism and James Forbes's Romanticism would be a moralising Romanticism.

## *Nostalgic meditations on ruins and bleak battlements*

To begin with ruins and bleak battlements, these were a theme often used by Romantic poets and Gothic novelists to reflect on the residences of formerly powerful chiefs or the vestiges of ancient temples. The literary texts quoted in Tod's narratives on this theme of ruins and bleak battlements are from various evocations by (pre-)Romantic poets of violent invasions or fallen edifices and statues, from Byron's poems 'The Dream' (1816) and *Childe Harold's Pilgrimage* (1812–18), as also from the prose fictions of Samuel Johnson (1709–84), Ann Radcliffe (1764–1823) and Walter Scott (1771–1832).

Thus while referring to ruins at Pushkar near Ajmer, where Aurangzeb and before him 'the illiterate and mercenary Afghan', descendant of Ishmael, had destroyed most of the numismatic treasures in the region, executing the Islamic injunction to destroy all graven images,[105] Tod resorts to a line from an ode by the Cambrian minstrel Thomas Gray (1716–71), entitled *The Bard*, which is an imprecation by a solitary, surviving Welsh bard against Edward I, who invaded Wales in 1283 and was reputed to have ordered the suppression of all the Welsh bards: 'Ruin seize thee, ruthless king'. The ruins of the ancient Jain temple at Ajmer, adjacent to Hindu shrines and a 'Saracenic arch', inspire Tod to quote a sonnet published in 1805, by Edward Coxe, a little-known poet who imitated Italian sonnets in his own poetic creations:[106]

> I saw OBLIVION pass with giant stride;
> And while his visage wore Pride's scornful smile,
> Haply Thou know'st, then tell me WHOSE, I cried,
> Whose these vast domes that ev'n in ruin shine?
> I reck not whose, he said: THEY NOW ARE MINE.

The ruins at the ancient Chauhan capital at Chittore,[107] as also the ruins at the ancient Rajput capital of Chandravati, south of Mount Abu,[108] lead Tod to quote on 'columns strewn' and 'statues fallen' from 'The Ages', by the American poet William Cullen Bryant (1794–1878), who published two volumes of poems in 1821 and 1832.

To continue with Tod's use of lines from Byron's poems, under the theme of ruins and bleak battlements, they are always associated with ancient Rajput capital cities. Mundore, the ancient capital of the Puriharas, who later established themselves at Jodhpur in Marwar, contains a rude altar to Nahur Rao, also known as Tiger Rao Purihara, who met Prithviraj Raj Chauhan, Emperor of Delhi, in equal combat in a pass of the Aravalli mountains in the 1170s. Tod honours this monument to the memory of Nahur Rao Purihara with a quotation on ruined walls from Byron's 'The Dream' (1816), stanza IV.[109]

Also at Mundore, Tod evokes the ancient ruined Tuscan and Etruscan cities of Cortona, Volterra and Todi, and quotes Byron's *Childe Harold's Pilgrimage*, canto IV, stanza 129, to depict the ruined battlement which gains its public dignity only with the passage of many years.[110] The Chauhan king Ajipal's fortress at Ajmer, with its antique towers,[111] as also the ruined castle of the Pramaras on Mount Abu in his later *Travels in Western India*,[112] call forth from Tod a quotation from *Childe Harold's Pilgrimage*, canto III, stanza 47, on deserted bleak battlements which 'shall bear no future blow'.

Similarly, with the empty castle of the Haras under the chief of Bumaoda, *Childe Harold's Pilgrimage*, canto III, stanza 47, enables Tod to conjure up the atmosphere of the deserted castle precincts:[113]

> All tenantless, save to the crannying wind
> Or holding dark communion with the cloud.

The Chittor ruins are also conveyed through a quotation from *Childe Harold's Pilgrimage*, canto III, stanza 67 that links 'deeds which should not pass away' though forgotten, with 'a just decay'.[114]

Tod was tempted to carry away the statue of Adi Pala from the Akhileshwar temple on Mount Abu. He ironically compares his impulse to Lord Byron's horror at the plunder of the Parthenon by Lord Elgin, in *Childe Harold's Pilgrimage*, canto II, stanza 13.[115]

Dilwarra, among the twelve hamlets of Mount Abu, constituted a beautiful scene of ruins among greenery, also mentioned in *Childe Harold's Pilgrimage* (canto III, stanza 46), where 'ruin greenly dwells'.[116]

So Byron helps Tod to elevate his reader to the poetic heights of nostalgia on ruins and on the fragmented vestiges of past glories, while also expressing support for the cause of freedom from plunder and tyrannical oppression.

Walter Scott's historical novels and narrative poems were very popular in Tod's period. He mentions *Rob Roy*, *Ivanhoe* and Roderick Dhu, the Red Reaver of Scott's widely read poem *The Lady of the Lake*. Doongur Singh, the rebel chief of Ruttungurh and Beygoo, is compared to Scott's rebel Highland chief Roderick Dhu, as being ready to die defending his clan's honour.[117]

This theme of ruins and bleak battlements is thus heightened by Tod's device of using quotations from poems and literary works. The appeal to the imaginary realm introduces nostalgic overtones, while bringing the distant Rajput lands onto familiar, literary ground for British and European readers.

## *Dark, cosmic elements and death*

The second theme I will illustrate is dark cosmic elements and death, since they were an important part of the world view of the Romantic writers of Tod's time. Tod quotes Thomas Campbell's *The Pleasures of*

*Hope* (1799), part I, line 7, to advocate toleration, distance and respect for Rajput virtues to his British counterparts, rather than any harsh imposition of their British 'rod' on their new colonised subjects: "'Tis distance lends enchantment to the view'.[118]

This use of a visual trope from landscape painting to underline the need for gentle British intervention in Rajasthan can be seen as an example of Tod's readiness to use all the means available to him to make a point. It is perhaps interesting also to note that Thomas Campbell (1777–1844) was a native of Glasgow, among the founders of the non-Anglican, pro-Utilitarian University College London in the 1820s, and is otherwise remembered for his war songs and ballads.

In the same way, in connection with dark cosmic elements and the danger of death, Tod refers to the prose fictions of Samuel Johnson, Ann Radcliffe and Walter Scott, all these being well-known texts of his time, to endow his own texts with familiar British cultural references. As David Arnold has argued, the imaginary Africa of Samuel Johnson's *Rasselas* (1759), as also of James Bruce's and Mungo Park's travel accounts, was a common motif in early nineteenth-century travel writings,[119] which was naturally quoted in contemporary writings on India. So Tod while in India refers several times to the 'happy valley' of the native Abyssinia of Johnson's Prince Rasselas, with which the prince is, however bored and from which he wishes to escape,[120] the allusions to *Rasselas* help convey the ambivalence of the feelings of British officers like Tod in India – a feeling of material comfort and privilege, but also an awareness of climatic discomfort and health hazards.

Tod's single mention of Ann Radcliffe's 'scenes seasoned with romance' occurs when Tod is on the banks of the Bunas River, and harks back to his younger days in Gohad among playful wild wolves, with his colleague Lieutenant-Colonel T.D. Smith. While Tod's cook roasts a leg of mutton before blazing logs, Tod is aware that his Romantic reminiscences are perhaps not in tune with the emotional reactions of his Indian followers.[121] So human feelings of terror and isolation, associated with Gothic tales of love and danger, remain within Tod's inner self, since he cannot share them with his Indian travel companions. This is one exceptional instance where the allusion to a British literary text is a cause for Tod's momentary withdrawal from communion with his Indian counterparts, though in his travel narrative it certainly serves the purpose of establishing a bridge between the rural Rajput scene and Ann Radcliffe's Gothic settings for Tod's British readers.

On the heights above the river at Bhynsrorgarh, Tod quotes *Childe Harold's Pilgrimage*, canto III, stanza 94.[122] Here, Byron's mention of the River Rhône winding through cliffs that appear like passionate lovers who now stand starkly apart as a result of their destructive ('mining') feelings towards each other, endows Tod's evocation of the Kotah Plateau at Bhynsrorgarh with a cosmic atmosphere.

When Tod passes through Kaira, between Ahmedabad and Baroda, in Gujarat, he witnesses 'the pitiless torrent' of the 'wrath' of the monsoon season, and his text includes lines from one of the earliest Bengali poets to use the English language for his poetry, Kasiprasad Ghose, whose poems were first published in 1839 after Tod's death (see note 82).[123] Adding poetic lines at a point when all Tod could think about was that his paraphernalia were soaked, and that his companions were 'shivering, silent and sulky', gives a wider perspective to Tod's account.

## Heroic, epic tone

Tod's texts also deliberately adopt a heroic, epic tone in the course of their unfolding, through the use of learned references. The effect created can be understood as consciously sought-after sophistication and refinement.

In the 'Annals of Mewar',[124] and in his 'Personal Narrative' in the first volume of his work on Rajasthan,[125] Tod evokes the dramatic tragedy of Princess Krishna Kumari, daughter of Rana Bheem Singh of Mewar (r.1772–1828) and victim of the political rivalries between Marwar (the Rathore Raja Maun Singh of Jodhpur, r.1803–43) and Jaipur (the Cuchwaha Raja Jagat Singh of Jaipur, r.1803–18). In a context of conflicts between the British and the Marathas, which included the defeat of General Monson at Garot and Mukundwara Pass by Holkar in August 1804, the Rajas of Jodhpur and Jaipur tried to use a marriage link with the very beautiful daughter of Rana Bheem Singh of Mewar, compared by Tod to Helen of Troy,[126] in order to outdo each other, while also gaining a hold over Mewar, the foremost political kingdom in Rajasthan. While both the Maratha chiefs, Jeswunt Rao Holkar and Daulat Rao Sindhia, attempted to arbitrate in this Rajput dispute with their respective military forces, Tod was present (as assistant to Graeme Mercer, the British envoy to Sindhia's court between 1805 and 1810) 'at the interview, in June 1806, between the Rana of Mewar, Bheem Singh, and Dowlut Rao Sindia, at the shrine of Eklinga, about six miles from Oodeypore, during the memorable transactions which ended in the inhuman sacrifice of the Rana's daughter, Kishna Komari, "the Flower of Rajasthan", the whole of which dreadful drama was acted before his eyes'.[127] In the mean time, in April 1806 Jagat Singh of Jaipur married his younger Cuchwaha sister to Raja Man Singh of Jodhpur, and the latter married his Rathore daughter, Sira KunwariBai, to the Cuchwaha Jagat Singh of Jaipur. The Jodhpur and Jaipur rulers thus became each other's brother-in-law and son-in-law respectively!

## TOD'S USE OF ROMANTICISM

After Sindhia withdrew from Rajasthan to Malwa in May 1810, having exacted huge money tributes from both Jagat Singh of Jaipur and Man Singh of Jodhpur, the Pathan mercenary Amir Khan used the Jodhpur–Jaipur marriage feud to his own advantage by imposing his Pathan subsidiary force in Udaipur and insisting that Krishna Kumari's life be terminated in order to avoid the plunder of Mewar.[128] Thus it was that in desperation Rana Bheem Singh ordered that his very dear daughter Krishna Kumari should be poisoned on 21 July 1810, and that she willingly accepted the sacrifice of her life for the preservation of her father's kingdom, in a supreme act of daughterly devotion. Tod cannot find words hard enough to condemn Amir Khan's role in this episode, comparing him to Judas who 'kissed whom he betrayed'[129] and qualifying him as 'the rapacious and blood-thirsty Pathan'[130] and 'the Caligula of the Desert'.[131] After his return to England, Tod was reminded of Krishna Kumari's sacrifice on two occasions, when he attended two separate performances in mid-1823: one in York Cathedral with 'the sublime recitations of Handel in "Jephtha's Vow"' and the representation shortly after 'of Racine's tragedy of "Iphigénie", with Talma as Achille, Duchesnois as Clytemnestre, and a very interesting personation of the victim daughter of Agamemnon'.[132] Handel's oratorio of 1751 depicting the moving situation of the biblical character Jephtha, an Israelite judge who vanquished the Ammonites, as described in Judges 11, but then had to put his own daughter to death in fulfilment of the vow he had made that he would sacrifice the first person he met after the battle if he was victorious, as also Racine's 1674 reinterpretation of Euripides' classical tragedy set in ancient Greece, of a daughter sacrificed by her own father in order to secure political advantage, enable Tod to situate the circumstances of the death of the Princess of Mewar in a universal context, with probable resonances in the minds of all his British readers. It appears evident here that Tod is not in any way disadvantaging or minimising the enormity of Krishna Kumari's tragic plight by making these literary comparisons. On the contrary he seems to be using these textual allusions in order to convey to his readers his own emotion as a witness of such a heart-rending scene in the depths of far-flung Rajasthan.

Tod uses biblical references on three occasions. He compares the reversal of the destiny of Chittor to that of Jerusalem by quoting a passage from Lamentations 1:11.[133] This sets in parallel the trajectories of Jerusalem and of Chittor, both subject to dreary forebodings, by prophetic observers concerned with the respective destinies of these two cities.

Again, Tod quotes the biblical book of Ecclesiastes to underline his awareness of the vanity of all his undertakings in India, at the time of his departure for Britain,[134] when several of his dear friends were either dead or ill: 'I looked upon all the works that my hands had wrought and on the labour I had laboured to do; and behold all was vanity and vexation of spirit' (Ecclesiastes 2:11). The insertion of this biblical verse adds a zest of venerable trustworthiness to Tod's text, while also showing his own actions in India in a tragic light of futility.

In his travels through Gujarat, Tod remarks ironically on the acceptance of the British yoke of 'subsidiary alliance' by Indian powers who had only an underaged, minor prince to take over the reins of power, as in the case of the Jharejas of Cutch[135] (having mentioned a similar incident in his *Annals* concerning the accession to the Mewar throne of the infant Rana Udai Singh at the age of twelve, r.1541–71). His quotation from Ecclesiastes 10:16, 'Woe to thee o Land, when thy king is a child', confirms Tod's warning that these alliances most often led to the destruction of every semi-barbarous state that accepted such a foreign yoke.

In Tod's texts on Rajasthan and Gujarat, I have traced four references to Shakespeare. One such reference occurs as a quotation by Zalim Sing of Kotah, nicknamed by Tod the Nestor of Rajputana (Nestor was the wise adviser in Homer's *Odyssey*), in connection with the superficial effect of trappings. With a slight distortion of Shakespeare's text, Zalim Sing is reported to have said to Tod: 'The World is e'er deceived by ornament'.[136] In fact, this expression occurs in *The Merchant of Venice*, act III, scene ii, when Bassanio is subjected to the test of opening the caskets at Portia's home in Belmont. Zalim Sing and Tod's text gain an aura of prestige by this quotation from Shakespeare on such a banal subject as the false attraction of external trappings.

Tod again resorts to Shakespeare during his sea voyage from Mandavi to Bombay in January 1823, this time with reference to the beneficial effect of sleep, much regretted when it is not accessible, quoting from Shakespeare's *Macbeth*, act II, scene iii:[137] 'Sleep that knits up the ravell'd sleeve of care, / The death [birth] of each day's life ...' This comes from a tormented Macbeth, abandoned by sleep, because of his own mental unease!

Again Tod, on leaving India, reflects on his fall from glory as he withdraws to England,[138] since he will no longer be at the fighting front of events, and quotes from Shakespeare's *Othello*, act III, scene iii, to underline his sense of bereftness: 'Othello's occupation's gone'. This quotation from *Othello* perhaps reveals the degree of Tod's own investment in his role as British political agent in the western Rajput states, and his feeling of destitution on relinquishing this position.

At Napoleon's tomb on the island of Saint Helena, Tod uses an adaptation of Shakespeare's *Henry IV, part I* by Dryden, Shadwell and

Thomas Betterton (1635–1710) to stress the gulf between the symbolic space occupied by a living person, and his relative physical smallness after his death:[139]

> Ill-weav'd ambition how much art thou shrunk?
> ...
> But now two paces of the vilest earth
> Is room enough ...

These lines are pronounced by Prince Hal (the future Henry V) after he has personally killed Percy Hotspur, and consigned him to a tomb. Tod quotes them in connection with Napoleon, whom he greatly admired, thereby underlining the tragic nature of Napoleon's death.

Tod also resorts to Milton, Pope and William Jones in his attempts to prove his literary worthiness and respectability. It is remarkable that Tod does not hesitate to quote Milton's description of the battle between Satan's evil angels and God's son, the Messiah, after the discovery of fire, in Milton's *Paradise Lost* (1674), when alluding to the abundance of volcanoes and hot springs in Gujarat.[140] The fortuitous nature of the discovery of the beneficial uses of fire is thus highlighted.

Alexander Pope's (1688–1744) doggerel presentation of Hercules'/Samson's story, as it appears in the *Prologue to the Wife of Bath's Tale*, line 382, in *The Canterbury Tales of Chaucer* (1741), published by George Ogle (1704–46), is used by Tod in order to compare Dejanira's killing of Samson with the unacceptable poisoning of the Rathore prince Pirthi Sing by Aurungzeb in the 1670s, through the use of an envenomed robe.[141]

Again, Pope's description of the episode of Sarpedon in the Trojan War, during the battle at the Grecian Wall where Sarpedon opened a breach in the fortified walls of Athens for Hector and the Trojans to enter the city, as translated from Homer's *Iliad* by Pope, is quoted by Tod to stress the tragic value of the sacrifice of one's life in a context of conflict, as in the particular case of Dilloh the Darawut during the battle by the Rahtores, all united against Aurungzeb's attacks.[142]

The Champa flower on Mount Abu inspires Tod to quote William Jones's poem 'Hymn to Camdeo'[143] in order to highlight the elegant appearance of this highly perfumed tropical flower, that had inspired poets and writers down the ages.[144]

Tod also referred to other poetical creations by William Jones in connection with the Rajput festival in honour of Gangaur, a river goddess,[145] and with Jones's observation of a possible link between the Hindu god Ganesha with the Roman god Janus,[146] where Tod extends Jones's observation of the nominal similarity between 'Ganes' and

'Janus' to a comparison of the fable of the birth and the celestial functions of this Hindu deity with those of the Roman deity.

These various erudite references, spanning the Bible, Latin authors, Shakespeare, Milton, Pope and William Jones, in heroic, epic contexts, can be perceived as adding cultural breadth and prestige to Tod's observations. As elsewhere, these non-Indian literary landmarks appear to be used by Tod to underline similarities and parallels between the histories and cultures of Europe and Rajasthan, blending them together and drawing them nearer to one another.

## *Conclusion*

To conclude on Tod's use of quotations from Romantic literary texts, it appears that they serve a number of aesthetic and ideological purposes. On the one hand, they widen the cultural reach of Tod's accounts, evoking literary favourites familiar to British readers, thus bringing what might have appeared as outlandish and unfamiliar experiences on to well-known imaginative terrain. On the other hand, they also highlight certain aesthetic aspects which Tod apparently intended to drive home. For example, certain quotations underline nostalgia about ruins and relics from the past. The attention to cosmic elements and death brings a universal tone to the whole. Finally, the literary quotations that accompany Tod's anecdotes about mythological figures and epic heroes can be perceived as attempts at cultural *métissage*, constructing parallels and transpositions in order to bridge differences. While conveying anecdotes of Rajput history and of his own years among the Rajputs, Tod seems to use the voices of European literary authors in order to introduce a new intercultural vision of the Rajput world, comprehensible to British readers, while also remaining authentic and true to the Rajput sources, and voicing his admiration for the age-old Rajput customs which had outlived 800 years of Muslim domination in India. He also blends in his liberal, political stand in support of a flexible British colonial regime that would ultimately recognise the right to the restoration of the independence of its colonised subjects, since in Tod's opinion the use of force and repression would lead only to a rejection of the foreign authority by the natives of India. His position can thus be qualified as pragmatic Romanticism.

On the whole, much can be speculated on the whys and the wherefores of Tod's particular selection of certain poetical and literary texts as extensions of his main narrative of the history of the Rajputs and of his own experiences in Rajasthan and Gujarat. For example, was he covering up his own difficulties in understanding the Rajput foundations of his texts through a show of Western literary erudition, or was this mixing of cultures merely superficial, amounting to a distortion of the real meaning of Rajput culture, or again was it a commercial stunt in order to ensure better sales of his works? On comparing Tod's literary quotations with those deployed by James Forbes and by Bishop Heber, it appears not only that Tod had genuinely moved deeper than either Forbes or Heber into understanding on its own terms that part of Indian culture and society he had personally encountered, but that he had made it his chosen task and 'a sacred obligation ... to awaken a sympathy for the objects of my work, the interesting people of Rajpootana'.[147] He comes over then as a British coloniser with at least one foot firmly in the camp of his colonial subjects.

## Notes

1 See Isaiah Berlin, *The Roots of Romanticism*, ed. Henry Hardy, Princeton: Princeton University Press, 1999, pp. 37–40, 84–90.
2 Nigel Leask, *Curiosity and the Aesthetics of Travel-Writing, 1770–1840*, Oxford: Oxford University Press, 2002, pp. 45–9, 170–8. Also Nigel Leask, *British Romantic Writers and the East*, Cambridge: Cambridge University Press, 1993 (1992).
3 Berlin, *Roots of Romanticism*, pp. 132–4.
4 Reginald Heber, *Narrative of a Journey through the Upper Provinces of India, from Calcutta to Bombay, 1824–5, with notes upon Ceylon*, London: John Murray, 1828, 3 vols, repr. New Delhi: Asian Educational Services, 1995, 3 vols.
5 James Forbes, *Oriental Memoirs, selected and abridged from a series of familiar letters written during seventeen years' residence in India: including observations on parts of Africa, and South America, and a narrative of occurrences in four India voyages*, London: White, Cochrane & Co., 1813, 4 vols, quarto.
6 Francis Buchanan, *A Journey from Madras through the countries of Mysore, Canara and Malabar*, London: T. Cadell & W. Davies, 1807, 3 vols, quarto.
7 William Tennant, *Indian Recreations consisting chiefly of strictures on the domestic and rural economy of the Mahomedans and Hindoos*, 2nd edn, London: Longman, Hurst, Rees & Orme, 1804–8, 3 vols, octavo.
8 Jason Freitag, 'Travel, history, politics and heritage: James Tod's 'Personal Narrative'", in: Carol E. Henderson and Maxine Weisgrau (eds), *Raj Rhapsodies: Tourism, Heritage and the Seduction of History*, Aldershot: Ashgate, 2007, pp. 47–60.
9 Lloyd Rudolph and Suzanne Hoeber Rudolph, 'Writing and reading Tod's Rajasthan: interpreting the text and its historiography', in: Jos Gommans and Om Prakash (eds), *Circumambulations in South Asian History:Essays in Honour of Dirk H.A. Kolff*, Leiden: Brill Publishers, 2003, pp. 251–82.
10 See Heber, *Narrative of a Journey*, vol. I, pp. 84, 114, 123, 126, 408; vol. II, pp. 62, 303, 417, 473, 479, 514; vol;. III, pp. 24, 109, 216.
11 James Tod, *Annals and Antiquities of Rajasthan*, vol. I, London: Routledge & Kegan Paul Ltd, 1829; repr. Delhi: Rupa & Co., 1997, p. 231; James Tod, *Annals and Antiquities of Rajasthan*, vol. II, London: Routledge & Kegan Paul Ltd, 1832; repr. Delhi: Rupa & Co., 1997, p. 609.
12 Tod, *Annals*, vol. I, p. 233.
13 Tod, *Annals*, vol. I, p. 535.
14 Tod, *Annals*, vol. II, pp. 526–7.
15 Tod, *Annals*, vol. I, p. 345.
16 Tod, *Annals*, vol. II, pp. 375–6, 378–80, 601.
17 Tod, *Annals*, vol. I, p. 346.

18 Tod, *Annals*, vol. I, p. 562.
19 Tod, *Annals*, vol. II, p. 472, and Norbert Peabody, *Hindu Kingship and Polity in Precolonial India*, Cambridge: Cambridge University Press, 2003, p. 118.
20 Tod, *Annals*, vol. I, p. 468.
21 Tod, *Annals*, vol. II, p. 470
22 Tod, *Travels*, p. 169, and tables pp. 150, 167.
23 Tod, *Travels*, p. 60–1.
24 Tod, *Annals*, vol. I, p. 496.
25 Tod, *Annals*, vol. II, pp. 37, 391.
26 Tod, *Annals*, vol. I, p. 495.
27 Tod, *Annals*, vol. I, p. 497.
28 Tod, *Annals*, vol. I, p. 502; vol. II, p. 380.
29 Tod, *Annals*, vol. I, p. 233.
30 Tod, *Annals*, vol. I, p. 535.
31 Tod, *Annals*, vol. I, p. 562
32 Tod, *Annals*, vol. I, p. 500.
33 Tod, *Annals*, vol. I, pp. 266–7, n.4; vol. II, pp. 384–5.
34 Tod, *Annals*, vol. I, pp. 141, 143.
35 Tod, *Annals*, vol. II, pp. 145, 287.
36 Tod, *Annals*, vol. II, p. 287.
37 Tod, *Annals*, vol. II, p. 286.
38 Tod, *Annals*, vol. II, p. 385.
39 Tod, *Annals*, vol. I, p. 267, n.4.
40 Tod mentions the heroic role played by one of the queens of Rana Udai Singh of Udaipur during Akbar's attack on Chittore in 1568: '[Rana Udai Singh's (r.1541–71) concubine queen] headed the sallies into the heart of the Mogul camp, and on one occasion to the emperor's headquarters. The imbecile Rana proclaimed that he owed his deliverance to her; when the chiefs indignant at this imputation on their courage, conspired and put her to death. Internal discord invited Akber to re-invest Cheetore [in May 1568].' *Annals*, vol. I, p. 260.
41 Tod, *Annals*, vol. II, p. 280, n.3.
42 Tod, *Annals*, vol. II, p. 601.
43 James Tod, *Travels in Western India*, London: William Allen & Co., 1839 (posth.) pp. 258–9; repr. Delhi: Munshiram Manoharlal Publishers, 1997.
44 Tod, *Travels*, p. 297.
45 Tod, *Travels*, p. 299.
46 Tod, *Travels*, p. 273.
47 Tod, *Annals*, vol. II, p. 145.
48 Tod, *Annals*, vol. II, p. 384.
49 Tod, *Annals*, vol. I, p. 260.
50 Tod, *Annals*, vol. I, p. xviii; also mentioned at *Annals*, vol. I, p. 471; and at *Annals*, Vol. II, p.582.
51 Tod, *Annals*, vol. II, p. 45, n.9; also *Annals*, vol. I, p. 471.
52 Tod, *Annals*, vol. II, pp. 581–2.
53 Tod, *Annals*, vol. I, pp. 199–200.
54 Tod, *Annals*, vol. II, pp. 596–7.
55 See Cynthia Talbot, 'Recovering the heroic history of Rajasthan – Tod and the Prithviraj Raso', in: Giles Tillotson (ed.), *James Tod's Rajasthan: The Historian and His Collection*, Mumbai: Marg Publications, 2007, pp. 97–117; simultaneously published as *Mārg*, 59.1 (2007).
56 Tod, *Annals*, vol. I, pp. 214–16.
57 Tod, *Annals*, vol. II, p. 609. Rudyard Kipling in his 'Letters of Marque', in: *From Sea to Sea*, Leipzig: Bernhard Tauchnitz, 1900, 2 vols, vol. I, p. 101, refers to Tod in connection with his own visit to Chittore's Gau-Mukh, where 'a passage led to the subterranean chambers in which the fair Pudmini and her handmaids had slain themselves'.
58 Tod, *Annals*, vol. I, pp. 243–6.

59 Tod, *Annals*, vol. I, pp. 261–3.
60 Tod, *Annals*, vol. I, pp. 269–78.
61 Tod, *Annals*, vol. I, p. 495; vol. II, p. 37.
62 Tod, *Annals*, vol. I, p. 309.
63 Tod, *Annals*, vol. II, p. 38.
64 Tod, *Annals*, vol. II, pp. 391–2.
65 Tod, *Annals*, vol. I, pp. 337–8.
66 Tod, *Annals*, vol. I, p. 338.
67 Tod, *Annals*, vol. I, pp. 351–3; also vol. I, pp. 596–8.
68 Tod, *Annals*, vol. I, p. 353, mention of the battle at Patun (1790, also mentioned at *Annals*, vol. I, p. 596) and of the battle at Merta (1791, also mentioned at *Annals*, vol. I, p. 581)
69 Tod, *Annals*, vol. I, p. 595.
70 Tod, *Annals*, vol. I, p. 596.
71 Tod, *Annals*, vol. I, pp. 599–600, n.1.
72 Tod, *Annals*, vol. I, pp. 598–9.
73 Tod, *Annals*, vol. I, p. 453, n.1.
74 Tod, *Annals*, vol. I, p. 206.
75 Tod, *Annals*, vol. I, pp. 123, 126.
76 Tod, *Travels*, p. 33.
77 Tod, *Travels*, p. 53.
78 Tod, *Travels*, p. 194.
79 Tod, *Travels*, p. 203.
80 Jason Freitag, 'Tod's *Annals* as history and archive', in: Giles Tillotson (ed.), *James Tod's Rajasthan: The Historian and His Collection*, Mumbai: Mumbai: Radhika Sabavala for Marg Publications on behalf of the National Centre for the Performing Arts, 2007, pp. 86–97; simultaneously published as *Mārg*, 59.1 (2007).
81 David Arnold, *The Tropics and the Travelling Gaze: India, Landscape and Science, 1800–1856*, Seattle and London: University of Washington Press, 2006, p. 91.
82 For example, in *Travels*, p. 239, Tod's description of the monsoon rain at Kaira, between Ahmedabad and Baroda, is accompanied by a quotation from a poem in English entitled 'Storm and Rain' by the Bengali poet Kasiprasad Ghose (1809–73). The first edition of Kasiprasad Ghose's poems in English appeared in Calcutta in 1839, four years after Tod had died, and in the very year of the posthumous publication of Tod's *Travels in Western India*, under the title *The Shair and other Poems*, Durrumtoollah (Calcutta): Scott, 1839. See Theodore Douglas Dunn (ed.), *The Bengali Book of English Verse*, Bombay: Longmans, Green and Co., 1918, pp. 3–4.
83 Forbes, *Oriental Memoirs*,. vol. I, p. v.
84 Robert Southey's review of James Forbes's *Oriental Memoirs* in *Quarterly Review*, 12.23 (October 1814), article IX, 180–227. See pp. 182, 227.
85 *Quarterly Review*, 12.23 (October 1814), p. 198: 'Mr. Forbes, who acted in the double capacity of chaplain to the British troops and secretary to the Commander-in-Chief [Colonel Keating, during the 1775 war in Gujarat between Raghunat Rao helped by the British against Holkar and Sindhia] was now in the midst of a Mahratta army.'
86 Forbes, *Oriental Memoirs*, vol. I, p. xii.
87 Heber, *Narrative of a Journey*. Reviews of Heber's travel narrative: (a) by J.J. Blunt and John Gibson Lockhart in *Quarterly Review*, 37 (January 1828), 100–19 (with general observations on India, pp. 119–47); (b) by Francis Jeffrey in *Edinburgh Review*, 48 (December 1828), 312–35.
88 Heber, *Narrative of a Journey*, vol. I, p. 7.
89 Heber, *Narrative of a Journey*, vol. II, p. 253.
90 Heber, *Narrative of a Journey*, vol. I, pp. 172–3.
91 Heber, *Narrative of a Journey*, vol. I, p. 123.
92 Heber, *Narrative of a Journey*, vol. I, p. 126.
93 Heber, *Narrative of a Journey*, vol. I, p. 272; also vol. II, p. 514.
94 Heber, *Narrative of a Journey*, vol. I, p. 249.
95 Heber, *Narrative of a Journey*, vol. II, pp. 52–3.

96 Heber, *Narrative of a Journey*, vol. I, p. 408.
97 Thomas Moore, *Lalla Rookh: an Oriental Romance*, London: Longman, Brown, Green, Longmans & Roberts, 1856 (1817), pp. 373, 374, 376. Moore adds in a note on p. 373 that there is an inscription in the cornice above Shah Alam's Diwan-i-Khas in Delhi's Red Fort in letters of gold in Persian, the equivalent of: 'If there be a paradise on earth, it is this, it is this'. I am grateful to Marc Rolland for this reference.
98 Heber, *Narrative of a Journey*, vol. II, p. 303.
99 Heber, *Narrative of a Journey*, vol. II, p. 418.
100 Heber, *Narrative of a Journey*, vol. II, p. 473.
101 Heber, *Narrative of a Journey*, vol. II, p. 479.
102 Heber, *Narrative of a Journey*, vol. II, p. 62.
103 Tod, *Annals*, vol. I, p. xi, 'Dedication to His Most Gracious Majesty George the Fourth'. A similar idea is repeated in Tod's dedication of his second volume to 'His Most Gracious Majesty William the Fourth': 'My prayer is ... that neither the love of conquest, nor false views of policy, may tempt us to subvert the independence of these States, some of which have braved the storms of more than ten centuries.' *Annals*, vol. II, p. v.
104 Arnold, *The Tropics and the Travelling Gaze*, pp. 94–8.
105 Tod, *Annals*, vol. I, pp. 613–14.
106 Tod, *Annals*, vol. I, p. 611.
107 Tod, *Annals*, vol. I, p. 610.
108 Tod, *Travels*, p. 132.
109 Tod, *Annals*, vol. I, p.573.
110 Tod, *Annals*, vol. I, p. 571.
111 Tod, *Annals*, vol. I, p. 612.
112 Tod, *Travels*, p. 98.
113 Tod, *Annals*, vol. II, p. 601.
114 Tod, *Annals*, vol. I, p. 604.
115 Tod, *Travels*, p. 91.
116 Tod, *Travels*, p. 115.
117 Tod, *Annals*, vol. I, p. 519; vol. II, pp. 514, 548.
118 Tod, *Annals*, vol. I, p. 102.
119 Arnold, *The Tropics and the Travelling Gaze*, p. 89.
120 Tod, *Annals*, vol. I, p. 505, n.1; vol. I; p. 519; vol. I, p. 521; vol. II, p. 612; and Tod, *Travels*, p. 500
121 Tod, *Annals*, vol. I, pp. 526–7.
122 Tod, *Annals*, vol. II, p. 523.
123 Tod, *Travels*, p. 239.
124 Tod, *Annals*, vol. I, pp. 366, 369.
125 Tod, *Annals*, vol. I, p. 564.
126 Tod, *Annals*, vol. I, pp. 366, 564.
127 Tod, *Travels*, p. xxiv.
128 R.K. Saxena, *Maratha Relations with the Major States of Rajputana, 1761–1818*, New Delhi: Chand & Co., 1973, pp. 200, 225.
129 Tod, *Annals*, vol. I, p. 367.
130 Tod, *Annals*, vol. I, p. 368.
131 Tod, *Annals*, vol. I, p. 564.
132 Tod, *Annals*, vol. I, p. 369, n.1.
133 Tod, *Annals*, vol. II, p. 604.
134 Tod, *Annals*, vol. II, p. 611.
135 Tod, *Travels*, p. 492; also Tod, *Annals*, vol. I, p. 255
136 Tod, *Annals*, vol. II, p. 473.
137 Tod, *Travels*, p. 495.
138 Tod, *Travels*, p. 499.
139 Tod, *Travels*, p. 501.
140 Tod, *Travels*, p. 37.
141 Tod, *Annals*, vol. II, p. 40, n.1.

142 Tod, *Annals*, vol. II, p. 45.
143 Lord Teignmouth (ed.), *The Works of Sir William Jones,* London: John Stockdale and John Walker, 1807, 13 vols, vol. XIII, pp. 235–9, esp. p. 238.
144 Tod, *Travels*, p. 79.
145 Tod, *Annals*, vol. I, p. 458. See also Lord Teignmouth (ed.), *Works of Sir William Jones*, vol. XIII, pp. 328–33, esp. p. 328, William Jones's 'Hymn to Ganga'.
146 Tod, *Annals*, vol. I, p. 469.
147 Tod, *Annals*, vol. II, p. vii.

CHAPTER FIVE

# Tod's Romantic approach as opposed to James Mill's Utilitarian approach to British government in India

Despite their common Scottish origin, James Mill (1773–1836) and James Tod (1782–1835) were poles apart in their perception and approach of things Indian. James Mill grew up in Montrose and Aberdeen and only moved to London in 1802 at the age of twenty-nine, after seven years of university education, where he came into contact with leaders of the Scottish Enlightenment like John Millar and Dugald Stewart. James Tod was born in Islington near London, of partly Scottish parents, underwent a brief education at the Woolwich military academy in England, and left for India at the young age of seventeen in 1799, where he remained for twenty-three years until February 1823. While James Mill never ever set foot in India, he was Examiner of Correspondence at the London headquarters of the East India Company for eighteen years, from 1818 to his death in 1836. He was also a close associate of Jeremy Bentham (1748–1832), for over twenty years from 1808 until about 1830, and participated actively in spreading Bentham's political philosophy of Utilitarianism, with the foundation of University College London, and the Society for the Diffusion of Useful Knowledge in order to educate the adult working classes. The foundation in 1824 of the *Westminster Review* was another platform for propagating the Utilitarian creed. He took twelve years (1806–17) to compile his major work, *The History of British India*,[1] which was published in London in 1817, in three quarto volumes, based on published reports of Parliamentary Proceedings, the East India Company records and other published works on British contacts with India between 1600 and 1805. In his preface, Mill did not conceal that he had not visited India and did not have any knowledge of any Indian languages, brazenly claiming these characteristics as guarantees of his detached objectivity in his historical compilation.

In contrast, Tod was fascinated by the Indians he met during his twenty-three-year sojourn in India, in particular the Rajputs, whose

7 Painting of the East India Company building, Leadenhall Street, London, 1800, by James Malton (1761–1803).
(By kind permission of the British Library)

history and customs he studied in detail during his five years as the British Governor-General in India's political agent to the western Rajput states between 1818 and 1823. After his return to England he spent a large amount of his time putting together his two large volumes on the *Annals and Antiquities of Rajasthan*, which appeared in 1829 and 1832, some ten years after his departure from India. They are based on the numerous records, inscriptions, coins and translated local chronicles he had collected in Rajasthan. In his text he gives several quotations from British poets, among whom feature contemporary Romantic poets. More than his textual allusions to Romantic poetry, Tod's work on the Rajputs contains several qualities that are associated with European Romanticism, for example, his attention to written Indian texts, religious and non-religious, as well as to oral narratives that he encountered along his way. Not only had he learned the local dialect of Urdu, but through his learned Jain guru he was able to obtain explanations, translations and copies of manuscripts in Sanskrit, Pali and Persian. In this, he was undoubtedly following the example of the British Sanskrit scholar William Jones, who lived in India from 1784 to his death in 1794, but also the path of German Romantic scholars like Johann Wolfgang von Goethe (1749–1832), who collected local popular songs and ballads in the company of Johann Gottfried Herder (1744–1803) in Alsace, and Friedrich Schlegel (1772–1829), who learned Sanskrit in Paris in 1803 with the British Sanskritist Alexander Hamilton. Hamilton went on to become Britain's first professor of Sanskrit at the East India Company's Haileybury College in England in 1808. In the same year, 1808, Schlegel published his essay 'On the Language and Wisdom of the Ancient Indians'.[2] All these Romantic scholars showed great respect for and interest in the languages, texts and cultures of the civilisations of Asia, to the extent that a twentieth-century scholar, Raymond Schwab, labelled the phenomenon within European Romanticism the 'Oriental Renaissance'.[3]

Johann Gottfried Herder (1744–1803) went even further in his incorporation of the world's different cultures and civilisations in his philosophical world view. In his *Ideas for the Philosophy of the History of Humanity* (1784–91), Herder claims an equal dignity for all cultures, warning against judging any culture by measuring it against another culture.[4] Herder developed a flexible reinterpretation of the Universality of the Enlightenment by incorporating what he saw as irreducible cultural singularities of different nations and civilisations within a rational, universalist whole, held together by a Great Divine Plan that ensured equilibrium between antagonistic forces and the triumph of Reason and Equity over stupidity and irrationality. Despite his latent pro-European racism that offered caricatural representations of certain peoples like the Chinese and the Japanese, he definitely postulated a more inclusive and less hierarchised view of world cultures than did the philosophers of the Scottish Enlightenment. On the universal scale of human civilisation of the late eighteenth century, according to Scottish thinkers like Millar and Reid, there were four stages of civilisation, no more no less, and all the world's civilisations had to be fitted into them, being thus given a label of lesser or greater human advancement.[5]

Though I have no proof that Tod was acquainted with Herder's thinking, his texts display a receptive openness to cultural difference (in relation to the Rajputs for example) that reflect the Romantic *Zeitgeist*. In contrast, James Mill not only explicitly mentions the Scottish Enlightenment's rigid classification of human societies, but also systematically applies Bentham's principle of Utility, which ensures the greatest happiness for the greatest number, as an absolute criterion to determine India's position on the universal scale of human civilisation. It is also interesting to note that James Mill's *History of British India* obtained such commercial success, in 1817, that by 1818 he had a secure, well-paid job with the East India Company in

London, and the Company's Directors initially presented his work as a premium to all the newly qualified East India Company officials on their leaving the Company's Haileybury College for appointments in India. Later, Mill's work was introduced as a standard textbook in the Haileybury College curriculum. Despite its erroneous, disparaging views on Indian civilisation, the Sanskrit scholar Horace Hayman Wilson (1786-1860), who occupied the first Sanskrit chair at Oxford University, considered it worthwhile to republish James Mill's *History* between 1840 and 1848, with a few corrections, and three supplementary octavo volumes extending Mill's narrative from 1805 to 1835. In his 'Editor's Preface' to the new edition, Wilson declares it to be 'the most valuable work on the history of India which has yet been written',[6] though in the volumes that he added to Mill's work he did correct some of Mill's harsh opinions on the low state of Indian civilisation, judging them to be 'not unfrequently erroneous and unjust'.[7] In comparison, Tod's work on Rajasthan, though it was reviewed in various learned journals upon its release, and though it was held in the libraries of certain learned societies in London connected with India, like the Royal Asiatic Society, it certainly cannot be expected to have reached a readership as wide as Mill's *History of British India* did. Within the limited circles of British-India-lovers though, it can be understood to have left its marks as an introduction to the antiquities and social anthropology of Rajasthan, very little known in Britain and Europe until the 1830s.

Having presented the two authors, their respective ideological contexts and their respective publications, I will now proceed to compare the ways in which they each treated India's past, and their respective recommendations to the British Government in India. In addition to their published works, especially concerning their assessment and conception of the future of British rule in India, I will refer to the testimonies both Mill and Tod gave to the British House of Commons Select Committee on the Affairs of the East India Company in 1831 and 1832, in preparation for the British Government's renewal of the East India Company's Charter in 1833-4.[8]

About India's past, the views of Mill can be understood to differ widely from the views expressed by Tod, especially in the attention they each accorded to the historical records available in India, and to their pertinence for a reconstitution of past events there. Mill's approach shows signs of his 'spirit of positive dogmatism',[9] in its sweeping generalisations and systematic application to the Indian context of the Utilitarian programme for a rational and just reorganisation of society, through legal reform, through judicial reform and through electoral reform (the latter only in principle, since the first real elections in India under the British Government were held only in 1937, some hundred years after Mill's death). In his *History of British India*, Mill traces the arrival, installation and expansion of the British in India from 1600 till 1805, stressing throughout that excepting British documents on India, there was little or no indigenous, historical record of India's past, apart from myths and legends, which could explain why India was mired in unchanging, stagnant social processes. His whole demonstration is intended to show that it was only through the imposition of British supremacy, and the superior system of British administration, laws and judicial proceedings, that India could be dynamised towards modernisation and progress, since civilised, British standards would ensure the triumph of reason over superstition and despotic tyranny. Mill repeatedly underlines the absence of reliable historical records among India's annals of her past:[10]

> This people indeed, are perfectly destitute of historical records. Their annals, however, from that era [the visit of Alexander the Great and his Greek troops in 325 BCE] to the period of the Mohammedan conquests [already from 725 CE, but mainly from 998 CE on], are a perfect blank.

From which premise, Mill logically concludes that India's civilisation was sunk in a rude, primitive stage, according to the universal scale of human civilisation of the Scottish Enlightenment:[11]

> It is accordingly found that all rude nations, even those to whom the use of letters has long been familiar, neglect history and are gratified with the productions only of the mythologists and poets. It is allowed on all heads that no historical composition whatever appears to have existed in the literature of the Hindus; they had not reached that point of intellectual maturity, at which the value of a record of the past for the guidance of the future begins to be understood.

Mill goes on to reproach William Jones (1746–94) and other British scholars of the Asiatic Society of Bengal like Francis Wilford, for wrong, exalted notions of the high level achieved by ancient Indian civilisation, since according to the harsh, rationalist yardstick of Utility, the grand test of civilisation according to Mill, India was not more advanced than other oriental civilisations of the past (Egypt, China ...) and was most definitely below the civilisational level of Europe in the Middle Ages. In the absence of valid historical records, Mill uses the laws and institutions of Hindu civilisation to judge the state of its advancement: '[Hindu laws and institutions seem] such as could neither begin nor continue to exist, under any other than one of the rudest and weakest states of the human mind.'[12] Mill also quotes Adam Smith's *Essay on the History of Astronomy*, in order to illustrate that despotism is a proof of low civilisation:[13]

## TOD'S ROMANTIC APPROACH

The opinion by which [Adam Smith] supports his disbelief in the ancient civilisation of Asia is at once philanthropic and profound. That 'despotism [which prevailed over the East] is more destructive of leisure and security, and more adverse to the progress of the human mind, than anarchy itself'.

For his part, Mill, adhering to the views of Scottish conjectural history, firmly believed in blind social progress, even without the intervention of individual reason, as a philosophy of history in human society, a sort of inevitable working out of improvement throughout the world, according to immutable natural laws. However, like Adam Smith, he seems to perceive despotism and superstition as factors that obstruct the working of natural laws, needing therefore to be neutralised by civilised laws and government.

In opposition, James Tod, in his *Annals and Antiquities of Rajasthan*, appears determined to disprove James Mill's claim (widely in circulation by the mid-1820s when Tod wrote his work on Rajasthan) that India had no historical records, and therefore could be relegated to the level of a primitive, rude civilisation. In a similar vein to William Jones before him,[14] Tod states that in spite of the mythology and fantastic legends that obscured so many narratives of India's past, they would nevertheless 'serve to banish the reproach, which India has so long laboured under, of possessing no records of past events'.[15] His aim then appears to be to exhibit the glories of India's past, and to draw lessons from it for a better administration of its present, as opposed to Mill's goal to critically assess, reform and improve India according to British rational parameters. David Arnold perceives in Tod's impulse to '[give] India a history ... with lively characters and stirring events' a characteristic common to much Romantic writing about India, seen also in John Malcolm's and Mountstuart Elphinstone's inspiring historical accounts of the regions adjoining Rajasthan, of Malwa and Afghanistan respectively; also a frequent feature in Romantic writing in Europe.[16] Indeed, much Romantic writing shows attention to and respect for local, popular cultures (as with Shelley, Byron, Southey and Moore), while in their search for self-definition, the Romantics seem to have adopted a pluralist, progressive and universalist view of history and human societies, as advocated by J.G. Herder's cosmopolitan humanism.[17] Tod expresses a solid optimism in the advantages to be gained by Britain through the pursuit of the painstaking deciphering, collating and diffusing of the contents of India's hidden lore, begun in the 1780s by Britain's early Orientalists:[18]

> Much disappointment has been felt in Europe at the sterility of the historic muse of Hindustan. When Sir William Jones first began to explore

> the vast mines of Sanscrit literature, great hopes were entertained that the history of the world would acquire considerable accessions from this source. The sanguine expectations that were then formed have not been realised; and as it usually happens, excitement has been succeeded by apathy and indifference. It is now generally regarded as an axiom, that India possesses no national history. ... Although the labours of Colebrooke, Wilkins, Wilson and others of our own countrymen, emulated by many learned men in France and Germany, have revealed to Europe some of the hidden lore of India; still it is not pretended that we have done much more than pass the threshold of Indian science; and we are consequently not competent to speak decisively of its extent or character. Immense libraries, in various parts of India, are still intact, which have survived the devastations of the Islamite.

Tod goes on to affirm the specificity of Rajput culture and the non-European uniqueness of Rajput historical chronicles:[19]

> Those who expect from a people like the Hindus a species of composition of precisely the same character as the historical works of Greece and Rome, commit the very egregious error of overlooking the peculiarities which distinguish the natives of India from all other races, and which strongly discriminate their intellectual productions of every kind from those of the West. Their philosophy, their poetry, their architecture, are marked with traits of originality; and the same may be expected to pervade their history, which like the arts enumerated, took a character from its intimate association with the religion of the people. It must be recollected, moreover, that until a more correct taste was imparted to the literature of England and France, by the study of classical models, the chronicles of both these countries, and indeed of all the polished nations of Europe, were, at a much more recent date, as crude, as wild, and as barren, as those of the early Rajpoots.

In Tod's approach to the history of the Rajputs, then, we can observe his awareness of their differences from European cultural norms, and his eagerness to respect these specificities in his study of their historical chronicles, with the aim of establishing a coherent, historical narrative of the past exploits of their various clans. This is in marked distinction to James Mill's sweeping tendency to perceive all civilisations within an all-encompassing universality, while also situating European civilisations as more advanced, and non-European civilisations (in particular the Indian civilisation) as retarded and lagging behind on the scale of universal progress.

I will base my assessment of James Mill's and James Tod's recommendations to the British Government on the best policies to follow in the administration of Britain's Indian territories, drawing on their respective testimonies before the House of Commons Select Committee on the Affairs of the East India Company, prior to the renewal of the East India Company's Charter in 1833–4. James Mill gave personal answers orally in the House of Commons on various dates in 1831 and 1832, while Tod submitted a letter dated 23 March 1832 answering a series of questions on the recent developments of the East India Company in India, addressed to T. Hyde Villiers, who in 1832 was the Secretary of the British Parliament's India Board of Control.

In their testimonies to the House of Commons, both James Mill and James Tod clearly denounce the system of subsidiary alliances, under which the British government appointed a British military resident with British troops in those native states that accepted British protection. The reasons for their respective denunciations, however, are far from similar. James Mill was convinced that this mixed system of government, with the military affairs under British control and the civil administration under the native prince's own staff, resulted only in 'misgovernment' and 'mismanagement', in particular because it eliminated the traditional forms of political checks and balances against the tyrannical abuse of power:[20]

> It has been found by experience (and the same was predicted) that misgovernment under this divided rule does go to its utmost extent, far beyond its ordinary limits, even in India. ... In the ordinary state of things in India, (though under such governments as that of India there was little of anything like a regular check), the princes stood in awe of their subjects. Insurrection against oppression was the general practice of the country. The princes knew that when mismanagement and oppression went to a certain extent, there would be revolt, and that they would stand a chance of being tumbled from their throne, and a successful leader of the insurgents put in their place. This check is, by our interference, totally taken away, for the people know that any attempt of theirs would be utterly unavailing against our irresistible power. Accordingly, no such thought occurs to them, and they submit to every degree of oppression that befalls them.
> 
> [...]
> 
> It appears to me that the subsidiary alliance does not take away the spirit of sovereignty by degrees, from these princes; this is taken from them, along with the sovereignty, at the first step. It does not remain to be done by degrees. We begin by taking the military power, and when we have taken that, we have taken all. The princes exercise all the power that is left them to exercise, as mere trustees of ours, and unfortunately they are very bad trustees.

After affirming that certain upper-class Indians 'who have held the power of government, or might hope again to held them [sic] under native princes', are understandably 'averse to our rule', James Mill states that most Indians are indifferent to which power rules them, being totally absorbed in resolving their own day-to-day problems:[21]

> The mass of the people, I believe, care very little by what sort of persons they are governed. They hardly think about the matter. They think of the present pressure and of relief from that pressure; but if they find themselves at peace in their dwellings and the fields, and are not burthened by too heavy an annual exaction, they are equally contented whether their comfort is under rulers with turbans or hats.

James Mill concluded that from the perspective of the greatest happiness of the greatest number of the native people of India, the best system of government would be a completely British system of justice, with exclusively British revenue collectors, in order to avoid extortion by native officials, which led only to the impoverishment and the desolation of the country,[22] and with purely British modes of administration, deliberately reducing all the native princes to a state of complete dependency like that which had been imposed on the Rajah of Tanjore.[23]

In comparison, Tod concedes (like James Mill) that the subsidiary alliance system had destroyed the traditional means of resistance against political tyranny:[24]

> Already have the evil effects of our alliances received practical illustration, in a variety of ways, in almost every state of Rajpootana. The first effect is the abolition of all those wholesome checks which restrained the passion of the princes. ... The sufferers have not even emigration left as a refuge. ... The ancient balance of power which often ended in the deposal or death of a tyrant, we have thus completely destroyed.

Tod is convinced that the result of British military intervention in the native states was a slow process of decay:[25]

> The whole history of our subsidiary alliances has practically illustrated their denationalising influence upon the princes and the people, who have been made to purchase our protection. The principle is immutable; even if it insure not sudden annihilation, it operates with equal certainty, in a slow process of decay.

However, unlike James Mill, Tod recommends a remodelling of the subsidiary alliances, precluding any outright British conquest or takeover, in order to better arrive at the 'mutual benefit and support' of both the protected native states, and of the British Government in India, thus ensuring the military cooperation of the native princes against 'any foreign foe' like Russia:[26]

The only safe alternative therefore is a re-modelling of the alliances, lessening the causes of interference, by diminishing the tributes, and providing for their realisation in a manner to prevent the least chance of collision, and rendering the alliance, as far as possible, one of mutual benefit and support.

Concerning the level of land revenue impositions, which constituted a major source of income for the British Government in India, both James Mill and James Tod advocate a lowering of the level of land taxes, but for very different reasons. James Mill affirms that the means of levying the revenue were more objectionable than the precise amount raised, especially because 'there is endless fraud and exaction by the subordinate people, who are under little or no control',[27] being 'a great source of oppression' and tending to 'the distress of the inhabitants'. Here, Mill's negative opinion of the native systems of administration and of the corrupt zemindars is manifest, whereas he proposes lower levels of land tax to be collected by uncorrupted British revenue collectors, leaving the peasant cultivators with sufficient means to invest in the following year's crops and to improve their land. This was Mill's Utilitarian method of applying Ricardo's rent theory to the land-revenue system in India, while also attacking the aristocratic zemindars, made all-powerful by Cornwallis's Permanent Settlement Act of 1793, and thus of taking measures to protect the peasant cultivators. Tod's reasoning on the best way to conduct revenue collection was more political and less economic. He felt that a respect for traditional Rajput land practices and institutional autonomy, while avoiding undue tributary exactions, would consolidate Rajput support for and trust in the British administration:[28]

> But in addition to these causes, with two of the most important states, Mewar and Jeipoor, we left the door open to interference by the undefined nature of our tributary exactions, which were to increase in the ratio of their reviving prosperity. It was then, but at all events, it is now, in our power to close this door, which leads to the worst kind of interference in their financial and territorial arrangement; for there cannot be a shadow of independence, where such a system is tolerated; which, moreover, will not fail to generate hatred and mistrust of the protecting power.

By avoiding unduly high tributes and land rents in Rajputana, and by recognising the Rajputs as Britain's 'important allies',[29] Tod hoped to uphold the friendship of the Rajputs for the British Government in India, thus honouring the Rajput sense of Rajput honour while also benefiting the British Government.

On the subject of monopoly duties on agricultural products from India, as well as on the nature of the relationship between British employees and Indian employees of the East India Company, James Mill implements rational, Utilitarian ideas in recommending the greatest advantage of the largest number of parties involved, while Tod seems to take into account the prosperity of the Indians and the mutual feelings of loyalty that could be developed among the East India Company's multi-ethnic staff. For example, James Mill recommends the continuation of the monopoly duties imposed in India on the sales of salt, opium and tobacco, revealing that he accorded more importance to the maintenance of substantial returns to the British Government through these duties, over and above the well-being of the Indian producers and traders:[30]

> The result of this comparison [of the free sale of salt and of the monopoly sale of salt by the British Government in India] seems to be in favour of the monopoly, unless the very name monopoly is considered a make-weight, and a counterbalance to real and substantial advantages; advantages gained by it, not as an instrument of commerce, but of taxation, raising great revenue through sale of salt.
> ...
> I am satisfied that the monopoly of opium has had no injurious effect on the agriculture or commerce of the country. ... I do not consider any other mode of raising a large revenue by opium feasible.
> The mode of realising the revenue [on tobacco] by monopoly appears to have been resorted to, as in the case of salt and opium, for the greater facility of coping with the smuggler. It would appear that the means employed have not been successful in the prevention of abuse. ... It is said the people of Malabar and Canara are poor, and already overtaxed. That may be a very good reason for lessening the amount of taxation, without being any reason for abolishing the tax on tobacco. It is no reason for abolishing the tax on whiskey, that the people of Ireland are miserably poor, seeing the consumption of whiskey tends only to make them poorer.

In answer to the Parliamentary India Board of Control's question about the employment of natives in the service of the East India Company, James Mill uses the rational arguments of the cheaper rate at which natives could be paid, and of the need to employ the fittest candidates (native or not) in order to ensure the efficacy of government business.[31]

In contrast to Mill's rational approach, Tod's answers appear more humane. Tod wishes to see the elimination of monopoly duties on salt and opium, judging these taxes to be unjust, impolitic and inquisitorial, with the added disadvantage of permitting fraud:[32]

The produce of the salt lakes in Rajpootana has long since found its way into our provinces, and might be rendered highly beneficial to the allies and the inhabitants of our own provinces, but for our Bengal salt monopoly and our protecting duties. It is the same with opium, the cultivation of which, in consequence of our monopoly, produced an activity, both in Malwa and lower Rajpootana, quite unexampled, though the policy of this measure was very questionable, whether in a financial or moral point of view. The history of this monopoly will show the danger with which our alliance encircles these states, and may enable the paramount power to protect them against it, according to the spirit of the treaties. It affords another of the too many instances where public faith is lost sight of in the pursuit of financial or mercantile interest.

As for the relationship between British officials and Indian employees in India, Tod recommends the creation of cadetships and appointments for the family members of retired British officials with the aim of maintaining human ties of loyalty across generations between Britain and India:[33]

There should be a certain number of appointments reserved for the children or near relatives of those who have served the Company long and faithfully. Neither would this course be impolitic; for the native soldiers, who are creatures of sympathy and strong feeling, would rejoice to see the children of their old officers amongst them, thus keeping up ties of ancient standing.

These various examples tend to show that while James Mill adopted abstract, rational Utilitarian principles in his recommendations to the British Government on their future policies in India, James Tod used his ground knowledge and field experience to urge respect for local Indian customs and to underline the need to enlist the support of the ruling Indian elites for the emerging British administration.

However, things were perhaps not so clearly cut and dried between disparaging Utilitarian views on India on the one hand, and respectful, Romantic attitudes on the other. For example, both Mill and Tod were caught up in a vast colonial bureaucracy, with multiple pressures from the East India Company Directors, from the British Government, from the vagaries of the political climate in Britain and the evolution of British public opinion, while also being exposed to changing circumstances, personal rivalries and hierarchical obstacles on the Indian side.

To give James Mill the benefit of the doubt on the aims of his *History of British India*, Javed Majeed reads in his work a 'rhetoric of reform', with the genuine goal of improving and remodelling Indian society through a Utilitarian form of British rule.[34] Defending James Mill from the reproach of only negatively and destructively attacking the social and administrative institutions of India, Majeed credits him with deploying a politically oriented, imitative imagination (as distinct from the aesthetic, poetic imagination of the Romantics), in order to rationally create a new society, by applying universal, constitutional and legal principles and by adopting polemical positions in what was intended perhaps as a 'liberating critique'.[35] Majeed adds in James Mill's defence that he was writing his work as a philosophical radical in the Opposition against the 'revitalised Conservatism'[36] of the early decades of nineteenth-century Britain under George IV, using the alien background of India to indirectly criticise the dominant elites in his home country, as Montesquieu had done in *Lettres Persanes* (1721). Majeed claims Mill can be understood to have also attempted to articulate a new secular idiom for the comparison, contrast and improvement of existing cultures, cutting through constraining, tradition-bound identities, and restrictive, age-old, aesthetic attitudes, since the Utilitarians were more concerned with transforming the here and now, unlike the Romantics, who gave importance to the reconstitution of each nation's past in unifying its national culture through a sense of heroic and inspiring continuity. Through the 1830s controversy between the Orientalists and the Anglicists in India, concerning which languages should be adopted for the British colonial government's administration and government-financed educational institutions, James Mill surprisingly sided with the vernacularist stance of the Orientalists, despite his earlier reservations about the philological endeavours of the pioneer Orientalist William Jones and the Asiatic Society of Bengal (founded in 1784). In this, Mill was opposed by the Governor-General, Lord William Bentinck (1828–35), and Thomas Babington Macaulay, legal member of the Bengal Council (1834–8), who both advocated the adoption of the more functionally convenient English language, with the elimination of Sanskrit and Persian from all official transactions and documents. James Mill supported the Conservative Orientalist Horace Hayman Wilson, who was aware of a practical and cultural advantage in preserving the use of Indian languages for official purposes. Majeed states that James Mill was motivated by ideas of improvement and liberating change in his views on education in general, and on education in India in particular.[37] Besides, while parrying a too-extreme condemnation of Mill's views on India, Christopher Bayly has underlined the fragile nature of the British colonial power in India, with its wide reliance on Indian networks for support, and with the ultimately limited impact of its reform programmes probably as a result of a lack of overall consistency of purpose.[38] Bayly has also drawn attention to the active agency of Indian society in the colonial process, involving a constant adaptation and self-consolidation of the Indian elites.[39] So, Javed Majeed finally attributes an 'innovative, reformist spirit' to James Mill's formulations on India.[40]

Adopting a similarly ambivalent position to James Mill's, which we have just seen above, James Tod expressed the desire to see material improvements in the agricultural prosperity, in the exploitation of the mineral wealth and in the transport links of Rajputana, following upon the introduction of Pax Britannica in 1817. David Arnold qualifies this as 'combining the ethos of Romanticism with the doctrine of improvement',[41] observing that Tod linked his 'Romanticising' with 'a more Utilitarian agenda',[42] since while immersed in feudalist folklore, he simultaneously championed 'the seemingly contrary cause of capitalist modernity'.[43] For example, Tod joyfully reports the return of prosperity to territories brought under Pax Britannica in 1817, on passing through the towns of Bunera and Bhilwara in early December 1819:[44]

> All required a long period of toleration and unmolested tranquillity, to emerge from their impoverished condition. ... [O]ur good town of Bhilwara, which was making rapid strides to prosperity, notwithstanding drawbacks from sectarian feuds.

Again, at Heentah and Khyroda on 30 January 1820, Tod notes that 'the peasantry were smiling at the sight of the luxuriant young crops of wheat, barley and gram, aware that no ruthless hand could now step between them and the bounties of heaven'.[45]

Apart from this applause for material improvements thanks to the blessings of peace under British protection, Tod also indulges in wishful thinking about later introducing modern, technological improvements in the Rajputana countryside, while observing the landscape between Chittore and Udaipur, from the tablelands at Kunairoh on 13 February 1820:[46]

> The rich flat we have passed over ... appears as a deep basin, fertilised by numerous streams, fed by huge reservoirs in the mountains and studded with towns, which once were populous, but are for the most part now in ruins, though the germ of incipient prosperity is just appearing. From this height I condensed all my speculative ideas on a very favourite subject – the formation of a canal to unite the ancient and modern capitals of Mewar, by which her soil might be made to return a tenfold harvest, and famine be shut out for ever from her gates. My eye embraced the whole line of the Bairis, from its outlet at the Oodisagur, to its passage within a mile of Cheetore, and the benefit likely to accrue from such a work appeared incalculable. What new ideas would be opened to the Rajpoot, on seeing the trains of oxen, which now creep slowly along with merchandise for the capital, exchanged for boats gliding along the canal; and

his fields for many miles on each side, irrigated by lateral cuts, instead of the cranking Egyptian wheel, as it is called, but which is indigenous to India. ...

But I cannot relinquish the conviction that the undertaking, if executed, would not only enable the Rana to pay his tribute, but to be more merciful to his subjects, for whose welfare it is our chief duty to labour.*

[Tod's note: * Even now, as I transcribe this from my journal, I would almost (when 'The Annals' are finished) risk a couple of years' residence in 'the Happy Valley', where I scarcely ever enjoyed one day of health, to execute this and another favourite project – the reopening of the tin-mines of Jawura.]

Although amounting to only a few interludes, these passages reveal a pragmatic, forward-looking aspect of Tod, also concerned with down-to-earth improvements in the territories under his supervision, in addition to his literary and antiquarian pursuits.

## *Conclusion*

To conclude, we can observe that neither the Romanticist nor the Utilitarian approach won complete sway in the policy decisions of the East India Company in India during the period between 1817 and 1857. While the Utilitarians (like James Mill) considered India's social condition to be backward and immature, because of the Indian people's strong attachment to their ancient traditions, these Utilitarians, in all sincerity, attempted to recommend rational reforms covering the political administration, the judicial system, the marriage laws and the status of women, the revenue collection and the education facilities in India. These reforms were perceived in a variety of ways in Britain and in India, but did not, in fact, leave any deep imprint on Indian society. For their part, the Romanticist administrators (like James Tod) showed a more humane involvement with the Indian population, expressed a greater respect for Indian perceptions of their own past and a tendency to uphold Indian social institutions and customs, but were also tempted to conceive plans for the modernisation and material improvement of India's territories, in the light of the emerging capitalist technologies available in Britain. Finally, both the Utilitarian and the Romanticist ways of exercising authority through the application of knowledge gathered in the colonial, political context of British India, appear to have been inspired by high ideals, and a desire to conduct colonial government in the least harmful and most advantageous manner for all concerned. They can be understood to have been two different ways in which British ideologies engaged with Indian conditions and participated in the reciprocal fashioning of mentalities and attitudes on both sides of the colonial divide, through the nineteenth century.

## Notes

1. James Mill, *The History of British India*, London: Baldwin, Cradock & Joy, 1817, 3 vols, quarto, vol. I, 'Author's Preface'.
2. Friedrich Schlegel, *On the Language and Wisdom of the Ancient Indians*, first published in German, Heidelberg: Mohr & Zimmer, 1808. Reissued in *The European Discovery of India: Key Indological Sources of Romanticism*, selected and with new introductions by Michael Franklin, London: Ganesha Publishing Ltd., 2001, 6 vols, see vol. IV.
3. Raymond Schwab, *La renaissance orientale*, Paris: Payot, 1950.
4. Johann Gottfried Herder, *Histoire et cultures: Une autre philosophie de l'histoire; Idées pour la philosophie de l'histoire de l'humanité (extraits)*, trans. and ed. Max Rouché; presentation, bibliography and chronology by Alain Reinaut, Paris: Garnier Flammarion, 2000, pp. 7–39.
5. James Mill, *Selected Economic Writings*, introduced and ed. Donald Winch, Edinburgh and London: Oliver & Boyd, 1966, pp. 1–22.
6. James Mill, *History of British India*, ed. Horace Hayman Wilson, London: James Madden & Co., 1840–8, 9 vols, 'Preface of the Editor', vol. I, p. x.
7. Mill, *History of British India*, ed. Wilson, vol. I, p. ix.
8. 'Minutes of Evidence taken before the Select Committee on the Affairs of the East India Company, Session of 6th December 1831 to 16th August 1832', in: *British Parliamentary Papers in 18 Volumes, India Office Records*, vol. XIV, section vi, Political and Foreign, OIOC Shelfmark: V/4/1831-2, No. 735-VI, London: House of Commons, 1832, pp. 3–10 (James Mill); pp. 122–35 (James Tod). See also *British Parliamentary Papers*, vol. V (1831), vol. VII (1831), vol. IX (1832) and vol. XI (1832), quoted in: Mill, *Selected Economic Writings*, ed. Winch, pp. 423–43.
9. James Mill, *An Essay on Government*, with an introduction by Ernest Barker, Cambridge: Cambridge University Press, 1937, pp. vii–xx, in particular p. xiv.
10. Mill, *History of British India*, vol. I, pp. 99–100, Book II, chapter 1.
11. Mill, *History of British India*, vol. I, p. 374, Book II, chapter 9.
12. Mill, *History of British India*, vol. I, p. 428, Book II, chapter 9.
13. Mill, *History of British India*, vol. I, p. 455, Book II, chapter 10.
14. Javed Majeed, *Ungoverned Imaginings: James Mill's 'The History of British India' and Orientalism*, Oxford: Clarendon Press, 1992, pp. 31–40.
15. James Tod, *Annals and Antiquities of Rajasthan*, vol. II, London: Routledge & Kegan Paul Ltd, 1832, p. viii; repr. Delhi: Rupa & Co., 1997.
16. David Arnold, *The Tropics and the Travelling Gaze: India, Landscape and Science, 1800–1856*, Seattle and London: University of Washington Press, 2006, p. 88
17. Herder, *Histoires et cultures*, p. 18.
18. James Tod, *Annals and Antiquities of Rajasthan*, vol. I, London: Routledge & Kegan Paul Ltd, 1829, p. xiii; repr. Delhi: Rupa & Co., 1997.
19. Tod, *Annals*, vol. I, p. xv.
20. *British Parliamentary Papers*, vol. XIV, pp. 4, 7.
21. *British Parliamentary Papers*, vol. XIV, p. 8.
22. *British Parliamentary Papers*, vol. XIV, p. 4.
23. *British Parliamentary Papers*, vol. XIV, p. 10.
24. *British Parliamentary Papers*, vol. XIV, p. 131.
25. *British Parliamentary Papers*, vol. XIV, p. 131.
26. *British Parliamentary Papers*, vol. XIV, p. 132.
27. *British Parliamentary Papers*, vol.XIV, p. 10.
28. *British Parliamentary Papers*, vol. XIV, p. 125.
29. *British Parliamentary Papers*, vol. XIV, p. 130.

30 *British Parliamentary Papers*, vol. XI (1832), pp. 278–81, in: Mill, *Selected Economic Writings*, ed. Winch, pp. 437–41.
31 *British Parliamentary Papers*, vol. VII (1831) and vol. IX (1832) in: Mill, *Selected Economic Writings*, ed. Winch, pp. 441–3.
32 *British Parliamentary Papers*, vol. XIV, p. 125.
33 *British Parliamentary Papers*, vol. XIV, p. 135.
34 Javed Majeed, 'James Mill's *The History of British India* and Utilitarianism as a rhetoric of reform'. *Modern Asian Studies*, 24.2 (1990), 209–24.
35 Majeed, *Ungoverned Imaginings*, p. 200.
36 Majeed, *Ungoverned Imaginings*, p. 195.
37 Majeed, *Ungoverned Imaginings*, pp. 138–45. Mentions of Mill, *Essay on Education* (1824); Mill, *Analysis of the Phenomena of the Human Mind* (1828); and Mill, *Recent Changes in Native Education* (1836).
38 Christopher A. Bayly, *Indian Society and the Making of the British Empire*, Cambridge: Cambridge University Press, 1988, pp. 200–6.
39 Bayly, *Indian Society*, pp. 45–78.
40 Majeed, *Ungoverned Imaginings*, p. 149.
41 Arnold, *The Tropics and the Travelling Gaze*, p. 90.
42 Arnold, *The Tropics and the Travelling Gaze*, p. 92.
43 Arnold, *The Tropics and the Travelling Gaze*, p. 92.
44 Tod, *Annals*, vol. I, p. 617.
45 Tod, *Annals*, vol. II, p. 482.
46 Tod, *Annals*, vol. II, pp. 504–5.

CHAPTER SIX

# Tod's knowledge exchanges with his contemporaries in India

The aim of this chapter is to use such manuscript details as are available at the British Library and at the Public Record Office at Kew, as well as the mentions of Tod's other writings (in addition to his two published works, *Annals and Antiquities of Rajasthan* in two volumes, 1829, 1832, and *Travels in Western India*, 1839 (posth.)) that appear in various learned journals of his time, in order to arrive at as complete a picture as possible of Tod's knowledge exchanges in India, through his miscellaneous writings and relationships with his colleagues, friends, subordinates and hierarchical superiors in the field.

In order to carry this out, I will use biographical details on Tod prior to his departure for India from various archival sources, in order to arrive at an estimation of Tod's intellectual baggage; then, I will study Tod's mentions of friends and colleagues in the course of his two major published texts, *Annals and Antiquities of Rajasthan* and *Travels in Western India*, as illustrations of his knowledge exchanges; Tod's correspondence and field account book in Rajputana will further demonstrate Tod's efforts to gather scholarly information in India.

One of the earliest documents that mentions Tod's existence is his baptism certificate, dated 11 February 1799, and signed by the vicar of Islington of that time, G. Abraham, certifying that James Tod, son of James Tod and Mary [Heatly], born on 19 March 1782, had been baptised in Islington Church [near London] on 5 May 1782.[1] The date of the baptism certificate, February 1799, perhaps could be understood to indicate that Tod required a certificate of the date of his birth prior to his departure for India, which took place in March 1799. In fact, Tod had obtained a cadetship with the East India Company in 1798, through his maternal uncle, Patrick Heatly, an employee of the Bengal Civil Service. Tod was formally nominated to the infantry of the Bengal Presidency by an East India Company official in London named Grant, in association with an East India Company patron named Wilkinson.[2]

8 Miniature attributed to Deogarh Chokha, 1817, entitled 'Captain Tod riding on an Elephant with his companions and Escort'.
(With permission from the Victoria & Albert Museum, London)

Tod's forebears on the paternal as well as on the maternal side were among the Scots who had migrated to the American colonies either during the English civil wars of the 1650s or in the early eighteenth century (1720s). On both sides, the families had connections with the minor Scottish aristocracy.[3] Tod's own father, James Tod Senior (born 26 October 1745), the son of Henry Tod (b.1717) of Borrowstonness or Bo'ness on the Clyde,[4] migrated to Newport, Rhode Island, where he married Mary Heatly, daughter of Andrew Heatly, on 4 November 1779. Tod's parents apparently moved back to England soon after their marriage, because Tod's elder brother, Suetonius Henry Tod, was born in England in 1780, and our James Tod was born in Islington in March 1782. James Tod Senior, together with his brother John Tod, moved to India in the 1780s (leaving his children Suetonius and James Tod Junior, who were still infants, with their mother in London). Tod's father and paternal uncle set themselves up as indigo planters in the region of Agra and Mirzapur.[5] Our James Tod Junior spent his early years in England, before his departure for India as an engineering officer cadet of the East India Company's Army in March 1799.[6]

Tod's maternal uncles, Patrick Heatly and S. Heatly, were both members of the Bengal Civil Service.[7] They must have been in India at least since the 1780s, since a manuscript letter from Patrick Heatly, dated Patna, 9 December 1788, is addressed to Governor-General Cornwallis, Knight of the Garter, in Calcutta.[8] In this letter, Patrick Heatly seeks to exculpate himself in the Governor-General's eyes of any disloyalty to his employer, the East India Company, concerning the arrival in Calcutta of an American trading vessel, with a trade consignment for sale in Calcutta, together with a request to Patrick Heatly to promote the American merchant vessel's trading schemes in the Orient. However, Patrick Heatly admits that 'many other of my relations remained in America and are still there', but that he had 'scarcely any intercourse' with the American branch of his family. This letter enables us to situate Patrick Heatly with certainty in Patna in December 1788, and to confirm the links between the Heatly branch of Tod's family in England and India, and the trader Heatlys of Rhode Island, America.

## Tod's human contacts in India

Tod makes several mentions of his British friends and colleagues through his two published texts.[9] A close look at these allusions will enable us to situate Tod in his professional setting, as an ardent, knowledge-collecting member of the East India Company bureaucracy in India. Tod's texts contain reminiscences of striking historical moments in which we can observe Tod in interaction with his colleagues; episodes about wild animals, hunting and fishing that provide light relief in his dense narratives; a suspicious distrust of Tod spread by his superior, Sir David Ochterlony; Tod's experience of illness in India; Tod's contacts with the British Residents in various cities across western India; and tributes to Tod's qualities expressed by his colleagues.

Tod's reminiscences of historical turning points include his visit to Benoît de Boigne in Chambéry in 1826. Although Tod did not encounter de Boigne in India, since de Boigne left Daulat Rao Sindhia's court and India in 1795, whereas Tod was attached to Daulat Rao Sindhia's court only from 1805 onwards, de Boigne had enjoyed an illustrious military reputation as the commander of Sindhia's troops from 1785 to 1795, particularly at the 1791 Battle of Merta, where the Maratha troops under de Boigne defeated the Rajput forces, thanks to their European artillery (eighty cannon as against the twenty-five of the Rajputs) and the European training of the Maratha infantry, with use of the hollow square formation.[10]

Tod was present in 1806, with Graeme Mercer, the British envoy and resident at Sindhia's court between 1805 and 1810, at the interview in the Eklinga shrine, six miles from Udaipur, between Bheem

Singh, Rana of Mewar, and Daulat Rao Sindhia, in which the rival claims of Raja Jagat Singh of Jaipur and of Raja Maun Singh of Jodhpur, for the hand of Bheem Singh's daughter, Princess Kishna Komari, were discussed. The transactions, during which Bheem Singh's humbled condition struck Tod and inspired him to work towards the regeneration and restoration of 'this descendant of a hundred kings' of the Hindus, had ended in the tragic poisoning of Kishna Komari in 1810.[11] Tod evokes his role during the 1817–18 Pindari War, during which Governor-General Hastings decisively defeated the Marathas and the Pindaris in western and central India. Tod was based at Rowtah, near Kotah, 'in the very centre of movements of all the armies, friendly and hostile',[12] contributing towards reorienting the British troops from Bombay under General Grant Keir, and the Malwa contingent under General Sir Thomas Browne, towards Ujjain and Mewar, thus saving them from massacre by the Pindari Roshan Beg's forces, ensconced in the gorge of the River Cali Sind.[13] Tod also succeeded in killing 150 of the 1,500 men under the son of the Pindari chief, Kureem Khan, with only thirty-two armed men of his 25th Native Infantry, using the funds from the sales of the Pindari booty confiscated on this occasion, to construct the fifteen-arch 'Hastings Bridge' or *Hasteen-Pool* in honour of Lord Hastings, the Earl of Mornington, over the river to the east of Kotah.[14]

Tod narrated in the *Asiatic Journal* of London of 1835 an anecdote that took place at the end of the Pindari War of 1817–18, concerning the surrender of the Kumbalgarh fortress, held at the time by Pathan sirdars, formerly employed by Sindhia. Tod's British colleagues, General Donkin, Colonel Casement and Major Macleod, were weighing the difficulty of laying siege to the Kumbalgarh fortress, situated on a steep mountainside, when Tod managed to negotiate its surrender without a shot being fired. Tod worked this wonder by promising to pay the Pathan sirdars the considerable amount of arrears due to their troops, thanks to a bill of exchange drawn on a native banker, known to Tod. The atmosphere of mutual confidence established by Tod with the Pathan sirdars succeeded in defusing the conflict, to the advantage of all concerned.[15] Here, Tod was using his practical knowledge of the needs of the Pathan soldiers and their chiefs in order to avoid violent conflict with them.

As through all his writings, Tod appears here in his ambivalent double role as a British officer who did his best to uphold the honour of the Rajputs, while also defending the military and political interests of his employers, the British East India Company.

In his travel accounts entitled 'Personal Narrative' in the two volumes of his *Annals and Antiquities of Rajasthan*, more than in his other writings, Tod mentions several incidents of hunting, fishing and encounters with wild animals. These can be understood to have been included for the entertainment of Tod's readers, in order to lighten what otherwise would have been an unalleviatedly dense account. For example, the spectacle of an eight-year-old elephant who inserted 'his proboscis into the sepoy's baggage', or the scene of Tod's faithful old elephant Futteh floundering with his load in a bog at Oosurwas (between Udaipur and Jodhpur) in October 1819, appear comical.[16] Tod also mentions his camel Manika (a gift from the Prince of Bundi) rolling down a steep slope, when he lost his footing.[17] The 'Personal Narrative' of the first volume of Tod's work on Rajasthan closes in December 1819, with Waugh and Duncan fishing for trout with rods in the Bunas River, near Poorh, southwest of Bhilwarra, while Tod set the net and obtained several dozen trout,[18] of which 'the largest measured seventeen inches, and weighed seventy rupees [sic], or nearly two pounds [in weight]'.

The second volume contains relatively fewer of these light, sporting incidents, with a mention of Tod hunting for pigeons near Neembaira, east of Udaipur in February 1820, while Waugh chased after a *nilgaé* (or blue cow) astride his Arab horse;[19] a description of Tod's friend David Stewart successfully fishing for trout in the same Bunas River in late October 1820 at Merowlee, near Rasmy;[20] and an account of Tod, Waugh and Duncan managing to make a 'huge bear' withdraw, near the Bhil fortress of Ekailgurh (near Kotah) in December 1821.[21] Tod expresses several times his attachment to horses, having had occasion to possess four different horses himself through his career in Rajputana (1818–23): Bajraj, a gift from the Rana of Mewar, which horse had died in Kotah (in 1821); another horse from the Raj Rana Zalim Sing of Kota, named Javadia, who was still with Tod even through his trip in Gujarat; then a 'white courser' from the Raja of Bundi; and a horse named Hargaz. In one of his letters (in Devanagari script) from Gujarat to Rana Bheem Sing of Mewar, dated late 1822, shortly before Tod finally quit the shores of India in February 1823,[22] he requested the Rana to ensure that good care was taken of his beloved horses Hargaz and Javadia.[23] This confirms an image of Tod as a dignified British official in Rajasthan, taking part in elite sporting pursuits like riding and in familiar, personal contact with the Rana of Mewar, the Raja of Bundi and the Raj Rana of Kota, beyond the strict limits of officialdom.

Another set of circumstances which reveal Tod's interactions with his colleagues are related to his difficult relationship with his immediate hierarchical superior, General Sir David Ochterlony (1758–1825), the Resident of the British Government in Delhi from 1815 onwards. Several indications of mutual suspicion and a lack of trust between these two men can be observed in Tod's text on Rajasthan, in Bishop

Heber's travel account and in the official correspondence of Tod and Ochterlony with the Calcutta authorities (which I will study later in this chapter). For example, Tod's relations with the court of Jodhpur (the Rathores of Marwar) were rendered difficult thanks to interference by Ochterlony. In Tod's initial instructions of February 1818, Marwar was apparently not attributed to his supervision, coming under his administrative control only in February 1819, 'in addition to Mewar, Jaisalmer, Kota, Bundi, and Sirohi'.[24] However by late 1821, Marwar had been removed from Tod's care and entrusted to Francis Wilder, the British Superintendent at Ajmer, directly under the supervision of Ochterlony in Delhi.[25] In Tod's travel journal in his two volumes on Rajasthan, these hierarchical tensions appear only indirectly, in connection with the British superintendent of Ajmer, Francis Wilder, appointed in this position in December 1818, ten months after Tod's appointment in Udaipur,[26] and immediately deputed by Ochterlony (in December 1818) to visit the court of Jodhpur, where Wilder was 'very courteously received' by Raja Maun Singh of Jodhpur.[27]

Subsequently, Tod was given instructions as the British envoy to Marwar in February 1819, to report on Marwar's administration, finances, police and commerce, which led to Tod making the journey from Udaipur to Marwar and back, between October and December 1819.[28] Until this point, relations seem to have been cordial between Tod and Wilder, since on his return journey from Marwar, on 2 December 1819, Tod halted in Ajmer, and 'breakfasted with Mr. Wilder'.[29]

The mental tension that Tod underwent from the middle of 1821 is further borne out by the fact that the 'Personal Narrative' in volume I of Tod's work on Rajasthan hardly has any references to illness. Tod describes his first official entry into Udaipur in February 1818 without any reference to health problems: 'the prince received the Agent and suite in a manner at once courteous and dignified'.[30] When Tod's party left Udaipur for the journey to Marwar in October 1819, he only briefly mentions the health hazards in Mewar as 'the prevalent fevers of the monsoon'.[31] However, we learn from Graeme Mercer that right from Tod's early days in India, he had suffered from 'a state of health which, from rheumatic affection, frequently disabled him from taking even common exercise'.[32]

By contrast, in the second volume of Tod's work on Rajasthan, his mentions of illness are more frequent. These can be perceived as signs of the wear and tear of Tod's strenuous knowledge-hunting, in addition to the burden of his official responsibilities, on his general health. Near Morwun and Neembaira to the east of Udaipur, in February 1820, Tod suffered 'a severe pulmonary affection'.[33] At Jehajpur in October 1820, Tod suffered food poisoning, probably from 'datura' introduced in a maize cake he ate, bringing Tod 'to the verge of death'. After being treated with 'ether and compounds' by Dr Duncan, Tod recovered, confessing that 'this is about the fourth time that I have been "upon the brink" (*canari ponchâ*) since I entered Mewar'.[34] Tod mentions his diseased spleen, requiring him to be bled by leeches, in mid-October 1820, at Mandelgurh, between Jehajpur and Rasmy.[35]

Cholera raged in Bundi and in Kota during the monsoon season.[36] Tod refers to the suffering state of his travelling companions on several occasions in his second volume.[37] For example, Tod uses terms such as 'looking very ill', 'in despair and ready to die', 'in a very precarious condition' and 'sinking rapidly' to convey the difficulties presented by various illnesses during his party's journeys across Rajasthan. Tod felt great sadness at having to bury his companion Lieutenant Carey in 1821.[38]

After his return to England in September 1823, Tod suffered attacks of apoplexy,[39] in 1825 and in November 1835, of which he finally died. In between, he made trips to Europe for health reasons in 1826,[40] and for a whole year, between September 1834 and September 1835, Tod was in Italy because of a 'chest complaint'.[41] Since Tod died at the young age of fifty-three, he can be understood to have succumbed to the stress and fatigue of the Indian climate, aggravated by his unrelenting pace in collecting and compiling knowledge about the Rajputs throughout his active life, and most probably also worsened by certain hierarchical tensions that he had to face.

Tod availed himself of the assistance of a network of British residents across western India during his travels. His exchanges with these British representatives in various Indian cities mentioned in his texts reveal Tod's scholarly affinities with his contemporaries in India. For example, he mentions his visits to Hissar in Haryana (at the northeast frontier of Rajputana), where his Scottish friend James Lumsdaine was posted, near the ruins of the castle of the former Muslim chief Feroz. Tod refers to Lumsdaine as 'a beloved friend' who had already died by 1829 when Tod's first volume was published, adding that it was partly thanks to Lumsdaine's 'ardent and honourable' urgings that he had undertaken the compilation of his *Annals*.[42] Tod mentions his younger cousin, John Tod (1796–1818), whose scholarly talents Tod had hoped to direct towards realising his own dream of 'the "Aravulli delineated" by the hand of science', but who had died prematurely, at the young age of twenty-two, barely six months after arriving in India.[43] On the occasion of Tod's passing through Rasmy in 1820, he reminisces about his early years in Mewar from 1805, confirming that he had spent all his time in India since 1805 gleaning details on the history of the Rajputs and their Gujarati neighbours.[44]

Through Tod's journeys across Gujarat (between June 1822 and February 1823) in particular, he includes many details about his contacts with the British residents at various Gujarati cities. Not only did they offer Tod hospitality under their roofs, but they also shared with him their own antiquarian pursuits and concerns for local reforms. This knowledge-sharing with his British counterparts in Gujarat, just prior to his final departure from India in February 1823, seems to have heartened Tod considerably. For example, Colonel Lincoln Stanhope, the British Resident at Kheda (Kaira), south of Ahmedabad in 1822, turns out to have been a classmate of Tod's during their year of training at the Woolwich Military Academy in Kent, where they both attended the mathematics, geography and philosophy classes of John Bonnycastle (1750–1821).[45] This also informs us about Tod's intellectual formation prior to his departure for India. All his historical and antiquarian interests apparently dawned while he was in India, since he does not seem to have had any early training in history or architecture. Lincoln Stanhope was the brother of Leicester Stanhope, an official of the East India Company in Calcutta, known for his memoir on the press in India,[46] both being nephews of the illustrious Lady Hester Stanhope who lived and died on her own in Damascus, on the banks of the River Libanus.[47] Tod had had to abandon for health reasons his 'long-cherished plan' of returning to Europe overland, in the company of Lincoln Stanhope, together with his dreams of halting in Damascus and comparing the religion and architecture of the Hindu, the Egyptian and the Syrian, along the way.[48] Tod's friend Colonel Lincoln Stanhope had accomplished the feat of dislodging the Wagair pirates of Dwarka and the Badhail pirates of Bate Island in 1820, by a spectacular armed attack.[49] Although from Tod's text on Gujarat it is not clear whether he actually met Major Walker, Tod mentions him (as 'the benevolent Walker' and 'the philosophical Walker') in reference to his pacific measures to reclaim the piratical Waghairs of Dwarka and the equally piratical Badhails of Bate, prior to Stanhope's military attack on them in 1820.[50] Walker's peace treaties before 1820 with these piratical groups had not been effected at all. Tod refers later in his text to Walker's attempts to reform female infanticide among the Summa-Jharejas of Kutch, which probably took place while Walker was the British resident at Baroda between 1802 and 1813.[51] Walker, who wrote a memoir on this subject of female infanticide in Gujarat, is mentioned in Bishop Heber's travel narrative, as well as in Alexander Kinloch Forbes's late nineteenth-century account of the history of Gujarat.[52] The British Resident at Baroda in 1822 appears to have been James Williams, who used his influence to facilitate Tod's visit to Junagadh and to Mount Girnar (a place revered by the Jains), and who died around the same time as Tod (d.1835), while Tod's *Travels in Western India* was in the press.⁵³ At Pahlanpur (between Baroda and Junagadh), the British Resident in 1822 was Major William Miles, whose expertise on the Jain community is acknowledged by Tod, with a mention of Miles's memoir on the Jains published in the third volume of the *Transactions of the Royal Asiatic Society*.⁵⁴

Major Barnewell, the British Resident at Jamnagar (in the peninsula of Cutch) in 1822, cooperated with Tod and helped him to obtain historical details on the local dynasty of the Jaitwa Ranas of Goomli and Porbunder, known as the Pooncheria Ranas, or long-tailed Ranas.⁵⁵ This Major Barnewell had become Lieutenant-Colonel Barnewell by 1831–2, and was among the witnesses who gave testimony to the House of Commons Select Committee on East India Affairs, prior to the renewal of the East India Company's Charter in 1833.⁵⁶ Tod also makes a brief allusion to Barnewell's predecessor in Cutch, Captain MacMurdo, who held this office until his death in 1820. Tod refers in particular to MacMurdo's report on the earthquake that shook western India in 1819. MacMurdo also compiled his observations on the Cutch tribes, with which Tod seeks to differ, refuting MacMurdo's distinction between the Rajput mentality and the Cutchi mentality as being almost opposed, while Tod prefers to underline the similarities between these two peoples of Western India.⁵⁷ Tod's furthermost stop in the Cutch peninsula of Gujarat was at Bhuj, where he was assisted by Mr Gardiner, the British Resident there. Thanks to Gardiner's help, Tod was able to visit the necropolis of the Bhuj rulers and to gather information on these Jhareja Raos of Cutch.⁵⁸

Despite Tod leaving India at the relatively young age of forty-one, and despite his departure having been under the cloud of hierarchical difficulties with Calcutta, Tod seems to have remembered his contacts with the British residents in the course of his journeys in western India for the encouragement they afforded him in his own antiquarian pursuits, these apparently having been shared by several of his British counterparts in various local capitals. Far from being a unique example of a British colonial with a passion for history and information about Indian society and culture, Tod, through his exchanges with his British counterparts during his journeys, appears as one of many British explorers of knowledge about India's past and present.

In publications assembled after Tod's death in November 1835, we come across tributes to Tod's obsession for acquiring human knowledge, from several of his colleagues. For example, one of Tod's comrades from his young days in India, a Lieutenant-Colonel W. Nicholl, stated that Tod had great talents, an 'amiable disposition', and was 'beloved by all his brother-officers'.⁵⁹ The anonymous author of the biographical memoir on Tod at the beginning of his *Travels in Western India* praised Tod for his detailed study of the Rajputs and for his 'irrepressible' energy.[60]

Graeme Mercer (under whose orders Tod worked between 1805 and 1810) seems to have admired Tod considerably since he paid a tribute as a fellow Scot to Tod's perseverance and enthusiasm in the tasks he undertook.[61] Tod in turn acknowledges Graeme Mercer's encouragement of his own efforts as having 'stimulated my exertions with his approbation'.[62] A tribute from another friend of Tod concerns his modesty and wide vision.[63] Bishop Heber was astonished to discover, in 1825, two years after Tod had left India, feelings of concern and attachment for Tod among the people of Rajasthan.[64]

From these glowing expressions of admiration for Tod, we can conclude that he did in fact possess several scholarly qualities which were appreciated by many of his contemporaries, despite certain moments of human friction and unpleasantness during his active career. Also, contrary to certain accusations about Tod's arrogance and refusal to cooperate with his superiors, in the field, Tod seems to have enjoyed the warm friendship and wholehearted support of most of his colleagues.

## *Correspondence*

Another aspect of Tod's relations with his contemporaries can be observed in the letters he exchanged with colleagues while he was in India. These fall into three groups: (a) Tod's official correspondence on political and military matters, including Tod's disputes and differences with General Sir David Ochterlony; (b) Tod's field account book; (c) Tod's letters in Devnagiri script to Rana Bheem Singh of Mewar.

To begin with Tod's official correspondence on political and military matters, we can identify four themes for the purposes of our analysis of Tod's relationships with his contemporaries. These are (i) the disputed villages in the Mhairwarra region, between Mewar and Marwar (1819–23); (ii) the succession at Jaipur in 1819; (iii) Kota affairs from November 1819, when Maharao Umed Singh of Kotah died, till the battle of Mangrol in October 1821; (iv) East India Company appointments in Rajasthan between 1818 and 1822.

The Mhairs were a tribe of plunderers who lived in the Aravalli hills to the west of Udaipur. Since it was their place of dwelling, this hilly region was referred to as 'Mhairwarra' or region of the Mhairs. The Mhairs appear in Tod's letters from November 1820, when one of the Mhair chiefs, the khan of Athoon, attacked a British police post at Jhak (instigated by the corrupt Deewan of Mewar, Ajit Singh, according to Tod) and massacred several British and Indian persons there.[65]

However, Tod, in his report of November 1821, expresses a divergence in approaches between himself and the British Superintendent in Ajmer, Francis Wilder: Wilder wished to rivet together the interests of the Mhairs with the interests of the Mewar Thakurs, while Tod was convinced that it was preferable to sever all links and alliances between the Mhairs and the Mewar chiefs, in order to better consolidate the authority of the Rana of Mewar.[66] Also, Wilder wished to resettle the hill-dweller Mhairs in the plains to the west of Mewar, while Tod believed that the Mhairs' attachment to their mountainous locality would have to be respected.[67] In Swinton's letter to Ochterlony dated 10 May 1822 (after Tod had submitted his final resignation to the Calcutta government on 12 April 1822), Swinton formally denounces Tod's conduct on the Mhairwarra question as 'reprehensible', in particular because Tod had unilaterally attributed the disputed Mhairwarra villages to the Mewar chiefs who had occupied them, before any inquiry had been conducted, while Tod had also introduced numerous obstacles to the carrying out of the inquiry into who could legitimately claim possession of the disputed Mhairwarra villages. Swinton suggests that a speedy settlement of the question should be reached after the inquiry was completed by Wilder.[68] However, we learn that the inquiry was finally conducted by Captain Hall (of the Quarter Master General's division), who was then entrusted with the supervision of the new armed corps of Mhairs,[69] not without difficulties, since Hall reported to Ochterlony in 1823 (after Tod's final departure from Rajasthan in mid-1822) on increasing misrule and mismanagement in the Mhairwarra districts ceded to the British Government's control.

Tod's clear understanding of the stakes for the Mhairs, as well as his outright partisanship for Mewar interests, seem to have been misunderstood by his colleague Wilder (in Ajmer), by Ochterlony (in Delhi) as well as by the Calcutta government. The type of knowledge Tod had accumulated through his interactions with the authorities of Mewar and its wider region seems to have been perceived by his British colleagues in Rajasthan, Delhi and Calcutta as too subversively distant from what were perceived as the official British interests.

The 1819 succession to the Jaipur throne, after the death of the Kucchwa Raja Jagat Singh of Jaipur without any legal heir, constitutes another example where Tod's opinions, solicited by his superior Ochterlony, demonstrate his deep knowledge of the complicated questions of legal rights, personal ambitions and political stakes in Rajasthan. Following upon a request from Ochterlony to Tod, dated 8 April 1819, announcing that he had left Delhi for Jaipur, in order to deal with the Jaipur succession, and requesting Tod to convey the 'views of Mewar and of the Rajpoot states in general' on this question,

Tod replied to Ochterlony on 12 April 1819, laying out clearly the different claims to the Jaipur throne: (a) of the ruling prince of Gwalior in 1819, named Man Singh, who was a cousin of the deceased Jagat Singh of Jaipur, and who was favoured by the Vazir of Jaipur for the succession; (b) of the Jhalaye chief, who via the Nirwar branch of the Kucchwa family of Jaipur had acceded to the throne of Bikaner, and then to Jhalaye and to Parone, and stood next in right of succession to the Jaipur throne; (c) thirdly, the Bhattrani widow of the deceased Raja Jagat Singh of Jaipur, who was announced to be pregnant in 1819, and could give birth to a son who would be the ideal successor to the Jaipur throne, while she could alternatively give birth to a daughter who could not succeed to the Jaipur throne. However, in Ochterlony's letters to Tod on this subject, certain tensions appear indirectly. While Ochterlony had declared in his letter of 8 April 1819 to Tod that he esteemed and respected the Vazir of Jaipur, who supported Man Singh of Gwalior for the succession, but who would also certainly favour the adoption of an appropriate child, in case of the birth of a daughter to Jagat Singh's widow, Tod stated to Ochterlony on 12 April 1819 that he considered Man Singh of Gwalior to be unfit to occupy the throne of Jaipur, since he was little short of a fool and at the age of forty-five had no legitimate children.[70]

The question of the Jaipur succession in 1819 illustrates a difference of approach to Rajasthan matters on the part of Tod and of his superior Ochterlony.[71] Tod's comments always show a desire to understand the background and motivations of the Rajput leaders, while Ochterlony's remarks seem to proceed from a more superficial basis of hearsay and from public demonstrations to the native chiefs and to the Calcutta government of his concern for 'the lustre of the British Government's present brilliance' in India.

The very contentious issue of the Kota succession, after the death of Maharao Umed Singh of Kota in November 1819 with the problematic status of the Regent or Raj Rana Zalim Singh of Kota in Kota's politics, contributed to Tod's fall from grace in the eyes of the Calcutta government. The two sources that enable us to understand the complexities of the questions at stake in this matter are Tod's letters to Ochterlony and to the British Government in Calcutta,[72] and his reconstitution of the events in his 'Annals of Kotah' in his second volume on Rajasthan.[73] In a letter from Swinton, Secretary to the British Government in Calcutta, to Ochterlony, dated 31 October 1821, Swinton denounces Tod's inaction at Mangrol against Kishore Sing (the titular prince of Kota) in September 1821, accusing Tod of wasting time in 'protracting negotiation' and in 'fruitless persuasion', while Kishore Singh had invaded Kota with his own armed force, in outright violation of the

1818 British treaty with Kota. Thereupon followed two despatches from Tod to the British Government in Calcutta, dated 18 February 1822 and 12 April 1822. Tod's February 1822 despatch contains his reasons for his delay in commencing his attack on Kishore Singh's forces at Mangrol, which began only on 1 October 1821: in short, these reasons were the heavy monsoon rains and the rise of the Kali Sind River, which delayed the junction of the British forces from Neemuch and Nusseerabad with Tod's forces from Udaipur, on the one hand; and Tod's respect for Zalim Singh's long defence of Kota (from Maratha spoliation, for example) with his Pathan mercenaries, as opposed to Tod's disgust with Kishore Singh's show of ingratitude towards the British, on the other hand. In Tod's despatch of 12 April 1822 (he having returned to Udaipur on 8 March 1822, after his prolonged stay in Kota) he expresses disappointment at having caused 'repeated displeasure' to Government, and his sadness at being unable to 'yield satisfaction' to Government, requesting therefore he be relieved of his duties as agent for the western Rajput states. Four days after Tod's resignation letter of 12 April 1822, Swinton wrote to Ochterlony on 16 April 1822 about the circumstances leading to Tod's resignation, specifying that the Governor-General was 'happy to exonerate' Tod from any imputation of delay in commencing the Kota operations against Kishore Singh in September–October 1821, and reprimanding Ochterlony for the brashness of his announcement to Tod in Udaipur in early 1822 of the Residency of Malwa and Rajputana having been vested entirely, as of October 1821, in Ochterlony's hands, thus impairing Tod's authority at Udaipur. In this letter to Ochterlony of 16 April 1822, Swinton also stated the British Government's suspicions of Tod having withheld from Government's notice his own correspondence with various indigenous agents concerning the Kota intrigues of 1821, declaring finally that the Governor-General's agent in Delhi, named Ross, had been instructed to conduct an inquiry into these 1821 Kota intrigues.

Three earlier letters from Ochterlony reveal certain differences with Tod about the British administration in Rajputana.[74]

There is an ellipsis about the events of August–September 1821 in Kota in Tod's 'Personal Narrative' of his travels in his *Annals*.[75] He devotes twenty-five pages, however, to these succession affairs of Kota in his 'Annals of Kotah' in his second volume,[76] first published in 1832, some eleven years after the 1821 Kota events, allowing Tod time to re-evaluate what had actually happened on the ground. It is interesting to note that in this later version, Tod suggests that the supplementary articles to the initial treaty of 26 December 1817 between Kota and the British Government,[77] signed separately some months after this initial treaty, between Zalim Singh and Tod in March 1818, maintaining the executive authority of Kota in the hands of the Raj Rana (Zalim Singh) on a hereditary basis, had probably been provoked by Zalim Singh's younger son Govurdhan Dass.[78] Then, Tod reports his own complex negotiations in September 1821, with the titular prince of Kota (Kishor Singh) on the one hand, and with the Regent (Zalim Singh) on the other hand, necessitating two pageants of sovereignty, one *de facto*, and the other *de jure*.[79] Tod confesses that since all his efforts to reason with Kishor Singh 'proved ineffectual and hopeless', and because Kishor Singh persisted in his demand for 'death or the full sovereignty of his ancestors', Tod was reduced to the ambivalent measure of merging his Udaipur-British troops with the mercenary army of the Regent of Kota, Raj Rana Zalim Singh, against the official Kota forces of Maharao Kishor Singh.[80]

Tod goes on to expose 'the role of the wily Regent', whose aim was 'to have all the benefit which the alliance compelled us to afford, with none of the obloquy it entailed', summing up the outcome of the dilemma as a triumph of the Regent's 'love of dominion' over 'every scruple'.[81] Tod even pays homage to the loyalty of the Kota troops of the Hara Rajput tribe in supporting their legitimate sovereign Kishor Singh of Kota, claiming that he personally 'tempered punishment with clemency' in dealing with these rebellious/loyal Hara troops.[82]

Tod expedites in a note the dismissal of the two native advisers who had contributed to the conflict. These were 'the native treasurer in Delhi', Soogun Chund, who worked under the orders of Ochterlony, and 'the chief *moonshi* of the Persian secretary's office at the seat of government', that is Mirza Mohammed Khan, who was based in Calcutta but had been active in Delhi through this crisis.[83] Ochterlony had, for his part, tried to cast blame on Tod's native delegate in Kota, Chund Khan, whom the Calcutta government authorised Ochterlony to deal with as he 'may deem most fit', after Tod's departure from Rajputana.[84] In this opposition over blame due to their respective native advisers, an antagonism between Ochterlony and Tod is also obvious.

Tod concludes his account of the Kota conflict of October 1821 in his 'Annals of Kotah' with a passing mention that the Rana of Udaipur was concerned for a peaceful settlement of the Kota hostilities, since he himself had as one of his wives a sister of Maharao Kishor Singh of Kota, and then describes his own role as 'Agent' in restoring Kishor Singh to the throne of Kota, in order 'to strengthen the good understanding now introduced'.[85]

Tod deliberately adopts a literary register in his assessment of the person of Raj Rana Zalim Singh of Kota (1739–1826, who died at the age of eighty-seven, three years after Tod's departure from India).[86] As a preamble to the complexity of the role of this court adviser to the monarch of Kota, who in fact wielded the real political power from behind the Kota throne, Tod refers to the image of the biblical David as a victim of usurpation, and then to the instance of the Frank *maire du palais*, Pépin, who founded the new Carolingian dynasty in the wake of the stagnant Merovingian dynasty in France in 751 CE, acceding to the title of power.[87]

Tod also uses the term 'Nestor of Rajwarra' while justifying his own indulgence towards the *de facto* ruler of Kota in the December 1817 treaty, and again in the March 1818 supplementary articles between the British Government and Kota, while also acknowledging that this indulgence was undoubtedly the road to future conflicts within Kota.[88]

That this paragraph has a self-justificatory intention on Tod's part is evident in the fact that Nestor in the Trojan War, mentioned in the *Odyssey*, was known for his circumspect advice to the Greek kings and for his mediations towards restoring harmony in the Greek camp, thanks to his insider's knowledge. Tod's sympathy towards Raj Rana Zalim Singh of Kota appears again when Tod compares Zalim Singh to the biblical figure of Job, known for his loyalty to God through the most trying experiences, a model of the upright believer even in the face of extreme suffering.[89]

That Raj Rana Zalim Singh revealed the secret of his political genius to nobody is expressed by Tod through a comparison with Machiavelli (1469–1527), the cunning royal adviser of the Italian Renaissance.[90]

Tod goes further in his parallels to illustrate for his European readers the basic goodness of Raj Rana Zalim Singh's political astuteness, by imagining Zalim Singh's possible (but unrealised) abdication, and hypothetically comparing it with the abdications of Diocletian and of Charles V. On the one hand, the Roman emperor Diocletian (245–315 CE, r.284–305 CE, when he abdicated, ten years before his death), maintained the unity of the Roman Empire, despite its division into the empire of the Orient and the empire of the Occident, thus sharing the purple imperial cloak with another until his voluntary exit from power, and on the other hand, the European emperor Charles V (or Charles Quint, 1500–58, r.1519–56), abdicated in favour of his son (Philip II of Spain, r.1556–98) and his brother (Ferdinand, Emperor of Germany, r.1556–64), two years before his own death, after a long and eventful reign.[91]

The historico-literary comparisons Tod deploys to depict the character and political career of Raj Rana Zalim Singh of Kota contribute to explain the compromising consequences for Tod himself of his unhesitating support to Zalim Singh throughout his years as the political agent for the western Rajput states, since Tod's loyalty to Zalim Singh ended by provoking criticism and loss of trust in his own usefulness among Tod's hierarchical British superiors.

To complete this section on Tod's official correspondence on political and military matters, I will review the East India Company appointments in Rajasthan between 1818 and 1822. First, concerning Tod himself, after his initial appointment by the Calcutta government as the British political agent in the western Rajput states, based in Udaipur, in February 1818, we learn that while Tod was confirmed in his office of political agent with the western Rajput States in February 1819, the charge of Jodhpur was added to Tod's charges of Udaipur, Kota and Bundi, and that Francis Wilder was appointed as superintendent of Ajmer under Tod's orders.[92] A few months later, in August 1819, Tod was notified that Jodhpur had been reverted to Ochterlony's charge on account of a desire expressed by the Raja of Jodhpur.[93]

Francis Wilder, after being appointed as Superintendent of Ajmer in February 1819, was put in charge of Kishengurh, Jodhpur and Jaisalmer, in addition to his charge over Ajmer, on 11 April 1822, at the time of Tod's resignation.[94] In Jaipur, Captain Stewart was appointed to make a report on the Jaipur finances in May 1821, whereas when Bishop Heber visited Jaipur in January 1825, the British Resident in Jaipur was Colonel Raper.[95] Captain Cobbe replaced Tod in Udaipur, taking over as political agent in the western Rajputana states in September 1822. Cobbe was assisted by Captain Ferguson, who replaced Tod's assistant in Udaipur, Captain Patrick Waugh, (who died seven years later, in 1829, in Shahpura, Rajasthan, northeast of Bhilwara,)[96] right from June 1822, three months before Cobbe's arrival in Udaipur.[97] Captain Caulfield was appointed in June 1822 as the British Resident in Kota after the Battle of Mangrol of October 1821 and after Tod's resignation in April 1822.[98] Ochterlony continued in Delhi as the Resident for Malwa and Rajputana from October 1821 until his death on 13 July 1825, barely two years after Tod's final departure from India.[99]

This brief summary of the various East India Company appointments in Rajputana between 1818 and 1822 illustrates the overlapping issues and decisions taken by the British authorities in Delhi and in Calcutta, making clear the difficulties and differences of opinion encountered by all the persons in the field during this period. It shows also Tod's single-minded pursuit of what he considered to be the best interests of those Indian dignitaries he respected (Rana Bheem Singh of Mewar and the Raj Rana Zalim Singh of Kota), without losing sight of his instructions as a representative of the British Government, and despite disapproval and obstacles from his hierarchical superiors.

The next document that gives us a glimpse of Tod in the field in Rajasthan is the manuscript account book kept by Tod from November

1819 till April 1822 (or at least that is the portion of it that is available today).[100] This period of thirty months corresponds to the latter part of Tod's stay in Udaipur as the British political agent for the western Rajput states (from February 1818 till May 1822). Tod's accounts cover folios 1 to 105, and folios 105 to 108 contain the charges for May 1822, signed by Captain Patrick J. Waugh, assistant political agent in Udaipur, confirming the fact that Tod did indeed depart from Udaipur in May 1822.

The manner in which these accounts are presented on the pages conveys useful information. They are entitled 'Monthly Accounts current with the Political Agent, western Rajpoot States', and are addressed to the 'Civil Auditor' or to the 'Accountant General' of the British Government in Calcutta, with 'accompanying bills' and 'vouchers sent in accompaniment'. The accounts are separated under two headings: on the one hand 'Amount of Bills Granted' or the money authorised for expenditure in Udaipur, by the Calcutta government, and on the other hand 'Amount of Bills Drawn', which shows under what headings the money was actually spent. The bills drawn were most often on account of: Charges General, Durbar Charges, Contingent Charges and Extra Charges.[101] In order for Tod to get access to this money, the bills for expenditure had to be drawn on the various British Treasuries in north India: either on the General Treasury (based in Calcutta), via the Presidency Pay Master, or via the Collector of Benares, or via the Collector of Cawnpore (Kanpur) or via the Deputy Pay Master at Muttra (Mathura); alternatively the bills for expenditure could be drawn on the Agra Treasury via the Collector of Agra, or again on the Farrukhabad Treasury via the Collector of Farrukhabad.[102]

The currencies used were Sonal rupees, Sicca rupees, Udaipur rupees, Kota Rupees[103] or even 'Hoondian' or bills of exchange encashed against a charge of 29¼ per cent paid to the local Indian agent of exchange.[104] This illustrates the fact that different currencies were in circulation and that their value fluctuated according to market conditions, for example Sicca rupees could yield a higher exchange in Udaipur rupees at a given time, and perhaps a slightly lower exchange in Udaipur rupees at a later time.

The headings of Tod's field expenses are particularly revealing. For example, the persons to whom he made regular payments were the British surgeon attached to his political agency, Dr J. Duncan, his assistant, Captain Patrick J. Waugh, and various Indian agents, such as Devychand Sait, Narain Dass, Jugannath Doss, Hurpershaud Bannerjee and the nine members of what Tod calls his 'office establishment',[105] being made up of Indian clerks and scribes. Exceptional payments were made to Indian dignitaries like Sewai Singh and Bheebut

Singh.[106] Tod also inscribes the functions of several Indian persons to whom he made payments: a Gomastah (or agent of a mercantile firm) attached to the Commissariat (or department charged with furnishing provisions); servants of the Thakoors (or local chiefs) in Rajputana; Moonshees (clerks or scribes); Hircars (messengers or carriers); Dufter(i)s (or office clerks who were experts in the Persian or the Hinduee languages); Jemadars (guards or head soldiers); Mootsuddies (scribes or accountants). This shows us Tod in interaction with a host of varied persons for different reasons, all of them requiring payment for the services they rendered.

Relatively large amounts are inscribed as having been paid to Indian agents (for services not elucidated): Narain Dass received 2,000 Sonal rupees in November 1820, and Hurpershaud Bannerjee received 1,000 Sonal rupees in the same month.[107] Narain Doss and Herpershaud Bannerjee were perhaps commercial agents, which would explain the big difference in the amounts paid to them, as compared to the monthly salaries paid to Indian messenger-carriers and to Tod's Indian office staff.

In all, these 105 folios of Tod's field accounts reveal him dealing with various British and Indian subordinates, maintaining official relations with a series of local chiefs, dignitaries and princes, and obtaining supplies, means of transport and all the articles necessary for the job he was appointed to do. They also show him as part of a British bureaucracy that already stretched across most of India by the 1820s, with collectors, treasuries, local exchange agents and very punctilious officials like the 'Civil Auditor' and the 'Accountant General' who required justificatory evidence (bills and vouchers) for expenses declared.

A set of thirteen letters from Tod to Rana Bheem Singh of Mewar, running from March 1820 to November 1822 (roughly two and a half years, corresponding to the latter part of Tod's stay in Rajasthan and Gujarat) were transcribed in Devanagari script and published in *Anusheelan*, the research journal of the Maharana Mewar Research Institute, in January 1989.[108] Tod's letters in the local Urdu-Marwari language were prepared for publication from their manuscript form by Shree Laxmisinha Purohit.[109] Of these thirteen letters, two are signed by Captain Patrick Waugh (written 'Waak' in the Devanagari script), both date from 25 July 1822, after Tod's departure from Mewar in May 1822, and they concern the crown prince of Mewar, Kunwar Juwan Singh, son of Rana Bheem Singh of Mewar, who had been sent to Benares on a pilgrimage, which Waugh apparently considered pointless, urging his early recall to Udaipur. The remaining eleven letters are not presented in a strictly chronological manner in the

*Anusheelan* research journal, so we have opted to study them in a chronological manner, for easier comprehension of the evolution of Tod's views expressed in them over his stay in Udaipur. Three points occur through these letters: (a) four of the eleven letters deal with political matters of collection of dues, the cost of maintaining an armed force in a particular region or the grounds on which fines could be imposed on offenders; (b) three of the eleven letters concern the approaching marriage of Kunwar Juwan Singh of Mewar, arranged for the early months of 1822, though the provenance of the bride is not mentioned; (c) four of the eleven letters touch on personal matters between Tod and Rana Bheem Singh of Mewar, for example Bheem Singh's liking for pomegranates, Bheem Singh's difficulties in saving money in the course of his expenditures or Tod's preparation of a military camp with full comforts for the benefit of Bheem Singh of Mewar. All eleven letters from Tod to Bheem Singh are written from field positions, in the course of Tod's peregrinations through Rajasthan, while he was away from his base at Udaipur.

The final letter from Tod to Bheem Singh (number thirteen of thirteen) from the Dwarka Shankhodwar (at the extreme western end of the Saurashtra peninsula in Gujarat), is dated around November 1822 (or the fourth day of the Hindu month of Paush in the year 1879 of the Vikram era). In this final letter, Tod announces to Bheem Singh his forthcoming boat trip from Dwarka to Mandvi and Bhuj (in the Kutch peninsula). Tod informsCed Bheem Singh that within ten days he was to reach the Bombay coast for final embarkation for England. Tod encloses objects of personal attachment for Bheem Singh. He movingly expresses his concern for the welfare of his two beloved horses (Jawadia, to be presented to the younger Shree Deewanji or minister of Mewar, and Hargaz, to be given to any fit person as a remembrance of Tod). In an ultimate sentence of emotion, Tod requests Bheem Singh to accord due consideration to his (Tod's) memory in Udaipur, since his entire life was left suspended in the middle of Udaipur. This is the only document which unveils Tod's deep personal disturbance at leaving Udaipur in 1822–23.

The significance of these thirteen letters from Tod in the local language (a mixture of Hindustani, Urdu and Marwari) is immense. Not only do they show us Tod at ease in the local language, but we can also observe in them Tod actively involved in the internal, family and personal affairs of the Rana of Mewar, despite all the Rana's reported weaknesses. Here the official Tod, in relentless negotiation with the British authorities in Neemuch, Delhi and Calcutta, is in abeyance, leaving space for the more humane and personally involved Tod to express himself.

## Conclusion

Various facets of Tod's personality and action in India emerge in this attempt to construct a picture of him through archival sources on his life, in his mentions of his friends and colleagues in his two major published texts and in different letters and written documents by Tod himself and by his official associates while he was in India. The Scottish link, through members of his family and through friends and acquaintances encountered during his career in India, situates Tod among the Scottish contingent of the British administration in India. His firm views on Rajput affairs despite official disapproval from his hierarchical superiors show the degree of Tod's commitment to defending what he had understood to be the interests of his Rajput friends, even at the cost of considerable mental tension, health problems and professional risks. His field account book and camp letters in the local dialect of Urdu to his Indian patron, Rana Bheem Singh of Mewar, allow us to glimpse Tod amidst the myriad transactions and human relationships he had to maintain while he was in India. We are left, then, with an impression of a tormented but courageous Tod, who followed his personal convictions through to their ultimate conclusion.

## Notes

1 Tod's Baptism Certificate, IOR/L/MIL/9/07 #155. At the end of his 'Personal Narrative' in vol. II of *Annals*, Tod remarks on the significance of the month of March in his life: 'By a singular coincidence, the day on which I closed these wanderings, is the same on which I have put the last stroke to a work that has afforded me some pleasure and much pain. It was on the 8th March 1822 I ended my journey and entered Oodipoor; on the 8th March 1832 I am transcribing this last page of my journal: in March my book appears before the public; I was born in March; embarked for India in March; and had the last glimpse of its land, the coast of Ceylon, in March. But what changes has not the ever-revolving wheel produced since that time!'

2 See IOR/L/MIL/9/255/folio 144 v., List of the Cadets for the Year 1798; and IOR/L/MIL/9/255/149 #35, Certificate of the Age of the Cadets, Season 1798. According to Anthony Farrington, *Guide to the Records of the India Office Military Department*, London: India Office Library, 1981, p. 132, the procedure of nomination of officer cadets to the East India Company's armies was by the patronage of members of the East India Company Court of Directors and Board of Control in London. The nomination was followed by an application by the concerned candidate, and final approval (in Tod's time) until 1809 was by the East India Company's Committee of Correspondence, for a training appointment at the Royal Military Academy, Woolwich. After 1809, the Company established its own Military Seminary at Addiscombe, near Croydon. In fact, only the artillery and engineering recruits were afforded a technical training in England before their departure for India. The other trainee officer cadets obtained their training in the field, directly with their regiments in India. Tod was apparently an engineering trainee at the Royal Military Academy, Woolwich. (See Jason Freitag, *Serving Empire, Serving Nation: James Tod and the Rajputs of Rajasthan*, Leiden: Brill Publishers, 2009, p. 35, n.10.)

3 See 'Memoir of the Author' in: James Tod, *Travels in Western India*, London: W.H. Allen & Co., 1839 (posth.) pp. xvii–xviii; repr. Delhi: Munshiram Manoharlal Publishers, 1997.
4 See BL MSS. Add. 38226, folio 18, Petition dated 21 December 1790, addressed to the Earl of Hawkesbury and the Lord Treasurers of the Pitt Government, in order to obtain trading privileges for Borrowstonness on the Clyde, as a port for foreign trade, under the new Corn Law. Among the signatories is a 'James Tod', probably James Tod Junior's father, James Tod Senior, since the Tod family were natives of Bo'ness and were involved in trade.
5 See 'Introduction', in: William Crooke (ed.), *Annals and Antiquities of Rajasthan or the Central and Western Rajput States of India, by James Tod*, London: Oxford University Press, 1920, 3 vols, vol. I, pp. xxv–xlv, at p. xxv.
6 See 'Memoir of the Author' in: Tod, *Travels*, pp. xvii–xviii.
7 See 'Introduction', in: Crooke (ed.), *Annals*, vol. I, p. xxv.
8 PRO/30/11/27, folios 258–59, being part of Packet No. 27, 'East India Papers of November and December 1788'.
9 James Tod, *Annals and Antiquities of Rajasthan*, vol. I, London: Routledge & Kegan Paul Ltd, 1829; repr. Delhi: Rupa & Co., 1997; James Tod, *Annals and Antiquities of Rajasthan*, vol. II, London: Routledge & Kegan Paul Ltd, 1832; repr. Delhi: Rupa & Co., 1997; and Tod, *Travels*.
10 Tod, *Annals*, vol. I, p. 599, n.1. This encounter between Tod and de Boigne in Chambéry probably took place in 1826, since the note ends with a quote from de Boigne's *Memoirs*, published by his son in 1829, and this note begins 'Three years ago, I passed ...'.
11 Tod, *Annals*, vol. I, p. 366, n.1. Also Tod, *Travels*, p. xxii.
12 Tod, *Annals*, vol. II, pp. 561–2.
13 Tod's unpublished 'Memorandum on the Pindari War', quoted in *Travels*, p. xxxii.
14 Tod, *Annals*, vol. II, p. 561, n.2.
15 Tod, *Travels*, p. lviii; also *Asiatic Journal*, 16 (1835), 262–70, and Tod, *Annals*, vol. I, p. 531.
16 Tod, *Annals*, vol. I, pp. 521, 526.
17 Tod, *Annals*, vol. I, p. 536.
18 Tod, *Annals*, vol. I, p. 619.
19 Tod, *Annals*, vol. II, p. 497.
20 Tod, *Annals*, vol. II, p. 548.
21 Tod, *Annals*, vol. II, p. 593.
22 See 'Memoir of the Author', Tod, *Travels*, p. xlvi.
23 Tod, *Annals*, vol. I, p. 615; vol. II, p. 612; Tod, *Travels*, p. 445; *Journal Asiatique*, first series, 11 (January–June 1827), p. 288, n.1; *Annsheelan*, the research journal of Maharana Mewar Research Institute, 1.1 (January 1989), Letter no. 13, dated the end of 1822: 'My horse Javadia should go to the younger Shree Deevanjee. Let Hargaz be given to nobody inappropriate, my mind is very keen about this. Please keep an eye on to whom this horse Hargaz is given so that that person may remember me – someone who appears to you fit to ride Hargaz, and don't allow anyone else to mount Hargaz. If Shreeji would be so kind as to meet Shree Deevanjee, then let him take Javadia my horse, and please make sure that Javadia is kept with the utmost care and affection' (translation from the Devnagiri is mine).
24 Tod,*Travels*, p. xxxvii.
25 Reginald Heber, *Narrative of a Journey through the Upper Provinces of India, from Calcutta to Bombay, 1824–1825, with notes upon Ceylon*, London: John Murray, 1828, 3 vols, repr. New Delhi: Asian Educational Services, 1995, 3 vols, vol. II, p. 456: 'He was on terms of close friendship with Zalim Singh of Kotah, and has left a name there, as honourable as in Oodeypoor. His misfortune was that, in consequence of his favouring the native princes so much, the Government of Calcutta were led to suspect him of corruption, and consequently to narrow his powers and associate other officers with him in his trust, till he was disgusted and resigned his place. They are now, I believe, well satisfied that their suspicions were groundless.'

26 Tod, *Annals*, vol. II, p. 116.
27 Tod, *Annals*, vol. I, p. 556, n.1.
28 Tod, *Annals*, vol. I, pp. 519–621.
29 Tod, *Annals*, vol. I, p. 609.
30 Tod, *Annals*, vol. I, p. 376.
31 Tod, *Annals*, vol. I, p. 520.
32 Tod, *Travels*, p. xxii.
33 Tod, *Annals*, vol. II, p. 497.
34 Tod, *Annals*, vol. II, p. 541.
35 Tod, *Annals*, vol. II, p. 544, n.1.
36 Tod, *Annals*, vol. II, pp. 534, 552, 591.
37 Tod, *Annals*, vol. II, pp. 537, 544, 547, 551 and 611–13.
38 Tod, *Annals*, vol. II, pp. 551, 611.
39 Tod, *Travels*, p. xlvii.
40 Tod, *Annals*, vol. I, p. 599, n.1.
41 Tod, *Travels*, p. lv.
42 Tod, *Annals*, vol. I, p. 602; vol. II, p. 233.
43 Tod, *Annals*, vol. I, p. 538, n.2.
44 Tod, *Annals*, vol. II, p. 549.
45 Tod, *Travels*, p. 241.
46 Leicester Stanhope, *Sketch of the history and influence of the press in British India*, London: C. Chapple, 1823.
47 Tod, *Travels*, p. 242.
48 Tod, *Travels*, p. 242.
49 Tod, *Travels*, pp. 428, 440.
50 Tod, *Travels*, p. 440.
51 Tod, *Travels*, p. 475.
52 Colonel Alexander Walker, 'Suggestions for effecting the abolition of the practice of Female Infanticide', 28 June 1819, IOR/H/521, folios 637–47. Heber, *Narrative of a Journey*, vol. II, pp. 518–19, in connection with Walker's efforts to reduce female infanticide in Gujarat between 1802 and 1813 when he was British Resident in Baroda. A.K. Forbes, *Raas Mala*, London, 1856, repr. London: Oxford University Press, 1924, 2 vols, makes mention of Colonel Walker's reports on the history of the Baroda region of 1804, 1806, vol. I, p. 343; vol. II, pp. 50, 73, 300, and mention of Walker's entry into his functions as Resident in Baroda in June 1802, vol. II, p. 43.
53 Tod, *Travels*, pp. 244, 363, 376, 444.
54 Lt Col William Miles, 'On the Jains of Gujerat and Marwar'. *Transactions of the Royal Asiatic Society*, London, 3 (1835), 335–71. See also, Tod, *Travels*, pp. 140, 302.
55 Tod, *Travels*, p. 408.
56 *Minutes of Evidence taken before the Select Committee on the affairs of the East India Company*, London: J.L. Cox & Sons, 1833.
57 Tod, *Travels*, p. 316.
58 Tod, *Travels*, pp. 448, 458, 459.
59 Tod, *Travels*, p. xviii.
60 Tod, *Travels*, p. xxxiii.
61 Tod, *Travels*, p. xix.
62 Tod, *Annals*, vol. I, p. 3, n.2.
63 Tod, *Travels*, p. xxxv, n.*.
64 Heber, *Narrative of a Journey*, vol. II, p. 456.
65 IOR MSS EUR E/293/47, 22 folios, Being a letter-report from Tod to George Swinton, Secretary to the British Government in Calcutta, dated 25 November 1821, on the Mhairs and Mhairwarra. See Appendix III.
66 IOR MSS Eur E/293/47, paragraph 59 of 71 paragraphs.
67 IOR MSS Eur E/293/47, paragraph 66 of 71 paragraphs.
68 N.K. Sinha and A.K. Dasgupta (eds), *Selections from Ochterlony Papers, 1818–1825*, Calcutta: University of Calcutta, 1964, Letter no. 119A, p. 237.

69 Sinha and Dasgupta (eds), *Ochterlony Papers*, Letter no. 165, pp. 319–21. Also, Board's Collections, IOR MSS F/4/810/21725, folio 17, from Bengal Government to Resident of Malwa and Rajputana, dated 12 September 1823.
70 IOR/Home Miscellaneous/738: Document No. 32, folios 823–6, Ochterlony to Tod, dated 8 April 1819; Document No. 12, folios 685–706, Tod to Ochterlony, dated 12 April 1819; Document No. 13, folios 709–11, Ochterlony to Tod, dated 18 April 1819.
71 Heber, *Narrative of a Journey*, vol. II, p. 412, mentions that a month before his own passage through Jaipur, in January 1825, that is, in December 1824, another Jaipur palace revolution had been tolerably settled. The British Resident in Jaipur in 1824–5, Colonel Raper, had sided with the Jaipur Minister or Dewan, an honourable Rawul of Rajput stock, against the queen mother of Jaipur (one of the widows of the deceased Jagat Singh of Jaipur, who had given birth to a son after the death of Jagat Singh in early 1819) supported by Jaipur's troops. However, Sir David Ochterlony, in December 1824, despite military support from British troops in Mhow, and from the aged Pathan Ameer Singh based in Neemuch: 'probably in consequence of directions from Calcutta, thought it best to give up all the points in dispute, rather than run the risk of a new war in Western and Central India. …The chance now is, that the British will be called on to mediate between the parties; but before this takes place, some further mischief may be looked for.'
72 Sinha and Dasgupta (eds), *Ochterlony Papers*.
73 Tod, *Annals*, vol. II, pp. 451–76.
74 Sinha and Dasgupta (eds), *Ochterlony Papers*, Letter no. 29, dated 18 November 1818, Ochterlony to Tod, pp. 55–6; Letter no. 80, dated 12 December 1820, Octherlony to Prinsep, pp. 141–2; Letter no. 112, dated 20 January 1822, Ochterlony to Swinton, pp. 207–8.
75 Tod, *Annals*, vol. II, pp. 563–81, especially Chapter XI and Chapter XII of Tod's 'Personal Narrative' in vol. II.
76 Tod, *Annals*, vol. II, pp. 448–76, i.e. Chapter X and Chapter XI of 'Annals of Kotah'.
77 Tod, *Annals*, vol. II, p. 451.
78 Tod, *Annals*, vol. II, p. 456, n.1.
79 Tod, *Annals*, vol. II, p. 462.
80 Tod, *Annals*, vol. II, p. 464.
81 Tod, *Annals*, vol. II, p. 465.
82 Tod, *Annals*, vol. II, pp. 468–9.
83 Tod, *Annals*, vol. II, p. 468, n.3.
84 Sinha and Dasgupta (eds), *Ochterlony Papers*, Letter no. 120A, dated 17 May 1822, Swinton to Ochterlony, p. 239.
85 Tod, *Annals*, vol. II, pp. 470–1.
86 Tod, *Annals*, vol. II, pp. 454–5, 472–6.
87 Tod, *Annals*, vol. II, p. 454.
88 Tod, *Annals*, vol. II, p. 455.
89 Tod, *Annals*, vol. II, p. 472. See Job 31.
90 Tod, *Annals*, vol. II, p. 472.
91 Tod, *Annals*, vol. II, p. 476.
92 Sinha and Dasgupta (eds), *Ochterlony Papers*, Letter no. 33, dated 6 February 1819, Metcalfe to Tod, pp. 62–3.
93 Sinha and Dasgupta (eds), *Ochterlony Papers*, Letter no. 43, dated 7 August 1819, Metcalfe to Tod, p. 86.
94 Sinha and Dasgupta (eds), *Ochterlony Papers*, Letter no. 115A, dated 11 April 1822, Swinton to Wilder, pp. 214–15.
95 Heber, *Narrative of a Journey*, vol. II, p. 412.
96 Tod, *Annals*, vol. II, p. 613.
97 Sinha and Dasgupta (eds), *Ochterlony Papers*, Letter no. 128, dated 7 June 1822, Swinton to Ochterlony, p. 253.
98 Sinha and Dasgupta (eds), *Ochterlony Papers*, Letter no. 127, dated 31 May 1822, Swinton to Ochterlony, p. 252–3.

99 Sinha and Dasgupta (eds), *Ochterlony Papers*, Letter no. 237, dated 15 July 1825, Captain Gerard to Swinton, p. 432.
100 Tod's Account Book covers folios 1–105 in a folio-sized fascicule containing 158 folios, found in Udaipur, and of which a photocopy is held at the library of the Royal Asiatic Society, London. I am grateful to Kathy Lazenbatt, librarian of the Royal Asiatic Society, London, for having made this document available to me.
101 Tod, Account Book, folio 18.
102 Tod, Account Book, folios 27–30.
103 Tod, Account Book, folio 19.
104 Tod, Account Book, folios 12, 15.
105 Tod, Account Book, folio 15.
106 Tod, Account Book, folio 13.
107 Tod, Account Book, folio 4, 6.
108 See Appendix I.
109 Laxmisinha Purohit, 'Maharana Bheemsingh jee kay naam, Mewar Mitra James Tod kay Mewari Patra' (Mewar Letters addressed to Maharana Bheemsinghjee by his friend James Tod), in: Purushottam Lal Menaria (ed.), *Anusheelan*, the research journal of the Maharana Mewar Research Institute, 1.1 (January 1989), 46–51. This set of letters was very kindly made available to me by Kathy Lazenbatt. the Royal Asiatic Society librarian, in the summer of 2008.

CHAPTER SEVEN

# Tod among his contemporaries in London, 1823–35

After his departure from India in February 1823, Tod returned to London and became the librarian of the recently founded Royal Asiatic Society from April 1825.[1] His travels through Gujarat (from May 1822 to February 1823) had been his way of putting some distance between himself and the unpleasant circumstances of the termination of his services with the East India Company at his own request in April 1822, since his immediate hierarchical superiors as well as the East India Company authorities in Calcutta had apparently considered his close relationships with the Rajput princes under his jurisdiction as going against the interests of the British Government in India. In London therefore, Tod tried to turn the page on his abrupt separation from India, by turning to advantage his knowledge of the dialects of northwest India, as well as his personal collection of historical artefacts, texts and inscriptions, assembled through the twenty-two years he had spent in India (1800–22). His declared aim was henceforth to bring the history, the manners and character of the Rajputs to the knowledge of the public in Britain and Europe.[2]

With this awareness of his own pioneering role in making known details of western India in Britain, Tod published his two major works (*Annals and Antiquities of Rajasthan*, in two volumes, and the account of his travels through Gujarat under the title *Travels in Western India*). In addition, with the same goal of diffusing information on the Rajputs, he read and published twelve short compilations in learned circles in London and Paris, between May 1824 and his death in November 1835 (one of these twelve publications appeared posthumously in 1838).[3] These twelve articles fall roughly into three categories: (a) the presentation of inscriptions, medallions, sculptures and artefacts, accompanied by Tod's reflections on the possible migrations of Central Asian peoples from ancient times; (b) Tod's anthropological comments on the

**9** Five initial seals of the Royal Asiatic Society in 1823, from the uncatalogued RAS collections.
(By kind permission of the Royal Asiatic Society of Great Britain and Ireland)

traditional practices, social institutions, manners and festivals of the Rajputs; (c) historical chronicles of the Rajputs in English translation.

In order to study Tod's manner of providing examples of his field observations on the Rajputs in London and Europe, I will proceed in two steps: first, Tod's packaging of his locally gathered information with learned references and an apparatus of erudition (illustrations, tables, explanatory notes); then, Tod's attention to language in his respect for the rhetoric and imagery of the Rajput texts he translated.

## *Tod's packaging of his information gathered locally in India for learned London and European audiences*

To begin with Tod's recourse to learned references, illustrations and explanations, these seem to be chosen in order to envelop his compilations with seriousness, even when these erudite additions appear digressive and superfluous. The first paper that Tod read before the Royal Asiatic Society in London on 1 May 1824, published in 1827,[4] contained his translation of a Sanskrit inscription from Hansi-Hissar (to the northwest of Delhi) and concerned the victory in 1168 CE, over adversaries belonging to the Doda race (traced by Tod to Kasondi situated west of Ajmer), of Prithviraj Chauhan, the last Hindu emperor of Delhi, through two of his faithful Rajput vassals, Kilhana Gelhote (Prithvi Raj's own maternal uncle) and the valiant Hammir Hara. Among the erudite details furnished by Tod in this article, we can note his mention of the Agnicula race, produced from the element of Fire, as being among India's most ancient races of the Sun (Suryavansha) and the Moon (Chandravansha). Tod further gives the four best-known branches of the Agnicula (or fire-engendered) race: Chauhan (to which Prithvi Raj Chauhan belonged); Solanki (who ruled in Saurashtra); Pramara (who ruled in central India around Dhar); and Purihara (who ruled in Allahabad-Kanauj and then moved to Jodhpur in Marwar in the early thirteenth century, as a result of Muslim invasions in the valley of the Ganga River). Further, in a note within Tod's article signed by Henry Thomas Colebrooke, Sanskritist and first President of the Royal Asiatic Society (1823–37), we have various spellings of Prithiraj and of Chauhan, as well as of his capital Delhi,[5] showing the 'uncertainty in the proper orthography of names'. Then, with a series of references to European scholars like de Guignes, Gibbon and Cosmas, together with a mention of Chinese and Greek histories, Tod alludes to invasions of India by an Indo-Scythian or Tartar tribe called 'Yuechi' or 'Assaceni' between 200 BCE and 150 BCE, and again in 550 CE. This is to demonstrate that the Chauhans of North India had long been accustomed to external invasions. With a considerable mastery of archaeological knowledge, Tod gives as parallels to the 1168 CE inscription from the Hissar fortress commemorating a victory, three other inscriptions which used characters similar to those in the Hissar fortress inscription: the Firoz Lath pillar in the palace of Emperor Firoz in Delhi dated around 1162 CE; a rock inscription at Girnar in Junagadh; and a triumphal pillar in a lake in the Rajput kingdom of Mewar. Tod adds that around 1794, William Jones had laid before the Asiatic Society of Bengal a translation of the inscriptions on the Firoz Lath pillar of Delhi.[6] Using writings by the Moghul historian of the Deccan, Ferishta, Tod refers to Mahmud of Ghazni's failed attack on Ajmer, on his way to plunder Somnath (around 1000 CE) and to Alaudin Khilji's attack in 1316 CE, on Rinthambor near Jaipur, during which a Hammir Chauhan was killed, this being a different Hammir, and not Prithvi Raj Chauhan's vassal Hammir Hara of Tod's inscription, who had lived a century and a half earlier.[7] After these learned excursions, Tod terminates his comments on the Sanskrit inscription from the Hansi-Hissar fortress near Delhi with a summary of its literal contents, including its date.[8]

Tod read his paper 'Comments on an Inscription in marble at Madhucargarh, and on three grants inscribed on copper found at Ujjaiyini' before the Royal Asiatic Society on 19 May 1824.[9] This paper presents a marble inscription from Madhucargarh which Tod states to be in 'Harouta', is dated 1108 CE and concerns the inauguration of a temple to the Hindu divinity Siva, declared to be descended from Mahadeva and Sri Hara. The position of Madhucargarh in the inscription is described as 'between the Northern region and the Southern region'. The officiating monarch is mentioned as Nara Varma, descended from Raja Sindhula and his son Bhoja, and Bhoja's son Udayaditya, who was Nara Varma's father. The occasion of the temple inauguration was an eclipse of the sun and H.T. Colebrooke had found out for Tod that there had been an eclipse of the sun in June 1108 CE, which fixes the inscription in time and in space. This is followed by Tod's presentation of three incomplete copper plates 'found at Ujjaiyini'. These contain land grants made (a) in 1136–7 CE by Yaso Varma Deva; (b) in 1144 CE, by Lacsmi Varma Deva, one of the two sons of the above-mentioned Yaso Varma Deva; (c) and without any date, the latest of the three grants is signed by Jaya Varma Deva, another son of Yaso Varma Deva, who perhaps succeeded his father. This chronologically latest of the three copper plate grants is addressed to the inhabitants of the village of Mayamodaca, described as part of the thirty-six villages of Vata.

Tod deploys his acquired knowledge about the four royal tribes of the Agnicula race (already exhibited in his paper on a Sanskrit inscription from Hansi-Hissar),[10] as well as the royal chronicles of the twelfth-century Solanki king, Kumar Pal (known as the 'Kumar Pal Charitra') and of the late eleventh-century Pramara-Powar king Bhoj (known as the 'Bhoj Charitra'), to demonstrate that the dynasty in these four inscriptions was of the Pramara-Powar tribe of the Agnicula race, who had reigned from three capitals: Avanti or Ujjain (far west of Bhopal and NNW of Indore), Dharanagari or Dhar (west of Indore) and Arbuda or Chandravati (near Mount Abu). This situates the Pramara-Powars alongside the Chauhans of Delhi, Ajmer and Chittore, the Purihara-Rathores of Kanauj, Mandaur and Jodhpur and the Solankis of Ballabhipura and Anhulwara-Patan.

What adds even more learned prestige to Tod's presentation of these four inscriptions is that some seven months later, on 4 December 1824, H.T. Colebrooke read before the Society and published an English translation, with a verbatim transcription into the Devanagiri script, of the three original copper grants in the Pali script, found by Tod at Ujjaiyini.[11] Colebrooke corroborates Tod's conclusion about the succession of this part of the Pramara-Powar dynasty.

## TOD AMONG HIS CONTEMPORARIES IN LONDON

In Tod's next paper, read before the Royal Asiatic Society on 18 June 1825, and published in 1827, he bases his speculations on possible migrations of the Greek Bactrian kings on five series of medals gathered in north India by his foraging teams between 1810 and 1822.[12] He begins with his coin of Apollodotus, found near Baitasor on the Yamuna River, and continues with his coin of Menander, found near Mathura and Agra, also on the Yamuna River. These could be understood to form the first series of medals presented in this article. The obverse and reverse of the medals in all his five series are shown in engraved drawings alongside the article.[13] A total of some twenty medals are thus exposed. They contain human faces and figures, symbols and undecipherable characters. Among the learned details Tod includes in his study of these medals, there is a speculation on their similarity with the ancient Persian characters visible in the medals of the Sassanian Sapor, as mentioned by the French scholar of Persian, Silvestre de Sacy, and other ancient Persian characters studied by the French scholar of antiquity, Mionnet.[14] Tod then explores the various views on the extent of the territories governed by Alexander the Great's successors in Asia, in accounts by historians of Alexander's exploits, such as Arrian's *Periplus of the Erythrean Sea* (of 200 BCE), reproduced in English in Vincent's *Navigation of the Ancients*, the learned Bayer's *Historiae Regni Graecorum Bactriani*, the compilers of the *Ancient Universal History*, Sainte-Croix's *Carte des Marches d'Alexandre* and even Marsden's edition of *Marco Polo's Travels*. Tod mentions other authors from antiquity to the eighteenth century who wrote on Greek Bactria. Taking support from this plethora of learned works, Tod develops his hypothesis that the coins of Greek Bactria and of Parthia (situated to the west of Greek Bactria, according to Tod) found in India show that there were Hindu princes both to the east and to the west of the Indus, and that the Greek Bactrian dynasty known to have lasted from 256 to 134 BCE (almost a century and a quarter) was finally overthrown by Indo-Scythic (or Central Asian) tribes. Tod takes things a bit far by affirming that these same Indo-Scythic tribes invaded India, Greek Bactria and even Scandinavia. He states that Balkh, the residence of Cyrus the Great, was also known as Am-ul-Belad or the mother of towns. Tod observes that the relative abundance of Parthian coins as contrasted with the rareness of Greek Bactrian coins in north India, 'is a decided proof of the extent of their [respective] conquests and influence'.[15] Tod points out also that the *Puranas*, the mythological compendiums of ancient India, contained mentions of the Yavan or Greek kings. He goes into detail about whether the capital of the lower Indus in 323 BCE was 'Sambhus' or 'Minagara' or 'Alaor' or 'Tatta' (and whether these were other names for Bukhara). Based on Strabo and

Bayer, Tod favours the view that Apollodotus and Menander did indeed cross the Sutlej and reached eastern India. However Elphinstone quoted Plutarch to conclude the contrary, namely that Menander's funeral monument in Bactria was at Sangala or at Taxila, and was found to be 'entirely Grecian', implying that Menander never visited India.[16]

In this same article, Tod presented a fifth series of medals that belonged to a dynasty that ruled from Avanti (Ujjain) to the Indus. Tod assigns these coins to the Saurashtra dynasty of the Solanki-Balhara sovereigns, who had even founded their own Balhara era, which began 375 years after the Vikramaditya era, corresponding to 431 years after the Common Era. This discovery of the Balhara era (although it had nothing to do with the Greek Bactrians) was one of Tod's personal breakthroughs in India. Tod concludes this article by formulating the hope that others will use the historical materials he collected in order 'to throw new light on Indian history'.

This article by Tod on Greek, Parthian and Hindu medals which he had collected in north India caught the attention of the German philologist August Wilhelm Schlegel, who learned Sanskrit in Paris, where he resided for several years in the early part of the nineteenth century. Schlegel published an article in French in the official journal of the *Société Asiatique* of Paris in November 1828,[17] in which he critically evaluated Tod's presentation of the ancient medals he had assembled in north India, which had appeared in 1827 in the first volume of the *Transactions of the Royal Asiatic Society* (analysed above). Schlegel's approach to Tod's hypotheses about possible occupations of the Indus Valley and even of the Ganga Valley by Greek Bactrian authorities is very cautious. Schlegel points out the many false conjectures advanced by so-called experts on Alexander's exploits in Asia (Arrian, Trogus-Pompeius, Justin, Strabon, Photius, Diodorus of Sicily and Bayer of much later date). Schlegel favours the idea that Menander might have conquered the regions up to Lahore, but is convinced that Menander definitely did not reach the Ganges or the centre of India. Schlegel then studies Tod's second series of medals, and using the voyages into Bukhara and Sogdiana (Balkh) of the baron de Meyendorf,[18] claims that the Tartar Khan of the Indo-Scythic empire might have reigned over provinces of ancient India and ancient Persia, and might even have adopted certain religious practices of the Hindu Brahmins, since on the coins in question, the diagrams of incense being offered and the depiction of a halo with radiating beams seemed to indicate a form of sun worship. After denouncing certain false hypotheses put forward by European scholars like Bayer, Lassen and the baron de Meyendorf, all leaning towards a separateness and a superiority of the marks of Greek civilisation in Balkh and Bactria, Schlegel concludes his article on Tod's coins with great prudence concerning the nomadic peoples of Central Asia, comparing their migrations to the moving sands of their deserts.[19]

Finally, Schlegel neither corroborates nor invalidates Tod's ideas of widespread migrations towards Europe and towards Asia of certain Indo-Scythic peoples of Central Asia, leaving the avenues open to later historians to find further evidence on this question. I have mentioned Schlegel's article simply to illustrate that Tod's learned articles did indeed attract comment from reputed European scholars of his time.

Tod himself went further in his speculations on the possible migrations of Central Asian peoples in an article he published in French, in the same French journal of the Paris *Société Asiatique* used by Schlegel.[20] In this article, Tod uses analogies and quotations from the writings of authors from antiquity to underline similarities between settlements in pre-Roman Italy, Asia Minor and northern India. In this perspective, Tod situates the origin of Buddhism in Central Asia, and draws parallels between cults of the earth goddess in north and south Europe as well as in India (Hertha in Scandinavia, Laxmi in India and Cybele among the Celts and the Romans). Tod develops the resemblances between these different geographical regions, with examples of similarities among their words and names, their common adoration of the horse, their common use of particular weapons (the bow and arrow) and certain common agricultural festivals. Here Tod unfolds an array of learned authors and concludes by linking the Rajputs and the ancient tribes of Europe, through their heroic poetic legends, their emblems, their architectural ornaments and their temples, in order to support his idea that these far-flung peoples had perhaps issued from a common origin. As we know, this was a controversial question at the time, with scholars like Elphinstone denying it, and other scholars like Schlegel stating that further investigation was needed.

Tod read his next learned paper before London's Royal Asiatic Society on 6 December 1828, and it was published in the second volume of the Society's *Transactions* in 1830.[21] It concerned the religious establishments and land grants for religious purposes in Mewar. In the year following his reading of this paper before the Society, Tod incorporated this article (in 1829) into the first volume of his *Annals and Antiquities of Rajasthan*, expanding it into a lengthier essay which made up an entire section of this volume. In the published volume, Tod included in this section a description of Rajput festivals, the social practices of Rajput women and his reflections on female immolation or 'sati' in Rajasthan. Already in his shorter version presented the Royal Asiatic Society, Tod had added an impressive apparatus of learned references and a series of twelve appendices, which were his own translations of original land grants and endowments for religious purposes in Mewar down the ages. Among the learned references cited in this paper, Tod uses the classical Sanskrit text translated by William Jones, the Laws of Menu, in 'Haughton's edition', to explain the legal conditions of certain territorial endowments.[22] Later in this article, while describing the trade caravans that passed from Central Asia via the temple of Nathdwara in Rajasthan into the plains of India, Tod uses an infrapaginal note to mention his pet ideas on the common origin of the peoples of Central Asia and of north India, this time along the lines opened by William Jones in relation to linguistic similarities between the ancient languages of Greece, Italy and India. Here, Tod uses the flimsy basis of 'nominal resemblances' to make his point, and cites works by European Orientalists (Klaproth and Rémusat) to corroborate his ideas.[23]

Although it must be admitted that subsequent research has not yet revealed evidence of the exact location from which these various Central Asian peoples migrated and spread, and that philologists have so far established only superficial links between the different 'Indo-European' languages,[24] these questions were indeed part of a contemporary debate among European scholars in Tod's time.

On the same day on which Tod read his paper 'On the Religious Establishments of Mewar', Tod also read before the Royal Asiatic Society his 'Remarks on certain sculptures in the Cave Temples of Ellora'.[25] The special feature of this paper was that it was intended to comment upon drawings made in western India in 1813 and assembled as *Cave Temples of Ellora*, by Tod's contemporary, Captain R.M. Grindlay.[26] Some examples of Grindlay's drawings are included in Tod's article as illustrations of his comments. Tod states that his explanations were 'according to the wishes of the Royal Asiatic Society', thus underlining the fact that his effort was a response to an official request, and not of his own initiative. Referring to the learned Dr G. Babington, Tod outlines two ways of explaining mythological drawings: either by astronomical allusion or from mythological allegory. After a brief mention of certain constellations of the zodiac, and of 'some particular position of the heavens',[27] Tod opts clearly for explanation of the drawings through mythological allegory. Tod identifies the central figure in the series of engravings selected by him for comment as Mahadeva, such as he is represented in the legend of the sacrifice of Sati and the metamorphosis of Sati's father Daksha. Tod bases his comments on the rendering of this legend as it was extracted from ancient mythologies by the twelfth-century Rajput bard Chand in his major work 'Prithvi Raj Raso' (or chronicle of Prithvi Raj Chauhan).[28] Tod briefly recounts the ceremony of Daksha's ritual sacrifice to which neither Mahadeva nor

Mahadeva's wife Sati was invited, leading to the self-consumption in flame of Sati, resulting in Mahadeva cutting off his locks in grief, from which the giant Virabhadra emerged and proceeded to avenge Sati's death by decapitating her offending father Daksha. Mahadeva eventually restored Daksha to life with the head of a goat. Tod compares this account of the sun god Mahadeva to Volney's *Ruins of Empire*, where mention is made of Zoroastrian sun worship depicted on a cavern wall.[29] Tod also refers to the Theban Jupiter appearing in a ram's skin to Hercules, as mentioned by Herodotus.[30] Tod then proceeds to use the pretext of the legend of Mahadeva and Sati opposed to Daksha in the caves of Ellora to elaborate on his favourite subject: 'the last great struggle which the Hindu emperor of Delhi maintained against the arms of Islam', as portrayed by the Bard Chund, in order 'to enliven a dull, mythological speculation'.[31]

And all of a sudden we have Tod launching into the occasion when Prithvi Raj Chauhan in the late twelfth century had managed to avoid his own deposition for certain follies he had committed, by liberating his vassal Chaond-Rae Dahima, with forgiveness for Chaond-Rae Dahima's having killed Prithvi Raj's favourite elephant Har-Sengar. Chand evokes the cosmic writhing of the serpent of time, Sehesnaga, in the form of the giant Virabhadra, at this tremendous event of the liberation of Chaond-Rae Dahima. Chand terminates this episode with 'an invocation to Time (Kal)', in other words Sehesnag.[32] Was Tod using the only solid textual knowledge he possessed of Rajput mythology (Chand's *Prithvi Raj Raso*) to compensate for the inadequacy of his knowledge of the sculptures of Ellora? This is one possible reason for Tod's digression.

Despite his valid perception of points of intersection between ancient Greek and ancient Hindu mythology, Tod was not able to substantiate these further by more detailed explorations in comparative mythology.

Tod's next paper concerned his observations on a gold ring of Hindu fabrication found at Montrose in Scotland, dating back to the sixteenth century during the absence from Scotland of Mary Queen of Scots while she was in France.[33] Since Tod was considered an expert on things Hindu in his time by virtue of his prolonged stay in India, he was consulted on the origin and significance of the symbolic figures in this gold ring by its Scottish owner, through the good offices of one of Tod's fellow members at the Royal Asiatic Society, G. Fitzclarence. An illustration of the ring, drawn and engraved by J. Sarraine, in its side-view and in its front-view, shows the symbol of the union of the human sex organs, called the 'Linga-Yoni' in Hindu terms, against a backdrop of the head of a hooded cobra, with an elephant on either side at the base of this group. Tod begins with the double possibility of an astrological interpretation and of a mythological interpretation of the ring. He relates Shiva's phallus (depicted in the union of the Linga and the Yoni) to the sun god Balanath, often depicted as wreathed by a serpent guardian with two bulls as supporters. He links Balanath to Celtic sun worship, as visible in the pillar of Belenus, and to the fictitious monsters called wyverns, bearing features of the dragon, the griffin and the eagle, which supported the Roman god of war, Mars, as well as to 'the Mithraic worship of the Transoxianic nations'.[34]

Tod concludes his remarks on the mysterious ring found in Scotland with a reiteration of his ideas about common features in the symbolic worship of peoples in Europe and in Asia, however leaving uncertain the historical traces of the 'successive migrations' which would explain these common features of worship.[35]

The last paper that Tod personally presented at the Royal Asiatic Society in London was a study of an ancient Hindu engraved medallion, enabling Tod to make further parallels between Hindu mythology and Greek mythology.[36] Tod first describes the engraved medallion as representing the Hindu god Baldev, bearing a lion's hide, a bird on one of Baldev's arms, showing Baldev with a coronet, a club in one of Baldev's hands and a monogram with two undecipherable letters.[37] Then, Tod traces Baldev as a founder of the Pandu race, through genealogies in the epic *Mahabharat* (by way of the learned articles of Bentley in *Asiatick Researches*), and in Arrian's *Periplus in the Erythrean Sea*. He also points out (with two comparative tables) a 'perfect accordance' between the Hindu genealogy of the Pandu race as it appears in the *Puranas* and the cosmography of the Jains or Buddhists of India.[38] After recounting various legends from the *Mahabharat*, Tod alludes to the 'discourse on the horrors of civil dissension' between Hari and Arjuna, as presented in the *Bhagvad Gita*, translated into English by Charles Wilkins ('yet amongst us'),[39] who was a respected member of the Royal Asiatic Society through the 1820s. Tod justifies these digressions into the *Mahabharat*, as being a source of inspiration for the moral doctrines of the Rajputs of his time.[40]

Tod develops an analogy between India's Baldev and Hari Krishna, and the Persian hero Rustam, named 'the Persian Hercules', supposed to have been a contemporary of Cyrus the Great by Sir William Jones and further developed by Sir William Ousely in his *Travels in Persia*.[41]

A nine-page article by Tod entitled 'The Feudal System in Rajasthan', published in the May–August 1831 issue of the *Asiatic Journal and Monthly Register*, was in fact a letter to the Editor in which Tod justifies and defends himself against 'an illiberal and insidious attack upon my work' that had appeared as part of a critical review of Mr Gleig's

*History of India* in the journal.[42] In a spirit of fair play, Tod first quotes the passage from the review of Gleig's text that had so upset him in its evaluation of Gleig's and Tod's and Wilford's[43] work by the 'anonymous censor':[44]

> 'We have already noticed Mr. Gleig's propensity to assume the speculations of fanciful writers as unquestionable facts, and upon those frail and sandy foundations to build up the most important references of the early part of his compilation. The philosopher of Laputa busied himself in the experiment of extracting sun-beams from cucumbers; by a process as felicitous, Mr. Gleig extracts them from the wildest theories of Oriental Scholars. The dreams of Colonels Tod and Wilford seem, in Gleig's estimation, to be "strong as proofs of Holy Writ".'

Tod retorts to this learned doubting of his own verified and recorded facts concerning a possible analogy between the martial polity of the Rajputs and the feudal system of Europe on the one hand, and concerning Tod's observation of primogeniture in India on the other, with a series of equally learned defensive arguments. For example, Tod reinterprets the aphorism of the ancient Indian legislator Menu on the nature of land occupation in India (land ownership being traditionally accorded in ancient India, according to Menu, to those who first and constantly tilled it), used by the anonymous critic to invalidate Tod's analogy between a feudal allotment of land in Rajasthan and in medieval Europe, as well as to dispute Tod's claim that Indian polity invariably incorporated foreign tribes and foreign laws into the more anciently established governments of India. Tod's counter-argument is based on his field experience, during which he had observed that the Rajputs circumvented the 'trammels' of system by 'practical deviations' from 'the theory of the Divine Code of Menu'. To further support his own claims of the presence of a feudal system in India, Tod quotes other British historians of India, such as Stirling on Orissa,[45] Colonel Briggs on the land tax system in the Maratha territories (Briggs, *On the Land Taxes of the Hindoos*) and John Malcolm on the government in central India, as well as two reviews of his own first volume, which accepted Tod's hypothesis of a feudal system in Rajasthan.[46] Concerning the second point on which Gleig's reviewer had attacked Tod, about the existence of primogeniture in India, Tod dismisses this attack by showing that it was founded on 'sweeping generalisations', which used 'inconclusive and antiquated authorities' like Menu, the temple of Jagannatha and the ancient Greek Megasthenes, without alluding to a single original Hindu chronicle which might have offered concrete historical details. Here again, Tod opposes existing practice to the vague theories and canonical generalities of ancient texts, thereby also paying tribute to the flexible adaptability of Indian polities to new and changing circumstances down the ages.

In the July–December 1831 issue of the French *Journal Asiatique*, there appeared an edited version in French translation of the first chapter (fifteen octavo pages in the original) of Tod's first volume on Rajputana, entitled 'Geography of Rajasthan or Rajpootana'.[47] The French text omits five pages from the original and deletes Tod's humble declaration that his field explorations were intended to fill 'the blanks' in the existing topographical descriptions of Rajasthan, while waiting for the 'grand trigonometrical survey of India' to reach Rajasthan.

The French text thus divests Tod's original essay of much of its learned content, conveying with some accuracy Tod's remaining topographical descriptions, which were conducted from the vantage point of Mount Abu, and focused mainly on Medpat or Mewar. There are five threads in Tod's presentation of the geography of Rajasthan: (a) the alpine Aravalli Mountains; (b) the central Indian plateau or Pathar; (c) a second steppe further east (in today's Madhya Pradesh); (d) the various tributaries of the Chumbul River; (e) the sandy desert region west of the Aravulli Mountains. This last section on the sandy deserts of Rajasthan and the Rann of Kutch brings to mind Tod's regrets in *Travels to Western India* at having left unfulfilled his longstanding ambition to personally visit the Indus River Valley.[48] It must have been written, therefore, from maps and descriptions left by other travellers who had actually been there.

The last of Tod's papers published while he was alive is entitled 'Indo-Grecian Antiquities'.[49] It is in fact a letter to the editor of the *Asiatic Journal* that Tod wrote from Piazza Barberina, Rome, dated 2 March 1835. In it, Tod can be understood to have been trying to affirm his presence in the nascent field of Oriental numismatology and archaeology. Tod begins by quoting two scholars who deplored the absence of the British in the discoveries of ancient treasures in the regions of Bactria and Central Asia in the early nineteenth century: (a) Augustus Wilhelm Schlegel, who lamented the 'lethargy of years' in Indological Oriental research, especially in Britain, since the death of William Jones in 1794, and (b) an Indian assistant named Mohun Lall, who had accompanied the British explorer Dr J.G. Gerard to Kabul in the 1830s, and who had expressed surprise at why 'the English power never consider of such valuable discoveries respecting the old Grecian provinces, which history tells us existed in these very tracts'.[50] Tod's comments appear under two headings in this letter: ancient coins on the one hand, and ancient tombs on the other. In connection with coins, Tod underlines similarities between Honigberger's findings of coins in Afghanistan and Persia and his own findings of the ancient Greek coins of Apollodotus and Menander, which he had presented to the Royal Asiatic Society on 18 June 1825.[51] On the basis of these coins he had found and studied, Tod claims 'the paternity' of this growing Indo-Getic numismatical family.[52] In further corroboration of his own serious contribution to the field, Tod also mentions his meeting in Florence (Italy) in 1825 with the Italian Orientalist Sestini, who had found coins in countries bordering the Persian Gulf. In connection with ancient tombs, Tod refers to Elphinstone's account of burial topes at Manikyala in Afghanistan, which the French Chevalier Ventura had further explored in 1830, with the supposition that Ventura had probably, like Tod himself, in his study of the Afghanistan region, used the baron de Sainte-Croix's map attached to his *Critique des Historiens d'Alexandre*.[53] Since the date of 2 March 1835 when Tod wrote this letter was just eight months before his demise, it is understandable that he was perhaps keen to gain acknowledgement for his labours in the field of collection and collation of knowledge about Indian and Asian history.

In his display of references to works of erudition and in his personal use of the apparatus of scholarly learning (tables, notes, illustrations of artefacts studied, comparisons), Tod seems to be creating a place for himself among London's select specialists on the history and culture of India. This circle was just establishing itself in Tod's time, with the creation of the Royal Asiatic Society in London in 1823 and the launching of learned journals for research publications on India (and other parts of the Orient) (such as the *Transactions of the Royal Asiatic Society* and the *Asiatic Journal*). He can also be understood to have been situating his own discoveries about India in the intellectual landscape of his time, a time during which new ground was covered in several fields of knowledge (geology, botany, comparative mythologies, history, comparative linguistics, etc.). Thus, not only can Tod be seen to have been prudent in the conclusions he drew from the information he had gathered in India, but his hypotheses can be observed to have been part of ongoing debates in his time, even if some of his ideas ultimately proved (by comparison with those of contemporary scholars like Schlegel and Elphinstone) to be far-fetched and without foundation.

## *Tod's attention to the language of the Rajput texts he presented in London*

In the second part of this account of Tod's short essays, I would like to study Tod's use of language in his translations from source texts in the Rajput dialects, as it appears in his respect of the original Rajput imagery and rhetoric. In Tod's translation of 'The Vow of Sunjogta' from the fifth book of the bard Chand's sixty-nine books constituting his *Pirthi Raj Raso*, some images portrayed by Tod in English have a distinctly non-English ring about them. For example, when Prithvi Raj Chauhan's Guru Raj exhorted him to embark on his chosen path of action, the image used is of the unconcealable sparkle of the real gem:[54]

> Though the water-cloud may obscure, it cannot hide the rays of the sun; though numerous the constellations, they conceal not the moon, neither can the warrior, the man of science or of virtue, the real Rajpoot or true prince remain concealed. Like the real gem, they will sparkle however they are set.

The parallels between images from nature (clouds and constellations) and from a jeweller's collection of gems show the poet Chand's inventiveness based on his personal experiences. A little further on in the text, Chand compares Prithvi Raj's braves around him to a lotus rising with the water, to a flood, as well as to rays of light intended to dispel the darkness of the foe.[55]

Then, the poet compares the enthusiasm of Prithvi Raj's braves before the battle to the young bride fleeing the marriage bed on the morning after her wedding night, desiring 'the departure of night that day might witness their deeds in arms'.[56]

Tod respects the poet's original language of victory breaking 'like the sun from the cloud-bound sky', to depict the field defeats of the troops of the adversary Jychund of Kanouj.[57]

In a series of onomatopoeic evocations, Tod renders Chand's version of the cosmic sounds of war:[58]

> The din of shields, the neigh of steeds, the heroes' shouts, made ocean exclaim that his roar was eclipsed.

Tod terminates his extract from 'The Vow of Sunjogta' with a typically Indian expression of ambivalence, of joy splintered by grief:[59]

> On a throne of gold were seated the Chohan and his bride, while the damsels raised the song of love. Round the neck of Delhi's Lord was a garland of gems, the gift of Jychund. Love and harmony were restored. ... But sorrow dwelt in the heart of the Chohan, when he recalled the price paid for his prize, of Kahn, and the heroes ever present to his mind. Like the tiger excluded from the abode of his mates, Pirthi Raj pined for the companions of his glory, even though blessed with the fair of Kanouj.

This series of images at various moments of the Battle of Kanouj and of Prithvi Raj's marriage to the Rathore princess Sunjogta of Kanouj, convey the richness and the specific, local inspiration of the bard Chand's composition, perceptible even through Tod's English translation of Chand's text.

To conclude this analysis of Tod's short essays, I will mention brief reviews of three of Tod's compilations that appeared in the *Asiatic Journal and Monthly Register*. The first review concerns Tod's essay 'On the Religious Establishments of Mewar in Rajputana', and praises Tod's presentation of the privileges of the Saivas, the Jainas and the Vaishnavas of Mewar, and his appendix with translations of inscriptions.[60] In the same issue of the *Asiatic Journal and Monthly Register*, there is a review of Tod's essay 'An Account of some sculptures in the Cave Temples of Ellora'.[61] Here the reviewer is very economical with his words, commending the 'beautifully executed' figures that give evidence that the art of sculpture formerly existed in India in a much higher state of perfection than is generally supposed and furnish a 'further pledge of the [Royal Asiatic] Society's labours'. The third review appeared in the last quarter of 1830 and concerned Tod's article on 'Observations on a Gold Ring of Hindu Fabrication found at Montrose in Scotland'.[62] In this review, tribute is paid to 'Colonel Tod's archaeological researches', and far from criticising Tod's attempts to establish links between the mythological characters of ancient Italy and the rock inscriptions of Saurashtra, the reviewer concludes with praise for Tod's antiquarian knowledge.

On the basis of these reviews, we can perhaps state that Tod seems to have succeeded in his goal of establishing himself as a scholar of Rajput antiquities among the learned circles of Britain and Europe. In his manner of constructing his shorter compilations we can perceive his basic rootedness in Enlightenment rationality, as evidenced by his constant use of empirical observation with abundant reference to concrete details available in inscriptions, regional chronicles and oral details from the local people. Tod also demonstrated scientific prudence and respect for the rhetoric of the original Rajput texts he translated into English.

## *Reviews of* Annals and Antiquities of Rajasthan

Now let us move on to the reviews of Tod's *Annals and Antiquities of Rajasthan*.[63] These appeared in six learned journals during Tod's lifetime. We will not take into account later reviews that appeared after Tod's death, since these deal with a completely different dimension (later reinterpretation, reutilisation) of Tod's work. We have been unable to trace any reviews of Tod's posthumous work *Travels in Western India* (1839). Our concern here is solely to study the impact and reception of Tod's *Annals and Antiquities of Rajasthan* immediately upon its publication. Two of the six learned journals we will focus on published reviews of the first volume only of Tod's work on Rajasthan (the *Oriental Herald* and the *Journal Asiatique*). The remaining four (the *Edinburgh Review*, the *Quarterly Review*, the *Asiatic Journal* and the *Journal des Savans*) published reviews of both the volumes of Tod's *Annals*: the *Edinburgh Review* in two separate issues in 1830–1 and in 1832–3; the *Quarterly Review* in a single, combined review in 1832; the *Asiatic Journal* in two separate issues, in July–December 1829 and in May–August 1832; and the *Journal des Savans* in six parts between 1830 and 1834.[64]

The *Oriental Herald*, though begun in 1824 by the anti-establishment free trader James Silk Buckingham, was closely linked to the affairs of the East India Company. The anonymous *Oriental Herald* review of the first volume of Tod's *Annals* appeared in the July–September 1829 issue.[65] The *Oriental Herald* reviewer seems to have gone deeply into the context in his insistence (like Tod) on the need for the Rajputs to enjoy 'perfect internal independence and their ancient institutions', in order to be 'useful friends' to the British Government (in case of outside aggression against the British Indian Empire, by the Russians, for example). After initial praise for Tod's insightful incorporation of copious data into his depiction of the genius and manners of the Rajputs through minute description, the *Oriental Herald* reviewer makes a brief allusion to the political importance of Tod's contribution to the formulation of future British policy in India. He then refers to what has become a cliché concerning Tod's work: the rectification of the relative geographical positions of Cheetore and Udaipur (Cheetore being to the northeast of Udaipur, and not to the southwest of Udaipur, as it was frequently believed to be in Tod's time). Then, the *Oriental Herald* reviewer wholly approves of Tod's theory of a possible common origin of the two types of feudalism, in Europe and in Rajputana. Claiming to be receptive to analogies, the *Oriental Herald* reviewer accepts Tod's claim that knowledge and customs must have accompanied the tide of migration from 'higher Asia' into Europe on the one hand and into India on the other. Mentioning Tod's use of Henry Hallam's study of European feudalism, the *Oriental Herald* reviewer, however, raises the point that this work includes endless definitions of the duties of the European vassal, while the Rajput vassal seems to maintain an ambivalence in his loyalties, giving priority to his immediate chief, over and above the more distant sovereign lord (*Raj ca malik veh/ Pat ca malik yeh* or the sovereign of the kingdom is the distant lord, but the head of our ancestral land is our immediate chief). Moving on to Tod's 'Annals of Mewar', the

## TOD AMONG HIS CONTEMPORARIES IN LONDON

*Oriental Herald* reviewer pays tribute to the *Asiatic Journal*'s critic in August 1829, who had 'with skill and fidelity' given an accurate analysis of Tod's version of the history of Mewar (see below). The *Oriental Herald* reviewer, in contrast, chooses to select only 'a few characteristic specimens of Tod's style' in his review. These selected extracts illustrate three points: (a) the *noble origins* of the Rajput race including comparisons with the celebrated dynasties of Europe, (b) the *expansion* of the Mewar Sesodias and the Marwar Rathores, through allodial or freehold vassalage, as also through an emphasis on all Rajputs' *attachment* to their horse, their plough and their lance as their only inheritances, which consolidate the idea of their martial identity, followed by (c) the *delicacy* of the Rajputs as visible in their devotion to the fair sex, in their high sense of honour, and in their sensitivity to the respect of their Rajput customs.

As an example of the sensitivity of the Rajputs to the upholding of their honour, the *Oriental Herald* reviewer cites the dissolution of the Jaipur–Jodhpur alliance, which had left them both vulnerable to the depredations of the Marathas, following upon aspersions cast on the virility of the Cuchwahas of Jaipur (because of their submission to the Mughals)! Another example of the proud respect by the Rajputs of their honour and prejudices, mentioned by the *Oriental Herald* reviewer, is the sacrifice of his right to primogeniture by the Mewar heir Chonda in 1398, after the Marwar Rathores had proposed a Marwar princess for marriage to the Mewar Sesodias. Chonda's father Lakha Rana (r.1373–98), following upon his light-hearted jest about which marriageable groom (the ageing Rana himself, or his young son and heir Chonda) the Marwar princess was precisely intended for, the elderly Lakha Rana ended up by marrying the young Marwar princess, since his son Chonda was absent from Mewar at the time the Jodhpur marriage proposal had been made. A son, Mukul, was born of Lakha Rana's union with the Marwar princess, so Chonda sacrificed his own right to the Mewar throne as a result of Lakha Rana's trivial jest, in order to allow the infant Mukul to succeed Lakha Rana in 1398. According to Freitag, the *Oriental Herald* reviewer distinctly subordinates the glorious history of the Rajputs to his stress on the conservative argument for the preservation of a positive British alliance with the Rajputs, through the respect by the British of the independence of the Rajputs which was 'sacred' to the latter.[66]

The *Oriental Herald* reviewer limits his mentions of Rajput warriors' exploits to quotation of a few anecdotes on Rajput eccentricities. He expresses receptivity to Tod's theories on the common origins of the practices of feudalism and the obligation to supply military service in exchange for the right to exploit land in medieval Europe and in Rajasthan, without wholeheartedly endorsing Tod's claims, however.

This brings us to the second review of the first volume of Tod's *Annals*, in French this time, by the French Orientalist Eugène Burnouf, in the *Journal Asiatique*, published by the Société Asiatique of Paris in 1829,[67] at about the same time that the review of Tod's work appeared in the British *Oriental Herald* (in late 1829). Burnouf begins by praising Tod's highlighting of new information on the Rajputs in a purely historical narrative (refuting Tod's humble claim of not attaining the academic level of 'strict history') that successfully makes selections between sterile and pertinent details. Burnouf undertakes to make only a summary presentation of the main points in Tod's work, under four headings: (a) Tod's geographical description of Rajasthan, (b) the history of the Rajput tribes, (c) Tod's essay on the feudal system of Rajasthan and (d) the 'Annals of Mewar'.

Under his evaluation of Tod's geography of Rajasthan, Burnouf only points out the well-known error on the precise position of Chittore in relation to Udaipur (ENE and not WSW of Udaipur). Tod's history of the Rajput tribes, according to Burnouf, presents reliable information on the two ancient royal races (the descendants of the Sun and the descendants of the Moon), and on the thirty-six principal tribes of Rajputana. Here however, Burnouf expresses doubts on the acceptability of Tod's etymologies, citing the examples of 'genesis' as linked to 'djanam', of 'bahuman' as stemming from the Persian 'Bahman', or great soul, and of 'Rawul' associated by Tod with the Norman Radulf or the French king Raoul, all dismissed by Burnouf as implausible. Nevertheless, Burnouf acknowledges the value of Tod's linking of the famous families of Rajasthan with the ancient heroes of the Puranas (legendary accounts of the Hindu divinities).

On Tod's essay on the Rajput feudal system, Burnouf does not enter into details. He simply salutes the novel and extensive information provided by Tod concerning the military organisation of Rajputana in relation to the feudality of medieval Europe.

In connection with the historical section of Tod's first volume, entitled the 'Annals of Mewar', Burnouf selects a summary chronological outline from Tod's historical presentation of the princes of the Gehlote family of Mewar that is more condensed than the outline presented by the reviewer of the *Asiatic Journal* (see below) and thus reveals Burnouf's priorities. After a brief mention of the Gehlote prince Keneksen (or Kanyaka Sena, as specified by Burnouf) in Saurashtra (perhaps in Somnathpur, near Veraval and Diu, in south Saurashtra), in 144 CE, and the foundation of the capital city of Balabhipura (to the west of Bhavnagar) in 431 CE (Burnouf had perhaps associated Balabhipura with Tod's discovery of the Balabhi era, which began in 431 CE), he moves on to 524 CE, when Balabhipura was attacked by barbarian, White Huns, reducing the Chohan child crown prince, Goha, to clandestinity, and then to 728 CE, when the Gehlote family moved their capital from Idar (in the north of today's Gujarat) to Chittore, under Bappa Rawal, who conquered Chittore from the King of Ujjain. Alluding to the obscure period between the ninth and twelfth centuries on which there are few details concerning the history of Mewar (judged by Burnouf to be sparsely described because the period presents little historical interest), Burnouf halts at 998 CE, when, according to the Muslim historian Ferishta, there was a war between Mahmud of Ghazni and the Rajput king of Lahore, and then at 1192 CE, when the Rajput king of Delhi was defeated by Mahmud of Ghor. Burnouf points out the comprehensiveness of Tod's historical account, which covers the period from the second century CE to the nineteenth century CE. Then Burnouf refers to the 1290–1303 attack on Chittore by Allaudin Khilji, against Rana Lakhamsi, his uncle Bheemsi and the latter's wife, Princess Padmini. The huge massacre of the Rajput braves, the flight into hiding of Crown Prince Ajaysi and his nephew Hamir, and the immolation of Princess Padmini with hundreds of Rajput princesses, were testified to by all the bards of Rajasthan, but Burnouf considers these events closer to fantastic adventure than history, properly speaking. Burnouf groups together the two centuries between the attacks of Allaudin Khilji and of Babar (1303–1526) as perhaps 'the most interesting' part of the history of Mewar. He rapidly sketches the reigns of Rana Koombho, Rana Raemal and Rana Sanga, who confronted the Moghul Babar at the Battle of Kanua in 1526. Burnouf qualifies the years from 1526 onwards as filled with energetic efforts by the Rajputs to escape the domination of the Mughals, in defence of their independence and Hindu identity. According to Burnouf, 1533 marked the second fall of Chittore to the forces of Sultan Bajazet of Gujarat, and after the defeat of the Rajputs at Haldighati in 1576 by Moghul forces, in 1614 the Mughals forced the heroic Rana Pratap (r.1576–1621) to accept a Muslim settlement in Ajmer, which amounted to a formal submission to the Moghul emperor Jehangir. Burnouf finds 'uncontestable merit' in Tod's relation of the history of Mewar, since it highlights the survival of the pride of the Rajputs despite the victories of the Moghuls, internal Rajput dissensions, plunderings by the Marathas and the peaceful imposition of supremacy by the British East India Company. Burnouf praises Tod's mention of the Shaivites and Jains of Rajasthan in Tod's essay on the religious institutions, festivals and customs of Mewar. He finds interest in Tod's depiction of the native races of Rajasthan (Bhils, Gonds and Meras), as opposed to the Rajputs, who were themselves invading outsiders when they entered Rajasthan (in 728 CE, under Bappa Rawal), mentioned in Tod's personal travel narrative of his journey to Marwar in 1819. In his overall assessment of Tod's 'Annals of Mewar', Burnouf salutes Tod's allusions to the constant virtues of the Rajputs (courage, loyalty and a detestation of submission to foreign domination), while never concealing their defects (civil discord, a lack of unity, and a constant breaking of their mutual links of loyalty). Burnouf considers that this attempt at comprehensiveness by Tod is a proof of his commitment to precision and truth, never giving in to one-sided admiration for the Rajputs, and never omitting to mention positive qualities among their Muslim enemies (the Mughal leaders' upholding of promises made, honourable impartiality and leadership qualities).

There is, however, no political involvement on Burnouf's part in Tod's arguments about Rajput honour and independence. The brevity of Burnouf's mention of Tod's essay on the feudal system of the Rajputs shows perhaps that he did not attach much importance to it. His doubts about the solidity of Tod's etymologies reveal wider philological concerns in France at the time, where a serious study of Sanskrit, Arabic, Persian and other oriental languages was launched from the 1820s.

The third review of Tod's *Annals* appeared in two separate issues of the *Edinburgh Review*.[68] The author of this review has been identified as William Erskine (1773–1852).[69] He was, like Tod, an East India hand who served in Bombay from 1804 to 1823, being associated with the Scot Sir James Mackintosh, who also served in Bombay, whose second daughter Erskine married in 1809. After returning to Scotland in 1823 (not long after Tod left India in February 1822), Erskine lived in Edinburgh (1823–7), in Pau in France (1827–31), in various places in Scotland (1831–44), in Bonn (1844–8) and then spent his final years in Edinburgh (1848–52). Erskine is remembered for his translation into English from the Persian original of Babur's memoirs (1826), and for a history of Babur and Humayun (published posthumously by his son in 1854). The views expressed in Erskine's review of *Annals*, armed with his Orientalist field experience of the Bombay region in western India, are predominantly in keeping with the Whiggish, liberal line of the *Edinburgh Review*, tending clearly towards anti-imperialism, with support for the natives' self-government and autonomy from British domination. According to his biography,[70] Erskine was residing in Pau in France (1827–31) in 1829 when Tod's first volume was published. By the time Tod's second volume was released in 1832, Erskine had moved back to Linlithgow in Scotland (from 1831 on).

In comparison with the other reviews of Tod's volumes, Erskine's reviews seem to allot equal importance to their historico-literary weight on the one hand, and to their political significance on the other. In the first place, Erskine begins his review of Tod's first volume[71] with an overview of textual mentions of Rajasthan before the appearance of Tod's volumes: he includes Thucydides and Arrian from ancient Greece, seventeenth-century Europeans like Thomas Roe, Thomas Herbert, Mandelslo, William Hawkins, Nicholas Withington and François Bernier, before rounding off his list with the Mughal historians Abul Fazl and Ferishta. Even if these predecessors of Tod on the subject of Rajasthan had mentioned certain Rajput characteristics – their military virtues, their lack of order and discipline and their bloody struggles to defend their territory, for instance – Erskine considers that they lacked precision and conveyed only vague generalisations, without 'awareness of differences between Indians'. Then, strangely for a Whiggish liberal who would normally have been championing the intrinsic value of native groups (with the Rajputs among them), Erskine denounces the absence of Indian historical works, since Rajput texts seemed to him to show an inconsistent and 'imaginative stamp'. Erskine goes so far as to cite other known Indian historical chronicles, like the Kashmiri *Rajtarangini* (translated by H.H. Wilson), the chronicle of the kings of modern Orissa and the *Rajavalli*, which traced events in Bengal from 56 CE to 1550 CE, but dismisses them all for being debased with improbably long reigns of several centuries each, and 'absurdities' such as the historicised personification of musical modes like 'ragas' and 'raginis', concluding that there was 'no equivalent in India' of true historians like Thucydides and Titus Livy of ancient Europe. He attributes to Tod the role of an adventurer in unknown terrain in his compilation of the annals of the kingdoms of Rajasthan, thus explaining Tod's unorthodox use of legendary tales and bardic poems among his historical sources.

Erskine then reveals his own literary sensibility in his 'concise epitome' of Tod's 'Annals of Mewar'.[72] While passing over the key dates of the history of the Gehlote-Seesodias, he labels Prithvi Raj Chauhan, who died at the Battle of Tarain in 1192 CE, as 'a Hindu Rolando', Rolando being the nephew of the French emperor Charlemagne, who died heroically in 778 CE in the Pyrenees, while resisting an attack by the Saracens. Again, Erskine compares the heirs to the Mewar throne in 1298 CE, Prince Ajaysi and his nephew Hammir, who reigned from 1301 to 1361 CE, to the English king Alfred (r.878–99, known for his resistance to invasions by the Danish Vikings), since they were preserved from extinction by hostile enemies, thanks to their concealment during their youth in a nearby forest. While noting the beneficial influence in Rajasthan of the presence of heterodox beliefs (Shaivism and Vaishnavism alongside Jainism), Erskine mentions the 'beautiful odes' of Jydeva.

Erskine continues by commenting on Tod's 'curious parallels' between Henry Hallam's details on Saxon feudalism in England and land tenures in Rajasthan, further bringing in also the Mughal Jagirs, the Zamindars of Hindustan and the Timariots of Turkey. Erskine concludes with the prevalence of more differences than similarities between the feudalism of the Rajputs and the feudalism of medieval Europe, since while in Europe the king was the universal lord and original proprietor of all the lands in his kingdom, in Rajasthan the prince's rights appeared to be limited to the revenues levied on the lands in his kingdom, making his land grants merely 'revenue share grants'.

Concerning the 'exquisite' architecture of the Rajputs, Erskine compares the temple at Ajmer to the Duomo at Milan, extending his architectural appreciation to encompass both Europe and Rajasthan in the same lens. Finally, anticipating his later review of Tod's second volume, Erskine adopts the same position as Thomas Munro and Tod himself, in denouncing the evils of the British subsidiary alliance system, advocating instead a restoration of the Rajputs' independance. This corroborates the general anti-imperialist stand of the Whiggish liberals of the time (and also of the *Edinburgh Review*). Erskine concludes his review of Tod's first volume with a repetition of his reservations against Tod's 'irregular and diffuse' arrangement and style, acknowledging nevertheless his 'valuable' oriental information and the quality of the book with its 'beautiful plates'.

Erskine begins his review of Tod's second volume[73] with appreciation for Tod's filling in of the existing blank about the geography and history of western India, as Colonel Wilks had done for south India, Malcolm for the countries between the Narbada and the Chambal, Elphinstone for the region between Kabul and Khorassan and Captain Pottinger for Baluchistan and the Indus Valley. He thus situates Tod among the emerging British historians of the different regions of India. After a quick, renewed summary of the various sections of Tod's volume one, Erskine announces the contents of this second volume as including the annals of all the other Rajput states, and touching on the paradoxical character of the Rajputs as observed by Tod: soldierly and gentlemanly with attachment to tribe or clan on the one hand, while on the other hand revealing an incomplete state of civilisation in their 'immoderate use' of opium. Erskine in this later review seems to have overcome his initial doubts about the validity of Tod's parallels between Rajput feudalism and medieval European feudalism, acknowledging here 'resemblances' between these two spaces of historical experience.

Erskine goes on to present his selection of anecdotes from the second volume of Tod's *Annals* around three themes: (a) the stern soul force of the Rajputs; (b) their barbarous superstition; (c) their bouts of remorse. Erskine illustrates the Rajputs' soul force with the anecdote of 1615 CE when two clans of the Gehlote-Seesodias, the Chondawuts and Suktawuts, were competing for the attribution of the honour to lead the Mewar army van at Ontala fortress. The condition laid down by the Mewar Rana was that the honour would be given to that tribe which succeeded in entering the Ontala fortress before the other. Both the chiefs of the Chondawuts and of the Suktawuts sacrificed their lives in their attempt to obtain first entrance into the ramparts of Ontala for the honour of their respective tribes, so the Mewar Rana had the difficult task of personally deciding the issue, which he did in favour of the Chondawuts.

To explain the extent of barbarous superstition among the Rajputs, Erskine chooses the struggle to maintain possession of their territory of Khandela (the chief city of the Shekhawat confederation) by the brothers Kesuri Singh and Futteh Singh,[74] during the reign of Aurangzeb, 1658–1707, under attacks by the Muslim Vizir of Delhi (Syed Abdullah). Kesuri Singh murdered his own brother Futteh Singh, permitted the sacrifice of his uncle to the local goddess Awini Mata and sent his other brother Oody Singh into clandestine retreat, in order to sacrifice himself to the invading army from Delhi. Kesuri Singh was indeed slain, while his brother Oody Singh was held captive for three years in Ajmer, after which Oody Singh recovered Khandela, but was soon after expelled from his own capital, being forced to accept submission to the Rajas of Jaipur-Amber, allies of the Mughal forces, by 1716.

As a typical example of Rajput remorse, Erskine selects Omeda Singh of Bundi (b.1731, r.1736–71, d.1804), since this son of Budh Singh of Bundi spent the first fourteen years of his reign (1736–49) as an exiled wanderer, while the interfering Jey Singh of Jaipur (d.1744) gifted Bundi to a pro-Jaipur usurper, Duleel Singh. After regaining his Bundi throne in 1749, Omeda Singh brutally killed Deo Singh of Indergurh in 1757, together with his son and grandson, in revenge for Deo Singh's earlier collaboration with Jey Singh of Jaipur. Then, as if in remorse for this brutality, Omeda Singh of Bundi renounced his throne in 1771 and spent the rest of his life (till 1804), that is thirty-three years, as a wandering mendicant. Erskine states that he has cited the case of the Bundi Raja 'from a persuasion that one such detailed sketch will convey a better notion of the manners and history of the Rajpoots, than any dry outline of the various dynasties which have ruled over them'.[75]

Erskine goes on to refute Tod's theory of the common Central Asian origin of all nations, affirming that 'uncertainty' regarding 'the origin of nations' is not confined to Asia.[76] Then Erskine praises Tod's 'meritorious' history writing, asserting his preference for Tod's use of original documentary evidence including the texts of Muslim historians, above what he considers as less reliable sources, such as bards' songs, legends from the Puranas and romantic ballads. Erskine finds four reasons to explain why the Rajputs never attained military supremacy over all of India: (a) want of union among Rajputs; (b) inappropriateness of feudal militias for conquest; (c) polygamy among the Rajputs as a melancholy cause of disunion and intrigues; (d) Maratha plunder of Rajput territories as a cause of the decline of the Rajputs.

Erskine proceeds to make (as he had done in his review of Tod's first volume in the *Edinburgh Review*) an explicit denunciation of British subsidiary alliances with the Indian princes. He even makes clear his preference for self-government and autonomous action among the native peoples, rather than any 'far extended Empire' such as the Romans and the Persians and the British had had occasion to establish. He concludes his review of Tod's second volume with repeated praise for Tod's 'labour of love' and for his 'valuable and laborious work',[77] since he finds it 'the only source we know from which an acquaintance with the varied relations of the British interests and policy in the northwest of India can be drawn'. Thus, in spite of Erskine's marked anti-imperialism, even he is forced to take into account the presence of the politically oriented imperial interests of Britain in all discussions about India at the time.

The fourth contemporary review of Tod's *Annals* encompassed both volumes in the same issue of the *Quarterly Review*, and was authored by Henry Hart Milman (1791–1868).[78] This reviewer was an Anglican historian of Christianity and of the Roman Empire, having also participated with the Sanskritist H.H. Wilson in a translation into English of the ancient Indian epic of the *Mahabharata*, from the original in Sanskrit. According to Jason Freitag, Milman's review shows his conviction that true history was impossible in India without European or foreign influences; his opinion that only British rule could prevent native degradation and relapse into oriental despotism; his view that Tod's study of feudalism in India and in Europe revealed only 'dubious results' to the effect that all societies show the same universal tendencies when subjected to oppressive chivalry and that, in fact, the only possibility for 'advancement and progress' of political culture in India lay in a continuation of the British presence.[79]

Milman's biography places him in the anomalous category of a liberal Anglican conservative, a friend of both the conservative Bishop Heber and of the liberal reformer T.B. Macaulay (1800–59).[80] His publications show an ambition to combine contemporary historical techniques (as demonstrated by Gibbon, Thomas Arnold and Macaulay) with a Christian interpretation, taking into account material progress as well as religious doctrine and scriptures.

Milman does affirm the absence of historical records in India (contrary to Tod's determined claim of the existence of historical chronicles in Rajasthan), observing that miraculous legends (as in the *Puranas*) and poetic fiction restrained by religious awe could never result in serious history such as Herodotus had practised in ancient Greece. Even if there were historical chronicles like the *Raja Tarangini* or annals of Kashmir, these were always encumbered by mythology. Then Milman expresses disagreement with Tod's theory about the common origin of the tribes of Asia and Europe, in particular with the possibility of the Rajput tribes having a Scythian, Tartar origin, linking the Asian Jit tribes with the Getic tribes of Europe. Milman similarly dismisses Tod's conclusion of a possible common ancestry of the feudal system of medieval Europe as described in Henry Hallam's study and of the feudal system of the Rajputs as unfounded and unconvincing.

In his assessment of Tod's annals of the various Rajput kingdoms, Milman confesses an interest in 'the characteristic national poetry of all nations'. This is borne out in his comparison of Alaudin Khilji's infatuation for Princess Padmini in 1298 CE, with the evil king Agramant before Albracca trying to win Angelica, the beloved of Rolando, in Ariosto's *Orlando Furioso* (1516–32), and in his observation on the tragic death of Princess Kishna Kumari in 1810, an instance of 'a blameless Helen', signifying that Kishna Kumari had no share of blame in the tragedy and drama that surrounded her betrothal and death, quite like the legendary Spartan-Greek Helen of Troy. Having thus expedited Tod's 'Annals of Mewar', Milman does likewise with the 'annals of the rival states of Rajpootana', mentioning only the case of the Rathore prince Ajit of Marwar, celebrated for his resistance to Aurangzeb, with a quotation from Tod's 'Annals of Marwar' depicting the tragic scene of all Ajit's faithful queens who 'laded their bodies in the flames' with Ajit's heroic soul 'as it went to inhabit Amritpura at the age of forty-five years three months and twenty-two days'.[81] About Zalim Singh of Kota, Milman finds that his ministerial despotism, especially concerning taxation and the police force, 'might have moved the jealousy of M. Fouché himself', further acknowledging that the superior political talent of 'the wily chieftain of Kotah' might have made him, had he been in the anti-British league, 'a more formidable antagonist even than Scindia, Hyder or Tippoo'.

Milman concludes his review with two negative remarks: first, in relation to Tod's style, criticised as 'occasionally stiff and formal'; then the inordinate length of Tod's work, which unavoidably puts the patience of the reader 'to a severe trial'. He pays tribute, however, to

Tod's diligence and industry in collecting materials for history. Thus, in keeping with his personal approach to writing history, Milman's review of Tod's two volumes upholds the conservative Tory position on the British Empire (in line with the conservative editorial stand of the *Quarterly Review*), showing the importance of taking into account material conditions on the ground along with pro-imperialist ideological underpinnings.

The fifth review of Tod's *Annals* appeared in the *Asiatic Journal and Monthly Register* and contained presentations of both Tod's volume I (in 1829) and of Tod's volume II (in 1832). The *Asiatic Journal* (begun in 1816 by the East India Company itself) was an official press organ of the East India Company. As Jason Freitag has pointed out, the *Asiatic Journal* review[82] is marked by its focus on 'promoting the national interest' of Britain, putting 'the problem of imperial security at the forefront of its concerns', even to the point of highlighting only those sections of Tod's observations that could advance 'good government for the administrators', while ignoring Tod's interest in the benefit of the governed in India.[83] After paying tribute to the antiquarian interest of Tod's account of the Rajputs, in particular his genealogical table of the Rajput courts, and his description of the ancient manners of the early Rajput tribes, the anonymous *Asiatic Journal* reviewer expresses reservations about Tod's theory of a common origin and an original identity between the early Rajputs and the northern tribes of Europe, despite Tod's 'abundant evidence' in support of 'striking analogies' between the feudal system of the Rajputs and the feudal system in medieval Europe. He concludes this part of his review by insisting on the absence of stability and dependability among the vassals of the Rana of Mewar, thereby pointing to the greater stability and dependability of European serfs in their relations with their local lord. In a detailed summary of Tod's 'Annals of Mewar', the *Asiatic Journal* reviewer presents some of the salient dates and royal names of the history of Mewar which has in all probability contributed to the presence of these dates and royal names in the collective memory of most people interested in Indian history, even today. After 928 CE under the reign of Sakti Komar, the reviewer notes a 'lamentable chasm in the domestic annals of Mewar', of around 200 years, until 1150 CE, with the reign of the Gehlote Samarsi in Cheetore, who was killed at the Battle of Khaggar in Central Asia, together with his brother-in-law Prithvi Raj Chauhan, the Rajput king of Delhi, in 1198 CE, by Mahmud Shahbudin of Ghor. The next episode mentioned by the *Asiatic Journal* reviewer is the 1298 CE massacre of Rana Lakhamsi of Cheetore, together with his uncle Bheemsi and the wife of the latter, Princess Padmani, by Allaudin Khilji.[84] The narrative of the reviewer then skips ahead to 1419–69 CE, the reign of Rana Koombho. Koombho having been killed by his own son 'Oodo Hatiaro' (r.1469–74), Koombho's other son Raemul (r.1474–1509) fathered three sons, of whom Rana Sanga (r.1509–28) distinguished himself in the Battle of Kanua in 1528, defending Cheetore against the Moghul Babar. Sanga's son Rutna (r.1530–5) was the father of Bikramjeet (r.1535–42), who was the father of Udai Singh, who founded Udaipur. Udai Singh (r.1542–71) is, however, remembered as a coward, since he was in charge of the Rajput forces during the loss of Cheetore in 1567 to Emperor Akbar. Udai Singh's son, Rana Pratap, led the Rajput forces at the Battle of Haldighati in 1576, when Akbar's son, Prince Salim (the future Emperor Jahangir), caused the death of several thousands of Rajputs.[85] Rana Pratap is the unforgettable hero of the Rajputs, though most of his reign (1571–97) was spent in exile. Pratap's son, Umra, ruled from 1597 till 1621, and recovered Cheetore from the Mughals, at the cost of a humiliating compromise in 1614, allowing a permanent Mughal seat in Ajmer. Umra was succeeded by his son Kurrun (r.1621–8), in turn succeeded by Kurrun's son Jagat Singh (r.1628–54), who constructed the Jagniwas palace and the Jagmander temple on islands in the Udaipur lake. The next Rana of Mewar, Rana Raj Singh (r.1654–81), is remembered for having written a letter of protest against the anti-Hindu 'Jezeya' tax imposed by Emperor Aurangzeb on the Rajputs. Between 1681 and 1778, when Tod's friend Rana Bheem Singh succeeded to the throne of Mewar (r.1778–1828), the reigns of Jai Singh of Mewar, Umra II, Sangram Singh II, Jagat Singh II, Rana Pertap II, Rana Raj Singh II and Rana Ursi II were shadowed by Mughal exactions and predatory incursions by the Marathas, according to the *Asiatic Journal* reviewer. He praises Tod's personal implication in the rapid growth of Mewar to prosperity, after the introduction of Pax Britannica in Rajasthan in 1818. The *Asiatic Journal* reviewer endorses Tod's view that this 'meagre outline of the History of Mewar' serves to show that 'materials for history *do* exist in India'. He ends by expressing the hope that Tod's 'magnificent work' will contribute to making the Rajputs 'better known and appreciated'.

The anonymous reviewer prolongs his moderately reserved though enthusiastic views, already expressed about the first volume of Tod's *Annals*,[86] in his review of Tod's second volume.[87] This review skims over Tod's annals of the various Rajputana states, apart from Mewar (presented in Tod's first volume): Marwar, Bikaner, Jessulmer, Amber, Kotah and Bundi, with attention to the origin of each of these Rajput kingdoms.

Thus he traces the origins of the state of Marwar to 1212 CE, when Seoji Rahtore shifted the Rahtore capital from Kanauj (in the valley of the Ganga) to the valley of the Sutlej in western India, followed by shifts to Mundore in Marwar and then to Jodhpur, also in Marwar, under Joda Rahtore in 1432 CE. The reviewer reports that Maun Sing Rahtore succeeded to the Marwar throne in 1804. Blinded by a demoniacal spirit of revenge, Maun Sing Rahtore became 'one of the most sanguinary monsters that ever disgraced the *gadi* (or throne)'.[88]

The foundation of the Rajput state of Bikaner in the desert lands of the Yadu Bhattis is traced by Tod to around 1450 CE, by Beeka, one of the sons of the Marwar Rahtore Joda. But the *Asiatic Journal* reviewer reports Tod's pessimism owing to 'the prevailing general disorganisation in Bikaner' noted by Tod.[89]

The country proper of the Yadu Bhattis, while possessing the castle of Tunnote from 731 CE, had its capital Jessulmer founded only in 1156 CE, by Rawul Jessul, illustrating 'the gradual peopling of a great portion of the Indian desert'.[90]

The Annals of Amber or Jaipur report the founding of the Jaipur kingdom in 967 CE, by the leader Dhola Rae of Nurwar, who usurped the lands of the aboriginal mountaineers known as the Meenas. About 600 years later, Bhagwandas Cuchwaha gave his daughter in marriage to the future Mughal emperor Jehangir in 1586. After incursions by the Jats and the Marathas, Jagat Sing of Amber-Jaipur was forced into an alliance with the British, against his wishes, in 1818.

The *Asiatic Journal* reviewer devotes much attention to the kingdoms of Haravati (Kotah and Bundi). Tracing the origin of the Haras to Manik Rae of Ajmer, the founder of the Chohans of the North, he reports Tod's mention of Visaladeva (r.1010–74), as the progenitor of the Haras, and comments on Rao Budh Sing of Bundi's choice to remain faithful to his ally the Mughal emperor Shah Alam I in the 1720s, despite invitations to join rival Mughal factions. The reviewer then turns to the Regent of Kotah, Zalim Sing, whose political acumen was noted by Tod in the 1820s.

The reviewer praises Tod's use of lively anecdotes and colourful delineations of character and manners in his annals of the various kingdoms of Rajputana.

The second part of the *Asiatic Journal*'s review of Tod's second volume of *Annals* is devoted to Tod's 'Personal Narrative' at the end of this volume. The reviewer contrasts Tod's appreciation and detailed study of ancient Rajput monuments with the superficial, disparaging remarks on specimens of Hindu sculpture by the British chaplain Tennant (*Indian Recreations*),[91] who inspired James Mill (in *The History of British India*), to make similar negative comments about Hindu arts and manners. The *Asiatic Journal* reviewer illustrates the Rajput character with a few anecdotes from Tod's text: their heroic form of patriotic devotion, their inclination to superstition and the 'Ossianic style' of their historical chronicles, with poetic accounts of their battles by their bards. The *Asiatic Journal* review closes its presentation of this second volume of Tod's *Annals* with a tribute in superlative terms to Tod's contribution of 'a mass of entirely new information' on the history of Rajputana and 'the flood of light' that Tod's works had poured on the arts of India.[92]

We can conclude therefore that these *Asiatic Journal* reviews of Tod's two volumes of *Annals* highlight Tod's revelations as historiographer, art historian, anthropologist and geographer, while glossing over the controversial aspects of Tod's writings, in particular, his speculations about the common origins of the European and Asiatic peoples, as also his insistence on the close similarities between European and Rajput forms of feudalism.

The sixth and final review of Tod's work included both Tod's volumes of *Annals* in the French *Journal des Savans*. Silvestre de Sacy, a well-established French Orientalist, published a six-part review of the *Annals* in this learned Paris journal between 1830 and 1834.[93] Like certain other reviewers of Tod's work on Rajasthan that we have presented above, Sacy touches on Tod's sources and his wide use of Rajput historical chronicles, he adheres to Tod's advocacy of autonomy for India's native peoples as opposed to a top-down imposition of British supremacy and he notes certain paradoxes in Tod's perception of the Rajput mentalities where qualities jostled with defects. Sacy also accepts Tod's view of the existence of parallels between the Rajput form of feudalism and Europe's medieval feudalism, but firmly rejects Tod's hypothesis of a common ancestry descending from migrant Central Asian tribes between various European peoples and the peoples of Rajasthan.

In the first part of his six-part review, Sacy regrets that a solid base for a history of pre-Islamic India (the earliest Muslim invasion of India can be dated from approximately 700 CE) may not ever be possible. In order to trace the beginnings of the Rajput races according to their own perceptions of their origins, Sacy follows Tod's explorations of the mythological *Puranas* and the heroic poems about various Indian princes. Sacy endorses Tod's outline of the uninterrupted rule of Yadav kings (reputed to be descendants of the lunar branch of Pandu of the epic *Mahabharata*) on the throne of Delhi over some 2,500 years (from 1179 BCE, when the rule of Yudisthira of the *Mahabharata* began, until 1192 CE, when the rule of the Rajput king Prithvi Raj Chauhan ended).

Like Eugène Burnouf in his review of Tod's work on Rajasthan in the *Journal Asiatique*, Sacy makes a brief mention of the 'curious details' supplied by Tod in support of his hypothesis of strong similarities between the Rajput feudal system and European medieval feudalism, revealing his own lack of interest in such far-flung comparisons.[94]

The second part of Sacy's review deals with Tod's 'Annals of Mewar'. If Tod begins his history of the Gehlote dynasty of Mewar in 145 CE, with the installation of the founder, Keneksen, in the south of Gujarat (probably in Somnathpur), Sacy prefers to focus on the 800 years of Mewar's resistance to Muslim attacks (from the invasion of Chitore by Mahmud of Ghazni in 997 CE to 1818, when the Mewar alliance with the British put a stop to Muslim and Maratha depredations of their lands). This brings Sacy to acknowledge the truth in Tod's claim that the alliance treaty between the British authorities and Mewar, dated January 1818 and clinched by Tod himself, did indeed mark a turning point in Mewar's circumstances, since it enabled Mewar's British protectors to introduce much-needed reforms and administrative stability.

The third part of Sacy's review goes to the end of Tod's volume I, covering his essay on Rajput festivals and customs followed by the author's 'Personal Narrative' of his journey of 1819–20, from Mewar to Marwar and back. Sacy criticises Tod's tendency to establish parallels between the religious customs of the Rajputs and those of a whole host of other peoples (from the Egyptians to the Scythians), which Sacy finds unconvincing. While alluding to Tod's final halt at Ajmer, Sacy mentions the goatherd Aja Pal, who, according to legend, was the founding ancestor of the Chauhans of Ajmer, at an undetermined date, and whose descendants resisted Muslim invasions of Ajmer in the eighth and eleventh centuries. Sacy concludes his review with regrets that it does not thematically separate the subjects treated, that it does not follow a regular plan and that it does not include an index.

In the latter three parts of his review in the *Journal des Savans*, Sacy concentrates on Tod's second volume, in which he chooses to focus on the 'Annals of Marwar'. Tod's particular sketch of the history of the Marwar Rahtores begins from 470 CE, when they conquered Kanauj in northern India, continues to the late twelfth–early thirteenth century, when Shivji Rahtore moved from Kanauj to Gujarat under the Solankis of Anhalwarra and extends to the 1820s, when Tod returned to England. Despite inconsistencies in certain dates given by Tod, noted by Sacy,[95] the latter concurs with Tod that: 'It is impossible to ignore that there are important parallels between the European feudal system and the political institutions of Rajasthan, whatever the cause might be for this resemblance.'[96] Sacy thus fully endorses Tod's hypothesis of links and similarities between the European and the Rajput systems of feudalism. Sacy then dwells on the tragic forty-year rule of Ajit Singh Rahtore (r.1681–1724), of which he actually ruled only during the last seventeen years (1707–24).

The next chapters of Rahtore history were marked, according to Tod, by assassinations and intrigues between rival claimants to the Marwar throne (1724–1843).[97] Sacy closes the fifth part of his survey with comments on the *panchaiets* or indigenous civil juries that dealt with all the local civil cases of litigation, playing the role of 'tribunals of equity' and allowing the plaintiffs a possibility of appeal to their Raja.

In the sixth and final part of his review, Sacy deals with Tod's personal account at the end of his second volume. This includes Tod's two voyages to Kotah and Bundi in 1820, and again in 1821–2. Silvestre de Sacy closes this final part of his six-part review of *Annals* by reiterating his regrets at its lack of a complete list of contents, of a glossary of Indian terms and of coherent, internally cross-referenced dates. He emphasises again, however, the lively interest awakened in him by Tod's work, which he considers of 'great importance'.[98]

On the whole, Silvestre de Sacy's review is the longest contemporary review that covered both of Tod's volumes on Rajasthan, extending to some seventy-seven pages, since William Erskine in the *Edinburgh Review* totalled forty-eight pages, Henry Hart Milman in the *Quarterly Review* ran to thirty-nine pages and the *Asiatic Journal* included in all thirty-three pages. This greater length is mirrored in the immense detail of Sacy's coverage of the contents of Tod's volumes, which Sacy carefully considers, before accepting or rejecting their claims. Sacy's review is also, together with Burnouf's review in the French *Journal Asiatique*, one of the rare reviews of Tod's work on Rajasthan that appeared in French. This confirms that Tod's publication had reached across the English Channel into Europe at the time of its release.

Considered together, the above six reviews of Tod's work on Rajasthan show similarities and divergences. Among the similarities, we can note attention to Tod's historiographical pioneering, and a foregrounding of his 'Annals of Mewar' to the detriment of the annals of the other Rajput kingdoms, detailed most thoroughly by the *Asiatic Journal*. Also, with the exception of the *Oriental Herald* which expressed some support for Tod's views of a possible common origin of the Euro-Asian tribes and which with the *Journal des Savans* showed approval of Tod's comparison of the feudal systems of Europe and Rajasthan, the other four reviewers remained sceptical on these points. Finally, the only two reviewers to follow Tod's exhortations to respect for the Rajputs' ancient institutions and attachment to independence through to the anti-imperialist conclusions they implied, were William Erskine of the *Edinburgh Review* and Silvestre de Sacy of the *Journal des Savans*. All the others reinterpreted Tod's presentation of Britain's political stakes in Rajasthan in a strictly pro-imperialist light.

## Conclusion

Tod's shorter publications and the reviews in contemporary journals of his volumes on Rajasthan reveal his efforts (at the cost of considerable personal energy) to make known to the British and European public some of the vast amount of information he had gathered on the Rajputs while he was in India. His adherence to the norms of presentation at learned Orientalist societies (the Royal Asiatic Society in London and the Société Asiatique in Paris) as also his exchanges with reputable scholars and reviewers of his time (H.T. Colebrooke, Charles Wilkins, A.W. Schlegel, William Erskine) permit us to observe his gradual acceptance and recognition as an erudite authority on his beloved Rajputs.

## Notes

1. See Proceedings of the Minutes of the RAS Council, vol. I, March 1823–March 1827; folios 35–9, Council of 15 March 1824: Tod was elected as a Member of Council of the RAS; folios 85–8, Council of 16 April 1825: Tod was confirmed as the RAS librarian.
2. James Tod, *Annals and Antiquities of Rajasthan*, vol. I, London: Routledge & Kegan Paul Ltd, 1829; repr. Delhi: Rupa & Co., 1997, p. xviii.
3. See list of Tod's shorter publications in the Bibliography at the end of this volume.
4. James Tod, 'Translation of a Sanscrit Inscription relative to the last Hindu Monarch of Delhi, with comments thereon'. *Transactions of the Royal Asiatic Society*, 1 (1827), 133–54. Paper read 1 May 1824.
5. Tod, 'Translation of a Sanscrit Inscription', pp. 136–8.
6. Tod, 'Translation of a Sanscrit Inscription', p. 141.
7. Tod, 'Translation of a Sanscrit Inscription', p. 145, then p. 143.
8. Tod, 'Translation of a Sanscrit Inscription', p. 154.
9. James Tod, 'Comments on an inscription in marble at Madhucargarh, and on three grants inscribed on copper found at Ujjaiyini'. *Transactions of the Royal Asiatic Society*, 1 (1827), 227–9.
10. Tod, 'Translation of a Sanscrit Inscription'.
11. Henry Thomas Colebrooke, 'Three Grants of Land, inscribed on copper, found at Ujjaiyini, and presented by Major James Tod, to the Royal Asiatic Society, translated by Colebrooke, Henry Thomas'. *Transactions of the Royal Asiatic Society*, 1 (1827), 230–9. Read 4 December 1824. See esp. p. 231.
12. James Tod, 'An Account of Greek, Parthian, and Hindu Medals, found in India'. *Transactions of the Royal Asiatic Society*, 1 (1827), pp. 312–42. Read 18 June 1825.
13. Tod, 'An Account of Greek, Parthian, and Hindu Medals', p. 312.
14. De Sacy, *Mémoires sur diverses antiquités de la Perse* and Mionnet, *Description de Médailles Antiques*, cited in Tod, 'An Account of Greek, Parthian, and Hindu Medals', p. 313.
15. Tod, 'An Account of Greek, Parthian, and Hindu Medals', p. 320.
16. Tod, 'An Account of Greek, Parthian, and Hindu Medals', p. 330, n.
17. A.W. Schlegel, 'Observations sur quelques médailles bactriennes et indo-scythiques nouvellement découvertes'. *Journal Asiatique*, second series, 3 (November 1828), 321–49.
18. Baron de Meyendorf, 'Voyage en Boukharie et en Sogdiane (Balkh)'. *Journal Littéraire de Gottingue*, 108 (1828).
19. Schlegel, 'Observations', p. 342.

20 James Tod, 'De l'origine asiatique de quelques-unes des anciennes tribus de l'Europe, établies sur les rivages de la mer baltique, surtout les Su, Suedi, Suiones, Asi, Yeuts, Juts ou Getes-Goths' [par le Major Tod]. *Journal Asiatique*, first series, 11 (January–June 1827), 277–309.
21 James Tod, 'On the Religious Establishments of Mewar'. *Transactions of the Royal Asiatic Society*, 2 (1830), 270–325. Read 6 December 1828.
22 Tod, 'On the Religious Establishments', p. 270.
23 Tod, 'On the Religious Establishments', p. 295, n. *.
24 See Thomas R. Trautmann (ed.), *The Aryan Debate*, New Delhi: Oxford University Press 2008 (2005).
25 James Tod, 'Remarks on certain sculptures in the Cave Temples of Ellora'. *Transactions of the Royal Asiatic Society*, 2 (1830), 328–40. Read 6 December 1828.
26 The same Robert Melville Grindlay, had also published *Scenery, Costumes and Architecture chiefly on the western side of India*, London: Smith, Elder & Co., 1820.
27 Tod, 'Remarks on certain sculptures', pp. 328–30.
28 Tod, 'Remarks on certain sculptures', p. 330.
29 Tod, 'Remarks on certain sculptures', p. 329.
30 Tod, 'Remarks on certain sculptures', p. 331.
31 Tod, 'Remarks on certain sculptures', p. 332.
32 Tod, 'Remarks on certain sculptures', pp. 332–5.
33 James Tod, 'Observations on a Gold Ring of Hindu Fabrication found at Montrose in Scotland'. *Transactions of the Royal Asiatic Society*, 2 (1830), 559–72. Read 15 May 1830.
34 Tod, 'Observations on a Gold Ring', p. 561.
35 Tod, 'Observations on a Gold Ring', p. 571.
36 James Tod, 'Comparison of the Hindu and Theban Hercules, illustrated by an ancient Hindu intalgio'. *Transactions of the Royal Asiatic Society*, 3 (1835), 139–59. Read 4 December 1830.
37 Tod, 'Comparison of the Hindu and Theban Hercules', p. 140.
38 Tod, 'Comparison of the Hindu and Theban Hercules', p. 144, with tables on pp. 143 and 148.
39 Tod, 'Comparison of the Hindu and Theban Hercules', p. 153.
40 Tod, 'Comparison of the Hindu and Theban Hercules', p. 154.
41 Tod, 'Comparison of the Hindu and Theban Hercules', p. 157.
42 James Tod, 'The Feudal System in Rajasthan'. *Asiatic Journal and Monthly Register*, new series, 5.17 (May–August 1831), pp. 40–8.
43 Colonel Wilford was the author, among other texts, of 'The Geography of the Puranas', and of an 'Essay on Vicramaditya and Salivahana' in *Asiatick Researches*.
44 Tod, 'The Feudal System', p. 40.
45 In *Asiatick Researches*, 15 (1825).
46 Review by Silvestre de Sacy, *Journal des Savans*, November 1830, and anonymous review in the *Asiatic Journal*, 28 (1829).
47 M. le Colonel Tod, 'Géographie du Radjasthan'. *Journal Asiatique*, new series, 8 (July–December 1831), 46–66.
48 Also James Tod, *Travels in Western India*, London: William Allen & Co., 1839 (posth.),pp. 459, 499; repr. Delhi: Munshiram Manoharlal Publishers, 1997.
49 James Tod, 'Indo-Grecian Antiquities'. *Asiatic Journal and Monthly Register*, new series, 17.65 (May–August 1835), 9–15.
50 Tod, 'Indo-Grecian Antiquities', p. 9.
51 Tod, 'An Account of Greek, Parthian, and Hindu Medals'.
52 Tod, 'Indo-Grecian Antiquities', p. 10.
53 Tod, 'Indo-Grecian Antiquities', p. 12.
54 James Tod, 'The Vow of Sunjogta', from Chand's chronicle, was published after Tod's death, in 1838, in *Asiatic Journal or the Monthly Register*, 25.1 (January–April 1838), in three sections: pp. 101–12; pp. 197–211; and pp. 273–86. See p. 103.
55 Tod, 'The Vow of Sunjogta', p. 110.
56 Tod, 'The Vow of Sunjogta', p. 112.

57 Tod, 'The Vow of Sunjogta', p. 204.
58 Tod, 'The Vow of Sunjogta', pp. 207–8.
59 Tod, 'The Vow of Sunjogta', pp. 285–6.
60 Anonymous review of Tod's 'On the Religious Establishments of Mewar', in *Asiatic Journal and Monthly Register*, 27 (January–June 1829), 328–30.
61 Anonymous review of Tod's 'An Account of some sculptures in the Cave Temples of Ellora', *Asiatic Journal and Monthly Register*, 27 (January–June 1829), 328–30.
62 Anonymous review of Tod's 'Observations on a Gold Ring of Hindu fabrication found at Montrose, Scotland', *Asiatic Journal and Monthly Register*, new series, 3 (September–December 1830), 33–4.
63 I am indebted to Norbert Peabody, 'Tod's *Rajast'han* and the boundaries of imperial rule in 19th century India'. *Modern Asian Studies*, 30.1 (1996), 185–220, and to Jason Freitag, *Serving Empire, Serving Nation: James Tod and the Rajputs of Rajasthan*, Leiden: Brill Publishers, 2009, pp. 131–70, and bibliography, for the references to the reviews of Tod's *Annals and Antiquities of Rajasthan*.
64 See Freitag, *Serving Empire*, for an analysis of mainly the political content of these reviews of Tod's work, pp. 131–55. The *Asiatic Journal* published a review of Tod's volume I in its issue of July–December 1829 (vol. 28), pp. 187–98, which is mentioned by Freitag, followed by a review of Tod's volume II in vol. 8 of its new series in its issue of May–August 1832, pp. 57–66, and pp. 108–18, not mentioned by Freitag. The review in six parts in the French *Journal des Savans*, all by the French Orientalist scholar Silvestre de Sacy, is mentioned neither by Peabody nor by Freitag. See *Journal des Savans*, November 1830, pp. 643–57; January 1831, pp. 65–81; and April 1831, pp. 225–38 which cover the first volume of *Annals and Antiquities of Rajasthan*; while May 1834, pp. 257–69; July 1834, pp. 394–404; and November 1834, pp. 641–9 are the three parts that deal with the second volume of *Annals and Antiquities*.
65 *Oriental Herald*, 22 (July–September 1829), 505–17.
66 Freitag, *Serving Empire*, p. 137.
67 *Journal Asiatique*, new series 2, 4 (July–December 1829), 374–89.
68 *Edinburgh Review*, 52 (October 1830–January 1831), 86–108; and 56 (July 1832–January 1833), 73–98, by William Erskine, represent forty-eight pages in all.
69 See Freitag, *Serving Empire*, p. 139, and W.E. Houghton, *The Wellesley Index to Victorian Periodicals: 1824–1900*, London: Routledge & Kegan Paul, 1966.
70 See biographical note on William Erskine (1773–1852), by Katherine Prior, www.oxforddnb.com/articles/8/8880-article.html?back, accessed 12 November 2010.
71 *Edinburgh Review*, 52 (October 1830–January 1831), 86–108.
72 Tod, *Annals*, vol. I.
73 *Edinburgh Review*, 56 (October 1832), 73–98.
74 Tod, *Annals*, vol. II, p. 321, 'Annals of Amber', under the reign of Aurangzeb, 1658–1707.
75 *Edinburgh Review*, 56, p. 84.
76 *Edinburgh Review*, 56, p. 85.
77 *Edinburgh Review*, 56, p. 98.
78 *Quarterly Review*, 48.95 (December 1832), 1–39, review by Henry Hart Milman of thirty-nine pages.
79 See Freitag, *Serving Empire*, pp. 142–50.
80 See biographical note on Henry Hart Milman (1791–1868), by H.C.G. Mathew, www.oxforddnb.com/articles/18/187778-article.html?back, accessed 12 November 2010.
81 The name 'Amritpura' is among those used in Hindu mythology for the celestial spheres to which a person's soul departs after his/her death.
82 *Asiatic Journal and Monthly Register*, 28 (July–December 1829), 187–98.
83 Freitag, *Serving Empire*, pp. 132–3.
84 See Ramya Sreenivasan, *The Many Lives of a Rajput Queen: Heroic Pasts in India c.1500–1900*, Seattle: University of Washington Press, 2007, esp. chapter 4, 'Tales of past glory under early colonial indirect rule (c.1750–1850)', pp. 117–56.
85 Tod's text, at *Annals*, vol. I. p. 270, mentions 14,000 Rajput deaths, while the reviewer of the *Asiatic Journal* gives '32,000' Rajput deaths at the 1576 Battle of Haldighati.

86 *Asiatic Journal and Monthly Register*, 28 (July–December 1829), 187–98.
87 *Asiatic Journal and Monthly Register*, new series, 8 (May–August 1832), 57–66; 108–18.
88 *Asiatic Journal and Monthly Register*, new series, 8 (May–August 1832), p. 59.
89 *Asiatic Journal and Monthly Register*, new series, 8 (May–August 1832), p. 60.
90 *Asiatic Journal and Monthly Register*, new series, 8 (May–August 1832), p. 62.
91 William Tennant, *Indian Recreations consisting chiefly of strictures on the domestic and rural economy of the Mahomedans and Hindoos*, 2nd edn, London: Longman, Hurst, Rees and Orme, 3 vols, octavo, 1804–8.
92 *Asiatic Journal and Monthly Register*, new series, 8 (May–August 1832), p. 118.
93 See *Journal des Savans*, November 1830, 643–57; January 1831, 65–81; and April 1831, 225–38, which cover the first volume of *Annals and Antiquities of Rajasthan*; while May 1834, 257–69; July 1834, 394–404; and November 1834, 641–9 are the three parts that deal with the second volume of *Annals and Antiquities*.
94 *Journal des Savanst*, November 1830, p. 657.
95 See Debra Diamond, Catherine Glynn and Karni Singh Jasol, with contributions by Jason Freitag and Rahul Jain, *Garden and Cosmos: The Royal Paintings of Jodhpur*, London: British Museum Press, 2009, p. 298.
96 *Journal des Savans*, May 1834, p. 264.
97 See Diamond *et al.*, *Garden and Cosmos*, p. 298.
98 *Journal des Savans*, November 1834, p. 649.

# CONCLUSION

# Tod's sympathetic understanding of Rajput difference

I intend to conclude by, first, comparing Tod's goals as expressed in the introductions to his major published works[1] with what we can show at the end of this study of his writings of how far he achieved these goals. Then, in a second step, I will present Tod's legacy to posterity through an overview of the documents and objects he bequeathed to the Royal Asiatic Society, by a special provision in his last will and testament. Finally, in order to situate Tod among the various scholarly British traveller-philanthropists who scoured Britain's colonial territories through the nineteenth century, in India and the Middle East in particular, I will compare Tod's particular knowledge-gathering efforts with the similar efforts of a few other British knowledge gatherers in eastern lands, in order to arrive at some understanding of Tod's individual position among this group of British colonialist, intellectual explorers. As throughout this study, my attention will be focused on ways of circumventing the too-neat binaries of a one-sided perception of top-down exchanges between West and East, or between colonisers and colonised, as spread by Edward Said's *Orientalism*, despite the undeniable contribution of this seminal work to the analysis of power relations between the Western and the non-Western worlds.

## Tod's declared goals

To begin with Tod's goals as they appear in the 'Author's Introduction' to each of the two volumes of his *Annals and Antiquities of Rajasthan* and to his *Travels in Western India*, they reveal him as entertaining the idealistic ambition of exciting the 'interest', 'sympathy' and 'enthusiastic delight' of his readers:[2]

> The struggles of a brave people for independence during a series of ages, sacrificing whatever was dear to them for the maintenance of the religion of their forefathers, and sturdily defending to death, and in spite of every

## CONCLUSION

10 Rana Bhim Singh of Udaipur installing the image of Srinathji in a tented enclosure.
(By kind permission of the Royal Asiatic Society of Great Britain and Ireland)

temptation, their rights and national liberty, form a picture which it is difficult to contemplate without emotion.

Tod also wishes 'to provoke further investigation', being conscious of the shortcomings of his own historiographical enterprise in relation to the available accounts of the Rajputs' past:[3]

> I have been so hardy as to affirm and endeavour to prove the common origin of the martial tribes of Rajasthan and those of ancient Europe. I have expatiated to some length upon the evidence in favour of the existence of

a feudal system in India, similar to that which prevailed in the early ages of the European continent, and of which relics still remain in the laws of our own nation. Hypotheses of this kind are, I am aware, viewed with suspicion, and sometimes assailed with ridicule. .... However, I submit my proofs to the candid judgment of the world: the analogies, if not conclusive on the questions, are still sufficiently curious and remarkable to repay the trouble of perusal and to provoke further investigation.

In addition to his satisfaction at having successfully carried out a cherished aim, Tod insists on the political slant to his writings on the Rajputs:[4]

> I have fulfilled what I considered to be a sacred obligation to the race amongst whom I have passed the better portion of my life: ... to awaken a sympathy for the objects of my work, the interesting people of Rajpootana. ... In the present circumstances of our alliance with these states, every trait of national character, and even every traditional incident, which, by leading us to understand and respect their peculiarities, may enable us to secure their friendship and esteem, become of infinite importance.

And despite not having executed the 'exact historical principles' of what was considered as serious, academic history,[5] Tod is confident that his 'copious collection of materials for the future historian',[6] and his specific historical anecdotes (*non historia sed particulae historiae*),[7] will indeed 'impart juster notions of the genius of the Asiatics',[8] as well as fulfil his hope 'of making the Rajpoots known by their works'.[9]

We have very few pointers from which to decide how far Tod did indeed achieve the above two goals he had set himself while compiling his publications on the Rajputs: namely, to arouse a sympathetic interest in the Rajputs in Britain and Europe, and also to inspire further investigation among British and European scholars into the history and customs of the Rajputs. One sign of the importance of Tod's *Annals* appears in the preface by Douglas Sladen to the 1914 reprint of this work by Routledge and Sons:[10]

> Tod's *Rajasthan* has for three quarters of a century been recognised as one of the chief English Classics upon India. It has for many years been out of print, and the price of a copy has been prohibitive. ... I approached Messrs. George Routledge & Sons Ltd, who ... make a speciality of resuscitating out-of-print Classics. ... The result is that the libraries of Great Britain and India and the Empire will be able to place on their shelves at a popular price this indispensable and immensely valuable Classic, which not one in a hundred of them has previously been able to include in its catalogue.

In Sladen's estimation, apparently, Tod's message had not fallen on deaf ears, since he considered that *Annals and Antiquities* had attained

## CONCLUSION

the status of an 'indispensable and immensely valuable Classic' about India in the English language.

Concerning the degree of Tod's success in inspiring new research on the Rajputs and western India, we find a hint in the publisher's 'Advertisement' at the beginning of his posthumously published *Travels in Western India*. The publisher mentions the continuing epigraphical research being conducted by British scholars in the late 1830s, in the wake of Tod's pioneering initiatives, into the ancient rock inscriptions in western India:[11]

> By the delay, an additional interest has been imparted to the subject of the work, by the flood of light which is now pouring upon the antiquities of Western India – the Girnar inscriptions, in particular, being now in a course of interpretation by the Asiatic Society of Bengal, whose learned secretary, Mr. James Prinsep, has already discovered the name of 'Antiochus the Greek', and that of one of the Ptolemies of Egypt, recorded in them.

The publisher's use of terms of abundance like 'the flood of light' and 'now pouring upon' demonstrates the view that Tod's successors in Indian learning were numerous and well-informed.

### The Tod Collection at the Royal Asiatic Society in London

The specific objectives Tod fixed upon, in the compilation of his two-volume work on the Rajputs and the dense travel narrative of his journeys through Gujarat, were further honoured through the documents and objects he bequeathed to the Royal Asiatic Society of London in his will. Upon Tod's death in November 1835,[12] the Council of the Royal Asiatic Society, which assembled on 6 February 1836,[13] recognised receipt of Mrs James Tod's letter making known Tod's donation to the Royal Asiatic Society of all his books and manuscripts and coins on oriental subjects. The Royal Asiatic Society acknowledged 'the liberal bequest of her late husband and assured her of the high respect the Royal Asiatic Society must ever entertain for [her late husband's] memory'. These objects became known in the Royal Asiatic Society as 'the Tod Collection'. There are at least three formal lists of the Tod Collection in the records of the Royal Asiatic Society. The first appeared scattered among the general list of donations to the Royal Asiatic Society published at the end of each of the three volumes of the Society's *Transactions* (1827, 1830 and 1835).[14] The second contains 120 items claiming to be the 'Sanskrit and Prakrit MSS (Todd [*sic*] Collection)' established by an anonymous researcher, and came out in the October 1890 issue of the *Journal of the Royal Asiatic Society*.[15]

The most recent list was compiled by L.D. Barnett and was published in the Society's *Journal* of April 1940.[16] Barnett's list contains 171 items presented in the order that they were registered in the Royal Asiatic Society general catalogue, followed by an alphabetical index of them, but Barnett in his brief introduction points out that twenty-one of these items were in fact donated by various donors other than Tod, leaving 150 items that can be indeed understood to have come 'from Colonel Tod's library'.[17] Despite Barnett's use of the label 'Indian Manuscripts', he admits that 'not all of them are manuscripts'. We will now make a synthetic analysis of the types of documents included in Tod's donations to the Royal Asiatic Society.

Apart from the objects Tod gifted to the museum of the Royal Asiatic Society, also mentioned in the three volumes of the *Transactions* –items in stone, plaster, copper, ivory, shell, velvet, horn, as well as portraits and drawings, rolls of canvas and glass – Tod presented, according to the lists in the three *Transactions* volumes, a total of forty-four documents to the Royal Asiatic Society. By 1890, these were listed as a total of 120 documents, and by 1940 they amounted to 150 documents. This threefold multiplication of Tod's donations of texts across the decades can perhaps be attributed to the fact that he made his donations piecemeal over several years, before the major bequest of 1836 (after his death in November 1835). Setting apart texts in English like Peter Heylyn's *Cosmography and history of the Whole World*, printed in Dublin in 1744, and A. de la Motraye's *Travels in Europe, Asia and Africa* of 1832, Tod's donations are made up mainly of texts from India. These are written in a variety of Indian languages, Sanskrit, Prakrit, Hindi, Gujarati, and other languages of northwest India such as Rajasthani-Hindi, Jaipuri-Hindi, Brajabakha-Hindi and Panjabi. Barnett classifies Tod's textual donations into three groups: (a) historical writings including panegyric compositions, pedigrees and miscellanea; (b) Jain doctrine in metrical tales or in prose stories; (c) Sanskrit classics and vernacular writings showing various phases of Indian culture. We can also note the absence of any Persian or Urdu documents of Muslim origin among Tod's donations. Although Tod refers constantly through his works to the texts of Muslim historians like Abul Fazl and Ferishta, these apparently did not feature among the texts he sought to collect and carry back to Britain. A rapid perusal of the various lists of Tod's textual donations convinces the observer of the eclecticism of Tod's collecting instinct, since it spanned ancient classics in Sanskrit to more contemporary texts like local histories, the lives of local saints (Mahatmya), innumerable versions of the *Prithviraj Raso* by the poet Chund and princely genealogies, while also covering Jainism, Vaishnavism and Shaivism, with the same enthusiasm. The paradox is that Tod could not read any

CONCLUSION

Indian language, although he was able to communicate orally in the Rajasthani dialects with ease.[18] So any analysis or 'translation' he made of the Indian texts he assembled was necessarily through the intermediary of his Indian counterparts, in particular his learned Jain guide, Yati Gyanchandra, who during Tod's sojourn in India 'was one of the great comforts of [my] exile'.[19] Tod had carried back to England his 'cargo of mutilated divinities, inscriptions, arms, manuscripts to the number of forty boxes'.[20] He makes explicit the motivation behind this vast collection in the Introduction to his first volume on Rajasthan:[21]

> The large collection of ancient Sanscrit and Bakha MSS, which I conveyed to England, have been presented to the Royal Asiatic Society, in whose library they are deposited. The contents of many, still unexamined, may throw additional light on the history of ancient India. I claim only the merit of having brought them to the knowledge of European scholars; but I may hope that this will furnish a stimulus to others to make similar exertions.

Thus, Tod seems to have been conscious of participating in an emerging trend of new 'Indological' scholarship, in the future flourishing of which he optimistically placed hope and confidence.

## Comparisons of Tod with other British travellers in the Orient

This brings me to comparisons between Tod's trajectory among the Rajputs and the experiences of other scholarly British traveller-philanthropists who scoured Britain's colonial territories through the nineteenth century, in India and the Middle East in particular. The aim of these comparisons is to situate Tod among the British gentlemen-scholars of his age, who wandered, as he did, among the peoples of eastern lands in search of historical, mythological, philological and literary information. In India, around the same time that Tod was the British political agent for the western Rajputana states (1818–22), at least three (among many) British administrators took advantage of their proximity to Indian circles of power in order to formulate in writing their personal understandings of the historical backgrounds and administrative particularities of the regions they administered. For example, Mark Wilks (1759–1831),[22] joined the Madras Army in India in 1777 at the age of eighteen, and had occasion to interact with Colonel Colin Mackenzie, who organised teams of Indian and British researchers in order to collect documents and conduct surveys of India over several decades.[23] Wilks, from his position as the British Resident at Mysore from 1782 to 1799, assembled information on the various political regimes that had functioned in Mysore from the beginnings of the Hindu Wodeyar dynasty, through its takeover by the Muslim military chiefs Hyder Ali (r.1769–82) and Tipu Sultan (1782–99). Since the British imposed their supremacy on Mysore from 1799 onwards, Wilks entitled his publication on Mysore as *Historical Sketches of the south of India in an attempt to trace the history of Mysoor, from the origin of the Hindoo Government of that state to the extinction of the Mohammedan dynasty in 1799. Founded chiefly on Indian authorities collected by Mark Wilks*.[24] Wilks can be compared to Tod in his attention to historical sources by 'Indian authorities', and in his attempt to render in English a coherent account of the details in the Indian documents he consulted, such as they appeared in Indian vernacular languages.

Another famous example of a British administrator who genuinely sought the welfare of the Indians who came under his administration is Thomas Munro (1761–1827).[25] Remembered for his reorganisation of the *ryotwari* system of land revenue collection in the Madras Presidency, with a view to reducing the exploitation of the Indian land cultivators while he was Governor of Madras between 1820 and 1827, he is included among the 'Romantics in India' by Thomas R. Metcalf.[26] Munro's major piece of writing, published in 1881, some fifty-five years after his death, is a pamphlet containing his reflections on his own experiences in south India as a British colonial administrator. The parallel between Munro and Tod is obvious in their common ambition to serve the best interests of the Indians under their administration, while also doing their utmost to loyally carry out their colonial responsibilities.

A final example of a British administrator in India, with sympathetic leanings towards the Indians under his administrative control, is James Grant Duff (1789–1858).[27] A devoted friend of Mountstuart Elphinstone, during the latter's residency in Pune, between 1808 and 1818, Grant Duff was appointed Resident at Satara between 1818 and 1822, during precisely the same years that Tod was the British political agent in Rajputana, the year 1818 having marked the final capitulation of the heads of several Indian princely states to British political supremacy. Like Tod, Grant Duff retired to Scotland in 1823, for health reasons, and during his retirement devoted his energy to publishing his three-volume work on the Marathas.[28] Both Tod and Grant Duff were careful to underline the respective particularities of the Rajputs and the Marathas in their historical presentations of these peoples.

The cases of Mark Wilks, Thomas Munro and James Grant Duff suffice to show that Tod was not alone in his views and efforts to gather sympathetic information on India and to make these details known to

## CONCLUSION

the wider world. Their deliberate crossing of the conventional borders between colonisers and colonised illustrates the varied types of relationships and exchanges that could exist between British officials and the peoples of the colonised countries they had to deal with.

Even farther afield than India, in the Middle East for example, and in periods other than the late eighteenth/early nineteenth centuries, certain British gentlemen-scholars made similar attempts to acquire eastern languages, and to compile their supportive views on the eastern peoples they chose to study at close quarters. Studies published by Gerald MacLean,[29] Rana Kabbani[30] and Geoffrey Nash[31] have been particularly useful to me in constructing this part of the conclusion of my reflections on James Tod.

For example, Gerald MacLean commends the seventeenth-century lawyer Sir Henry Blount (1602–82)[32] for his pragmatic method of gathering data during his travels to Constantinople and Egypt in 1634, in order to reach objective conclusions, since this went against the prevalent prejudices among English travellers to the Middle East at the time, who tended to use the Bible as their travel guidebook, and 'disbelieve anything [they] saw that was not confirmed by it'. MacLean applauds Blount's endeavours, since 'to expose just such prejudicial attitudes towards the East, Henry Blount travelled to the Levant in 1634, to see for himself and test received opinion by careful observation'.[33] The publication in London in 1634 of Blount's *Voyage to the Levant* established his reputation as a traveller and author.[34] According to his biographer in the *Dictionary of National Biography*, Blount showed 'sturdy independence of thought' and 'keen powers of observation of men and manners', pointing out the contrasts between the flourishing palaces and the oppression of the ordinary people in Egypt under Turkish Ottoman rule, based on evidence collected on the ground. Blount can be perceived as a forerunner of Tod, since they both seem to have bestowed a similarly sympathetic gaze on the peoples of the East they encountered, choosing to share the local food, language and living conditions, while assembling information at every opportunity along their way.

Another gentleman-traveller who can be compared to Tod is Edward William Lane (1801–76),[35] known for his two scholarly publications on the Islamic Middle East: (a) *Manners and Customs of the Modern Egyptians* (1836); and (b) his translation into English in three volumes of *One Thousand and One Nights* (1841). Lane shared with Tod an extreme attention to scholarly notes and details in the compilation of his texts. However, Rana Kabbani finds that Lane went perhaps a little too far in his erudite deliberations, to the point of excluding humaneness, and becoming a prey to the web of excessive, self-defeating scholarship. She also accuses Lane of having failed to free himself of tenacious Western biases about the East, since at times he seems simply to reiterate the patronising heritage of Western Orientalist learning.[36] So, the parallel between Lane and Tod has to be nuanced in favour of Tod, who did not labour under Western biases or the condescending tone of traditional Orientalism, using his energy, on the contrary, to dispel those biases and that patronising superiority, in order to establish the historical value and intellectual autonomy of Rajput learning in its own rights.

Wilfrid Scawen Blunt (1840–1922), although of a much later period,[37] shares in his own way certain characteristics with James Tod. Rana Kabbani finds in Wilfrid Blunt 'a staunch defender of Eastern rights against his own nation', since he based his patriotism on a universal love of the ancestral soil, common to peoples all over the world.[38] This rare trait of recognising that alien peoples have a right to the same privileges and consideration Europeans accorded themselves is a link between Wilfrid Blunt and Tod. Geoffrey Nash positions Blunt among the 'most vociferous' of the British travellers 'who consciously identified with the Eastern peoples whom they encountered', going to the extent of espousing Egyptian nationalism, thus 'cutting across established orthodoxies concerning the East'.[39] Politically, Blunt advocated a specialised British sponsorship of the self-determination and internal reform of the Eastern nations in contact with British administration, as opposed to the more non-committal approval of a benevolent, disinterested British patronage of their eastern territories by certain other British officials on the one hand, and the clear defence of the imposition of a beneficial, efficient Western rule over inferior races, by outright British imperialists, on the other, according to Geoffrey Nash.[40] Thus, both culturally and politically, Blunt's ambivalences towards the Egyptians he interacted with can be seen to reflect, although more virulently, Tod's ambivalences towards his Rajputs. Indeed, Tod bravely stood against the orthodox policies of the British Government of his time in Calcutta and Delhi, he espoused the particular interests of certain Rajputs, he upheld a British respect for the Rajputs' honour and pride against their eventual humiliation by British supremacy and he put forward ideas for internal, administrative reforms in the Rajput territories. In their published texts also, a certain similarity between Blunt and Tod can be observed. The very titles of Blunt's three published texts on the Middle East[41] exhibit Blunt's tolerance and favourable disposition towards Egyptian interests and Islam. For Tod's part, his *Annals and Antiquities of Rajasthan*, his *Travels in Western India*, as also his twelve shorter articles published in learned journals in London and Paris, all show

CONCLUSION

Tod's keen interest in the detailed history and in the defence of the interests of 'his' Rajputs.

## *Coda*

Throughout this study, as I have followed Tod's trajectory, I have tried to keep in mind his basic disposition in favour of a 'partnership' between the Rajputs and the British in India, rather than underline the contrast between the Rajput world view and the British colonialist world view. In this exploration of the avenues of intercultural dialogue and exchange that could exist within the complexities of the colonial situation, I have sought corroboration from other studies on British scholars in territories of the Orient. Thus, even Rana Kabbani, who tends to defend and illustrate Edward Said's top-down, binary approach to East–West relations, in a very negative vein since she speaks as an Easterner, acknowledges that[42]

> [o]bviously enough, not all the representations [of the East by Western visitors] that resulted were pernicious. There were some European minds that could perceive the common humanity in East and West. ... Although there was a determination on the part of the West to record all aspects of the Orient in order to facilitate its colonial designs, there was at the same time, a genuine and disinterested interest on the part of some individuals in the different reality which the Orient seemed to them to be. Such individuals contributed to an immense expansion of human knowledge, and were not handicapped by the perceptions they had inherited.

Gerald MacLean, for his part, defends 'mutuality' and 'reciprocity' in his study of Anglo-Ottoman exchanges.[43] Rather than focus on the tendency of European visitors to Eastern countries to hierarchise differences in favour of European superiority, MacLean prefers to turn attention to their 'remarkable capacity for *sympathetic understanding* of a society and a culture *quite different* from their own'.[44] This concept of 'sympathetic understanding' of difference has been very inspiring to me in my attempts to analyse Tod's portrayals of Rajput difference for British and European readers. Geoffrey Nash attempts to allow for possibilities of opposition to and contestation of the established discourses of Imperialism and Orientalism, in order precisely to show that Orientalism was not a monolithic construct, in his study of travellers to the Middle East between 1830 and 1926. Nash also conceptualises knowledge gathering as a two-way process:[45]

> In fronting the notion that travellers carry their stereotypes with them and return with them largely undisturbed, this study aims to open up the proposition that cross-cultural encounter did in certain instances result

in enhanced understanding of the target Eastern cultures. In these cases, the travellers brought back new vocabularies, influenced by if not directly acquired in the East.

The intermediary space in which this cross-cultural dialogue takes place, entailing the reciprocal transformation of both parties involved, has occupied me throughout the development of this reflection on Tod's contacts and relations with the Rajputs of his time.

As a final word, we can perhaps emphasise Tod's extraordinary versatility in overcoming difficulties of every imaginable kind (poor health, administrative hurdles, distrust by Rajputs and by British interlocutors, trying climatic conditions, language and cultural differences, the human gulf created by the colonial situation, to name only a few). Despite these restrictions, Tod confronted considerable risks and stepped across several lines that marked taboos and territories forbidden to 'outsider' British officials in India. That his optimism and enthusiasm about the people and culture of Rajasthan continue to live in his texts, in his donations to the Royal Asiatic Society and in the memories of innumerable individuals across the continents is perhaps the best and most lasting tribute to his unique contribution to intercultural dialogue and wider human understanding, despite the constricting context of growing British supremacy across the India in which he lived.

## Notes

1 James Tod, *Annals and Antiquities of Rajasthan*, vol. I, London: Routledge & Kegan Paul Ltd, 1829; repr. Delhi: Rupa & Co., 1997; James Tod, *Annals and Antiquities of Rajasthan*, vol. II, London: Routledge & Kegan Paul Ltd, 1832; repr. Delhi: Rupa & Co., 1997; and also James Tod, *Travels in Western India*, London: William Allen & Co., 1839 (posth.); repr. Delhi: Munshiram Manoharlal Publishers, 1997.
2 Tod, *Annals*, vol. I, p. xix.
3 Tod, *Annals*, vol. I, p xix–xx.
4 Tod, *Annals*, vol. II, p. vii.
5 Tod, *Annals*, vol. II, p. viii.
6 Tod, *Annals*, vol. I, p. xx.
7 Tod, *Annals*, vol. II, p. viii.
8 Tod, *Annals*, vol. II, p. viii.
9 Tod, *Travels*, p. vii.
10 Tod, *Annals*, vol. I, p. ix.
11 Tod, *Travels*, p. viii.
12 See Tod's Last Will and Testament, PRO, Kew: PRO/B/11/1857, folios 31–3, deposited by Tod with his solicitors on 11 August 1834.
13 Minutes of Council, Royal Asiatic Society, vol. IV, April 1833–April 1837, folios 185–8.
14 See Jason Freitag, *Serving Empire, Serving Nation: James Tod and the Rajputs of Rajasthan*, Leiden: Brill Publishers, 2009, appendix 2, pp. 203–7, which brings together these scattered mentions.
15 *Journal of the Royal Asiatic Society*, October 1890, 801–13.

## CONCLUSION

16 *Journal of the Royal Asiatic Society*, April 1940, 129–78, 'Catalogue of the Tod Collection of Indian Manuscripts in the possession of the Royal Asiatic Society', by L.D. Barnett.
17 *Journal of the Royal Asiatic Society*, April 1940, p. 130.
18 Tod, *Travels*, p. xxxiii, n.
19 Tod, *Travels*, p. 445.
20 Tod, *Travels*, p. 498.
21 Tod, *Annals*, vol. I, p. xviii.
22 See biographical note on Mark Wilks (1759–1831) at http://en.wikipedia.org/wiki/Mark_Wilks, accessed 3 November 2012.
23 See Jennifer Howes, *Illustrating India: The Early Colonial Investigations of Colin Mackenzie (1784–1821)*, New Delhi: Oxford University Press, 2010.
24 Mark Wilks, *Historical Sketches of the south of India in an attempt to trace the history of Mysoor, from the origin of the Hindoo Government of that state to the extinction of the Mohammedan dynasty in 1799. Founded chiefly on Indian authorities collected by Mark Wilks*, 3 vols, quarto, London: Longman, Hurst, Rees & Orme, 1810–17.
25 Thomas Munro, *Writings of Major-General Sir Thomas Munro, Governor of Madras*, ed. Alexander John Arbuthnot, London, 1889(1881). See also biographical note on Thomas Munro (1761–1827), at http://en.wikipedia.org/wiki/Sir_Thomas_Munro, accessed 3 November 2012.
26 Thomas R. Metcalf, *Ideologies of the Raj*, Cambridge: Cambridge University Press, 2001 (1995), pp. 25–7.
27 See biographical note on James Grant Duff (1789–1858), at http://en.wikipedia.org/wiki/James_Grant_Duff, accessed 3 November 2012. Also A.R. Kulkarni, *James Cunninghame Grant Duff, Administrator-Historian of the Marathas*, Kolkata: K.P. Bagchi, 2006.
28 James Grant Duff, *History of the Marathas*, London: Longman, Rees, Orme, Brown and Green, 3 vols, 1826.
29 Gerald MacLean, *The Rise of Oriental Travel: English Visitors to the Ottoman Empire, 1580–1720*, Basingstoke: Palgrave Macmillan, 2004. See also Gerald MacLean, *Looking East: English Writing and the Ottoman Empire before 1800*, Basingstoke: Palgrave Macmillan, 2007.
30 Rana Kabbani, *Imperial Fictions: Europe's Myths of Orient*, London: SAQI, 2008 (1986).
31 Geoffrey Nash, *From Empire to Orient: Travellers to the Middle East, 1830–1926*, London: I.B.Tauris, 2005.
32 See biographical note on Sir Henry Blount (1602–82), by Charles Henry Coote, in *Dictionary of National Biography*, ed. Leslie Stephen, London: Smith, Elder & Co., 1885–1900, vol. V.
33 MacLean, *Rise of Oriental Travel*, p. xiii.
34 Henry Blount, *A Voyage to the Levant, a briefe relation of a journey lately performed by Master H.B., gentleman, from England, by the way of Venice, into Dalmatia ... Rhodes and Egypt, into Gran Cairo, with particular observations concerning the moderne condition of the Turkes and other people under that Empire*, 2nd edn, London: A. Crooke, 1636.
35 See biographical note on Edward William Lane (1801–76), at http://en.wikipedia.org/wiki/Edward_William_Lane, accessed 3 November 2012.
36 See Kabbani, *Imperial Fictions*, pp. 42–6.
37 See biographical note on Wilfrid Scawen Blunt (1840–1922) at http://en.wikipedia.org/wiki/Wilfrid_Scawen_Blunt, accessed 3 November 2012.
38 Kabbani, *Imperial Fictions*, pp. 32, 46.
39 Nash, *From Empire to Orient*, p. 1.
40 Nash, *From Empire to Orient*, p. 20.
41 Wilfrid Scawen Blunt, (a) *The Future of Islam* (London: Kegan Paul, Trench, 1882); (b) the pamphlet, *Atrocities of British Justice under British Rule in Egypt*

(London: T.F. Unwin, 1906); and (c) *Secret History of the English Occupation of Egypt* (London: Knopf, 1907).
42 Kabbani, *Imperial Fictions*, p. 32.
43 MacLean, *Looking East*, p. x.
44 Gerald MacLean (ed.), *Reorienting the Renaissance: Cultural Exchanges with the East*, Basingstoke: Palgrave Macmillan, 2005, p. 20.
45 Nash, *From Empire to Orient*, pp. 2, 5.

# Appendix I

*Thirteen letters from James Tod (and Patrick Waugh), between early 1820 and late 1822, to Maharana Bheem Singh of Mewar*

Edited by Shree Lakshmishankar Purohit in: *Anusheelan*, the research journal of the Maharana Mewar Research Institute, City Palace, Udaipur, 1.1, January 1989 (46–51). Journal editor: Dr Purushottam Lal Menoriya. From the Introduction by Shree Lakshmishankar Purohit (in Hindi, translated into English by the author), p. 47:

> In the Library of the Udaipur Palace/Mewar's Research Centre and the Mewar Archives, there are several letters from James Tod addressed to Maharana Bheem Singh, never yet noticed by researchers. They include significant descriptions of Mewar's contemporary circumstances. Tod's letters also throw light on the close relationship between Tod and Maharana Bheem Singhji. These unpublished letters are being published here for the first time.

The thirteen letters are in Devanagiri script, and have been translated into English by the author.

\*\*\*

Letter no. 1. Place: MORWAN DHERA (military camp).

Dated: In the month of Phagun, the 6th day, in the year 1876, of the Vikram era [1820 CE].

Undersigned: James Tod Sahib, to Maharanaji Shree Bheem Singhji.

May Shree Bananath Assist us.

Greetings Maharaj Adhiraj, Maharanaji Shree Bheem Singhji, from MORWAN DHERA, Captain James Tod sends salaams, 18 pieces of good news. So even if the Maharana is ill, this good news will make him happy. For two months money has been coming in. It is an important issue, because all government matters are accomplished through money. We hope to return to Udaipur in six weeks, so by the month of Aashaad. Then a good aim will be accomplished even by those who haven't paid their dues. If you count the harvest of Udaipur under the harvest of Bhynsror, then you will not be able to check who exactly is cultivating the soil of Paanche, even if Paanche is your vassal.

If we are able to exercise superintendence then the dues of Paanche will be paid by Paanche, and we will not have the trouble of requesting those dues again and again, and everyone will be happier. And on your request, WAAK Sahib [Captain Waugh] will feel relieved, but if not [if you fail to make the request] our Residency will immediately be rendered useless.

\*\*\*

Letter no. 2. Place: From MERTA CAMP, near EJAN BEDNORE, including 11 villages with Rs. 10,000 collection.

Dated: In the month of Kartik, the 14th day, in the year 1877, of the Vikram era [19 November 1820 CE].

Undersigned: James Tod Sahib, to Maharanaji Shree Bheem Singhji.

Shree Ramji.

To Sidhishree Udaipur's uplifter, worthy of all praise, Shree Maharaj Adhiraj Maharanaji Shree Bheem Singhji, from the MERTA CAMP, Shree Captain James Tod Sahdb's salaams are expressed and good news conveyed, and your welfare always hoped for.

Eleven villages, eleven puras of the BEDNORE ZILLA, by forcing the cultivators, one village head named MEHTA RAMSINGH, forced other villages like MANDELGURH and others. So I removed all these villages from under his control, and fixed his dues for this year as Rs. 8,000, and for next year as Rs. 10,000, and made him sign a paper stating this. I am sending this paper to you and request you to send it back to me after signing it.

In the Vikram era year 1877, the 14th day of the month of KARTIK
On the 19th of November of 1820 [CE].

\*\*\*

Letter no. 3. Place: From RAEETHAL.

Dated: In the month of AASOJ [Aashvin], the ninth day, in the year 1878, of the Vikram era [26 September 1821 CE].

Undersigned: James Tod Sahib, to Maharanaji Shree Bheem Singhji.

Sidhishree Udaipur's Uplifter, worthy of praise, Shree Maharaj Adhiraj Maharanaji Shree Bheemsinghji, from the camp at RAEETHAL, Rajashree Captain James Tod Sahib's salaams are expressed, good news is conveyed, and your welfare is always hoped for.

In these days, Havaal Sah Sivlalji's paper and the paper in the name of Pacholi Nandlal, it is known that your request poses no problem. But you should keep in mind that everything will come right if you pay a fine of

## APPENDICES

Rs. 5/- and seek forgiveness. So whatever matter you keep in your thoughts and mind, it will gradually become possible – so don't worry about anything. And we will also soon return to your side, so that whatever you wish will be carried out. And from Haval Sah Ji's paper it will become clear who stands against your orders, and who has not executed your orders.

And we have come in order to explain your instructions.

Please keep the KAAMKAAJ [industrious busy activity] certificate ready.

In the month of Aasoj (Ashvin) Vikram era 1878 [26 September 1821 CE], from RAEETHAL.

\*\*\*

Letter no. 4. Place: Somewhere near KOTA.

Dated: In the month of Margasheesh, the 4th day, in the year 1878, of the Vikram era [late 1821 CE].

Undersigned: James Tod Sahib, to Maharanaji Shree Bheem Singhji.

To Sadashree Udaipur's Uplifter Maharaj Adhiraj Shree Bheemsinghji, from Captain James Tod Sahib Bahadur, Salaams, Good news and Wishes for your healthy meals and good health.

A packet sent by Raja Jai Singh Dev, Reva of Mukundpur, arrived for the Sahib of SAGAR, and the Sahib of SAGAR sent me a copy of it, and I am sending a copy of this packet to you. So you will be informed that for the good of RAJAJI, with the decorum/custom of the TEEKA of Ayodhya Prasad and 500 men camped in the KOTA Zilla, he can either move towards KOTA or move quickly towards you in Udaipur. So you should quickly decide on preparations for the Kunvar Prince's marriage and not delay with it. As you know, on your request, I put this question to the Sahib of SAGAR and assured him of our undertaking [Vachan] not to postpone the Kunvar Prince's marraige, but to definitely arrange for it in the SPRING. There is no doubt on this question, because I received the firm promise for it from the SAHIB OF SAGAR, it is no uncertain business. I also included in my missive to Raja JAISINGH Dev [of Mukundpur] a mention that the Kunvar Prince's marriage is being prepared, there is flexibility and looseness on the splendour of the TEEKA ceremony, so he will probably come over in 5 to 7 days, for the MEENAKH Teeka ceremony. In this way, no doubt will be left, and maybe he will go with Kunvarji to MEENAKH to conduct the marriage. Do not worry, he [the Sahib of SAGAR] will enter Udaipur with joy and will definitely order preparations for the marriage for the seventh day of KARTIK [October], though you have written to fix the undertaking for the TEEKA ceremony for Sravan [July], but so much of the deal took place, so the only pounding implement [means to convince them] was the PROMISE UNDERTAKING, so when MEENAKH is present at your court, you can get clarifications from him why there was this delay. Now the advantage of the MEENAKH ceremony is to conclude the marriage of the Kunvar Prince. So now you give orders for the marriage preparations and call for or write to me and I will join you, but since there have been delays in the work here, instead of in the month of

Margasheesh [November 1821], I will only be able to come in the month of PAUSH [December 1821]. But even if I have to leave aside the work here, there is no doubt about my coming and going, since the undertaking between myself and the Sahib of SAGAR is with your summoning us in view. In case of delay in the investigation, the marriage will not take place, so write to me in case of any requirement.

Day 4 of the month of Margasheesh, of the Vikram era year 1878 [late 1821 CE].

\*\*\*

Letter no. 5. Place: not mentioned.

Dated: not mentioned according to the Hindu calendar [25 November 1821 CE].

Undersigned: James Tod Sahib, to Maharanaji Shree Bheem Singhji.

Shree Bananathji.

With PRASAD from Shree Eklingji.

To Sadhashree, Udaipur's Uplifter, Maharaj Adhiraj Shree Bheem Singhji, from Captain James Tod Sahib Bahadur, salaams, good news and wishes for your healthy meals and good health.

The supervision and management of the TEEKA ceremony of Kunvarji, including the horse etc. presented some needs perhaps, so a good messenger came from Raja JAISING DEV [of Mukundpur] so that now even you will quickly proceed with the Kunvar Prince's marriage preparations. From the point of view of expenses, there is no atmospheric enmity remaining, so now it is appropriate for you to proceed quickly with the marriage preparations, and from the Rajput nobles, I have obtained contributions towards the marriage expenses and I am of a mind to go ahead with the Kunvar Sahib's wedding. If at your leisure you indicate when they should make the pilgrimage, both these sirdars will arrive [the Sirdar of SAGAR and Raja Jaising Dev of MUKUNDPUR], provided that you indicate how they should embrace you.

In the month of November, dated 25th, in the year 1821 [CE].

\*\*\*

Letter no. 6. Place: From the camp at PANDOLI.

Dated: The 8th day of the month of PHALGUN, in the year 1878 of the Vikram era [early 1822 CE].

Undersigned: James Tod Sahib, to Maharanaji Shree Bheem Singhji.

Praise to Shri Eklingji.

To Sidhashree Udaipur's Uplifter Maharaj Adhiraj, Maharaj Kunvar Shree JAVAN SINGHI, from Shree Captain James Tod Sahib Bahadurji, salaams, good news, and good wishes.

## APPENDICES

On reading your letter of Phagun 6th, VE 1878 [early 1822 CE], I felt happy and relieved from worry since from a shallow shape, arrangements have become abundant. On the third day from today, the camp will enter into its appointment/establishment.

Written on day 8 of the month of Phalgun, VE 1878, at the PANDOLI camp.

\*\*\*

Letter no. 7. Place: no place mentioned [Jhalrapatan?].

Dated: The month of VAISAKH, [no day mentioned] in the year 1878 of the Vikram era [26 April 1821 CE].

Undersigned: James Tod Sahib, to Maharanaji Shree Bheem Singhji.

Praise to Shree Ramji.

To Sidhashree Udaipur's Uplifter, Maharaj Adhiraj Maharaj Kunvar Shree JUVAN SINGHJI, from Rajashree Captain James Tod Sahib Bahadur, salaams, good news and wishes for your welfare.

The refusal of VADUGAD and the reply to it was read by Shree DURVAR, upon which your name was written, so Shree DURVAR's orders should be raised into your mind, so as to improve [enlighten] it. No other thought was expressed, so I will write more later. And at every response, I have twentyfold confidence that on your seeing the note from Shree Durvar, something will soon be done. And for your relaxation the camp at Jhalrapatan is ready and the certificate of the activity should soon be sent.

Vikram era year 1878, in the month of Vaisakh [26 April 1821 CE] [*sic* 1824 by error].

\*\*\*

Letter no. 8. Place: From the PACHOLI-UDAIPUR camp.

Dated: The 7th day of the month of SAAVAN, in the year 1879 of the Vikram era [25 July 1822 CE].

Undersigned: Captain WAUGH, to Maharanaji Shree Bheem Singhji.

Praise to Shree Ramji

Sidha Shree from the PACHOLI camp, Shree Gokulji and Pohat [Purohit] Ramnathji and Pacholi's Kisan Nathji and Mehta Savai Ramji JORPURE, from the Udaipur camp, Rajashree Captin VAAK [Waugh] Saheb all sing RAMRAM, send good news and wish you well.

We have obtained news that under instructions from VEENASHREE DARVAAR, you have sent the Kunvarji on a pilgrimage to KASHI, so this matter is of your own inspiration. So now please send word to the Kunvarji to return to Udaipur. If in the Kunvarji's return there is some delay, then you will be blamed with much uproar. They you will not see the young Lord of Udaipur, you can be sure of that.

By decision on day 7 of SAAVAN of the year 1879 of the Vikram era [25 July 1822 CE].

\*\*\*

Letter no. 9. Place: From the SUWOSHMA camp.

Dated: The 7th day of the month of SAAVAN, in the year 1879 of the Vikram era [25 July 1822 CE].

Undersigned: Captain WAUGH, to Maharanaji Shree Bheem Singhji.

Praise to Shree Ramji.

SidhShree at the camp at SUWOSHMA, to Rajashree Ravat Juvan Singhji and Ravat Shree Dulay Singhi, at the Udaipur camp, Rajashree Captain Waugh Sahib sends thousand salutations, good news, wishes for your welfare, may your friendship be preserved.

These days we have obtained news that under instructions from Veenashree Durvar, Kunvarji Saheb has been sent on a pilgrimage to KASHI, but this matter is not appropriate for the KINGDOM, so on reading this letter, the Kunvarji will be quickly called back to UDAIPUR, and in his return delay should be avoided, and an activity report should be sent.

Vikram era 1879, in the month of SAAVAN, day 7 [25 July 1822].

\*\*\*

Letter no. 10. Place: From the CHHATRAPURA camp.

Dated: [the Hindu calendar date is not mentioned] [7 September 1821 CE].

Undersigned: James Tod Sahib, to Maharanaji Shree Bheem Singhji.

With the assistance of Shree Bananath

Shree Nathji be praised.

From the garden of the CHHATRAPURA camp – 7th September 1821.

To Sidh Shree Maharaj Adhiraj Maharanaji Shree Bheem Singhji, from Rajashree Captain James TOD Saheb Bahadur, salaams, good news, your constant good health.

Your patch/plug/message arrived, and it was learned with much joy what you have written – that the people are without hatred or vengeance, and that an armed brigade will be raised, and by observing careful management in raising it, this brigade will provide protection, so if you maintain an army it is a good thing. So you are ready to do so, but an armed brigade also requires money. In addition if there is the extra burden of leaks, then if the money resources are not carefully managed, then there are also people for whom SAVING appears difficult and a weakness, for whom expense is like the state's income revenue, then it is a very good thing that there is an army, since it improves the state's appearance, but if there is a good manner of spending money, then eightfold useful jobs can be carried out.

So write and keep us informed.

## APPENDICES

In the garden of the Chhatrapura camp – 7th September 1821 [no Hindu calendar date].

\*\*\*

Letter no. 11. Place: From KOTA.

Dated: On the 11th day of the month of Vaisakh [the Hindu calendar year is not mentioned] [April 1821/22 CE].

Undersigned: James Tod Sahib, to Maharanaji Shree Bheem Singhji.

Praise to Shree Hari.

To Sidh Shree Shree Shree Shree Maharanaji, from KOTA, a letter from Rajashree Captain James Tod Sahib, salaams, good news and wishes for your constant good health.

Your letter arrived, its news was read and much happiness obtained from what you wrote – that MEHTA Seetaram Sadaram is arriving at KULAYTAY, so we will advance towards that place. When your own party arrives, then eightfold useful matters will be executed according to your wishes and instructions.

[No Vikram era year], Vaisakh, day 11 [perhaps April 1821/22 CE].

\*\*\*

Letter no. 12. Place: From KOTA.

Dated: On the 5th day of the month of Chaitra [the Hindu calendar year is not mentioned] [perhaps March 1821/22 CE].

Undersigned: James Tod Sahib, to Maharanaji Shree Bheem Singhji.

Praise to Shree Bananathji.

To Sidhashree Maharaj Adhiraj, Maharanaji Shree BheemSinghji, from the KOTA camp, a letter from Captain James TOD Saheb, with salaams, good news and wishes that through every minute and every hour you should continue in good health.

Your letter arrived through MEHTA RAM SINGHJI, and great happiness was felt on reading it. An oral answer to it was sent by Munshi Saroop Ram, so you will receive it soon.

Since you requested that pomegranates be sent from here [KOTA], much search has been made. When we find pomegranates, we will send them, and then they will reach you. In this way, an eightfold useful task will be executed. I will continue to send you our activity reports.

In the month of CHAITRA, day 5 [no mention of the Vikram era year] [perhaps March 1821/22 CE].

\*\*\*

Letter no. 13. Place: From DWARKA SHANKHODVAR.

Dated: On the 4th day of the month of PAUSH, in the year 1879 of the Vikram era [at the end of 1822 CE].

Undersigned: James Tod Sahib, to Maharanaji Shree Bheem Singhji.

Shree Jee Jaiyati.

Blessing on Shree of the Blessed Place of Udaipur, Maharaj Adhiraj Maharanaji Shree Bheem Singhji – from the place Shree Dwarka Shankhodvar, sent by Rajashree Captain James TOD Saheb Bahadur – many salaams.

You must have read my letter written in the hand of Yati Gyanchandraji. Tomorrow I will board a ship and make a pilgrimage to MANDVI / BHUJ / NARAYANSAR / KOTAYSAR. Then within ten days I will reach the Bombay coast; Now while leaving, I am sending you a few things of personal attachment.

My horse JAVEDIYAA should go to the younger Shree Deevanjee. Let HARGAZ be given to nobody inappropriate – my mind is very keen about this. Please keep an eye on to whom this horse HARGAZ is given, so that that person may remember me – someone who appears to you as fit to ride HARGAZ, and don't allow anyone else to mount HARGAZ.

Then if Shreeji would be so kind as to meet Shree Deevanjee, then let him take JAVEDIYAA my horse, and please make sure that he is kept with the utmost care and affection.

Please do not forget me – my life is left in the middle of Udaipur. Even though only a small thing, please give it due consideration.

From Dwarka Shankhodvar, in the Vikram era year 1879, in the month of PAUSH, day 4 [the end of 1822 CE].

# Appendix II

## Tod's Memorandum on the Mirs of Sind, IOR MSS EUR E 293/35 (9 folios)

C. METCALFE, Esq.                                                              Secret

Secretary to Government

[Date at end of dispatch: Kotah, 10 August 1820]

Sir,

At a moment when the insolence of the triumvirate Government of Sinde appears to render the Power of Peace or War no longer optional with the British Government, I should ill perform the duty of a public servant if I did not lay before you for the notice of the most noble the Governor General in Council such opinions as I possess in support of a point of such consequence, and an offer of my services to carry any which may be approved of into execution.

2. The forbearance of the British Government will only be the surer means to make hostilities with a race of Plunderers inevitable, as much from the individual character of the people as of its particular form of Government, nor will this annoyance cease but with their expulsion from the East bank of the Sinde.
3. If a war therefore takes place I shall argue upon this result, for nothing but a formidable attack is likely to avert a swarm of Invaders of the [Enemies? Armies?] of old from the wilds of Beelochistan, both to our Allies of Bhooj and those of the Guicawar and even our possessions in Guzerat.
4. The overflow of the Great Eastern Rin will prevent their putting their threats in execution [folio 2] till after the Monsoon, and though they might, but which can scarcely be expected, make an easterly movement by Mitnee and Karooi Kote from Hyderabad cross the Loony above its disimboguement into the Rin, [*Chamber's Dictionary*: 'disemboguement': to discharge at the mouth, as a stream] and thence descend into our Guzerat frontier, the only line by which they could invade. Yet this seems to have

been foreseen by the [Chief?] of Patun (Sidpoor Patun I suppose) for the point of assemblage of the field forces destined for Sinde.

5. By every appearance it is most likely the attack will be commmenced by the Sindis. Moreover it is the points of attack which I mean to advert to.
6. These it is evident from the nature of the valley, will be but few, confined on our part to a naval armament to either or both mouths of the Delta, and the Field Forces at Bhooj and Patun, which can be considered but as a single line of offensive moment.
7. To give effectual support to these movements from the South and South East, and cut off all support and retreat from the North is what I propose to submit to you.
8. With the possession of the island of Bukhur/Roree, on the Indus, the whole of Upper Sinde or that portion of it under one of the Triumvirate, Meer Sohrab would at once be taken possession of, and from the extreme narrowness of this part of the Eastern valley, easily defensible, and as a point of offensive combination with troops from the South, it requires no comment.**

> ** [note 1, folio 2: 17 miles from the River is the extremity of the Thal or Land Ridge terminating the Desert.]

[folio 3] 9. With the sanction of government, and being entrusted with the execution of my own plan, I may venture to [appear? offer?] I could erect the British standard on that island by the middle or end of November, and ready [*author's note*:verb, 'to ready'] to cooperate with the forces acting on the south.

10. Many circumstances conspire to render this plan not only feasible, but of no difficulty, indeed everything concurs to make it simple in execution; distant it certainly is, but this would soon be overcome, and throughout the whole line of space, not a point would be left in the river, but would be maintained by a Friend, and as will be detailed, his interest the best [Indian? Guardian?] to be faithful to his trust.
11. Jesselmere to the point I propose for the Rendesvus [sic] and place of preparation for crossing the Desert to Kary.
12. The anxiety of the Rawul of Jesselmere to be received under the Protective Alliance of the British Government is great, and he addressed me two letters on the subject from Oodipoor; and added indeed that it was this wish which was the principal inducement of his coming there and begged I would lay his wishes before the Most Noble the Governor-General.
13. It is the only state in Rajwarra out of the Pale of its protection and of which he is now most desirous: I in reply said I had understood he had formerly laid his wishes before Government, but it had not been then deemed expedient to grant them, [folio 4] but in reply he said that his Correspondence was merely hitherto friendly, and not having extended to this point. I said I would convey his wishes in this letter to Government, if he would send it. This is now on the road with a person in his confidence.

## APPENDICES

14. There are two points which the Rawul and his Minister are willing to accede to, to promote their wishes for the alliance. One the establishment of a commercial Depot. The other a small body of our own troops, if it was of consequence to us. Both are important and the latter particularly so at this moment.
15. The former might be an inducement even if we were not forced into a war with Sinde, to redirect this little state to our Protection, and it shows the penetration of the Minister Sulim Sing [Deewan of Jaisalmer], a man of great talents, though of a most severe character, inseparable, if the former are to be rendered useful in Rajwarra when there is constant re-action to overturn authority.**

    ** [note 1, folio 4: Reinforcement in Russia [*author's note*: ?reason], such as might be deemed requisite by the Commdr in Chief might be prepared to follow.]

16. Fifteen companies in two Battalions of Infantry would be ample with half a Regiment of Native Cavalry and a Regiment of Skinner's Horse, with a train of Light ordinance for there are few Forts of any consequence in Upper or indeed any part of Sinde.
17. Skinner's Horse could move at this season from Hansi direct on Jesselmere. It would require no extra aid, and [as?] there is now water and forage at every stage in abundance, and the authorities in [folio 5] the route under our protection, would furnish supplies.
18. Its [The?] best route could easily be ascertained, that by Rinnee Raghav on the mutual northern confine of Shekhawat and the Beekanaer state, thence by the high road by Buddanoo and Kaloo to the City of Beekanaer, from thence direct to Jesselmere, the route is perfectly good, though some of the stages are 18 or 20 miles, never more, often 12 to 14, and it is only 100 miles road distance between the capitals, which will be passed over in 10 days with ease, and from Hansi to Beekanaer 20 days would suffice, or a month altogether to Jesselmere to which may be allowed a week for halts or repairs of accidents.
19. The other details might be ordered from what other point was most convenient, if from the Rajpootana Field Force it would be the nearest and the Infantry Guns etc could mine [mire?] by Mairta on Jodpoor to Pokurn and Jesselmere, to be accomplished with perfect ease within the month, allowing for halts and the train [grain?]. The route to Jodpoor to [is?] free from any sand sufficient to obstruct; it is sandy thence to Pokurn, but from this to Jesselmere it is only a rocky ridge the whole way with water, forage and all requisites.
20. On the supposition that the most Noble the Governor General in Council would honour this plan with his approbation, orders might reach the Head [Zeemters?] of the Detachments by the 20th September. Two days would be [folio 6] the preparation; and by the end of October, both the Horse from Hansi and troops from Ajmere would unite at Jesselmere. If I proceeded myself to that capital, in advance, I should have ready the few preparations

necessary to cross the desert: collect an efficient contingent of the Bhatties, and arrange other points which I shall return to the consideration of.

21. In 6 long marches, I should from thence reach the banks of the Indus, and by some means or other take immediate possession of BAKHAR, a most important post as it commands the navigation of the river, the high road to the great Mart of Shikarpoor, and the whole of Upper Sind.**

> ** [note 1, folio 6: The Branches of the River are each from 6 to 700 yards in breadth. On the island are the remains of old fortifications. It would be necessary immediately to renew them.]

22. There is but a spane [sic] of 60 miles of desert of any difficulty, and this with the friendly aid of Jesselmere would easily be overcome.
23. There are two lines of route from Jesselmere: The one by Gotaroo and Oaden to Rory** the other lower by Shahgurh and [Gurpur?] to Khyrpoor** (Great), the capital of Meer Sohrab, 10 miles below Bakhur; which ever point might appear on a close inspection the most practicable could be adopted.

> ** [note // folio 6: Rory is on the Eastern bank of the Indus; Sukar on the West.]
> ** [note ** folio 6: Khyspoor: an open town of 300 houses.]

24. Thus by the 10th of November one effective force would strike a most important blow and in an unexpected quarter at a period when they would be drawing the greater part of their army to the point of conflict, in the south.
25. It is somewhat under 200 miles from [folio 7] from Bukhar to the Sinde capital Hydrabad, both admirable ports, and requiring but one or two intermediate to command the Eastern bank of the River, one of which it would be important to have opposite [Ichwan?].
25 [25A]. I had only a few days ago a communication merely complimentary from the Vakeel of Meer Sohrab. He accompanied the Rawul of Jesselmere to Oodipoor, and is anxious there should be an intercourse. In short, the whole of SINDE is split into factions, and self interest will enlist any individual of them into our service.
26. North of RANJ to Subsul Kote the Boundary of the Bhawalpoor state, there are some petty sirdars of no importance, nominally under Meer Sohrab.
27. Jesselmere would enter heartily into this course to recover some further places bordering the Valley seized by these Bulocches.
28. The Ruler of Bhawalpoor or Daodputra would be happy to aid and have us as his neighbours, which would dissipate all his fears of Runjit Sing and thus a route which he could not control would be open for the horses of the North West, which formerly formed our cavalry, but [are] all now grassed by him.
29. There is a second point of important co-operation, and a most efficient one at the disposal of Government, and which would threaten the very gates of Hyderabad. The Most Noble the Governor General is aware of the Maharajah Maun Sing's [folio 8] desire to recover OmerKote and by the

## APPENDICES

treaty he is left at liberty to do so when he pleases. The most favourable moment has arisen for this and in conjunction with our plan, it would cause him great happiness to get back this ancient possession, but in another point of view, the enterprize would be of UTILITY, for it would actually hurt every contending passion, and quiet all their discontent, which lately prevailed, by employing the chiefs in an expectation, where their minds would be amply employed and their self love gratified. The Rajah has also been pacifying them all, and even swearing to some that the ends of Justice were answered, and had only fallen on the guilty. He has now got upwards of 10,000 troops, half of which would be a good riddance for a short time, and to these 5 or 6,000 of his own class would soon unite in such an enterprize which would be entered into with all the spirit of national enthusiasm and there is a deep antipathy between the people of the States.

30. I could arrange with Rajah Maun the time of its departure, for preparation would be required and a European officer might be to his force attached to communicate with myself and the Division acting below.
31. I need not longer encroach on his Lordship's time by entering into further minutiae, if it is my good fortune that his Lordship should approve of my plan and will honor me with its execution, I can only offer [folio 9] that entire confidence I myself feel of its perfect practicability as the best [omen?] of success. The subject is as familiar as that passing under my eyes, and this confidence which is very opposite to VANITY, I never yet found to deceive me.
32. I presumed to specify Skinner's Horse from its known efficiency and being best adapted for that service while Lieut. Skinner's own experience among such a people would render his corps doubly valuable.

| | |
|---|---|
| KOTAH | I have the honor to remain, |
| 10 August 1820. | Sir, Your most obedient, humble servant, |
| | [signed] JAMES TOD. |

\* \* \*

# Appendix III

*Tod's Memorandum on the Tribal Mhairs of Mhairwarra, IOR MSS EUR E 293/47 (22 folios)*

Oodipoor, 25 November 1821.

GEORGE SWINTON, Esq.,

Secretary to Government in the Political Department.

Sir,

[MEYWAR AFFAIRS] 1. I have the honour to report at length on a subject which has nearly engrossed all my time and attention since my return to Meywar.

2. I mean my arrangements for the suppression of the Predatory Tribes of Mhairs, subject to this state in the extensive tract termed Mhairwarra.

3. It is a subject which involved so many changes in its progress to final success, requiring plans to be altered and adapted to circumstances as they arose, that I was averse to troubling the most Noble the Governor General in Council with progressive details, but to avoid encroaching on his Lordship's time by a condensed relation of the final, general result with remarks and observations towards the elucidation of the subject.

4. It will be in the recollection of the most Noble the Governor General in Council the anxiety with which I gave myself up to this subject from a very early period with the palliative measures I had seen adopted for checking an evil which the poverty or spirit of this state could not cure.

5. The various dispatches already before Government [folio 2] will render it unnecessary my employing much introductory matter to preface this dispatch, but as it is a subject of great importance extending far beyond mere locality and the result now obtained to be considered final, I shall take the liberty of prefixing a few remarks to obviate the trouble of general reference to former dispatches which were of date as per margin.**

## APPENDICES

** [note** folio 2: August 11, 1818, para 34, addressed, of the Resident Delhi. February 20, 1819, J. Adam Esq., with sketch.]

6. With the last of these dispatches a Sketch of Mairwarra accompanied such as I had been enabled to draw out from Information, and that on too small a scale to give a minute idea of these tracts or from the nature of the materials to be very correct, yet sufficiently so in both to elucidate my remarks. To this letter I may beg leave to refer to for the description of the Range and its inhabitants, with their mode of life.
7. I have little doubt that the Mhairs are the aborigines of the country, and that their Conquerors, the Rajpoots, expelling them the lowlands, compelled them to dependence on the Mountains for protection, and in these they have continued to maintain themselves against all their efforts, doubtless aided by the necessity of a mutual good understanding [in?] the long period of Musulman domination.
8. They are, prior to the conquest of Hindostan described as pursuing the same lawless habits of plunder as they continued to the present time, and in the Epic Poem of the Wars of Pirthi Raj, the Chohan Sovereign of Delhi, the opponent of Shahaboodeen, they withstand him for a whole day in defending the passes of the Arabullah in [folio 3] his march to attack the prince of Mundore.**

** [note ** folio 3: Capital of Marwar, previous to the settlement of the Rahtores, and some centuries ere Jodpoor was built.]

In this they are described as 'the manly Mhair', a Stranger to fear, who brings the spoils of the Plains to the recesses of the Mountains, who owns neither Lord or Law.

9. The most powerful of the Ranas of Mewar had compelled a sort of feudal subjection, and established a paramount authority or supremacy acknowledged in forms of fealty, homage and annual gifts in token of vassalage common to rude nations. The respect they paid the Princes of Meywar in honor of the ancient and noble birth of the Family is remarkably illustrated in the recorded vicissitudes of this House and perhaps to this respect may be attributed reasons for alacrity in performing service stronger than those which arose from their power.
10. There is besides singular coinsidence [sic] in religious tenets common to both: the inclusive worship of the Sun once common to this House is still the chief emblem of adoration and invocation amongst these mountaineers; and their spiritual directors are the Kanfutta Jogies still revered by the Seesodias, whose Head was himself styled, in ancient times, Jog-Ender or Lord of the Jogas.
11. In consequence in all reverses of this family [Seesodias], they were faithfully and honorably served by them [the Mhairs], and our understanding or compact on the basis of mutual aid was that which unites them superadded to a knowledge of supremacy. From their fidelity and the like sentiment of the other wild tribes in these tracts impossible to large armies, the Ranas of Oodipoor were indebted to the mountaineers, [folio 4] for their

independance; for independance it may be called, tho' destitute of power, which preferred the life of the Forrest Bheel to slavish subjection to the will, religious doctrines, and consequent debasement of another [Muslims], its antipode in every thing sacred or profane.

12. Alla Oodeen** attempted the subjection and conversion of the Mhairs tho' with but partial success and has left marks of the universality of his conquest even in this chain.

   ** [note 1, folio 4: about A.D. 1300]

13. The great Sowaee Jey Sing of Ambere in the zenith of his power when wielding all the forces of the Empire, failed in that [subjecting the Mhairs?]; and the repeated endeavours of the various Mahratta Soubadars since Ajmere fell into their hands were alike futile, they could not even protect Ajmere from their excesses [of the Mhairs]. [Sowaeejer?] Nanah, certainly one of the ablest officers of the Mahrattas, with every means at his disposal had but partial success, and without adding more, I shall conclude with Jesswunt Rao Holkar, who was compelled to pay for a free passage across the mountains during the League of 1806 against Jodpoor.

14. When the predatory Bands which roved over this distracted country had reduced its Prince to the condition of a Prisoner within this narrow valley, the miseries of the inhabitants were increased by the descent of the Mhairs, who then issued into the plains. At this period of general confusion, of which they took advantage, they adopted a measure of systematic exaction, which [folio 5] possibly [might?] have terminated in an establishment of Rule to the expulsion of the Rajpoots, becoming unwarlike in spirit and scanty in numbers, from increasing affliction and oppression.

15. Parallel with the range, each Community [of the Mhairs?] had its advanced post in the plains, from whence they carried on their depredations even to the Eastern and opposite mountainous confine. In these posts the head of a community resided, who exacted a regular contribution from all the villages in the neighbourhood. In some they held lands even, and the worn out Thakoors were compelled to pay them for abstinence from plunder. They had indeed exactly reversed the order of things. Estates [Escheats?] on their confines which were granted expressly for the purpose of protecting the interior and whose proprietor in better terms established marks of Paramount Controul over them, were now compelled to buy their goodwill by the surrender of a portion of what the Mahratta might spare them.

16. Such was the state of things before the events of /17 [1817?] These acted like a spell even on the savage of the Arabullah, or the Bheel of the West; they withdrew to their retreats and for a time seemed to forget the habits of rapine which sprung up with their birth. But as I remarked in a former dispatch, this impression could not be expected to be lasting, if the means to keep it alive were not exhibited, and with the causes of failure, my letter of the 29th November to Mr. Secy [Secretary] Metcalfe would fully have informed the most Noble the Governor General in Council.

## APPENDICES

17. I need not recapitulate here the plans adopted [folio 6] and detailed in my dispatch,** or the local means at disposal for carrying them into execution, and afterwards maintaining them, these are therein fully described, and were at best but a palliative to the evil and ceased even to be so from the motives described in my letter of 29th November last. I need not therefore go over this ground for in this dispatch is contained all the causes which led to failure and the necessity of adopting measures of a more rigorous description which should quel [sic] an evil which I felt assured the policy of Government both from desire of good order and humanity would not tolerate.

   ** [note ** folio 6: dispatch of 20th February 1819]

18. Strong therefore in the confidence of the support and approbation of the Most Noble the Governor General in Council, I determined to crush at once the evil, and tho' averse as I have always evinced to calling out our troops, its necessity was too invincible to make me hesitate when the massacre at SHAK [Jhak?] called for decision and prompt punishment. The supineness and apathy of the Courts on each side the range merited and received no delicacy of consultation for consent from me, and the note N6 which I addressed to the Ranah on the occasion will show the tone on which I took up the subject.

19. The suspicions I described in this letter, of Ajeet Sing [Deewan of Mewar] being the immediate tho' hidden cause of the revolt, appeared well founded, and the most circumstantial evidence short of proof was produced in the course of operations and which I shall revert to with transcripts of Information furnished by the Officer Commanding in the late operations in MAIRWARRA.

20. In the 10th, 11th and 12th paragraphs of this letter, [folio 7] will be found what more immediately relates to the result and massacre at JHAK. Therein I mentioned the superintendent of Ajmere [Mr Francis Wilder] having called for the aid of our own troops, and of my having furnished the unlimited permission of the Ranah to punish all those of Mcywar who had been associated in it.

21. The troops after the punishment of the villages of Ajmere, were rapidly withdrawn to Cantonment without any notice being paid to the equal capability of the MHAIRS here which compelled me to urge the necessity of return, that it might not be thus limited to the few villages dependent on Ajmere. Items 1 & 2**

    ** [note**folio 7: 21st and 29th November 1820]

    are copies of my letters to the Superintendent of Ajmere pointing out the necessity of a more general example being made.

22. Colonel MAXWELL was consequently sent with the disposable force of Hyderabad, with instructions from Brigadier General KER to correspond and attend to MY wishes.

23. ATHOON stood an assault but was abandoned in the night and on the 2nd December [1820?] in possession of our troops. The details of operations would have been communicated in the military department and are of consequence only for their result, for there was scarcely a show of opposition subsequent to that of ATHOON. The other place BORWAH implicated in the affairs of JHAK fled on the approach of the troops.
24. As however no adequate punishment had yet been inflicted either to person or property, I felt assured that without something more than merely expelling them from their haunts was done, it was less than useless; for it would only reanimate them [folio 8] and add to their audacity by impunity. Besides the case with regard to this extensive horde in Meywar was widely different from Ajmere, where a mere nook of Mairwarrah tracks that province with about half a dozen villages dependent on it. Here the whole Western frontier is inhabited by them.

No. 3**

** [note** folio 8: dated 5 December 1820]

contains my opinions at this period to Mr. WILDER, and I determined to complete the work I had begun by continuing the aid of the British troops.

No. 4**

** [note ** folio 8: 9th December 1820]

is a copy of my letter of Instructions to Lieut Col Maxwell directing his movement on the three principal communities of the Central part of the range. He reached Bairar on the 20th and its inhabitants fled almost on the formation for the attack after a few rounds from the guns. Bairwana and Mundilla were also similarly evacuated. Still no blow had been struck which could assure me of future tranquillity. They were merely roused and exasperated, for few had been killed.

25. During these operations in Meywar, I had been urging on Mr. WILDER's attention the necessity of attacking the places of MARWAR, especially culpable with the others and this officer had at long the instructions from the Resident at Delhi to carry this into execution. I found myself under the necessity however of detaining the force in MEYWAR for sometime after this permission was obtained for reasons detailed in No 5.**

** [note** folio 8: 2nd January 1821.]

Previous however to its movement towards the Marwar zone, an excellently well planned and well conducted alert was given, which reflected great credit on Captain HALL of the Quarter Master General's Department [folio 9] with whom it originated, and was conducted and proved of more use in installing dread with the Mhairs than all the previous operations. It taught them they were tangible, the first impression necessary to have the desired effect.

## APPENDICES

26. On the 11th January [1821], Lieut. Colonel Maxwell moved with his Force to chastise the Mhairs, and however leaving at my desire 5 Companies with a troop of Cavalry and Brigade of Guns at Mundilla, to prevent the chance of any reaction until the fortifications erecting were forward, and on the 20th of that month [January 1821] another right enterprize was undertaken, and most successfully executed against the Khan of ATHOON with his followers from Meywar, and in which he and about 200 men were killed, and many of their headmen made prisoners.
27. Added to the expulsion of the Marwar depredators, nothing was now wanting to complete the impression made by this well conducted affair under Captain Glover of the 17th Native Infantry. Again aided by the excellent infantry of Captain Hall in person. The moral effect produced by the death of the Khan of Athoon was in itself equal to the extermination of a whole community, and from the prominent part he had acted and his reputation as chief of the whole Range, it was putting the seal to complete success. It had its effect also with the suspected [Mhairs] at this capital who saw their plans not only frustrated but punished.
28. Shortly after this, the chief part of the Force under Lieutenant Colonel MAXWELL returned to Cantonment but I detained 5 Companies to complete my [folio 10] arrangements, which I shall now describe to you.
29. These arrangements may be considered as two fold, external and internal. External as regards the dependence of the Mhairs either from pecuniary obligations or those of mutual understanding in the chiefs whose Estates adjoin their respective communities.
30. I need not repeat the obstructions thrown in the way of my former or present plans, from the supineness in attention or interested view of the chiefs on the question so often alluded to, these have been often repeated. It is sufficient to state that with perhaps but one exception and this now doubtful, none received the measure of the [toll? total?] subjugation of this row to the Rana's authority with cordiality, and tho' each chief had a separate cause for dissent, yet they were all equally strong.
31. To some, a good understanding with the Mhairs was or had been of advantage in yielding a place either of refuge or defiance against their own Princes. To others, again it was profitable by sharing in the Plunder of Merchants, or by having established some marks of supremacy in tribute or Service. Rawut Gokul Dass of Deogurh had all these motives combined to make him dislike the plan. For three generations his family had been in rebellion. He has the regular chauth on all thefts even, since my arrival in Meywar, and had also established a certain right of revenue on various villages adjoining his estate. The stolen property found a ready market in his town of DEOGURH, and in one list of twenty-five Robberies committed, [folio 11] in his Estate, he pleaded inability to punish as the sole excuse.

This was admitted, and the whole of the villages inhabited by Mhairs in this Estate reclaimed to the Rana's authority. He had erected a fort about 30 years ago, when in rebellion in the centre of the Range, and here reside two desperate outlaws of Marwar, who conveyed to it the spoils and even inhabitants of Marwar who were ransomed for their liberty. The Rawut [of Deogurh] was repeatedly warned of this ere I went to KOTAH last year, but falsehoods in reply were all that could be urged, and when inquiry was warm, he managed to remove them. The Presence of the force was sufficent to arrange the Mhair community here and they are now in allegiance to the Ranah. The outlaws fled on the approach of the detachment to Mundilla, and the garrison of the Ranah took possession of Gokulgurh, thus left entirely unoccupied. It will be a most convenient Port, and completely keeps in subjection the Mhairs of the most southern part of the range.

32. Thus in some shape in either [or other?], all had some reasons for not wishing to see the plan executed to its full extent.

33. Such being the case, the first thing I urged to the Rana's notice was the indispensable necessity of separation in perpetuity of all community of interest between the chiefs and the Mhairs.

34. In effecting this, distinctions were drawn and a regard to Justice observed. As to Deogurh, his conduct was meriting the severest punishment, and [folio 12] all advantages he derived reverted to the Ranah, without any compromise or stipulation whatever. To those who have bravely maintained or conquered rights, notwithstanding the unsettled state of things, such will be preserved, tho' as well as those villages having Mhair population even if included by grant, it is intended to render KHALSA giving an equivalent elsewhere.

35. In the minor advantages tho' by any Thakoor of Pride still clung to, such as acknowledgement of supremacy by unusual force, from a sum of money to a Horse, a Bullock or Hare, such will be preserved, the remembrance recorded by a sealed attestation, but the personal rights of levy to cease and to be paid by the officer of Government. In short, every link of connection between them [between the Mewar chiefs and the Mhairs] to be severed, for by this alone can we hope for Peace and Tranquillity for the purpose of discharges of the defensive duties of the Thakoors, in which terms alone they held grants of their Estates. [Tod was careful to sever links of collaboration and combined insubordination to the Rana of Mewar, by the Mewar Thakoors and the Mhair chiefs.]

36. The Internal Arrangements are simple yet efficient, uniting sincerity for the future with the reclaiming of old habits to make their industry not only support themselves but the Force which keeps them in subjection and even to leave an annual increasing balance to the State.

37. All this is in a fair train of success, and I am not too sanguine when I say I have little doubt with other efficient charges in the Government, it will be permanent.

38. FEAR is the Engine which is to work this reform. Hopes on any other foundation would but lead to disappointment. This passion has had full sway [folio 13], for independent of the two brilliant [allowances?] specified, the LOSS in battle train and effects by every kind will outlive the present generation, and be handed down as the heaviest calamity which

## APPENDICES

ever befell a Race. The most obnoxious and turbulent and whose enormities were pro-eminent, had their houses levelled to the ground, their crops destroyed, and themselves only saved by flight. At one period the central and northern Communities were entirely expelled. But they soon found they had no refuge in Marwar for the capacity of the officers of that State, tho' the sole stimulus to exertion, was of use in shewing them this stay was gone.

39. Punishment having been complete, the impression deeply felt, which was to mould them to ulterior views, while the ends of Justice and society were attained by the suppression of crime, it became necessary on furnishing sufficient securities for the future to grant an amnesty for the past, and to heal those wounds which Justice had inflicted. [*Author's note*: Tod was in favour of reconciliation with the Mhairs.]
40. Proclamations were accordingly distributed throughout the [ZILLAH?] inviting them to return and people their dwellings on the following conditions:

    1. To give up their arms.
    2. To pay fines for their misconduct.
    3. To become Ryots to the Ranah and pay regular share of the harvest.
    4. To pay arrears of Revenue as might be demanded.
    5. To give up Hostages from each Community to be detained in Pledge for their conduct and fulfilment of all their stipulations.

    [folio 14] There was a 6th stipulation** which was at first demanded, but became inoperative when success gave the right to execute it without. I mean the erection of Posts in the Centre of their Communities.

    ** [note** folio 14: There might be added another stipulation, which will be [legally?] inforced with making good all thefts. Since I arrived in Meywar, it has been agreed and put in force.]

41. All these conditions were rapidly acceded to, and the work of disarming and repopulating has been going on with every success that could be expected.
42. The whole FINES is acted from the three central communities of [Beewar? Beawar? Bairar?], Bairewarra and Mundilla, of 5000 rupees each have been paid, with about 15,000 more of arrears of Revenue from these and smaller detached villages in their neighbourhood.
43. The early submission of the most southern MHAIRS saved them from a similar imposition and those to the North of ATHOON and Borwah have acceded to all the terms, given Bonds for their Fines, but are not sufficiently settled yet to have it collected.
44. The RANGE is for the present subdivided into three portions, the southern, central and northern. The two first are entirely settled and the Mhairs busily employed in repairing their losses and attending to CULTIVATION. The northern has been delayed as being the most guilty, to the last to be

## KNOWLEDGE, MEDIATION AND EMPIRE

received into terms, but their longer detention in misery would have compelled them to pursue the course these measures of severity were intended to destroy [plunder].

45. In this place I beg leave to refer you to the Schedule accompanying which is [in?] one view shews [shewing?] what an extensive arrangement this has been, which has brought a tract, [folio 15] which will in a short period equal in value any single possession of MEYWAR entirely under subjection to the Ranah.

46. It exhibits a total of 17 towns, 113 villages and 28 hamlets, having about 200 leaders or Rawuts, the population of which cannot be short of 35,000 souls, I might allow more, but I mentioned the smallest number till time supplies better information.

47. The Fines and arrears of Revenue which may be considered in the same light amount to 70,000 rupees, exclusive of what may be settled from ATHOON and BORWAH, but probably the whole of this may not be realized, while a settlement for the ensuing Sumbat Year has been made for Cheetore, Rupees 62,000.

48. It will require to be seen hereafter whether this has been or not too heavy: but happens what will a FUND has already been provided which has prevented the ruin of a body of 700 PATHANS, without the erection of three fortresses being any burthen whatever on the Rana's finances and in a like manner it is satisfactory to know the arrangement must benefit them for the future.

49. The list of ARMS** of which about 4000 of every kind have been surrendered is but a small portion of what ought to be expected, but not a fifth of the population has yet returned, and doubtless they will try to evade it as much as possible to prevent which heavy penalties have been attached.

   ** [note** folio 15:Many were taken by the troops and not included in this.]

50. In addition to this assessment or said tax, is the transit trade, which lawless as they were was never [folio 16] shut up, and whose duties were a great source of profit to these communities, and a part of which for its effectual protection, it may be wise to continue to conciliate the Mhairs, as give [conference? offence?] to the [CAREEN? caravan?]. This trade tho' confined to the internal consumption of the inhabitants in each side the Range, was very brisk, the general transit and foreign trade was always by the pass of DEOGURH.

51. Of the five Fortresses running along the ZILLOH, that of Gokulgurh, has been mentioned, which situated in the heart of the Southern communities, will keep them in awe. That with North BHEEMGURH, was the fortress of ATHOON, taken from the KHAN, and now called after the Ranah. The three central Forts are entirely new and almost finished and built on elevated Peaks commanding the three principal and hitherto most turbulent communities. His Highness the Ranah in sending his instructions to his relation who commands in that quarter, did me the honour to give

## APPENDICES

my name to one of them. As the Garrisons for three Forts, 700 foreign Rajpoots** and Puthans are distributed and the feudal quotas as amounting now to 800 Horse and Foot will be continually stationed under an officer of rank as to move on any point which may shew the slightest disposition of disaffection.

** [note ** folio 16: on monthly pay]

52. These arrangements have their importance, however chiefly by comparison, but should they be lasting as I expect, they will, I trust be considered by the Most Noble the Governor General in Council, as more worthy of his notice in their moral character and effect, than in their mere numerical, [folio 17] pecuniary result, which is a secondary consideration, and when it is asserted that not only the means will have been furnished by the EVIL itself for its permanent subjugation, but no small overplus left even, this will be [alluded? concluded? allowed?] to have been attained.
53. The vallies of Mairwarra, though not extensive, are fertile in the extreme, watered with numerous perennial rills, and the Mhairs are most industrious cultivators: It is a tract exactly resembling that of Komulmair and indeed a prolongation of it, tho' their bad habits have not allowed their industry to equal that Pergunnah.
54. Such have been the escape and end of my plans to bring a most turbulent and daring race of Public Robbers to become peaceful and quiet, tax-giving subjects: I hope [they?] succeeded, and shall be most gratified to learn if the mode pursued to this end shall meet the approval of the Most Noble the Governor General in Council.
55. In my settlement with this rude people, in 1818/19, the Bow and Arrow or the dagger was the symbol of the ratification of engagements, and it may be regarded as a pretty strong demonstration of internal feeling their having discarded this, and substituted a more peaceful and fitting emblem the PLOUGH. I subjoin a copy of one of these agreements, as a matter of curiosity.
56. Mr WILDER did me the favor to communicate to me his sentiments and intentions as respected three villages subject to his authority at the same time requesting mine in certain points of a more general plan; for the immediate interest [folio 18] of AJMERE, except as regards to welfare, is very slight in this people.
57. My arrangements were not sufficiently advanced to reply decidedly, nor did they correspond sufficiently with Mr. WILDER's intentions. These were giving those of AJMERE up to the Thakoor of Mussooda, stipulating that they should never be reinhabited by the MHAIRS, whom he should establish in the plains, and people their haunts with the agricultural tribes, Jats and GOOJURS from thence.
58. The Plan, if it succeeds, will doubtless be a good one, and there may be facilities in Ajmere which are here wanting, indispensible to success.
59. Our Plans however differ in this most essential point: his [fixes? serves?] the interests of the THAKOOR, with this class, while mine has the

object, whether their abode is in the plain or the mountain, entirely to sever whatever capacity any individual THAKOOR may possess to restrain the excesses of a race born to plunder. Yet it is on a general principal [sic] founded on experience equally visible to Mr Wilder as myself in all these operations that not one THAKOOR in whatsoever of these states who could be confided in, whose interests came in contact with this BANDITTI, and the principle was found equally true of those who had all their lives opposed them, as where they had acted with them, for the time bent under them. Such being the case, the base and foundation of my system and highly approved by the Ranah, has been to cut asunder for ever all ties which connected them, whether the collusion arose as in DEOGURH and most of the others [folio 19] from INTEREST, or as with BEDNORE from REVENGE, in a long prosecuted feud with Athoon, and it is a principle I am glad to say gratifying to the Mhairs, who have themselves confessed as being induced to hold out by surest advice of those interested.

60. It may be even expedient by and by to form a small corps of the Mhairs themselves of parties from the most orderly communities with their own Rawuts as officers, it will give employment and subsistence, and confidence thus placed in a judicious selection, may be of very great consequence to general amendment.

61. It is rare indeed to find a Thakoor with sufficient talent or energy to manage his own Estate, far less to curb the licentiousness of such Bands immersed in sloth or voluptuousness. They leave all to low agents of Buniahs, who only think of gain, and the shortest way to obtain this is considered the best. I have found few men of this class hypocritical enough to deny that they or their masters ever felt reluctance to this mode of adding to their means, such were the times. The moral change in Rajwarra is great as the Physical, and tho' still in Infancy, yet improvement in both is undoubted, and will proceed hand in hand. It is a common phrase which I may be pardoned giving as it conveys with full force what I describe 'you found us all thieves, and made us honest men' (Sahookars).

62. But we must not trust for such magical rapidity of reform, and I accordingly prefer not throwing them in the way of temptation so depending [folio 20] on their virtue in withstanding it.

63. But as it is situation and facility which make every class equally prone to a life of spoil and plunder, I should not expect with the absence of means of repressing it, either Jats or Goojurs, particularly the latter, would be less prone thereto than their predecessors.

64. Independent of these reasons and much stronger than either, are others which would operate to render the plan impracticable in Meywar.

65. Admitting that dread of extirpation could alter the habits of life, and that the native of the mountain transplanted to the plain, might in time become reconciled to his lot, there will be wanting the first incitement to success in abandoning the place of birth, equally [operating? operation?] on the cultivator of the plain supplanting them.

## APPENDICES

66. The strength of that first principle of nature, the attachment of LOCALITY are well known, but when subjoined to these you add the right of property in the soil, the chief and only efficient spur to industry, it may well be doubted that with the removal of this stimulus, habits of life could be altered. The Mhair might be driven down, but could the Tennant of Right not of will be made to ascend? Could he by any effort be brought to abandon his patrimonial fields which he could pledge, mortgage or sell, and do all but leave uncultivated at pleasure?**

   ** [note** folio 20: This he might even do paying the tax.]

67. Doubtless in Ajmere, the landed tenures under the Mogul Government underwent a change and the Right of absolute property in the soil [folio 21] might be frittered down to bare occupancy, which might induce the cultivators there to exchange, here the principle is too well understood 'Zumeen Ryot ka, Fussel Raj ka'**

   ** [note** folio 21: The land is the subject's, the tax to the Ruler.]

   to expect such, and were it otherwise, there is sufficient waste and fertile [infertile?] lands in the plain to stiffle [sic] all desire of emigration to [work it? towards it?].

68. Besides I never looked on the EVIL as one incurable, or where there existed efficient control in the Government, not only to be subdued, but to be kept under control, applications had already failed, but in the present the [Evil? ROOT?] was finally cut which could hinder success; and as this efficient control is also about being established, I trust to these arrangements being permanently answerable to the end.
69. The Ranah has given me perfect control to prevent their [these?] retrograding to disorder, and I trust experience from what the Mhairs have suffered, with the means to ensure obedience, will be effectual.
70. I had to regret being under the necessity of keeping out any part of the troops so long, but I felt anxious to see the fortresses finished ere they returned, and their presence materially added to the realization of the fines. In a week or 10 days I shall entirely dispense with the service of the detachment; but in a task of such magnitude I was desirous of being secure beyond doubt.
71. I fear I may have been led to occupy too much of the time of His Excellency, the most Noble [folio 22] the Governor-General in Council by these details. They have here caused a considerable sensation and it cannot be unimportant to notice, even in the chastisement of barbarous hordes, the charm which seems to operate from the late events, both as it affects physical and moral strength and opinion, nor is it any drawback to its intent, that our troops met no opposition, for this forms the Chief part of the wonder, while every one has his story of what these terrible communities had done, how they had fought against the kings, how Princes and Chiefs had fallen in attempting to subdue them, of the great Sowaee Jey Sing of Jeipoor

being foiled, and almost every Mahratta Subadar, and yet that they could not oppose but two Battalions of the British Government, this they say is wonderful, and from it extract a moral which may be turned to account, 'that in the cause of Justice and Humanity, numbers are of no account', throwing into the scale at the same time, however, the weight of compact physical FORCE.

I have the honor to be etc.
[signed]    JAMES TOD
Political Agent, Western Rajpoot States.

[Date at beginning of dispatch: Oodipoor, 25 November 1821]

# Appendix IV

## *James Tod's Last Will and Testament, deposited by him with his solicitors on 11 August 1834, PRO/B/11/1857, folios 31–3*

Records of the Prerogative Court of Canterbury. Name of register: STOWELL, quire numbers 51–100.

PRO/B/11/1857: Will of JAMES TOD, late Lieutenant Colonel in the service of the Honorable East India Company's Service, of Cumberland Terrace, Regents Park, Middlesex.

JAMES TOD ESQUIRE [folio 31 recto, following from folio 30 verso]

ACCT 1°.

I BEQUEATH to my wife during her life, provided she does not again marry, a life interest, in all the money estates I did possess of, for her use & maintenance

[folio 31 verso]

for the proper education of my children, my eldest son being abundantly provided for by the will of my uncle P. HEATLY, I bequeath to him out of all my property only my house, N° 6 Cumberland Terrace, its furniture, plate, books, and all its appurtenances, after his mother's death. The rest of my property of whatever kind, of which I may be possessor, or which may [revert?] to me after my death, I divide unto the rest of my children which I now have or may have, in equal proportions after their mother's death, should I die before my son attains the age of 21. I believe it is in the spirit and letter of my late uncle's will, that the property bequeathed should accumulate to that period, his mother [earning? winning?] for such period an ample sum to cover all his expenses, as education, clothing etc. which sum I fix at £300 annually, which with the advice of her Friends, my Executors, will be properly managed. Those Executors, whom I pray to act in her behalf, for her and my children's welfare, are as follows:

E.W. Blunt Esq., of Kompshut,
E. Mackintosh Esq., of Montgui Square,
John Melville Esq., of Upper Harley Street,
Alexander Melville Esq., of Upper Harley Street,
Rob Rowison Esq., of Upper Harley Street,
Srt. E.W. Clutterbuck,
Col. S.H. Tod, [see below, Colonel Suetonius Henry Tod]
J. Clutterbuck
And J. Russell Todd Esq.,                All of Whom I beg the acceptance
                                         Of Mourning Rings of 5 guineas value.

This draft of my will be put into proper form by Messrs Bromley, till which time it is to have all the weight and effect, annulling all former wills, ~~witness my hand~~,

Sd/- JAMES TODD [sic].

1ST CODICIL: As I know well that my beloved JULIA will wait the natural term of her existence in widowhood, to be committed to me, hereafter I have not deemed it necessary to make any provision against an improbable and almost impossible occurrence. Should she desire to forget my memory, she can have no desire to maintain with my children as my property, both and all of which would, in that event, be placed for their use, under the guardianship of the first four named executors, and my brother Colonel S.H. TOD.

Sd/- J. TOD, 11th August 1834, Upper Gloster Place, Dorset Square.

2D CODICIL: To the R.A. Society, I bequeath all my Books & Mss. & Coins on ORIENTAL SUBJECTS, of which they may not have duplicates.

Sd/- J.T. ENDORSED Draft of last will, to be considered as actual will, if not legally [DISTENDED? Oustended? Constituted?] by BROMLEY, Aug. 11th 1834.

In the Prerogative Court of Canterbury,

On the Goods of JAMES TOD, Esq., deceased.

APPEARED PERSONALLY, Julia Tod, at present waiting at the house of her father, Doctor Clutterbuck of the Crescent Bridge Street, Blackfriars, London, widow and made oath that she is the lawful [WIDOW?] of James Tod, late Lieutenant Colonel in the service of the Honourable East India Company's Service, and of Cumberland Terrace, Regents Park in the county of Middlesex, Esquire, [OCTOADOR?] who departed this life suddenly, on the seventeenth day of November last [1835], and she further says that a few days after the death of the said deceased, she sent to the East India House for certain [TEXTS?] and packages which had been deposited there, by him, previously to his leaving England for the Continent, in the month of August, one thousand eight hundred and thirty four, which he at such time did for the benefit of and in order to [Regain? Restore?] his health, and on receipt thereof she opened and examined the contents of a certain tin box, wherein she knew he had deposited his papers of importance and found therein certain paper writing loosely folded up. Purporting and which on inspection appeared to be and contain the last will and testament with two codicils. thereto, of the said deceased, all in his own handwriting, which are now hereunto annexed. The said will

beginning thus: 'ACCT 1°: I bequeath to my wife during her life, provided she does not again marry', …

ending thus: 'This draught of my will will be put into proper form by Messrs Bromley, till which time it is to have all the weight and effect of a regular will, annulling all former wills' and thus subscribed JamesTod.

The first of the two Codicils beginning thus: 'CODICIL: As I know that my beloved Julia will wait the natural term

[folio 32 recto]

of her existence in her widowhood',

Ending thus: '… all of which would, in that event, would be placed for their use, under the guardianship of the first four named Executors, and my brother Colonel S.H. TOD',
And thus subscribed and dated: 'J. TOD, 11th August 1834, Upper Gloster Place, Dorset Square'.

And the other of the said Codicils being written and comprized in the following words viz:

'2D CODICIL: To the R.A. Society, I bequeath all my Books, & MSS., & Coins on Oriental Subjects, of which they may not have duplicates'.

And subscribed with the initials: 'J.T.'.

Such will and codicils being endorsed in the following words, viz: 'Draft of the last will to be considered as actual will if not legally constituted by Bromley, 11th August 1834'. And which said will and codicils, she there handed to her father, the said Doctor Clutterbuck, who is out of the Executors thereby appointed, and [deponent?] at such time also found a certain other paper writing, which on inspecting appeared to be a former will of the said deceased, bearing date the ninth day of October, one thousand eight hundred and thirty, and she further saith that she hath since made the most diligent and careful search among the various papers left by the said deceased, with a view to discover whether he left any other will or testamentary disposition of his property, but being unable to find anything having the slightest relation thereto, and she lastly saith in exposure to the expressed intention of the said deceased, as contained in his aforesaid last will, and in the aforesaid underscribed version of his having the same legally [constituted?] by Mr. Bromley, that he the said deceased, a very few days after the date thereof, and as she believes on the 23rd day of the said month of August [1834] accompanied by deponent, left England and proceeded to Germany, where, and at various places on the Continent, he remained for a considerable period of time, and did not return to this country until the beginning of September last [1835], and only came to London with a view of taking up his final residence there, a few weeks before he was seized with the ILLNESS of which he died, and by reason she supposes of his health having been considerably improved during his absence abroad, he delayed consulting the said Mr. Bromley, on the subject of his said will, until his leisure and [disposition? condition?] would permit, [contending?] that unless he [RIONID?] gave instructions to put the same into legal form, the said will and codicils would as such in all respects have full and complete operation and effect.

Sd/- JULIA TOD, on the fifth day of Jan 1836, said Julia Tod was duly sworn to the truth of the aforegoing affidavit, before me: S.B. BURNABY, Surrogate, President P.C. MOORE, Not[ary]. Pub[lic].

In the Prerogative Court of Canterbury

On the Goods of James Tod, Esquire, deceased.

APPEARED PERSONALLY, WILLIAM BROMLEY, of No 3 Grays Inn Square, in the county of Middlesex, Solicitor, and JOSEPH WARNER BROMLEY of South Square Grays Inn, aforesaid Solicitor, and respectively made oath as follows, and first the said William Bromley for himself made oath that he knew and was intimately acquainted with James Tod late Lieutenant Colonel in the Service of the Honorable East India Company, and of Cumberland Terrace, Regents Park, in the county of Middlesex, Esquire, deceased, for several years prior, and down to the time of his death, which happened on or about the seventeenth day of November last [1835] and he further saith that he was also professionally entrusted for the said deceased down to the period of his decease, and had so been for several years previous thereto, and deponent referring to certain paper writings, now hereunto annexed, purporting to be and contain the last will and testament and two codicils of the said deceased, such will and codicils being written and comprised on a sheet and half of letter paper, the said will beginning thus: 'Acct 1: I bequeath to my wife during her life, provided she does not again marry'... ending thus: 'This draught of my will will be put into proper form by Messrs Bromley till which time it is to have all the weight and effect of a regular will annulling all former wills witness my hand', and thus subscribed 'James Tod', the first of the said Codicils beginning thus: 'Codicil: As I know well that my beloved JULIA will wait the natural term of her existence in her widowhood', ending thus: 'all of which would in that event be placed for their use under the guardianship of the first four named Executors, and my Brother Col. S.H. TOD', and thus subscribed and dated: 'J. Tod, 11th August 1834, 11 Upper Gloster Place, Dorset Square', and the other of the said Codicils being written and comprized in the following words viz: '2D CODICIL; To the R.A. Society I bequeath all my books & MSS. & Coins on Oriental Subjects, of which they may not have Duplicates', and subscribed wit the intials 'J.T.' and deponent referring also to the endorsement written on such will and codicils in the words following viz: 'Draft of last will to be considered as actual will if not legally CONSTITUTED by

[folio 55 (stamped page number 32 verso)]

... Bromley August 11th 1834', he deposes and says that shortly after the date of the said will, as he has been informed and believes the said deceased left England and proceeded to the Continent, in where he was for some time [absent?], and did not whence return again to this country until the beginning of the month of September last [1835] and although he hath had various meetings and consultations with the said deceased on matters of business and otherwise [since?] he so returned, he never [received?] any instructions whatever from the said deceased either to complete such aforesaid will or to prepare any other testamentary paper for or on his behalf, and he lastly saith that he alone hath a [hand?] in such his aforesaid professional capacity for the said deceased, since the dissolution of partnership between him and his brother, which took place on the twentieth day of September, one thousand eight hundred and thirty four [20 September 1834], and the said Joseph Warner BROMLEY for himself a saith that he knew and was well acquainted with the said deceased for several years previous to his decease, for whom [deponent?] and his said brother William Bromley were professionally sanctioned until the dissolution of their partnership as aforesaid, and referring to the aforesaid will, and all codicils of the said deceased as herebefore [cited?] and set forth, he deposes and says that he never at any time had any conversation whatever with the said deceased relating thereto, or any other will or Testamentary paper or disposition whatever. Sd/- W. BROMLEY and J.W. BROMLEY, on the sixth day of January 1836, the said William Bromley and Joseph Warner Bromley were duly sworn to the truth of the aforegoing affidavit before me JOHN. DANBERY SURRT [Surrogate], Presdt. G.S. NICHOLSON, Not[ary]. Pub[lic].

IN THE PREROGATIVE COURT OF CANTERBURY,

On the goods of James Tod, Esquire, deceased, 6th January 1836.

On which day appeared personally William Bromley, of No 3 Grays Inn in the county of a Middlesex solicitor, and Joseph Warner Bromley of South Square Grays Inn, aforesaid solicitor, and made oath that they knew and were well acquainted with JAMES TOD, late a Lieutenant Colonel in the service of the Honorable East India Company, and of Great Cumberland Street in Regents Park in the county of Middlesex, Esquire, deceased, who departed this life on the seventeenth day November last, and were likewise well acquainted with his manner and character, of handwriting and subscription, having frequently seen him write, and also write and subscribe his name to writings, and having now carefully and attentively viewed and inspected certain papers, Codicils thereto, of the said deceased, the said will beginning thus:

'Acct I° I bequeath to my wife during her life provided she does not again marry, a life interest in all the money and estates I died Possessed of'...

ending thus 'this draught of my will be put into proper form by Messrs Bromley, till which time it is to have all the weight and effect of a regular will, annulling all former wills, ~~witness my hand~~'

and having the word 'BOOKS' interlined between the fourth and fifth lines of the said will counting from the bottom thereof, and thus subscribed: 'James Tod',

the first of the said codicils beginning thus, 'Codicil ... as I know well that my beloved JULIA will wait the natural term of her existence in her widowhood' ... and ending thus: 'all of which would in that event be placed for their use under the guardianship of the first four named Executors, my brother Col. S.H. TOD,' and thus subscribed and dated: 'J. TOD, 11th August 1834, Upper Gloster Place, Dorset Square'.

And the second of such CODICILS being written and comprised in the following words viz: '2° CODICIL: To the R.A. Society I bequeath all my Books, MSS, Coins on oriental subjects, of which they may not have duplicates,' and subscribed with the initial letters 'J.T.' and having in like manner attentively viewed and inspected the [subservient?] written on such aforesaid paper writings viz: 'Draft of last will to be considered as actual will if not legally [constituted?] by Bromley, Augt 11th 1834',

They depose and say that they so verily and in their consciences believe the whole body series and contents of the said will and codicils so beginning, ending and comprized in the words before set forth, that word 'BOOKS' so as aforesaid interviews in the said will as well as the several signatures and initials so as aforesaid, set and subscribed thereto together with the subservient written thereon and herebefore cited, to be all of the PROPER handwriting and subscription of him the said JAMES TOD Esquire, deceased.

Sd/- W. BROMLEY and J.W. BROMLEY.

Signed: the said William Bromley and Joseph Warner Bromley were sworn to the truth of the aforegoing affidavit before inc: [John] DANBERY SURT [Surrogate], Prest G.S. NICHOLSON Not. Pub.[6 January 1836].

Resworn by the said William Bromley and Joseph Warner Bromley, the attestation as to the interlineation of the word 'BOOKS' having been first inserted, this 27th Jan 1836, before inc. JOHN DANBERY, Surt. [Surrogate]
Prdt R.W. JENNINGS N.P. [Notary Public].

[folio 33 recto]

PROVED at London, will and codicils, 27th January 1836, before the Worshipful Sherrard Brammont BURNABY, Doctor of Laws and Surrogate, by the oaths of Edward Walter BLUNT, Esq., of KOMPSHUT [name of place?] to whom ADINON was granted, having been first sworn only to administer

## APPENDICES

power, reserved of making the like to JOHN MELVILLE Esq., ALEXANDER MELVILLE, Esq., EDWARD CLUTTERBUCK Esq., SUETONIUS HENRY TOD, Esq., the Brother, and James Russell TODD, Esq., the other Executors, when they *** *** *** *** *** shall apply for the same.

[in margin on the right: BY MOTION AND DECREE.]

# BIBLIOGRAPHY

## *Manuscript sources*

### British Library, London

BL MSS. Add. 30356, by Colonel James TOD, History of Jessulmir, to 1702 (compiled c. 1816), 53 double folios.

BL MSS. Add. 34617, folios 254–5, letter from Tod to Macvey Napier, dated October 15 1835

BL MSS. Add. 38226, folio18, Petition dated 21 December 1790, addressed to the Earl of Hawkesbury and the Lord Treasurers of the Pitt Government, in order to obtain trading privileges for Borrowstonness on the Clyde.

BL MSS. Add. 71124 v., letter from Tod from Frankfurt on the Mayne to J. Klaproth in Paris, dated 20 September 1829.

BL MSS. EUR E83, folios 26–7, Tod to Major Frederick, dated 11 July [1824?].

BL MSS. EUR E83, folios 34–5, J. Tod to Major Frederick, 12 Hynde Street, Manchester Square, London, dated 13 November [1824?].

BL MSS. EUR E83, folios 37–9, letter from Tod to Frederick, dated January 10 1825.

### India Office Records

IOR/EUR E/293/35, 9 folios, being a letter-report from Tod to Charles Metcalfe, Secretary to the British Government in Calcutta, dated 10 August 1820, on the Mirs of Sind, with Tod's plan for the attack of Sind in November 1820.

IOR/EUR E/293/47, 22 folios, being a letter-report from Tod to George Swinton, Secretary to the British Government in Calcutta, dated 25 November 1821, on the Mhairs and Mhairwarra.

IOR/F/4/810/21725, Board's Collections, folio 17, from Bengal Government to Resident of Malwa and Rajputana, dated 12 September 1823.

IOR/H/521, folios 637–47, Colonel Alexander Walker, 'Suggestions for effecting the abolition of the practice of Female Infanticide', 28 June 1819.

IOR/Home Miscellaneous/738: Document No. 12, folios 685–706, Tod to Ochterlony, dated 12 April 1819.

IOR/Home Miscellaneous/738: Document No. 13, folios 709–11, Ochterlony to Tod, dated 18 April 1819.

## BIBLIOGRAPHY

IOR/Home Miscellaneous/738: Document No. 32, folios 823–6, Ochterlony to Tod, dated 8 April 1819.
IOR/L/MIL/9/01 #155 Tod's Baptism Certificate.
IOR/L/MIL/9/255/folio 144 v., List of the Cadets for the Year 1798.
IOR/L/MIL/9/255/149 #35, Certificate of the Age of the Cadets, Season 1798.
IOR MSS F/4/810/21725, folios 303–4, from Bengal Government to Resident of Malwa and Rajputana, dated 11 April 1822.

### Public Record Office, Kew

PRO/30/11/27, folios 258–9, being part of Packet No. 27, 'East India Papers of November and December 1788'.
PRO/B/11/1857, folios 31–3, James Tod's Last Will and Testament, deposited by Tod with his solicitors on 11 August 1834.

### Royal Asiatic Society of Great Britain and Ireland, London

Manuscript letter by Tod from the RAS archives (no reference allotted), communicated by the RAS librarian, Kathy Lazenbatt. Tod to H.T. Colebrooke, dated 15 November 1827.
Manuscript letter by Tod from the RAS archives (no reference allotted) communicated by the RAS librarian, Kathy Lazenbatt. Tod to W. Huttmann, Secretary, RAS, dated 14 December 1827.
MSS. ACCOUNT BOOK OF JAMES TOD, folios 1–105 in a folio-sized fascicule containing 158 folios, found in Udaipur (a photocopy of this manuscript document is held at the library of the Royal Asiatic Society, London).

## *Tod's two major published works*

Tod, James, *Annals and Antiquities of Rajasthan*, London: Routledge and Kegan Paul Ltd, vol. I (1829) and vol. II (1832); repr. Delhi: Rupa and Company, 1997.
—*Travels in Western India*, London: W.H. Allen & Co., 1839 (posth.); repr. Delhi: Munshiram Manoharlal, 1997.

## *Tod's shorter essays*

'An Account of Greek, Parthian, and Hindu Medals, found in India'. *Transactions of the Royal Asiatic Society*, 1 (1827), 312–42. Read 18 June 1825.
*Asiatic Journal*, 16 (1835), 262–70 (Tod's essay on General Donkin).
'Comments on an inscription in marble at Madhucargarh, and on three grants inscribed on copper found at Ujjaiyini'. *Transactions of the Royal Asiatic Society*, 1 (1827), 227–9. Read 19 June 1824.
'Comparison of the Hindu and Theban Hercules, illustrated by an ancient Hindu intalgio'. *Transactions of the Royal Asiatic Society*, 3 (1835), 139–59. Read 4 December 1830.

'De l'origine asiatique de quelques-unes des anciennes tribus de l'Europe, établies sur les rivages de la mer baltique, surtout les Su, Suedi, Suiones, Asi, Yeuts, Juts ou Getes-Goths' [par le Major Tod]. *Journal Asiatique*, first series, 11 (January–June 1827), 277–309.

'The Feudal System in Rajasthan'. *Asiatic Journal and Monthly Register*, new series, 5.17 (May–August 1831), 40–8.

'Géographie du Radjasthan'. *Journal Asiatique*, new series, 8 (July–December 1831), 46–66.

'Indo-Grecian Antiquities'. *Asiatic Journal and Monthly Register*, new series, 17.65 (May–August 1835), 9–15.

'On the Religious Establishments of Mewar'. *Transactions of the Royal Asiatic Society*, 2 (1830), 270–325. Read 6 December 1828.

'Remarks on certain sculptures in the Cave Temples of Ellora'. *Transactions of the Royal Asiatic Society*, 2 (1830), 328–40. Read 6 December 1828.

'Translation of a Sanscrit Inscription relative to the last Hindu Monarch of Delhi, with comments thereon'. *Transactions of the Royal Asiatic Society*, 1 (1827), 133–54. Read 1 May 1824.

'The Vow of Sunjogta', from Chand's chronicle, was published after Tod's death, in 1838, in *Asiatic Journal or the Monthly Register*, 25.1 (January–April 1838), in three sections: 101–12; 197–211; and 273–86.

## *Reviews of and critical comments on Tod's shorter compilations*

Anonymous review of Tod's 'An Account of some sculptures in the Cave Temples of Ellora'. *Asiatic Journal and Monthly Register*, 27 (January–June 1829), 328–30.

Anonymous review of Tod's 'Observations on a Gold Ring of Hindu fabrication found at Montrose, Scotland'. *Asiatic Journal and Monthly Register*, new series, 3 (September–December 1830), 33–4.

Anonymous review of Tod's 'On the Religious Establishments of Mewar'. *Asiatic Journal and Monthly Register*, 27 (January–June 1829), 328–30.

A.W. Schlegel, 'Observations sur quelques médailles bactriennes et indo-scythiques nouvellement découvertes'. *Journal Asiatique*, second series, 3 (November 1828), 321–49.

## *Minutes of learned societies*

*Journal Asiatique*, first series, vol. 10 (January–June 1827), 61–2. 'Nouvelles: Société Asiatique, séance du 9 janvier 1827'. Tod was present at this session of the Société Asiatique, and was elected as an overseas member.

*Royal Asiatic Society Minutes of Council*, vol. I, March 1823–March 1827, folios 35–9, Council of 15 March 1824, Tod was elected as a Member of Council of the RAS.

*Royal Asiatic Society Minutes of Council*, vol. I, March 1823–March 1827, folios 85–8, Council of 16 April 1825, Tod was confirmed as the RAS librarian.

## BIBLIOGRAPHY

*Royal Asiatic Society Minutes of Council*, vol. IV, April 1833–April 1837:

folio 22, Council of 15 June 1833, Tod stated his desire to resign the office of RAS librarian for health reasons.

folio 30, Council of 20 July 1833, Tod was replaced by Sir Graves Chamney Haughton as RAS librarian.

folios 185–8, Council of 6 February 1836, Mrs James Tod communicated Tod's bequest of his oriental possessions to the RAS.

folio 273, Council of 16 April 1837, Sir Graves Chamney Haughton was replaced as librarian of the RAS by Colonel Francklin.

### Reviews by learned journals of Tod's Annals and Antiquities of Rajasthan *(1829, 1832)*

*Asiatic Journal and Monthly Register*, 28 (July–December 1829), 187–98.

*Asiatic Journal and Monthly Register*, new series, 8 (May–August 1832), 57–66; 108–24.

*Edinburgh Review*, 52 (October 1830–January 1831), 86–108; and 56 (July 1832–January 1833), 73–98, by William Erskine.

*Journal Asiatique*, new series 2, 4 (July–December 1829), 374–89, review in French by Eugène Burnouf.

*Journal des Savans*, November 1830, 643–57; January 1831, 65–81; April 1831, 225–38; May 1834, 257–69; July 1834, 394–404; November 1834, 641–9; review in French by Silvestre de Sacy in six parts.

*Oriental Herald*, 22 (July–September 1829), 505–17.

*Quarterly Review*, 48.95 (December 1832), 1–39, by Henry Hart Milman.

### Other published works cited

Allan, David, 1993. *Virtue, Learning and the Scottish Enlightenment: Ideas of Scholarship in Early Modern History*. Edinburgh: Edinburgh University Press, 1993.

Archer, Mildred, 'India and natural history: the role of the East India Company, 1785–1858'. *History Today*, 9.11 (November 1959), 736–43.

Archer, Mildred and Lightbown, Ronald, *India Observed: India as Viewed by British Artists, 1760–1860*, London, 1982.

Arnold, David, *The Tropics and the Travelling Gaze: India, Landscape and Science, 1800–1856*, Seattle and London: University of Washington Press, 2006.

*Asiatick Researches*, 28 (1833), special volume on geology. Calcutta: Printed at the Bengal Military Orphan Press, by G.H. Whitmann.

Bakhtin, Mikhail, *The Dialogic Imagination: Four Essays*, Austin and London: University of Texas Press, 1981.

Barrell, John (ed.), *Painting and the Politics of Culture: New Essays on British Art, 1700–1850*, Oxford, 1992.

Bayly, Christopher A., *Indian Society and the Making of the British Empire*, Cambridge: Cambridge University Press, 1988.

## BIBLIOGRAPHY

—'Orientalists, informants and critics in Banaras, 1790–1860', in: Jamal Malik (ed.), *Perspectives of Mutual Encounters in South Asian History, 1760–1860*, Leiden: Brill, 2000, pp. 97–127.

Barnett, L.D., 'Catalogue of the Tod Collection of Indian Manuscripts in the possession of the Royal Asiatic Society'. *Journal of the Royal Asiatic Society*, April 1940, 129–78.

Berlin, Isaiah, *The Roots of Romanticism*, ed. Henry Hardy, Princeton: Princeton University Press, 1999.

Biographical note on Sir Henry Blount (1602–82), by Charles Henry Coote, in: *Dictionary of National Biography*, ed. Leslie Stephen, London: Smith, Elder & Co., 1885–1900, vol. V.

Biographical note on Wilfrid Scawen Blunt (1840–1922), at http://en.wikipedia.org/wiki/Wilfrid_Scawen_Blunt, accessed 3 November 2012.

Biographical note on James Grant Duff (1789–1858), at http://en.wikipedia.org/wiki/James_Grant_Duff, accessed 3 November 2012.

Biographical note on William Erskine (1773–1852), by Katherine Prior, at www.oxforddnb.com/articles/8/8880-article.html?back, accessed 12 November 2010.

Biographical note on Edward William Lane (1801–1876), at http://en.wikipedia.org/wiki/Edward_William_Lane, accessed 3 November 2012.

Biographical note on Henry Hart Milman (1791–1868), by H.C.G. Mathew, at www.oxforddnb.com/articles/18/187778-article.html?back, accessed 12 November 2010.

Biographical note on Thomas Munro (1761–1827), at http://en.wikipedia.org/wiki/Sir_Thomas_Munro, accessed 3 November 2012.

Biographical note on James Tod (1782–1835), by Stephen Wheeler and Roger T. Stearn, in: *Oxford Dictionary of National Biography*, Oxford: Oxford University Press, 2004, at www.oxforddnb.com/view/article/27486, accessed 12 November 2010.

Biographical note on Mark Wilks (1759–1831), at http://en.wikipedia.org/wiki/Mark_Wilks, accessed 3 November 2012.

Blount, Henry, *A Voyage to the Levant, a briefe relation of a journey lately performed by Master H.B., gentleman, from England, by the way of Venice, into Dalmatia ... Rhodes and Egypt, into Gran Cairo, with particular observations concerning the modern condition of the Turks, and other people under that Empire*, 2nd edn, London: A. Crooke, 1636.

Blunt, Wilfrid Scawen, *Atrocities of British Justice under British Rule in Egypt*, London: T.F. Unwin, 1906.

—*The Future of Islam*, London: Kegan Paul, Trench, 1882.

—*Secret History of the English Occupation of Egypt*, London: Knopf, 1907.

Bose, P.N., 'The history of the Asiatic Society of Bengal, 1784–1883', Part III, 'Natural Science, section of Geology', in: *Centenary Review of the Asiatic Society of Bengal from 1784 to 1883*, published by the Society, Calcutta: Thacker, Spink & Co., 1885, pp. 109–xcvi.

*British Parliamentary Papers in 18 Volumes, India Office Records*, vol. XIV, section vi, Political and Foreign, OIOC Shelfmark: V/4/1831-2, No. 735-VI, London: House of Commons, 1832.

## BIBLIOGRAPHY

Broady, Alexander, *The Tradition of Scottish Philosophy: A New Perspective on the Enlightenment*, Edinburgh: Polygon, 1990.

Buchanan Hamilton, Francis, '"Description of temples of the Jainas in South Bihar and Bhagalpur", by Dr. Francis Buchanan Hamilton, Member of the RAS' (read by Henry Thomas Colebrooke). *Transactions of the Royal Asiatic Society*, 1 (1827), article no. XXVIII, 523–6.

Buchanan Hamilton, Francis, '"Description of the ruins of Buddha Gaya", by Dr. Francis Buchanan Hamilton, Member of the RAS'. *Transactions of the Royal Asiatic Society*, 2 (1830), article no. II, 40–51.

Buchanan Hamilton, Francis, '"Inscriptions upon rocks in South Bihar", described by Dr. Buchanan Hamilton, Member of the RAS, and explained by Henry Thomas Colebrooke, Esq., Director of the Royal Asiatic Society'. *Transactions of the Royal Asiatic Society*, 1 (1827) article no. XI, 201–6.

Buchanan Hamilton, Francis, *A Journey from Madras through the countries of Mysore, Canara and Malabar*, London: T. Cadell & W. Davies, 1807, 3 vols, repr. New Delhi: Asian Educational Services, 1999, 3 vols.

—' "On the Srawacs or Jains", by Dr. Francis Buchanan Hamilton, Member of the RAS'. *Transactions of the Royal Asiatic Society*, 1 (1827), article no. XXIX, 531–6.

Burke, Edmund, *A Philosophical Enquiry into the Origin of our Ideas of the Sublime and the Beautiful*, Oxford, 1998 (1757).

Burton, Richard, *Sind, and the races that inhabit the valley of the Indus*, London: W.H. Allen, 1851.

Campbell, George, *Modern India: a sketch of the system of civil government, to which is prefixed some account of the natives and native institutions*, London: John Murray, 1852.

Carey, Daniel and Festa, Lynn (eds), *The Postcolonial Enlightenment: Eighteenth-Century Colonialism and Postcolonial Theory*, Cambridge: Cambridge University Press, 2009.

Chitnis, Anand C., *The Scottish Enlightenment: A Social History*. London: Croom Helm, 1976.

Crooke, William (ed.), *Annals and Antiquities of Rajasthan or the Central and Western Rajput States of India, by James Tod*, London: Oxford University Press, 1920, 3 vols.

Desmond, Ray, *The European Discovery of the Indian Flora*, Oxford: Oxford University Press, 1992.

Diamond, Debra, Glynn, Catherine and Jasol, Karni Singh, with contributions by Jason Freitag and Rahul Jain, *Garden and Cosmos: The Royal Paintings of Jodhpur*, London: British Museum Press, 2009.

Dodson, Michael S., *Orientalism, Empire and National Culture: India 1770–1880*, Basingstoke: Palgrave Macmillan, 2007.

Duchet, Michèle, *Anthropologie et histoire au siècle des lumières*, Paris: Flammarion, 1978.

Duchet, Michèle, *Le partage des savoirs: Discours historique et discours ethnologique*, Paris: La Découverte, 1985.

Dunn, Theodore Douglas (ed.), *The Bengali Book of English Verse*, Bombay: Longmans, Green and Co., 1918.

## BIBLIOGRAPHY

*Edinburgh Review*, 'Review of Heber's *Narrative of a Journey* by Francis Jeffrey'. 48 (December 1828), 312–35,

Elphinstone, Mountstuart, *An Account of the Kingdom of Caubul and its dependencies in Persia, Tartary and India, comprising a view of the Afghaun nation and a history of the Dooraunee monarchy*, London: Longman, 1815.

Farrington, Anthony, *Guide to the Records of the India Office Military Department*, London: India Office Library, 1981.

Forbes, Alexander Kinloch, *Raas Mala*, London 1856, repr. London: Oxford University Press, 1924, 2 vols.

Forbes, James, *Oriental Memoirs, selected and abridged from a series of familiar letters written during seventeen years' residence in India: including observations on parts of Africa, and South America, and a narrative of occurrences in four India voyages*, London: White, Cochrane & Co., 1813, 4 vols, quarto.

Franklin, Michael (ed.), *The European Discovery of India: Key Indological Sources of Romanticism*, selected and with new introductions, London: Ganesha Publishing Ltd, 2001, 6 vols.

Freitag, Jason, *Serving Empire, Serving Nation: James Tod and the Rajputs of Rajasthan*, Leiden: Brill, 2009.

—'Tod's *Annals* as history and archive', in: Giles Tillotson (ed.), *James Tod's Rajasthan: The Historian and His Collections*, Mumbai: Radhika Sabavala for Marg Publications on behalf of the National Centre for the Performing Arts, 2007, pp. 86–97; simultaneously published as *Mārg*, 59.1 (2007).

—'Travel, history, politics and heritage: James Tod's "Personal Narrative"', in: Carol E. Henderson and Maxine Weisgrau (eds), *Raj Rhapsodies: Tourism, Heritage and the Seduction of History*, Aldershot: Ashgate, 2007, pp. 47–59.

Ghose, Kasiprasad, *The Shair and other Poems*, Durrumtoollah (Calcutta): Scott, 1839; repr. in: Theodore Douglas Dunn (ed.), *The Bengali Book of English Verse*, Bombay: Longmans, Green and Co., 1918, the poem 'Storm and Rain', pp. 3–4.

Goguet, A.Y. and Fugere, A.C., *The Origin of Laws, Arts and Sciences, and their progress among the ancient nations*, translated from the French. Edinburgh: G. Donaldson & A. Donaldson, 1775 (1758).

Gommans, Jos and Prakash, Om (eds), *Circumambulations in South Asian History: Essays in Honour of Dirk H.A. Kolff*, Leiden: Brill Publishers, 2003.

Grindlay, Robert Melville, *Scenery, Costumes and Architecture chiefly on the Western Side of India*, London: Smith, Elder & Co., 1820.

Guest, Harriet, 'Curiously marked: tattooing, masculinity and nationality in 18th-century perceptions of the South Pacific', in: John Barrell (ed.), *Painting and the Politics of Culture: New Essays on British Art, 1700–1850*, Oxford, 1992, pp. 101–34.

Hallam, Henry, *A View of the state of Europe during the Middle Ages*, 2nd edn, London: John Murray, 1819, 3 vols.

Head, Raymond, *Catalogue of Paintings, Drawings, Engravings and Busts in the Collection of the Royal Asiatic Society*, London, 1991.

Heber, Reginald, Bishop of Calcutta, *Narrative of a Journey through the Upper Provinces of India, from Calcutta to Bombay, 1824–1825*, with notes *upon Ceylon*, London: John Murray, 1828, 3 vols, repr. New Delhi: Asian Educational Services, 1995, 3 vols.

Henderson, Carol E. and Weisgrau, Maxine (eds), *Raj Rhapsodies: Tourism, Heritage and the Seduction of History*, Aldershot: Ashgate, 2007

Herder, Johann Gottfried, *Histoire et cultures: Une autre philosophie de l'histoire; Idées pour la philosophie de l'histoire de l'humanité (extraits, 1784–1791)*, trans. and ed. Max Rouché; presentation, bibliography and chronology by Alain Reinaut, Paris: Garnier Flammarion, 2000.

Houghton, W.E., *The Wellesley Index to Victorian Periodicals: 1824–1900*, London: Routledge & Kegan Paul, 1966.

Howes, Jennifer, *Illustrating India: The Early Colonial Investigations of Colin Mackenzie (1784–1821)*, New Delhi: Oxford University Press, 2010.

Hume, David, *The History of England from the invasion of Julius Caesar to the revolution in 1688*. London: A. Millar, 1767, 8 vols.

Humphreys, S.C. (ed.), *Cultures of Scholarship*, Ann Arbor: University of Michigan Press, 1997

Inden, Ronald, *Imagining India*, London: Hurst & Co (1990) 2000.

Jordanov, Ludmilla and Porter, Roy (eds), *Images of the Earth: Essays in the History of the Environmental Sciences*, London: British Society for the History of Science 1997 (1979).

*Journal of the Royal Asiatic Society*, 'Sanskrit and Prakrit MSS (Todd [sic] Collection)'. October 1890, 801–13.

Jussieu, Antoine-Laurent de, *Genera Plantarum Secundum Ordines naturales disposita*, Paris: Académie des Sciences, 1795.

Kabbani, Rana, *Imperial Fictions: Europe's Myths of Orient*, London: SAQI, 2008 (1986).

Kipling, Rudyard, 'Letters of Marque', in: *From Sea to Sea*, Leipzig: Bernhard Tauchnitz, 1900, 2 vols.

Kennedy, Dane, 'Imperial history and postcolonial theory'. *Journal of Imperial and Commonwealth History*, 24.3 (September 1996), 345–63.

Klonk, Charlotte, *Science and the Perception of Nature: British Landscape Art in the Late Eighteenth and Early Nineteenth Centuries*, New Haven, CT: Yale University Press, 1996.

Kolff, Dirk H.A., *Naukar, Rajput and Sepoy: The Ethnohistory of the Miltary Labour Market in Hindustan, 1450–1850*, Cambridge: Cambridge University Press, 1990.

Kulkarni, A.R., *James Cunningham Grant Duff, Administrator-Historian of the Marathas*, Kolkata: K.P. Bagchi, 2006.

Leask, Nigel, *British Romantic Writers and the East: Anxieties of Empire*, Cambridge: Cambridge University Press,1992.

—*Curiosity and the Aesthetics of Travel Writing, 1770–1840*, Oxford: Oxford University Press, 2002.

MacLean, Gerald, *Looking East: English Writing and the Ottoman Empire before 1800*, Basingstoke: Palgrave Macmillan, 2007.

—*Reorienting the Renaissance: Cultural Exchanges with the East*, Basingstoke: Palgrave Macmillan, 2005.

## BIBLIOGRAPHY

—*The Rise of Oriental Travel: English Visitors to the Ottoman Empire, 1580–1720*, Basingstoke: Palgrave Macmillan, 2004.

Maine, Henry Sumner, *Ancient Law, its connexion with the early history of society and its relation to modern ideas*, London: J. Murray, 1861.

Majeed, Javed, 'James Mill's *The History of British India* and Utilitarianism as a rhetoric of reform'. *Modern Asian Studies*, 24.2 (1990), 209–24.

—*Ungoverned Imaginings: James Mill's 'The History of British India' and Orientalism*, Oxford: Clarendon Press, 1992.

Malcolm, John, *A Memoir of Central India, including Malwa and adjoining provinces: with the history of the past and present condition of that country*. London: Parbury & Allen, 1823, 2 vols, octavo.

Marshall , Peter James and Williams, Glyndwr, *The Great Map of Mankind: British Perceptions of the World in the Age of Enlightenment*, London: J.M. Dent, 1982.

Metcalf, Thomas R., *Ideologies of the Raj*, Cambridge: Cambridge University Press 2001 (1995).

Meyendorf, baron de, 'Voyage en Boukharie et en Sogdiane (Balkh)'. *Journal Littéraire de Gottingue*, 108 (1828).

Miles, Lieutenant-Colonel William, 'On the Jains of Gujerat and Marwar'.*Transactions of the Royal Asiatic Society*, 3 (1835), 335–71.

Mill, James, *An Essay on Government*, with an introduction by Ernest Barker, Cambridge: Cambridge, 1937.

—*The History of British India*, London: Baldwin, Cradock & Joy, 1817, 3 vols, quarto.

—*Selected Economic Writings*, introduced and ed. Donald Winch, Edinburgh and London: Oliver & Boyd, 1966.

Millar, John, *A historical view of the English government from the settlement of the Saxons in Britain to the accession of the House of Stewart*. London: J. Mawman, 1812 (1787), 4 vols, octavo.

*Minutes of Evidence taken before the Select Committee on the Affairs of the East India Company*, London: J.L. Cox & Sons, 1833.

'Minutes of Evidence taken before the Select Committee on the Affairs of the East India Company, Session of 6th December 1831 to 16th August 1832', in: *British Parliamentary Papers in 18 Volumes, India Office Records*, vol. V (1831), vol. VII (1831), vol. IX (1832) and vol. XI (1832), London: House of Commons, 1832; repr. in: James Mill, *Selected Economic Writings*, introduced and ed. Donald Winch, Edinburgh and London: Oliver & Boyd, 1966, pp. 423–43.

'Minutes of Evidence taken before the Select Committee on the Affairs of the East India Company, Session of 6th December 1831 to 16th August 1832', in: *British Parliamentary Papers in 18 Volumes, India Office Records*, vol. XIV, section vi, Political and Foreign, OIOC Shelfmark: V/4/1831–2, No. 735-VI, London: House of Commons, 1832, pp. 3–10 (James Mill); pp. 122–35 (James Tod).

Moore, Thomas, *Lalla Rookh: An Oriental Romance*, London: Longman, Brown, Green, Longmans & Roberts, 1856 (1817).

## BIBLIOGRAPHY

Munro, Thomas, *Writings of Major-General Sir Thomas Munro, Governor of Madras*, ed. Alexander John Arbuthnot 1889 (1881).

Nash, Geoffrey, *From Empire to Orient: Travellers to the Middle East, 1830–1926*, London: I.B.Tauris, 2005.

Obituary notice of Macvey Napier (1777–1848), *London, Edinburgh and Dublin Philosophical Magazine and Journal of Science*, 32 (January–June 1848), 220.

Peabody, Norbert, *Hindu Kingship and Polity in Precolonial India*, Cambridge: Cambridge University Press, 2003.

—'Tod's *Rajast'han* and the boundaries of imperial rule in 19th century India'. *Modern Asian Studies*, 30.1 (1996), 185–220.

Phillimore, R.H., *Historical Records of the Survey of India*, Dehra Dun: Office of the Geodetic Branch, Survey of India, 1945, 1950, 1954, 3 vols.

Porter, Roy, *The Making of Geology: Earth Science in Britain, 1660–1815*, Cambridge: Cambridge University Press, 1977.

—'The terraqueous globe', in: G.S. Rousseau and Roy Porter (eds), *The Ferment of Knowledge: Studies in the Historiography of Eighteenth-Century Science*, Cambridge: Cambridge University Press, 1980, pp. 285–324.

Purohit, Laxmisinha (ed.), 'Maharana Bheemsingh jee kay naam, Mewar Mitra James Tod kay Mewari Patra' (Mewar Letters addressed to Maharana Bheemsinghjee by his friend James Tod, = 'Thirteen letters from James Tod and Patrick Waugh to Rana Bheem Singh of Mewar, in the local Urdu dialect, transcribed and published in the Devanagiri script'), in: Purushottam Lal Menaria (ed.), *Anusheelan*, the research journal of the Maharana Mewar Research Institute, 1.1 (January 1989), 46–51

*Quarterly Review*, 'Review of Heber's travel narrative by J.J. Blunt and John Gibson Lockhart'. 37 (January 1828), 100–19 (with general observations on India, pp. 119–47).

*Quarterly Review*, 'Review of James Forbes's *Oriental Memoirs* by Robert Southey'. 12.23 (October 1814), article IX, 180–227.

Rendall, Jane, 'Scottish Orientalism: from Robertson to James Mill'. *Historical Journal*, 25.1 (1982), 43–69.

Rennell, James, *Memoir of a Map of Hindoostan*, 2nd edn, London, 1792 (1783).

Robertson, J. Logie (ed.) *The Poems of James Thomson*, London: Oxford University Press 1998 (1961).

Rousseau, G.S. and Porter, Roy (eds), *The Ferment of Knowledge: Studies in the Historiography of Eighteenth-Century Science*, Cambridge: Cambridge University Press, 1980.

Rudolph, Lloyd, 'Tod vs. Mill, clashing perspectives on British Rule in India and Indian civilization', in: Giles Tillotson (ed.), *James Tod's Rajasthan: The Historian and His Collections*, Mumbai: Radhika Sabavala for Marg Publications on behalf of the National Centre for the Performing Arts, 2007, pp. 122–33; simultaneously published as *Mārg*, 59.1 (2007).

Rudolph, Lloyd and Rudolph, Susanne Hoeber, 'Occidentalism and Orientalism: perspectives in legal pluralism', in: S.C. Humphreys (ed.), *Cultures of Scholarship*, Ann Arbor: University of Michigan Press, 1997, pp. 219–51.

## BIBLIOGRAPHY

Rudolph, Lloyd and Rudolph, Susanne Hoeber, 'Rajputana under British Paramountcy: the failure of indirect rule'. *Journal of Modern History*, 38 (1966), 138–60.

—'Writing and reading Tod's Rajasthan: interpreting the text and its historiography', in: Jos Gommans and Om Prakash (eds), *Circumambulations in South Asian History: Essays in Honour of Dirk H.A. Kolff*, Leiden: Brill Publishers, 2003, pp. 251–82.

Rushdie, Salman, 'Step across this line', in: *Step Across this Line: Collected Non-fiction 1992-2002*, London: Jonathan Cape, 2002, pp. 407–42.

Said, Edward, *Culture and Imperialism*, London: Vintage Books 1994 (1993).

—*Orientalism*, New York: Vintage Books 1979 (1978).

Sardesai, Govind Sakharam, *A New History of the Marathas: Sunset over Maharashtra, 1772-1848*, vol. III, Bombay: Phoenix Publications, 1968.

Saxena, R.K., *Maratha Relations with the major states of Rajputana, 1761-1818*, New Delhi: Chand & Co., 1973.

Schendel, Willem van (ed.), *Francis Buchanan in Southeast Bengal: His Journey to Chittagong, the Chittagong Hill Tracts, Noakhali and Comilla*, Dhaka: Dhaka University Press, 1992.

Schlegel, Friedrich, 'On the Language and Wisdom of the Ancient Indians', first published in German in Heidelberg: Mohr &Zimmer, 1808; repr. Michael Franklin (ed.), *The European Discovery of India: Key Indological Sources of Romanticism*, selected and with new introductions, London: Ganesha Publishing Ltd, 2001, 6 vols, see vol. IV.

Schwab, Raymond, *La renaissance orientale*, Paris: Payot, 1950.

Sinclair, John, *The Statistical Account of Scotland drawn from the communications of the ministers of the different parishes*, Edinburgh: William Creech, 1791-9, 21 vols.

Sinha, N.K. and Dasgupta, A.K. (eds), *Selections from Ochterlony Papers, 1818-1825*, Calcutta: University of Calcutta, 1964.

Sreenivasan, Ramya, *The Many Lives of a Rajput Queen: Heroic Pasts in India, c. 1500-1900*, Seattle: University of Washington Press, 2007.

Stanhope, Leicester, *Sketch of the history and influence of the press in British India*, London: C. Chapple, 1823.

Sterne, Laurence, *A Sentimental Journey through France and Italy by Mr. Yorick*, with *The Journal to Eliza* and *A Political Romance*, ed. Ian Jack, Oxford: Oxford University Press, 1968, 1984 (1768), section entitled 'The Pulse, Paris', p. 51.

Talbot, Cynthia, 'Recovering the heroic history of Rajasthan – Tod and the Prithviraj Raso', in: Giles Tillotson (ed.), *James Tod's Rajasthan: The Historian and His Collections*, Mumbai: Radhika Sabavala for Marg Publications on behalf of the National Centre for the Performing Arts, 2007, pp. 97–117; simultaneously published as *Mārg*, 59.1 (2007).

Teltscher, Kate, *India Inscribed: European and British Writing in India, 1600-1800*, Delhi: Oxford University Press, 1995.

Tennant, William, *Indian Recreations consisting chiefly of strictures on the domestic and rural economy of the Mahomedans and Hindoos*, 2nd edn, London: Longman, Hurst, Rees & Orme, 1804-8, 3 vols, octavo.

## BIBLIOGRAPHY

Tillotson, Giles (ed.), *James Tod's Rajasthan: The Historian and His Collections*, Mumbai: Radhika Sabavala for Marg Publications on behalf of the National Centre for the Performing Arts, 2007; simultaneously published as *Mārg*, 59.1 (2007).

Trautmann, Thomas R. (ed.), *The Aryan Debate*, New Delhi: Oxford University Press, 2008 (2005).

Vicziany, Marika, 'Imperialism, botany and statistics in early nineteenth-century India: the Survey of Francis Buchanan (1762–1829)'. *Modern Asian Studies*, 20.4 (1986), 625–60.

Viviès, Jean, *Le récit de voyage en Angleterre au XVIIIe siècle*, Collection Interlangues Littérature, Toulouse: Presses Universitaires du Mirail, 1999.

Washbrook, David, 'Orients and occidents: colonial discourse theory and the historiography of the British Empire', in: Robin W. Winks and Alaine Low (eds), *The Oxford History of the British Empire*, vol. V, *Historiography*, Oxford: Oxford University Press, 1999, pp. 596–611.

Waszek, Norbert, *The Scottish Enlightenment and Hegel's Account of 'Civil Society'*. Dordrecht and London: Kluwer Academic Publishers, 1988.

Weindling, Paul Julian, 'Geological controversy and its historiography: the prehistory of the Geological Society of London', in: Ludmilla Jordanov and Porter Roy (eds), *Images of the Earth: Essays in the History of the Environmental Sciences*, London: British Society for the History of Science, 1997 (1979), pp. 247–68.

Wheeler, James Talboys, *The history of India from the earliest ages*, London: Trübner, 1867–81, 4 vols in 5.

Wilks, Mark, *Historical Sketches of the South of India in an attempt to trace the history of Mysoor, from the origin of the Hindoo government of that state to the extinction of the Mohammedan dynasty in 1799, founded chiefly on Indian authorities, collected by Mark Wilks*, London: Longman, Hurst, Rees & Orme, 1810–17, 3 vols, quarto.

Wilson, Horace Hayman, *History of British India*, London: James Madden & Co., 1840–8, 9 vols.

# INDEX

Abhé Sing Rahtore (r.1725–50), 83
absence of historical records, 48, 120, 121, 122, 177, 180, 181
Addiscombe, 66, 152
Ad(i)nath (Jain deity), 25, 32, 55
aesthetical aspects/ function, 7, 96, 102
Ahar (ancient Chauhan capital), 28, 73
Ahmedabad, 52, 106, 113, 140
Aja Pal, founder of Chauhans of Ajmer at an undetermined date (Ajapal's fortress), 104, 186
Ajeysi, Prince 90
Ajit, Rathore prince of Marwar (b.1681, r.1711–25), 83, 88, 142, 186
Akbar, emperor, 86, 88, 90, 91, 101, 112, 183
Akhi Raj Gohil of Ghoga, 87
Akhileshwar temple, 104
Allaudin Khilji, 52, 55, 87, 90, 175, 182
allodial or freehold vassalage, 47, 56, 173
Amber (Jaipur), 3, 58, 70, 82, 86, 101, 183, 184, 190
ambivalences, 102, 129, 200
*AN* or allegiance, 95
ancient Etruscan cities of Cortona, Volterra and Todi, 24, 103
Andernach, 32, 69
anthropologist, 7, 14, 41, 43, 48, 49, 51, 185
*Anusheelan*, 150, 151, 153, 156, 205, 247
appointments in Rajasthan (1818–22), 142

Aravalli (Aravulli), 22, 26, 52, 67, 72, 76, 91, 103, 139, 142, 168
architectural styles, 30, 58, 59
Ariosto (*Orlando Furioso*, between 1516–32), 98, 101, 181
Arnold, David, 15, 19, 67, 75, 78, 102, 105, 113, 121, 129, 131
*Asiatic Journal*, 4, 9, 18, 136, 153, 166, 168, 169, 171, 172, 173, 174, 182, 183, 184, 185, 187, 189, 190, 191, 239, 240, 241
Asiatic Society of Bengal, 65, 71, 72, 78, 79, 120, 128, 159, 195, 242
*Asiatick Researches*, 65, 72, 79, 166, 189, 241
Aurungzeb, emperor, 85, 86, 88, 91, 92, 109

Baba Mohes, 67, 70
*babool*, 75
*Babur Nameh*, 90 (Eng.trans. as *Memoirs of Babur* 1826), 176
Badhail pirates, 140
Bakhtin, Mikhail, 10, 19
Balhara era (from 431 CE, capital at Balabhipura, west of Bhavnagar), 53, 162, 174
Banks, Joseph (1743–1820), 65, 70, 74
*Bapota*, 13, 47, 48, 56, 57
Bappa Rawal, conqueror of Chittore (728 CE), 175
Barnett, L.D., April 1940 list of Tod Collection at the Royal Asiatic Society, 195, 196, 203, 242

[ 250 ]

# INDEX

Barnewell, Major, British resident at Jamnagar, 141
Baroda (Vadodara), 43, 52, 53, 57, 84, 106, 113, 140, 141, 154
Barolli, 25, 29, 30, 67
barometer, 68, 69, 70
Battle of Cannae (216 BCE), 91
Battle of Cunaxa (401 BCE), 51
Battle of Haldighati (1576 CE), 90, 91, 183, 190
Battle of Kanouj (1172 CE), 170
Battle of Kanua (1528 CE), 44, 90, 175, 183
Battle of Lalsot (1788 CE), 93
Battle of Laswari (1785 CE), 94
Battle of Mangrole (Oct.1821), 2, 84, 142, 144, 145, 148
Battle of Marathon (490 BCE), 91
Battle of Merta (1791), 93
Battle of Nadole (1681), 88, 92, 95
Battle of Patun (1790), 93, 113, 214
Battle of Plassey (1757 CE), 65
Battle of Tarain (Khaggar) (1192 CE), 177
Battle of Thermopylae (480 BCE), 50, 88, 91
Bayly, C.A., 10, 19
Beejy Sing Rahtore (r.1765–96), 83
Benares, 10, 87, 98, 99, 100, 149, 150
Bengal, 6, 16, 34, 40, 60, 68, 71, 72, 78, 79, 98, 99, 127, 128, 133, 134, 155, 177, 238, 239, 241, 248
Bentinck, Gov.-Gen. William (r.1828–35), 128
Bernier, François 85, 177
Bhabha, Homi, 10, 11
*Bhagvad Gita*, 166
*Bhaibandh*, 57
Bhavnagar, 25, 32, 52, 56, 57, 59, 174
Bheem Sing Rahtore (r.1796–1802), 83
Bhils (tribals), 73, 95, 175
Bhilwara (town of), 45, 73, 129, 148
Bhola Bhimdeo of Anhulwarra Patan (r.1169–72), 95

Bhuj (town of), 25, 32, 33, 52, 53, 54, 57, 58, 59, 60, 141, 151
*bhyad*, 13, 58
Bhynsror(garh), 24, 25, 29, 30, 105, 106, 206
binary oppositions, 6, 9, 10, 18, 48
Blount, Sir Henry (1602–82), 199, 203, 242
Blunt, Wilfrid Scawen (1840–1922), 98, 113, 200, 203, 232, 242, 247
Boigne, General de, 94, 135, 153
Bonnycastle, John (1750–1821), 140
botany, 9, 14, 21, 40, 65, 66, 73, 74, 75, 77, 97, 169
Brahma, 3, 27, 49
Brahmin assistants, 67
Brande, W.T., 71
Briggs, Colonel on Maratha land taxes, 167
British Board of Agriculture (1799–1844), 68
British Mineralogical Society, 71
British Ordnance Survey, 68
British subsidiary alliances, 16, 108, 123, 124, 178, 180
Bryant, William Cullen (1794–1878), 103
Buchanan-Hamilton, Francis, 16, 22, 34, 38, 39, 40, 65, 74, 81, 82, 111, 243, 248, 249
Buckingham, James Silk, founder of *Oriental Herald* in 1824, 172
Buddhism, 163
Bukhara, 161, 162
Bumaoda, 104
Bunas River, 24, 105, 137
*Bunjarris*, 25
Burckhardt, Johann Ludwig (1784–1817), 70
Burnouf, Eugène, French Orientalist, 174, 175, 176, 185, 187, 241
Byron, George Gordon, 15, 80, 81, 103, 104, 105, 121

cairn, 22, 24, 25
Calcutta Botanic Garden, 65, 74
Cambay, 32, 52, 55

[ 251 ]

# INDEX

camel Manika, 137
Campbell, Thomas, 108, 109
Carey, Captain, 67, 139, 245
Carey, Daniel and Festa, Lynn, 11, 12, 13, 19
Caulfield, Captain, British Resident in Kota from June 1822, 148
Chakrabarty, Dipesh, 9
Chambal River, 29
Chandra Vansa (Chandravanshi), 3, 49
Chandravati (ancient Rajput capital in N.Gujarat), 52, 67, 103, 160
Charles V, European emperor (r.1519–56), 147
Chauhan dynasty (Agnicula race, Gehilote branch), 31, 49, 103, 104, 159, 160, 164, 165, 170, 177, 182, 185
Chavannes, Albert de, 41
Chavda dynasty (746–932 CE), 52, 84
Cheetore (Chittor / Chittore), 30, 31, 44, 49, 67, 68, 82, 85, 87, 89, 90, 91, 92, 94, 95, 101, 103, 104, 107, 112, 129, 160, 174, 175
Chund (bard Chand, late 12th century CE), 31, 45, 89, 95, 165, 168, 196
Chund Khan, Tod's native delegate in Kota, 146
Chund, Soogun, native treasurer in Delhi, 146
Claude Lorrain (17th century painter), 21
Cobbe, Captain, British political agent in western Rajput states from September 1822 (after Tod's resignation), 148
coins of Greek Bactria and Parthia (Menander, Apollodotus), 161, 174
cold societies, 43
Colebrooke, H.T. (1st Pres. Roy. Asiatic Soc. (1823–37), 40, 50, 122, 159, 160, 188, 239, 243
Coleridge, S.T., 80
colonial bureaucracy, 20, 127, 149, 150

colonial discourse, 9, 10, 11, 19, 249
common Central Asian origin, of martial tribes (Rajasthan & Europe), 95, 163, 164, 172, 179, 181, 182, 185, 187, 193
common-sense, 14, 65
comparison, 4, 17, 18, 21, 24, 33, 34, 35, 36, 37, 38, 41, 46, 49, 65, 69, 97, 107, 110, 119, 124, 126, 128, 147, 165, 169, 173, 176, 186, 187, 197
compass, 35, 68
connections, 9, 16, 17, 26, 49, 65, 134, 198
contact, 1, 5, 8, 11, 28, 41, 60, 116, 137, 200, 228
contemporaries in London, 7, 17, 157
contradictions, 5, 7, 10, 94
contrast, 6, 21, 23, 26, 27, 28, 30, 32, 35, 58, 60, 93, 100, 117, 118, 126, 138, 173, 201
contributions to British imperial science, 66
copper grants (Ujjaiyini) (12th century CE), 4, 160
copy of the *Siva Purana*, 67
correspondence, 4, 30, 133, 138, 142, 145, 148
cosmic elements, 15, 102, 104, 105, 110
Coxe, Edward, 103
crag, 22, 23
cross-/inter-cultural (dialogue/ encounter), 110, 199, 201, 202, 203, 204
Crown Prince of Mewar 1290 CE, 175, 177
cultural bridges (cultural *métissage*), 15, 96, 110
curiosity, 5, 227
Curtis, William, 73
Cutch (Kathiawar), 3, 23, 25, 32, 33, 52, 53, 56, 57, 58, 59, 60, 141
Cyrus the Great, 51, 161, 166

d'Hancarville, 21
d'Holbach, 48

# INDEX

Daksha, father of Sati, 164, 165
dale (glen), 22, 23, 24
Daniell, Thomas and William, 21
Davy, Humphrey, 71
dedication to King George IV, 1, 47
dedication to King William IV, 2
despotic (despotism), 16, 47, 94, 120, 121, 180, 181
Dhaulpur, south of Agra (1708), 91
dialects of Western India (based on Urdu), 41, 66, 85, 117, 152, 178, 197, 206
difference, 7, 9, 13, 17, 43, 46, 58, 78, 101, 110, 118, 122, 144, 145, 148, 150, 177, 178, 201
Dilloh the Darawut, 109
Dilwarra, 56, 104
Diocletian, Roman emperor (r.284–305 CE), 147
discontented uncle, 82
Dodson, Michael S., 10, 19
Donkin, General, 136, 239
Doongur Singh, rebel chief of Ruttungurh, 104
Dryden, John, 108
Duchet, Michèle, 41, 43, 61
Duncan, Dr., 66, 137, 139, 149
Dwarka, 24, 25, 52, 56, 140, 151, 212

earthquake, 33, 73, 141
*Edinburgh Review*, 98, 113, 172, 176, 178, 180, 187, 190, 244
Eklingji, 67, 208
El-Edrisi (12th century CE Arab traveller to India), 56
elephant Futteh, 137
elephant Har-Sengar of Prithviraj Chauhan (12th century CE), 165
elite sporting pursuits, 137
Ellora (caves of), 4, 164, 165, 171, 196, 198, 242
Elphinstone, Mountstuart, 98, 162, 163, 169, 178, 244
empirical observations, 14, 21, 27, 43, 65, 77, 158
engineering officer cadet, 134

Enlightenment, 9, 10, 11, 12, 13, 14, 19, 26, 29, 41, 48, 54, 61, 78, 80, 82, 116, 118, 120, 171, 241, 243, 246, 249
epic heroes, 99, 110
epic *Mahabharat*, 166
Erskine, William (1773–1852), 176, 177, 178, 179, 180, 187, 188, 190, 241, 242
established discourses of Imperialism and Orientalism, 201
Esuri Sing of Jaipur (r.1743–47), 92
Everest, George (of the Survey of India), 68

Falconer, Hugh, 74
*farkas* (parasite insect), 76
Fazl, Abul, 52, 177, 196
Fergusson, Adam, 48
Ferishta, 159, 175, 177, 196
feudalism, 1, 4, 7, 43, 46, 47, 57, 83, 85, 89, 94, 129, 167, 172, 173, 174, 176, 178, 180, 181, 182, 185, 186, 189, 193, 240
Fichte, Johann Gottlieb (1762–1814), 81
field account book, 133, 148, 152
field experience, 14, 43, 50, 65, 77, 127, 158, 167, 168
film *Joda-Akbar*, 86
Firoz Lath pillar (Delhi), 159
Fitzclarence, G., member Royal Asiatic Society, 165
flexible adaptability, 15, 77, 168
flying detachments (surveying parties), 67
Forbes, James, 15, 81, 97, 98, 102, 111, 113, 154, 244, 247
Forbes, Alexander Kinloch (author of *Raas Mala*), 140
Fouché, Joseph (1759–1820), French head of the Paris police force, 181
Frank *maire du palais*, 147
Franklin, Captain James, 65
Freitag, Jason, 5, 6, 11, 18, 82, 95, 111, 113, 152, 180, 182, 190, 191, 202, 245

[ 253 ]

# INDEX

friends and colleagues, 133, 135, 152
Futtehbad, south of Ujjain (1658), 91

Ganga Bheva, 2, 22, 29, 30
Gardiner, Mr., British resident at Bhuj, 141
gentlemen-scholars (traveller-philanthropists), 24, 193, 200, 204
geodetical (topographical) surveying, 14, 65, 66, 68
geography of Rajasthan, 1, 66, 168
Geological Society of London, 71, 249
geological strata, 9, 14, 21, 65, 66, 70, 71, 72, 73, 77, 79, 169, 241
Geological Survey of India, 71
George III (r.1760–1820), 59, 74
Ghassi (native Indian artist), 67
Ghoga, town of, 32, 87
Ghose, Kasiprasad (Bengali poet), 106, 113
Gibbon's (William) history of Europe, 53, 94, 102, 159, 180
Gleig, Robert, author of a *History of India*, 166, 167
Goethe, Johann Wolfgang von (1749–1832), 118
Goguet, A.Y., 50, 62, 244
Goha, Chauhan child prince (524 CE), 175
Govurdhan Dass, Zalim Singh's younger son, 84, 146
Grant (East India Company director), 133, 136, 203, 245
Grant-Duff, James (1789–1858), 198, 203, 242
Gray, Thomas (1716–71), 103
Great Trigonometrical Survey of India, 68, 72
Greenough, George, 71
Greville, Charles Francis, 71
Griffiths, William, 74
Grindlay, Captain, R.M., 164, 189, 244
Guha, Ranjit, 9
*gyan punchamee*, 55

Haileybury College (from 1809), 118, 119
Hall, Captain, of Quarter Master General's division, 143, 223
Hallam, Henry, 47, 57, 61, 172, 178, 181
Hamilton, Alexander, 34, 40, 118
Hamilton, William, 71
Hardwicke, Major-General, 71
Harun Al-Rashid, 52, 99
Heatly (family of Rhode Island), 16, 133, 134, 135
Heber, 14, 15, 22, 34, 35, 36, 37, 38, 39, 40, 63, 81, 82, 97, 98, 99, 100, 101, 102, 111, 113, 114, 138, 140, 142, 148, 153, 154, 155, 180, 244, 247
Hegel, Georg (1770–1831), 43, 61, 249
Herder, Johann Gottfried (1744–1803), 81, 118, 121, 131, 245
heroic spirit, 6, 9, 15, 60, 70, 81, 82, 83, 84, 85, 88, 89, 90, 91, 95, 102, 106, 110, 112, 128, 163, 175, 181, 184, 185, 248
historical (bardic) chronicles, 10, 14, 41, 54, 82, 117, 119, 158, 167, 171, 177, 181, 185, 196, 200
historical records available in India, 10, 14, 41, 119, 196, 200
Hodges, William, 21
Holkars of Indore, 48, 50, 92, 93, 106
hollow square (military technique), 94, 135
Hooker, William, 74
horse Bajraj, 137
horse Hargaz, 137, 151, 153
horse Javadia, 137, 151, 153
House of Commons Select Committee (1831–32), 119, 122, 141
human ties (of loyalty), 5, 17, 41, 97, 127, 152
Humayun, emperor, 44
Hume, David (1711–76), 47, 61
Hutton, James (1726–97), 71
hybridity, 10, 11, 59

## INDEX

Hyde Villiers, T., in 1832, Secretary of British Parliament's India Board of Control, 123
Hyderabad, 72, 213, 216, 221

idealised past values, 15, 20, 81, 101, 103, 136
illness, 16, 33, 135, 138
improvement, 8, 34, 67, 68, 77, 121, 128, 129, 130, 228
Inden, Ronald, 43, 61
Indian assistants, 14, 41, 70, 75, 105, 128, 145, 149, 197
Indian plant names, 76
Indian methods of recording distances, 70
Indo-European languages, 164
Indo-Grecian Antiquities, 4, 168, 189, 240
Indus River, 168
internal differences, 46, 94

Jagat (Juggut) Singh, Raja of Jaipur (d.1819), 60, 83, 106, 107, 111, 112, 113, 136, 143, 144, 184
Jahajpur, 46, 138, 139
Jahangir, 90, 183
Jahangir's Rajputni wife named Joda Baé, 86
Jain, Jains, Jainism, 3, 28, 32, 40, 44, 53, 55, 103, 140, 141, 154, 166, 171, 175, 196, 243, 246
Jaipur kingdom, founded by Dhola Rae of Nurwar (967 CE), 184
Jai (Jey) Singh II (Sowae), Raja of Jaipur (r.1699–1743), 92, 179
Jaitwas, 24, 25, 53
Janus, 109, 110
Jawad (town of), 73
Jeffrey, Francis, 98, 113, 244
Jessulmer (Jaisalmer), founded in 1156 CE by Rawul Jessul, 86, 183, 184
Jeswunt Sing Rahtore (r.1638–81), 85, 88
Jhak (town of), 142, 221
Jharejas, 25, 53, 54, 57, 108, 140

*joar*, 75
Johnson, Samuel (1709–84), 103, 105
Jones, William (1746–94), 8, 75, 79, 109, 110, 115, 117, 120, 121, 128, 159, 164, 166, 168
*joojurhs*, 25
*Journal Asiatique*, 4, 10, 18, 168, 172, 174, 185, 187, 188, 189, 190, 240, 241
*Journal des Savans*, 172, 186, 187, 189, 190, 191, 241
Juggut Singh I, Rana of Mewar (r.1628–54), 92, 144, 155, 183
Jumna (Yamuna river), 29
Junagadh, 3, 23, 24, 33, 52, 53, 58, 59, 140, 141, 159
Jussieu, Antoine-Laurent de (1748–1836), 75
Jydeva, beautiful odes, 177

Kabbani, Rana, 199, 200, 201, 203, 204, 245
Kailwara, 75
Kaira, 106, 113, 140
Keneksen, founder of Gehlote dynasty in south Gujarat (145 CE), 174, 186
Kennedy, Dane, 8, 9, 19
Ker Porter (artist painter), 98, 101
Khandela (Shekhawat confederation), 179
*khureel*, 75
*khyr*, 75
Kishangarh, 73
Kishor Singh, Maharrao of Kota, son of Umed Singh (r.from 1821), 84, 146
knowledge exchanges, 1, 4, 6, 7, 10, 16, 17, 133, 135, 138, 139, 141, 157, 193, 201
Kolff, Dirk, 57, 62
*Komar Pal Charitra*, 52
*koroo* tree, 30
Krishna Kumari (Princess, d.1810), 12, 106, 107, 136, 181
Kumbhalgarh (Komulmer), 8, 20, 22, 23, 26, 28, 69, 136

# INDEX

Kunwar Juwan Singh, crown prince of Mewar in 1822, 150, 151

Lambton, William (of the Survey of India), 68
land tenures, 41, 48, 125, 167, 178
landscape, 7, 14, 20, 21, 22, 23, 24, 25, 29, 34, 35, 36, 37, 38, 66, 67, 99, 105, 129
Lane, Edward William (1801–76), 199, 200, 203, 242
language strategies, 85, 128, 169, 170
Last Will and Testament, 7, 202, 231, 239
Laws (divine code) of Menu (*ManavaDhermashastra*), 47, 50, 164, 167
Lazenbatt, Kathy, librarian Royal Asiatic Society, 11, 156, 239
learned circles, 1, 6, 17, 65, 119, 133, 157, 158, 163, 164, 169, 171, 172, 240, 241
legacy to posterity, 96, 193
Leonidas I, 50, 88
Lévi-Strauss, Claude, 43
liberating change (liberalism), 16, 102, 128
Lindley, John, 74
Linga-Yoni, 165
Linnean Society of London (Linnaeus, Carl), 74
literary quotations, 15, 97, 98, 101, 102, 110
local brahmins, 28
London's Society of Arts (founded in 1757), 71
Lord Hastings (Gov-Gen.r.1813–23), 67, 136
Lord Minto (Gov-Gen.r.1807–13), 34
low state of Indian civilisation, 119
Lucknow, 76, 100, 101
Lumsdaine, James, 139

Macaulay, T.B., Bengal Council (1834–38), 128, 180
Machiavelli (1469–1527), 147

Mackenzie, Colin (1784–1821), 65, 68, 197, 203, 245
Mackintosh, Sir James, 176, 232
MacLean, Gerald, 199, 201, 203, 204, 245
MacMurdo, Captain, earlier British resident at Jamnagar, 141
Madhu Sing, Zalim Singh's elder son, 84
Magadha, 49
Mahadeva, 27, 28, 30, 160, 164, 165
Mahanal, 22, 31, 89
*Mahatmya* (local religious legends), 196
Mahi River, 35
Mahmud Khilji of Malwa, 82
Mahmud of Ghazni, 25, 52, 89, 159, 175, 186
Mahmud of Ghor, 31, 58, 84, 89, 175
*makhi* (Indian maize), 75
Malcolm, John, 8, 98, 121, 167, 178, 246
Mandalgarh, 29
Mandvi, 3, 52, 56, 73, 151
manuscripts in Sanskrit, Pali and Persian, 117
Maratha forces, 92, 93
Marwar Rahtores, conquered Kanauj (470 CE), 86
Maun Sing Rahtore, Raja of Marwar (r.1802–28), 83, 106, 136, 184
Meenas (tribals), 24, 46, 184
Meerabai (early 15th century CE), princess of Mewar, 82, 183
Mercer, Graeme, 106, 135, 138, 142
Merta, 6, 93, 113, 135
Metcalfe, Charles, 8, 238
Metcalf, Thomas R., 7, 8, 19, 198, 203
Mewar's resistance to Muslim attacks (997 CE to 1818 CE), 186
Mewari wife, Soojan-Kumari, 87
Mhairs of Mhairwarra (tribals), 7, 61, 142, 143, 154, 218, 219, 220, 222, 223, 225, 226, 227, 228, 229, 238
Miles, Major William, resident at Junagadh, 141, 154, 246

[ 256 ]

# INDEX

Military Academy, Woolwich in Kent (till 1809), 66, 117, 152
Mill, James (1773–1836) (examiner of correspondence, 1818–36) (associate of Jeremy Bentham (1808–30)) 7, 15, 16, 19, 65, 78, 81, 117, 118, 119, 120, 121, 122, 123, 124, 125, 126, 127, 128, 129, 130, 131, 132, 184, 246, 247
Millar, John, 47, 48, 61, 116
Milman, Henry Hart (1791–1868), 180, 181, 182, 187, 190, 241, 242
Milton, John (author of *Paradise Lost*), 102, 109, 110
Mohun Lall, Indian assistant of Gerard, J.G., to Kabul, 168
Mokundwarra (Mukundwara) Pass, 22, 29, 30, 50, 89, 106
monopoly duties, 126
Monson's retreat from Gurrote (1804), 50, 88
Montesquieu, 48, 50, 128
Montrose, 4, 116, 165, 171, 189, 190, 240
Moolraj Solankhi (r.932–88 CE), 84
Moore-Gilbert, Bart, 11
Moore, Thomas, author of *Lalla Rookh*, 80, 98, 100, 114
mother of Shah Jahan (prince Khurrum), 86
mother of Prince Khosroo, 86
mother of Prince Purvez, 86
Mount Abu, 3, 31, 32, 33, 52, 56, 69, 84, 103, 104, 109, 168
Mount Girnar, 3, 24, 32, 33, 58, 59, 140
Mount Halkin, 36
Mount Shatrunjaya, 25
Mount Sinai, 70
Mountstuart Elphinstone, 8, 121, 198
Mrs (Eliza) William Hunter Blair, 3, 21
Mughal siege of Ahmadnagar (slaughter of Chand Bibi) (1596–99), 88
Mundisore, 50, 89

Mundore (Marwar), 23, 24, 103, 184, 219
Munro, Thomas, 8, 185, 202, 203, 243, 252
Muslim Khan of Bhopal, 85
mutual interaction, 6, 9, 17, 126, 136
mythical-historical characters, 27, 54, 87, 110, 164

Nakhi (Nukhi) talao, 31, 32, 69
Napoleon, 108, 109
Nash, Geoffrey, 200, 201, 203, 204, 247
Nathdwara, 22, 72, 75, 164
native advisers, 146
natural history, 72
natural law, 97, 121
nature, 9, 29, 30, 36, 47, 49, 56, 57, 72, 76, 81, 97, 109, 170, 214, 219, 229
Neemuch, 100, 145, 151, 155
negative influence of the Marathas, 92
Neptunist theory, 71, 72
Nestor of Rajputana, 108, 147
new 'Indological' scholarship, 197
Nicholl, Lieutenant Colonel W., 141
non-Brahmanical Hindus, 43
nostalgia, 15, 104, 110
Nuddowaé, 48

Ochterlony, David, 11, 16, 60, 84, 135, 137, 138, 142, 143, 144, 145, 146, 148, 154, 155, 156, 238, 239, 248
Ogunah, 95
Oldham, T., 71
Omeda Singh, raja of Bundi (r.1736–71), 179
Ontala fortress, 1615 CE, 179
*Oriental Herald*, 9, 172, 173, 174, 187, 190, 241
Orientalist themes, 4, 7, 19, 81, 95, 96, 98, 118, 121, 128, 164, 168, 172, 242

[ 257 ]

# INDEX

Padmini (Princess/Queen end 13th century CE), 90, 175, 181
palace of Khengar, 33
Palitana, 23, 25, 32, 52, 55, 57, 58, 87
*pallia*, 24, 25, 26
*panchaiets*, 187
Pandu race, 166
paradoxes, 77, 185
parish of Callander (Buchanan-Hamilton), 34
parricide (Ooda Hatiaro), 82, 83
Parry, Benita, 11
Patan (Anhulwarra Patan in N.Gujarat), 52, 55, 95, 160
Pathan Ameer Singh, Khan of Rampur and Tonk, 48, 101, 107, 155
Pathan soldiers, 136
*Pax Britannica*, 92, 129, 183
Peabody, Norbert, 6, 7, 19, 61, 112, 190
Percy, Dr., 71
perambulator, 68, 70
Permanent Settlement Act (1793), 125
Pertabgurh, 50, 89, 100
picturesque, 21, 22, 23, 26, 27, 28, 30, 32, 33, 34, 35, 37, 38, 75
Pirtha Bae, 31, 89
Pirthi Raj in 1508, 83
Pirthi Singh, Rahtore (1670s), 109
Pope, Alexander, 109, 110
Postcolonialism, 8, 11
Pottinger, Captain, historian of Baluchistan, 178
practical deviations from ancient laws in Sanskrit, 167
pragmatic adaptations, 31, 43, 102, 130
Prakash, Gyan, 9
Pramara dynasty (Agnicula race of Dhar), 32, 52, 159, 160, 162
Pratap Sagar (lake), 30
primogeniture, 167, 173
Prince Ajit Sing Hara of Bundi, 83
Prince Azim Shah, 92

Prince Hal (the future Henry V), 109
Prince Lalji Ram Singh (of Bundi, r. from 1822), 45
Prinsep, James, Secretary of Asiatic Society of Bengal in 1830s, 155, 195
Prithviraj Chauhan (Sesodia, Gehilote, Agnicula dynasty, emperor of Delhi, d.1192 CE), 4, 26, 84, 103, 112, 159, 196, 248
*Prithviraj Raso (Pirthi Raj Raso)* (late 12th century chronicle), 4, 89, 112, 170, 196, 248
progress, 9, 45, 50, 62, 77, 102, 120, 121, 122, 181, 218, 244
*Puharees* or hill peoples, 100
*Puranas*, 161, 166, 174, 180, 181, 185, 189
Purihara dynasty (Agnicula race), 28, 103, 159, 160
Pushkar (town of), 22, 26, 27, 103

*Quarterly Review*, 97, 98, 113, 172, 180, 182, 187, 190, 241, 247
queen Kurnavati of Rana Sanga, 44
queen mother of Rao Soorajmul of Bundi, 85

Radcliffe, Anne (Gothic writing), 41, 82, 100, 102, 103, 105
Radcliffe-Brown (anthropologist), 41
Rae Sing of Bikaner (r.1573–1632), 86
Rahtore Doorgadas, 88
Rahtore Jeswunt Sing of Marwar (r.1638–81), 91
*Rajatarangini*, Kashmir chronicle, 177, 181
*Rajavalli*, Bengali chronicle, 177
Rajmahal (Bihar), 36, 100
Rajput festival in honour of Gangaur, 109
Rajput manners and customs, 15, 18, 41, 43, 44, 46, 85, 91, 94, 110, 125, 170, 173
Rajput princesses, 8, 16, 50, 51, 82, 86, 88, 95, 136, 175
Rajput queen of Ganora, 85

# INDEX

Rajput sense of honour/loyalty, 15, 85, 125
*Rakhi* (sisterly bracelet), 44, 45
Rana Bheem Singh of Mewar (r.1778–1828, friend of Tod), 12, 16, 44, 83, 106, 107, 137, 142, 148, 150, 151, 152, 183, 247
Rana Juggut Singh I of Mewar (r.1628–54), 92, 144, 155, 183
Rana Juggut Singh II of Mewar (r.1734–52), 83, 92
Rana Koombho of Mewar (r.1419–69 CE), 82, 83, 175, 183
Rana Pertap II of Mewar (r.1752–5), 83
Rana Pratap I (Pertap) of Mewar (r.1571–97 CE), 30, 83, 91, 175, 183
Rana Raemul of Mewar, 83, 90
Rana Raj Sing I of Mewar (r.1654–81), 85, 86, 91, 92
Rana Raj Sing II of Mewar (r.1755–62), 83
Rana Ruttun of Mewar, 85
Rana Sanga of Mewar (r.1509–28), 83, 90, 183
Rana Udai Singh of Mewar (r.1541–71), 88, 108, 112
Rana Ursi of Mewar, 83, 183
Rao Budh Sing of Bundi, maintained alliance with Mughal Emperor in 1720s, 184
Rao Maldeo Sing Rahtore (r.1532–69), 86
Rao Udai Sing Rahtore (r.1584–98), 86
Raper, Colonel, British Resident in Jaipur, Jan. 1825, 148, 155
Rasmy (town of), 137, 139
Reason and Equity, 118
reform, 8, 16, 21, 119, 121, 127, 128, 132, 140, 200, 224, 228, 246
render strange details familiar, 96, 99
Rennell, James (cartographer), 68, 69, 79
revenue collection, 125, 130, 198
reverse exoticism, 77
reviews (reception) of *Annals*, 6, 11, 17, 59, 61, 98, 167, 171, 172, 176, 185, 187, 188, 190
river Cali Sind, 136, 145
Robertson, William, 48
rocks and soils, 23, 65, 70, 72, 73
Romantic approach, 7, 8, 9, 12, 15, 16, 18, 80, 81, 82, 96, 97, 99, 102, 103, 104, 110, 111, 116, 117, 118, 121, 129, 130, 131, 242, 244, 248
Romantics in India, 8, 130, 198
Rosa, Salvator, 21, 32, 35, 36, 37
Roshan Beg (Pindari leader), 136
Roxburgh, William, 74
Royal Institution, 71
Royal Society of Edinburgh, 71
rude state of civilisation, 15
Rudolph, Lloyd, 6, 7, 11, 18, 19, 32, 111
Rudra Mala temple, 73
ruggedness, 30, 37
ruins, 15, 21, 26, 28, 31, 40, 44, 97, 102, 103, 104, 110, 129, 139, 243
rule of Yadav kings (1179 BCE to 1192 CE), 185
Rushdie, Salman, 5, 18

Sacy, Silvestre de, French Orientalist, 161, 185, 186, 187, 188, 189, 190, 241
Said, Edward, 7, 8, 19, 43, 61, 193, 201
Sakti Komar, Rana of Mewar (till 928 CE), 182
Samalkot, near Kakinada, 74
Samarsi (Chauhan), 31, 89, 94, 182
*sati*, 26, 50, 82, 85, 86, 87, 95, 163
Saurashtra, 52, 59, 60, 70, 151, 159, 162, 171, 174
Schelling, Friedrich von (1775–1854), 81
Schiller, Friedrich von (1759–1805), 81
Schlegel, Augustus Wilhelm (1767–1845), 162, 163, 168, 169, 188
Schlegel, Friedrich (1772–1829), 118, 131, 240, 248

# INDEX

Schwab, Raymond (*La Renaissance Orientale*), 118, 131, 248
scientific instruments, 14, 68, 70
scientific techniques practised by the Indians, 70
Scott, Walter, 15, 81, 82, 98, 99, 100, 101, 102, 103, 104, 105, 113, 244
Scottish Orientalism, 65, 78, 247
Scottish origin, 21, 65, 116, 152
*Scottish Philosophy*, 78, 243
Scottish terms, 22, 23, 26
Scottish universities (Edinburgh, Glasgow), 74
sculpture, 30, 171, 184
sea trade, 56
Ségur, comte de, 50
*Sehesnag*, serpent of eternity, 165
Seringapatam, 98, 101
Sesodia dynasty (Gehilote-Chauhans, Agnicula race), 49, 173, 177, 179
Sestini, Italian Orientalist in 1825, 169
Shah Alum (Mughal emperor), 92
short compilations, 1, 3, 4, 6, 14, 17, 157, 169, 171, 239, 240
Sibnibashi, 98, 99, 100
Sibpur, 74
siege of Bhurtpore (1815), 94
Sinclair, Sir John (1754–1835), 34, 68
Sindh, 52, 54
Sindhia, Daulat Rao, 27, 67, 93, 94, 106, 107, 113, 135, 136, 181
Sindia, Appajee, 92
Sira Kunwari Bai, 106
Sirohi, 52, 83, 84, 95, 138
sister of the Jessulmer wife of Raja Rae Sing of Bikaner (r.1573–1632), 86
Skinner, James, 94, 215, 217
Smith, Adam (1723–90), 120, 121
Smith, James Edward (1759–1828), 74
Smith, T.D., 105
Smith, William, 70
*Société Asiatique de Paris*, 4, 162, 174
Solankhi dynasty (Agnicula race), 2-, 52, 56, 84, 95, 159, 160, 162

Southey, Robert, 80, 82, 97, 98, 99, 100, 113, 121, 247
Spivak, Gayatri, 9
Stanhope, Colonel Lincoln, 140, 154, 248
Stewart, Captain, report on Jaipur finances, May 1821, 148
Stewart, David, 137
Stewart, Dugald, 116
Stock, John Ellerton, 74
Stirling on Orissa, 167
Stokes, Eric, 72
sublime, 21, 22, 26, 31, 32, 33, 34, 35, 37, 38, 39, 107, 243
succession conflicts (e.g. Jaipur), 82, 84, 85, 95, 142
Sunjogta, Princess of Kanauj (*Vow of Sunjogta*), 4, 84, 170, 189, 190, 240
superstition, 15, 120, 121, 179, 185
Surya Vansa (Suryavanshi), 3, 49
*swamdherma*, 13
Swinton, Sec to Gov.-Gen., Calcutta, 143, 144, 145, 154, 155, 156, 238
symbols and myths, 81
sympathetic information on India, 7, 9, 17, 198, 201
systems of kinship, 41

tableland (*Pathar*), 29, 30, 31
Tamba-Nagri, 28
Tara Bai of Bednore, 26
target Eastern cultures, 202
*Tarikh Mahmud-i-Ghazni*, 53
*teeba*s or sand-hills, 27
Tennant, William, 81, 111, 191
tensions, 16, 138, 139, 144
textual constructions, 7, 10, 16, 43, 48, 80, 107, 117
thermometer, 68
Thomason, Thomas, 74
Thomson, James 97
Tipu Sultan, 101, 181, 198
Tod, John (young cousin of James Tod), 67, 139
tolerance (toleration), 6, 17, 52, 105, 129, 200

# INDEX

top-down exchanges, 193, 201
traditional forms of political checks and balances, 123, 124
Tuar dynasty, 28

Udai Singh, Rana of Mewar (r.1542–71), 112, 183
Ujjain, 4, 85, 91, 136, 160, 162, 175
universality, 12, 22, 91, 96, 101, 118, 122, 220
usurpations, 48, 82, 83
Utilitarian approach, 7, 8, 15, 81, 116, 119, 127, 130

vegetation, 21, 25, 30, 69, 75
Ventura, 169
vernacular words/languages, 66, 85
Vikramaditya, 28, 49, 162
Virabhadra, giant, 165
Viswanathan, Gauri, 9
Viviès, Jean, 18
Volney, 165
Voltaire, 48
Voysey, Dr. H., 72
vulcanist theory, 71, 72

Waghelas, 52
Wales, 35, 36, 37, 103
Walker, Major, 115, 140, 154, 238
Wallich, Nathaniel 70
warm societies, 43
Washbrook, David, 9, 10, 11, 12, 19, 249

Waugh, Captain Patrick 1, 7, 21, 30, 39, 66, 137, 148, 149, 150, 205, 206, 209, 210, 247
Wellesley, Richard, Gov-Gen. (r.1798–1805), 34
Werner, Abraham Gottlob (1749–1817), 71
Western science (scientific classification), 15, 65, 77
*Westminster Review* (founded 1824), 117
Wilder, Francis, British superintendent of Ajmer, 138, 143, 148, 155, 221, 228
Wilford, Francis, 120, 167, 189
Wilks, Col. Mark, historian of Mysore, 178, 197, 198, 203, 242, 249
Wilson, Horace, Hayman, 50, 119, 128, 131
Winckelmann, Johann Joachim (1717–68), 21

Xenophon, 51, 88, 89
Xerxes, 51, 88

Yati Gyanchandra, 9, 44, 67, 89, 197
Young, Robert, 11

Zalim Singh (Raj Rana of Kotah), 44, 50, 84, 108, 144, 145, 146, 147, 148, 153, 181, 184
zodiac, 164
zone types: tropical, temperate and alpine, 75

EU authorised representative for GPSR:
Easy Access System Europe, Mustamäe tee 50,
10621 Tallinn, Estonia
gpsr.requests@easproject.com

www.ingramcontent.com/pod-product-compliance
Lightning Source LLC
Chambersburg PA
CBHW070236240426
43673CB00044B/1809